D1441954

AUTHORS
OF THE EARLY TO
MID-20TH
CENTURY

AUTHORS
OF THE EARLY TO
MID-20TH
CENTURY

EDITED BY KATHLEEN KUIPER, SENIOR EDITOR, ARTS AND CULTURE

Britannica
Educational Publishing

IN ASSOCIATION WITH

ROSEN
EDUCATIONAL SERVICES

Published in 2014 by Britannica Educational Publishing
(a trademark of Encyclopædia Britannica, Inc.)
in association with Rosen Educational Services, LLC
29 East 21st Street, New York, NY 10010.

Distributed exclusively by Rosen Educational Services.
For a listing of additional Britannica Educational Publishing titles, call toll free (800) 237-9932.

First Edition

Britannica Educational Publishing
J.E. Luebering: Director, Core Reference Group
Adam Augustyn: Assistant Manager, Core Reference Group
Marilyn L. Barton: Senior Coordinator, Production Control
Steven Bosco: Director, Editorial Technologies
Lisa S. Braucher: Senior Producer and Data Editor
Yvette Charboneau: Senior Copy Editor
Kathy Nakamura: Manager, Media Acquisition
Kathleen Kuiper, Senior Editor, Arts and Culture

Rosen Educational Services
Shalini Saxena: Editor
Nelson Sá: Art Director
Cindy Reiman: Photography Manager
Brian Garvey: Designer
Introduction by Adam Augustyn

Library of Congress Cataloging-in-Publication Data

Authors of the early to mid-20th century/edited by Kathleen Kuiper.—First edition.
    pages cm.—(The Britannica Guide to Authors)
"In association with Britannica Educational Publishing, Rosen Educational Services."
Includes bibliographical references and index.
ISBN 978-1-62275-002-3 (library binding)
1. Authors—20th century—Biography. 2. Authorship—History—20th century. 3. Literature, Modern—20th century—Bio-bibliography. I. Kuiper, Kathleen, editor of compilation.
PN451.A96 2013
809'.04—dc23

                                                            2013001095

On the cover, p.3: Ernest Hemingway, one of the most popular American authors of the 20th century, penned a number of works highly regarded by both critics and the public. *Alfred Eisenstaedt/Time & Life Pictures/Getty Images*

CONTENTS

346

379

431

441

INTRODUCTION

Early Modernist William Butler Yeats, c. 1902. George Eastman House/Archive Photos/Getty Images

Many of the most prominent features of the modern world—as well as much of its character—came into being during the first half of the 20th century. Well-known benchmarks include the proliferation of the automobile, the invention of television, and the development of atomic energy. But the political and cultural upheavals of this period (including two World Wars, the Great Depression, and the global rise of communism) had arguably even greater influence on contemporary society. As examined in the pages ahead, the impact of these cultural sea changes can be seen in the radical evolution of literature during the first five decades of the 20th century.

One of the first authors to reflect in his writing the seismic changes of this time was the Irish poet and playwright William Butler Yeats (1865–1939). Yeats started his literary career as a fairly traditional poet bent on using his medium to capture the beauty of the world. However, as he witnessed the massive political upheavals of the early 20th century, the themes of his poetry grew darker and more engaged in the concerns of the modern age, most famously in his apocalyptic free-verse poem "The Second Coming."

The literary movement that Yeats helped initiate was known as Modernism, and it flourished in the years following World War I (1914–18). In the wake of that geopolitical watershed, postwar Modernist literature reflected a sense of disillusionment and fragmentation, and the works themselves became more experimental than ever before. Modernism was the major literary movement of the first half of the 20th century and is perhaps best exemplified in the writings of Yeats, Marcel Proust (1871–1922), Virginia Woolf (1882–1941), James Joyce (1882–1941), Franz Kafka (1883–1924), T.S. Eliot (1888–1965), and William Faulkner (1897–1962).

The French author Marcel Proust is primarily known for his masterpiece *À la recherche du temps perdu (In Search of Lost Time)*, a seven-volume novel that tells the story of Proust's life as a symbolic quest for truth. The remembrance is famously touched off by the narrator's consuming a madeleine cake, which powerfully calls forth his unconscious memories. Through the painstaking examination of events in his life, Proust (through his narrator) shows that even the mundane and seemingly pointless moments in one's life are often suffused with vast import and beauty. It is not just the novel conceit of the plot and the book's massive scope that make Proust's magnum opus notable, but also the transcendent beauty of his prose, which is written in what has come to be regarded as among the most original and influential styles of the century.

Virginia Woolf was an English author of novels and nonfiction works who was one of the great innovators of narrative structure in the history of literature. Her major works include the novels *Mrs. Dalloway*, *To the Lighthouse*, and *The Waves*, as well as the landmark feminist essay *A Room of One's Own*. *To the Lighthouse* is especially noteworthy, as the book—which shows the Ramsey family at its summer home on the English seaside on two days a decade apart—has an innovative three-part plot that focuses on the affairs of Ramseys in the first and last thirds, but turns to the empty summer house in the middle. In that landmark middle section, Woolf meticulously describes the degradation of the house while off-handedly referring to major events in the Ramseys' lives such as deaths of characters from the first part of the novel. That drastic change of traditional narrative focus—which until then typically had followed the comings and goings of a work's characters—mirrored the widespread and unsettling indifference toward human life that came with World War I. A similar upending of assumed certitudes, but one that directly addresses the "real world," is seen in Woolf's *A Room of One's Own*. Her essay claims that centuries of prejudice and financial and economic disadvantage—arising from life in a patriarchal society—have inhibited women's creativity and resulted in the relative dearth of female writers over the years.

The Irish author James Joyce is arguably the greatest figure in 20th century literature. His reputation rests primarily upon his novel *Ulysses*, which is often regarded as the greatest novel ever written, but his other writings— notably *Dubliners*, *A Portrait of the Artist as a Young Man*, and *Finnegans Wake*—expressed the spirit of Modernism as well as any others of the time. *Ulysses*, which parallels events in the life of the Greek character for which it is named, unfolds on a single day (June 16, 1904). It is famous for its stream-of-consciousness narrative technique, wherein the actions of the book are relayed through the inner thoughts of its characters. Stream-of-consciousness was not a new literary device in the 1920s, but Joyce brought an unparalleled level of verisimilitude to it, explicating all the sudden digressions, lapses, and half thoughts that occur when one is seemingly thinking about a single subject. While the text is united by the stream-of-consciousness technique, *Ulysses* also stands out for its wide-ranging and cutting-edge stylistic and technical devices. In one chapter, for example, Joyce crafted his prose to reflect the evolution of the English language from Anglo-Saxon to Modern English. Another chapter consisted of just eight large, unpunctuated paragraphs. The breathtaking audacity of the book and its scintillating intelligence established it as a classic soon after its publication.

The German-language writer Franz Kafka's lasting literary reputation was based primarily on works that were published after his death. He published few of the works he produced in his spare time while holding down a series of white-collar jobs during his lifetime, but his literary executor went against Kafka's wishes. His decision to publish Kafka's remaining writings led to the establishment of one of the 20th century's literary giants. Kafka's works, notably *Der Prozess (The Trial)* and *Das Schloss (The Castle)*, are often set in surreal environments where the protagonists are beset on all sides by agents of alienation and bewilderment. These characters act as surrogates for Kafka (and for postwar humanity in general) as they search in vain for truth and meaning in worlds that mirror the moral anarchy that was triggered by World War I.

The disgust and disillusionment felt by many in the years after "the Great War" is perhaps best encompassed in the towering poem *The Waste Land*, by the American-English poet, playwright, and critic T.S. Eliot. Though Eliot produced a number of other modern classics—such as the poem *The Love Song of J. Alfred Prufrock* and the collection *Four Quartets*—that are arguably of greater literary merit, *The Waste Land* is his most famous work. This seminal Modernist piece consists of a series of vignettes that are loosely connected by the legend of the Holy Grail. The vignettes are underpinned by a search for redemption and renewal in a sterile and spiritually empty landscape. The complex and erudite style of the poem forces the reader to take an active role in interpreting the text, which would become another hallmark of Modernism.

William Faulkner brought the tenets of Modernism into the traditionally "folksy" settings of the American South, often in his famed fictional Yoknapatawpha County, Mississippi. His great novels—*The Sound and the Fury*, *As I Lay Dying*, *Sanctuary*, *Light in August*, and *Absalom, Absalom!*—use, among other experimental literary techniques, shifting narrative perspectives, complex structures, and stream-of-consciousness to a degree theretofore unheard of in literature outside of Europe. His works not only dazzle readers with their technical savvy but also feature richly realized characters that Faulkner uses to plumb the depths of human experience within an oft-belittled segment of the population.

Another consequence of the tumult of the first half of the 20th century was the massive demographic change of the countries of the Western world, specifically the United States. Millions of people moved to the U.S. in the wake of both World Wars, among them some of the greatest writers of the century. The most celebrated writer to settle in the U.S. during this period is the Russian émigré Vladimir Nabokov (1899–1977). One of the greatest literary gamesmen of all time, Nabokov wrote highly stylized novels—such as *Invitation to a Beheading*, *Pnin*, *Pale Fire*, and *Ada*—that investigate the subject of art itself through the use of unreliable narrators, doppelgängers, puns, and numerous other literary effects. His most-lauded work is *Lolita*, the tale of a middle-aged man who falls in love with the titular character, a 12-year-old girl. Nabokov used that unsettling conceit as a means of showing off his literary prowess, arguing that an artist of his caliber could fully express the beauty and nuance of romantic attachment in even the most disturbing circumstances imaginable. Moreover, the book, which was written in English by the trilingual Nabokov, also serves as something of a love letter to mid-century America. Like *Ulysses*, *Lolita* caused a scandal upon its initial publication, but it has since gained a reputation as possibly the greatest American novel of the 20th century.

A writer of similar inventiveness, though often far less playful than Nabokov, is the Argentinian Jorge Luis Borges (1899–1986). His fantastical short stories had a darker cast, not unlike the writing of Kafka. Borges began his literary career as a member of the Ultrarealist poetry movement (an innovative group of Spanish-speaking avant-garde poets that gained prominence after World War I) and then as a fairly traditional prose writer, but a traumatic head injury radically changed his writing style. His greatest achievements are his short stories, particularly those in the collection *Ficciones* ("Fictions"), which are thematically linked by featuring labyrinthine, convoluted worlds through which Borges explores the depths of human psychology.

While not as widespread and influential as the broader Modernism movement, the rise of the existentialist philosophy in the 1930s had a lasting impact on the literature of the era. Broadly defined, existentialism stresses the concreteness of human existence and acclaims the freedom of the individual human being. Existentialists do not believe that there are any grand unifying absolutes outside of each peculiar individual's existence within his immediate surrounds, which was a common reaction to living in a society from which the horrors of World War I stripped most conventional meanings and comforts. The leading figure of existentialism was the French author Jean-Paul Sartre (1905–80). His philosophy was first expressed in print in a nascent form in his novel *La Nausée (Nausea)*, but was best expounded upon in his influential essay *L'Être et le néant (Being and Nothingness)*, which posits that the human consciousness is "no-thingness" (in opposition to the "thingness" of the body) and thus can escape the determinism that limits individuals. However positive this message may seem, Sartre further notes that all achievements ultimately amount to nothing, grounded as they are in the actions of humans.

The Irish author Samuel Beckett (1906–89), who wrote in both English and French, was not a proponent of existentialism, but the underpinnings of that philosophy are often simply and beautifully expressed in his works. His writings explored the anguish of the human existence, but often concluded on an optimistic note, suggesting that an individual must strive on in spite of the fundamental meaninglessness of his existence. An accomplished novelist and short-story writer, Beckett is mostly known as a playwright of the "Theatre of the Absurd" school, which held that the human situation is essentially absurd and devoid of meaning. Artists in this informal group produced avant-garde plays featuring a lack of traditional dramatic action with a focus on the language spoken by the characters, which is itself dislocated, repetitious, and usually borderline nonsensical. Beckett reached his creative peak with the plays *En attendant Godot (Waiting for Godot)* and *Fin de partie (Endgame)*. Those two works best distill his outlook, which could be called a hopeful hopelessness. Though that is a seemingly preposterous notion, it is perhaps the most succinct expression of the literary reaction to the unprecedented foundational changes of the early to mid-20th century, and that attitude affected almost every aspect of human existence.

GEORGE BERNARD SHAW

(b. July 26, 1856, Dublin, Ireland—d. November 2, 1950, Ayot St. Lawrence, Hertfordshire, England)

I rish comic dramatist, literary critic, and socialist propagandist George Bernard Shaw was the third and youngest child (and only son) of George Carr Shaw and Lucinda Elizabeth Gurly Shaw. Technically, he belonged to the Protestant "ascendancy"—the landed Irish gentry—but his impractical father was first a sinecured civil servant and then an unsuccessful grain merchant, and the boy grew up in an atmosphere of genteel poverty, which to him was more humiliating than being merely poor. At first Shaw was tutored by a clerical uncle, and he basically rejected the schools he then attended; by age 16 he was working in a land agent's office.

Informal Education and Early Writing

Shaw developed a wide knowledge of music, art, and literature as a result of his mother's influence and his visits to the National Gallery of Ireland. In 1872 his mother left her husband and took her two daughters

George Bernard Shaw. FPG/Archive Photos/Getty Images

to London, following her music teacher, George John Vandeleur Lee, who from 1866 had shared households in Dublin with the Shaws. In 1876 Shaw resolved to become a writer, and he joined his mother and elder sister (the younger one having died) in London. Shaw in his 20s suffered continuous frustration and poverty. He depended upon his mother's pound a week from her husband and her earnings as a music teacher. He spent his afternoons in the British Museum reading room, writing novels and reading what he had missed at school, and his evenings in search of additional self-education in the lectures and debates that characterized contemporary middle-class London intellectual activities.

His fiction failed utterly. The semiautobiographical and aptly titled *Immaturity* (1879; published 1930) repelled every publisher in London. His next four novels were similarly refused, as were most of the articles he submitted to the press for a decade. Shaw's initial literary work earned him less than 10 shillings a year. A fragment posthumously published as *An Unfinished Novel* in 1958 (but written 1887–88) was his final false start in fiction.

Despite his failure as a novelist in the 1880s, Shaw found himself during this decade. He became a vegetarian, a socialist, a spellbinding orator, a polemicist, and tentatively a playwright. He became the force behind the newly founded (1884) Fabian Society, a middle-class socialist group that aimed at the transformation of English society not through revolution but through "permeation" (in Sidney Webb's term) of the country's intellectual and political life. Shaw involved himself in every aspect of its activities, most visibly as editor of one of the classics of British socialism, *Fabian Essays in Socialism* (1889), to which he also contributed two sections.

Eventually, in 1885, the drama critic William Archer found Shaw steady journalistic work. His early journalism ranged from book reviews in the *Pall Mall Gazette* (1885–88) and art criticism in the *World* (1886–89) to brilliant musical columns in the *Star* (as "Corno di Bassetto"—basset horn) from 1888 to 1890 and in the *World* (as "G.B.S.") from 1890 to 1894. Shaw had a good understanding of music, particularly opera, and he supplemented his knowledge with a brilliance of digression that gives many of his notices a permanent appeal. But Shaw truly began to make his mark when he was recruited by Frank Harris to the *Saturday Review* as theatre critic (1895–98); in that position he used all his wit and polemical powers in a campaign to displace the artificialities and hypocrisies of the Victorian stage with a theatre of vital ideas. He also began writing his own plays.

First Plays

When several of Henrik Ibsen's plays were performed in London beginning in 1890, the possibility of a new freedom and seriousness on the English stage was introduced. Shaw, who was about to publish *The Quintessence of Ibsenism* (1891), rapidly refurbished an abortive comedy, *Widowers' Houses*, as a play recognizably "Ibsenite" in tone, making it turn on the notorious scandal of slum landlordism in London. The result (performed 1892) flouted the threadbare romantic conventions that were still being exploited even by the most daring new playwrights. In the play a well-intentioned young Englishman falls in love and then discovers that both his prospective father-in-law's fortune and his own private income derive from exploitation of the poor. Potentially this is a tragic situation, but Shaw seems to have been always determined to avoid tragedy. The unamiable lovers do not attract sympathy; rather it is the social evil and not the romantic predicament on which attention is concentrated, and the action is kept well within the key of ironic comedy.

3

The same dramatic predispositions control *Mrs. Warren's Profession*, written in 1893 but not performed until 1902 because the lord chamberlain, the censor of plays, refused it a license. Its subject is organized prostitution, and its action turns on the discovery by a well-educated young woman that her mother has graduated through the "profession" to become a part proprietor of brothels throughout Europe. Again, the economic determinants of the situation are emphasized, and the subject is treated remorselessly and without the titillation of fashionable comedies about "fallen women." As with many of Shaw's works, the play is, within limits, a drama of ideas, but the vehicle by which these are presented is essentially one of high comedy.

Shaw called these first plays "unpleasant" because "their dramatic power is used to force the spectator to face unpleasant facts." He followed them with four "pleasant" plays in an effort to find the producers and audiences that his mordant comedies had offended. Both groups of plays were revised and published in *Plays Pleasant and Unpleasant* (1898). The first of the second group, *Arms and the Man* (performed 1894), has a Balkan setting and makes lighthearted, though sometimes mordant, fun of romantic falsifications of both love and warfare. The second, *Candida* (performed 1897), was important for English theatrical history, for its successful production at the Royal Court Theatre in 1904 encouraged producers Harley Granville-Barker and J.E. Vedrenne to form a partnership that resulted in a series of brilliant productions there. The play represents its heroine as forced to choose between her clerical husband—a worthy but obtuse Christian socialist—and a young poet who has fallen wildly in love with her. She chooses her seemingly confident husband because she discerns that he is actually the weaker man. The poet is immature and hysterical but, as an artist, has a capacity to renounce personal happiness in the interest of some large creative purpose. This is a significant theme for Shaw; it leads on to that of the conflict between man as spiritual creator and woman as guardian of the biological continuity of the human race that is basic to a later play, *Man and Superman*. In *Candida* such speculative issues are only lightly touched on, and this is true also of *You Never Can Tell* (performed 1899), in which the hero and heroine, who believe themselves to be respectively an accomplished amorist and an utterly rational and emancipated woman, find themselves in the grip of a vital force that takes little account of these notions.

The strain of writing these plays, while his critical and political work went on unabated, so sapped Shaw's strength that a minor illness became a major one. In 1898, during the process of recuperation, he married his unofficial nurse, Charlotte Payne-Townshend, an Irish heiress and a friend of Beatrice and Sidney Webb, friends of Shaw's and fellow members of the Fabian Society. The apparently celibate marriage lasted all their lives, Shaw satisfying his emotional needs in paper-passion correspondences with Ellen Terry, Mrs. Patrick Campbell, and others.

Shaw's next collection of plays, *Three Plays for Puritans* (1901), continued what became the traditional Shavian preface—an introductory essay in an electric prose style dealing as much with the themes suggested by the plays as the plays themselves. *The Devil's Disciple* (performed 1897) is a play set in New Hampshire during the American Revolution and is an inversion of traditional melodrama. *Caesar and Cleopatra* (performed 1901) is Shaw's first great play. In the play Cleopatra is a spoiled and vicious 16-year-old child rather than the 38-year-old temptress of Shakespeare's *Antony and Cleopatra*. The play depicts Caesar as a lonely and austere man who is as much a philosopher as he is a soldier. The play's outstanding success rests upon its treatment of Caesar as a credible study in magnanimity and "original morality" rather than as a superhuman hero on a stage pedestal. The third play, *Captain Brassbound's Conversion* (performed 1900), is a sermon against various kinds of folly masquerading as duty and justice.

International Importance

In *Man and Superman* (performed 1905) Shaw expounded his philosophy that humanity is the latest stage in a purposeful and eternal evolutionary movement of the "life force" toward ever-higher life forms. The play's hero, Jack Tanner, is bent on pursuing his own spiritual development in accordance with this philosophy as he flees the determined marital pursuit of the heroine, Ann Whitefield. In the end Jack ruefully allows himself to be captured in marriage by Ann upon recognizing that she herself is a powerful instrument of the "life force," since the continuation and thus the destiny of the human race lies ultimately in her and other women's reproductive capacity. The play's non-realistic third act, the "Don Juan in Hell" dream scene, is spoken theatre at its most operatic and is often performed independently as a separate piece.

Shaw had already become established as a major playwright on the Continent by the performance of his plays there, but, curiously, his reputation lagged in England. It was only with the production of *John Bull's Other Island* (performed 1904) in London, with a special performance for Edward VII, that Shaw's stage reputation was belatedly made in England.

Shaw continued, through high comedy, to explore religious consciousness and to point out society's complicity in its own evils. In *Major Barbara* (performed 1905), Shaw has his heroine, a major in the Salvation Army, discover that her estranged father, a munitions manufacturer, may be a dealer in death but that his principles and practice, however unorthodox, are religious in the highest sense, while those of the Salvation Army require the hypocrisies of often-false public confession and the donations of the distillers and the armourers against which it inveighs. In *The Doctor's Dilemma* (performed 1906), Shaw produced a satire upon the medical profession (representing the self-protection of professions in general) and upon both the artistic temperament and the public's inability to separate it from the artist's achievement. In *Androcles and the Lion* (performed 1912), Shaw dealt with true and false religious exaltation in a philosophical play about early Christianity. Its central theme, examined through a group of early Christians condemned to the arena, is that one must have something worth dying for—an end outside oneself—in order to make life worth living.

Possibly Shaw's comedic masterpiece, and certainly his funniest and most popular play, is *Pygmalion* (performed 1913). It was claimed by Shaw to be a didactic drama about phonetics, and its antiheroic hero, Henry Higgins, is a phonetician, but the play is a humane comedy about love and the English class system. The play is about the training Higgins gives to a Cockney flower girl to enable her to pass as a lady and is also about the repercussions of the experiment's success. The scene in which Eliza Doolittle appears in high society when she has acquired a correct accent but no notion of polite conversation is one of the funniest in English drama. *Pygmalion* has been both filmed (1938), winning an Academy Award for Shaw for his screenplay, and adapted into an immensely popular musical, *My Fair Lady* (1956; motion-picture version, 1964).

Works after World War I

World War I was a watershed for Shaw. At first he ceased writing plays, publishing instead a controversial pamphlet,

"Common Sense About the War," which called Great Britain and its allies equally culpable with the Germans and argued for negotiation and peace. His antiwar speeches made him notorious and the target of much criticism. In *Heartbreak House* (performed 1920), Shaw exposed, in a country-house setting on the eve of war, the spiritual bankruptcy of the generation responsible for the war's bloodshed. Attempting to keep from falling into "the bottomless pit of an utterly discouraging pessimism," Shaw wrote five linked plays under the collective title *Back to Methuselah* (1922). They expound his philosophy of creative evolution in an extended dramatic parable that progresses through time from the Garden of Eden to 31,920 CE.

The canonization of Joan of Arc in 1920 reawakened within Shaw ideas for a chronicle play about her. In the resulting masterpiece, *Saint Joan* (performed 1923), the Maid is treated not only as a Roman Catholic saint and martyr but as a combination of practical mystic, heretical saint, and inspired genius. Joan, as the superior being "crushed between those mighty forces, the Church and the Law," is the personification of the tragic heroine; her death embodies the paradox that humankind fears—and often kills—its saints and heroes and will go on doing so until the very higher moral qualities it fears become the general condition of man through a process of evolutionary change. Acclaim for *Saint Joan* led to the awarding of the 1925 Nobel Prize for Literature to Shaw (he refused the award).

In his later plays Shaw intensified his explorations into tragicomic and nonrealistic symbolism. For the next five years, he wrote nothing for the theatre but worked on his collected edition of 1930–38 and the encyclopaedic political tract "The Intelligent Woman's Guide to Socialism and Capitalism" (1928). Then he produced *The Apple Cart* (performed 1929), a futuristic high comedy that emphasizes

Shaw's inner conflicts between his lifetime of radical politics and his essentially conservative mistrust of the common man's ability to govern himself. Shaw's later, minor plays include *Too True to Be Good* (performed 1932), *On the Rocks* (performed 1933), *The Simpleton of the Unexpected Isles* (performed 1935), *Geneva* (performed 1938), and *In Good King Charles's Golden Days* (1939). After a wartime hiatus, Shaw, then in his 90s, produced several more plays, including *Farfetched Fables* (performed 1950), *Shakes Versus Shav* (performed 1949), and *Why She Would Not* (1956), which is a fantasy with only flashes of the earlier Shaw.

Impudent, irreverent, and always a showman, Shaw used his buoyant wit to keep himself in the public eye to the end of his 94 years; his wiry figure, bristling beard, and dandyish cane were as well known throughout the world as his plays. When his wife, Charlotte, died of a lingering illness in 1943, in the midst of World War II, Shaw, frail and feeling the effects of wartime privations, made permanent his retreat from his London apartment to his country home at Ayot St. Lawrence, a Hertfordshire village in which he had lived since 1906. He died there in 1950.

Assessment

George Bernard Shaw was not merely the best comic dramatist of his time but also one of the most significant playwrights in the English language since the 17th century. Some of his greatest works for the stage—*Caesar and Cleopatra*, the "Don Juan in Hell" episode of *Man and Superman*, *Major Barbara*, *Heartbreak House*, and *Saint Joan*—have a high seriousness and prose beauty that were unmatched by his stage contemporaries. His development of a drama of moral passion and of intellectual conflict and debate, his revivifying of the comedy of manners, and his ventures into symbolic farce and into a theatre of disbelief helped shape the theatre of his time and after. A visionary and mystic whose philosophy of moral passion permeates his plays, Shaw was also the most trenchant pamphleteer since Jonathan Swift, the most readable music critic in English, the best theatre critic of his generation, a prodigious lecturer and essayist on politics, economics, and sociological subjects, and one of the most prolific letter writers in literature. By bringing a bold critical intelligence to his many other areas of interest, he helped mold the political, economic, and sociological thought of three generations.

JOSEPH CONRAD

(b. December 3, 1857, Berdichev, Ukraine, Russian Empire [now Berdychiv, Ukraine]—d. August 3, 1924, Canterbury, Kent, England)

The English novelist and short-story writer christened Józef Teodor Konrad Korzeniowski and published as Joseph Conrad is best known for the novels *Lord Jim* (1900), *Nostromo* (1904), and *The Secret Agent* (1907) and the short story "Heart of Darkness" (1902). His initial reputation as a masterful teller of colourful adventures of the sea masked his fascination with the individual when faced with nature's invariable unconcern, frequent human malevolence, and the inner struggle with good and evil.

Early Life

Conrad's father, Apollo Nałęcz Korzeniowski, a poet and an ardent Polish patriot, was one of the organizers of the committee that went on in 1863 to direct the Polish insurrection against Russian rule. He was arrested in late 1861 and was sent into exile at Vologda in northern Russia. His wife and four-year-old son followed him there, and the harsh climate hastened his wife's death from tuberculosis in 1865. In *A Personal Record* Conrad relates that his first introduction to the English language was at the age of eight, when his father was translating the works of Shakespeare and Victor Hugo in order to support the household. In those solitary years with his father he read the works of Sir Walter Scott, James Fenimore Cooper, Charles Dickens, and William Makepeace Thackeray in Polish and French. Apollo was ill with tuberculosis and died in Kraków in 1869. Responsibility for the boy was assumed by his maternal uncle, Tadeusz Bobrowski, a lawyer, who provided his nephew with advice, admonition, financial help, and love. He sent Conrad to school at Kraków and then to Switzerland, but the boy was bored by school and yearned to go to sea. In 1874 Conrad left for Marseille with the intention of going to sea.

Early Voyages and Time at Sea

Bobrowski made him an allowance of 2,000 francs a year and put him in touch with a merchant named Delestang, in whose ships Conrad sailed in the French merchant service. His first voyage, on the *Mont-Blanc* to Martinique, was as a passenger; on her next voyage he sailed as an apprentice. In July 1876 he again sailed to the West Indies, as a steward on the *Saint-Antoine*. On this voyage Conrad seems to have taken part in some unlawful enterprise, probably gun-running, and to have sailed along the coast of Venezuela, memories of which were to find a place in *Nostromo*. The first mate of the vessel, a Corsican named Dominic Cervoni, was the model for the hero of that novel and was to play a picturesque role in Conrad's life and work.

Conrad became heavily enmeshed in debt upon return-ing to Marseille and apparently unsuccessfully attempted to commit suicide. As a sailor in the French merchant navy he was liable to conscription when he came of age, so after his recovery he signed on in April 1878 as a deckhand on a British freighter bound for Constantinople (now Istanbul) with a cargo of coal. After the return journey his ship landed him at Lowestoft, England, in June 1878. It was Conrad's first English landfall, and he spoke only a few words of the language of which he was to become a recognized master. Conrad remained in England, and in the following October he shipped as an ordinary seaman aboard a wool clipper on the London–Sydney run.

Conrad was to serve 16 years in the British merchant navy. In June 1880 he passed his examination as second mate, and in April 1881 he joined the *Palestine*, a bark of 425 tons. This move proved to be an important event in his life; it took him to East Asia for the first time, and it was also a continuously troubled voyage, which provided him with literary material that he would use later. Beset by gales, accidentally rammed by a steamer, and deserted by a sizable portion of her crew, the *Palestine* neverthe-less had made it as far as the East Indies when her cargo of coal caught fire and the crew had to take to the life-boats; Conrad's initial landing in the East, on an island off Sumatra, took place only after a 13 ½-hour voyage in an open boat. In 1898 Conrad published his account of his experiences on the *Palestine*, with only slight alterations, as the short story "Youth," a remarkable tale of a young officer's first command.

He returned to London by passenger steamer, and in September 1883 he shipped as mate on the *Riversdale*, leaving her at Madras to join the *Narcissus* at Bombay. This voyage gave him material for his novel *The Nigger of the "Narcissus,"* the story of an egocentric black sailor's deterioration and death aboard ship. At about this time Conrad began writing his earliest known letters in the English language. In 1886 two notable events occurred: he became a British subject in August, and three months later he obtained his master mariner's certificate.

In February 1887 he sailed as first mate on the *Highland Forest*, bound for Semarang, Java. Her captain was John McWhirr, whom he later immortalized under the same name as the heroic, unimaginative captain of the steamer *Nan Shan* in *Typhoon*. He then joined the *Vidar*, a locally owned steamship trading among the islands of the southeast Asian archipelago. During the five or six voyages he made in four and a half months, Conrad was discovering and exploring the world he was to re-create in his first novels, *Almayer's Folly*, *An Outcast of the Islands*, and *Lord Jim*, as well as several short stories.

After leaving the *Vidar*, Conrad unexpectedly obtained his first command, on the *Otago*, sailing from Bangkok, an experience out of which he was to make his stories "The Shadow-Line" and "Falk." He took over the *Otago* in unpropitious circumstances. The captain Conrad replaced had died at sea, and by the time the ship reached Singapore, a voyage of 800 miles (1,300 km) that took three weeks because of lack of wind, the whole ship's company, except Conrad and the cook, was sick with malaria. Conrad then discovered to his dismay that his predecessor had sold almost all the ship's supply of quinine.

Journey to the Congo

Back in London in the summer of 1889, Conrad took rooms near the Thames and, while waiting for a command, began to write *Almayer's Folly*. The task was interrupted by the strangest and probably the most important of his adventures. As a child in Poland, he had stuck his finger on the centre of the map of Africa and said, "When I grow up I shall go there." In 1889 the Congo Free State was four years old as a political entity and already notorious as a sphere of imperialistic exploitation. Conrad's childhood dream took positive shape in the ambition to command a Congo River steamboat. Using what influence he could, he went to Brussels and secured an appointment. What he saw, did, and felt in the Congo are largely recorded in "Heart of Darkness," his most famous, finest, and most enigmatic story, the title of which signifies not only the heart of Africa, the dark continent, but also the heart of evil—everything that is corrupt, nihilistic, malign—and perhaps the human heart. The story is central to Conrad's work and vision, and it is difficult not to think of his Congo experiences as traumatic. He may have exaggerated when he said, "Before the Congo I was a mere animal," but in a real sense the dying Kurtz's cry, "The horror! The horror!" was Conrad's. He suffered psychological, spiritual, even metaphysical shock in the Congo, and his physical health was also damaged; for the rest of his life, he was racked by recurrent malaria and gout.

Conrad was in the Congo for four months, returning to England in January 1891. He made several more voyages as a first mate, but by 1894, when his guardian Tadeusz Bobrowski died, his sea life was over. In the spring of 1894 Conrad sent *Almayer's Folly* to the London publisher Fisher Unwin, and the book was published in April 1895. It was as the author of this novel that Conrad adopted the name by which he is known: he had learned from long experience that the name Korzeniowski was impossible on British lips.

Career as a Writer

Unwin's manuscript reader, the critic Edward Garnett, urged Conrad to begin a second novel, and so *Almayer's Folly* was followed in 1896 by *An Outcast of the Islands,* which repeats the theme of a foolish and blindly superficial character meeting the tragic consequences of his own failings in a tropical region far from the company of his fellow Europeans. These two novels provoked a misunderstanding of Conrad's talents and purpose that dogged him the rest of his life. Set in the Malayan archipelago, they caused him to be labeled a writer of exotic tales, a reputation that a series of novels and short stories about the sea—*The Nigger of the "Narcissus"* (1897), *Lord Jim* (1900), *Youth* (1902), *Typhoon* (1902), and others—seemed only to confirm. But words of his own about the *"Narcissus"* give the real reason for his choice of settings: "the problem...is not a problem of the sea, it is merely a problem that has risen on board a ship where the conditions of complete isolation from all land entanglements make it stand out with a particular force and colouring." This is equally true of his other works; the latter part of *Lord Jim* takes place in a jungle village not because the emotional and moral problems that interest Conrad are those peculiar to jungle villages, but because there Jim's feelings of guilt, responsibility, and insecurity—feelings common to humankind—work themselves out with a logic and inevitability that are enforced by his isolation. It is this purpose, rather than a taste for the outlandish, that distinguishes Conrad's work from that of many novelists of the 19th and early 20th centuries. They, for the most part, were concerned to widen the scope of the novel, to act, in Balzac's phrase, as the natural historians of society; Conrad instead aimed at the isolation and concentration of tragedy.

In 1895 Conrad married the 22-year-old Jessie George, by whom he had two sons. He thereafter resided mainly in the southeast corner of England, where his life as an author was plagued by poor health, near poverty, and difficulties of temperament. It was not until 1910, after he had written what are now considered his finest novels—*Lord*

Jim, *Nostromo*, and *The Secret Agent*—that his financial situation became relatively secure. He was awarded a Civil List pension of £100, and the American collector John Quinn began to buy his manuscripts. His novel *Chance* was successfully serialized in the *New York Herald* in 1912, and his novel *Victory*, published in 1915, was no less successful. Though hampered by rheumatism, Conrad continued to write for the remaining years of his life.

Assessment

Conrad's view of life is deeply pessimistic. In every idealism are the seeds of corruption, and the most honourable individuals find their unquestioned standards totally inadequate to defend themselves against the assaults of evil. It is significant that Conrad repeats again and again situations in which such characters are obliged to admit emotional kinship with those whom they have expected only to despise. This well-nigh despairing vision gains much of its force from the feeling that Conrad accepted it reluctantly, rather than with morbid enjoyment.

Conrad's influence on later novelists has been profound both because of his masterly technical innovations and because of the vision of humanity expressed through them. He is the novelist of individuals in extreme situations. "Those who read me," he wrote in his preface to *A Personal Record*, "know my conviction that the world, the temporal world, rests on a few very simple ideas; so simple that they must be as old as the hills. It rests, notably, among others, on the idea of Fidelity." For Conrad fidelity is the barrier humans erect against nothingness, against corruption, against the evil that is all around them, insidious, waiting to engulf them, and that in some sense they bear within themselves unacknowledged. But what happens when fidelity is submerged, the barrier broken down, and the evil without is acknowledged by the evil within? At his greatest, that is Conrad's theme. Feminist and post-colonialist readings of Modernist works have focused on Conrad and have confirmed his centrality to Modernism and to the general understanding of it.

$\mathcal{S}$HOLEM $\mathcal{A}$LEICHEM

(b. February 18, 1859, Pereyaslav, Russia [now Pereyaslav-Khmelnytskyy, Ukraine]—d. May 13, 1916, New York, New York, U.S.)

$\mathcal{S}$ holem Rabinowitz (Shalom Rabinovitz), who later adopted the pseudonym Sholem Aleichem, was drawn to writing as a youth. He became a private tutor of Russian at age 17 and later served as a "crown rabbi" (an official record-keeper of the Jewish population, which, despite the word *rabbi*, was not a religious position) in Lubny. While there, he began writing in Yiddish. Earlier he had written articles in Russian and Hebrew, and his intention had been to write in those languages. Instead, between 1883, when his first story in Yiddish appeared, and his death in 1916, he published more than 40 volumes of Yiddish-language novels, stories, and plays. (He also continued to write in Russian and Hebrew.) A wealthy man through marriage, he used part of the fortune he and his wife inherited to encourage Yiddish writers and to edit the annual *Di yidishe folks-bibliotek* (1888–89; "The Jewish Popular Library") and lost the rest of it in business.

His works were widely translated, and he became known in the United States as the "Jewish Mark Twain." He began a period of wandering in 1906, established his family in Switzerland, and lectured in Europe and the United States. After the loss of his wife's inheritance, however, his many projects and extended travels began to take a toll on his health.

English translations from his *Verk* (14 vol., 1908–14) include *Wandering Stars*, translated by Aliza Shevrin (2009); *The Letters of Menakhem-Mendl and Sheyne-Sheyndl and Motl, the Cantor's Son*, translated by Hillel Halkin (2002); and *Stempenyu: A Jewish Romance*, translated by Hannah Berman (1913, reprinted 2007). Sholem Aleichem was the first to write in Yiddish for children. Adaptations of his works were important in the founding of the Yiddish Art Theatre in New York City, and the libretto of the musical *Fiddler on the Roof* (1964; film 1971) was adapted from a group of his Tevye the Dairyman stories, which have been translated many times over. *The Best of Sholem Aleichem*, a collection of tales edited by Irving Howe and Ruth R. Wisse, was published in 1979.

A.E. Housman

(b. March 26, 1859, Fockbury, Worcestershire, England — d. April 30, 1936, Cambridge)

Alfred Edward Housman, whose father was a solicitor, was one of seven children. He much preferred his mother; and her death on his 12th birthday was a cruel blow, which is surely one source of the Romantic pessimism his poetry expresses. While a student at Oxford, he was further oppressed by his dawning realization of homosexual desires. These came to focus in an intense love for one of his fellow students, an athletic young man who became his friend but who could not reciprocate his love. In turmoil emotionally, Housman failed to pass his final examination at Oxford, although he had been a brilliant scholar.

From 1882 to 1892 he worked as a clerk in the Patent Office in London. In the evenings he studied Latin texts in the British Museum reading room and developed a consummate gift for correcting errors in them, owing to his mastery of the language and his feeling for the way poets choose their words. Articles he wrote for journals caught the attention of scholars and led to his appointment in 1892 as professor of Latin at University College, London.

Apparently convinced that he must live without love, Housman became increasingly reclusive and for solace turned to his notebooks, in which he had begun to write the spare, simple poems that eventually made up *A Shropshire Lad* (1896). For models he claimed the poems of Heinrich Heine, the songs of William Shakespeare, and the Scottish border ballads. Each provided him with a way of expressing emotion clearly and yet keeping it at a certain distance. For the same purpose, he assumed in his lyrics the unlikely role of farm labourer and set them in Shropshire, a county he had not yet visited when he began to write the first poems. The popularity of *A Shropshire Lad* grew slowly but so surely that *Last Poems* (1922) had astonishing success for a book of verse.

Housman regarded himself principally as a Latinist and avoided the literary world. In 1911 he became professor of Latin at Cambridge, teaching there almost up to his death. His major scholarly effort, to which he devoted more than 30 years, was an annotated edition of the works of the Roman poet Marcus Manilius (1903–30), whose poetry Housman did not like but who gave him ample scope for emendation. Some of the asperity and directness that appear in Housman's lyrics are also found in his scholarship, in which he defended common sense with a sarcastic wit that helped to make him widely feared.

A lecture, *The Name and Nature of Poetry* (1933), gives Housman's considered views of the art. His brother

Laurence selected the verses for the posthumous volume *More Poems* (1936). Housman's *Letters* appeared in 1971.

ARTHUR CONAN DOYLE

(b. May 22, 1859, Edinburgh, Scotland—d. July 7, 1930, Crowborough, Sussex, England)

Scottish writer Arthur Ignatius Conan Doyle was the second of Charles Altamont and Mary Foley Doyle's 10 children. He began seven years of Jesuit education in Lancashire, England, in 1868. After an additional year of schooling in Feldkirch, Austria, Conan Doyle returned to Edinburgh. Through the influence of Dr. Bryan Charles Waller, his mother's lodger, he prepared for entry into the University of Edinburgh's Medical School. He received Bachelor of Medicine and Master of Surgery qualifications from Edinburgh in 1881 and an M.D. in 1885 upon completing his thesis, "An Essay upon the Vasomotor Changes in *Tabes Dorsalis*."

While a medical student, Conan Doyle was deeply impressed by the skill of his professor, Dr. Joseph Bell, in observing the most minute detail regarding a patient's condition. This master

Arthur Conan Doyle, c. 1900. © Photos.com/Thinkstock

of diagnostic deduction became the model for Conan Doyle's literary creation, the detective Sherlock Holmes, one of the most vivid and enduring characters in English fiction. Holmes first appeared in *A Study in Scarlet* in *Beeton's Christmas Annual* of 1887. Other aspects of Conan Doyle's medical education and experiences appear in his semiautobiographical novels, *The Firm of Girdlestone* (1890) and *The Stark Munro Letters* (1895), and in the collection of medical short stories *Round the Red Lamp* (1894). His creation of the logical, cold, calculating Holmes, the "world's first and only consulting detective," sharply contrasted with the paranormal beliefs Conan Doyle addressed in a short novel of this period, *The Mystery of Cloomber* (1889). Conan Doyle's early interest in both scientifically supportable evidence and certain paranormal phenomena exemplified the complex diametrically opposing beliefs he struggled with throughout his life.

Although public clamour prompted him to continue writing Sherlock Holmes adventures through 1926, Conan Doyle claimed the success of Holmes overshadowed the merit he believed his other historical fiction deserved, most notably his tale of 14th-century chivalry, *The White Company* (1891), its companion piece, *Sir Nigel* (1906), and his adventures of the Napoleonic war hero Brigadier Gerard and the 19th-century skeptical scientist Professor George Edward Challenger.

When his passions ran high, Conan Doyle also turned to nonfiction. His subjects include military writings, *The Great Boer War* (1900) and *The British Campaign in France and Flanders*, 6 vol. (1916–20), the Belgian atrocities in the Congo in *The Crime of the Congo* (1909), as well as his involvement in the actual criminal cases of George Edalji and Oscar Slater.

Conan Doyle married Louisa Hawkins in 1885, and together they had two children, Mary and Kingsley. A year after Louisa's death in 1906, he married Jean Leckie and with her had three children, Denis, Adrian, and Jean. Conan Doyle was knighted in 1902 for his work with a field hospital in Bloemfontein, South Africa, and other services during the South African (Boer) War.

Conan Doyle himself viewed his most important efforts to be his campaign in support of spiritualism, the religion and psychic research subject based upon the belief that spirits of the departed continued to exist in the hereafter and can be contacted by those still living. He donated the majority of his literary efforts and profits later in his life to this campaign, beginning with *The New Revelation* (1918) and *The Vital Message* (1919). He later chronicled his travels in supporting the spiritualist cause in *The Wanderings of a Spiritualist* (1921), *Our American Adventure* (1923), *Our Second American Adventure* (1924), and *Our African Winter* (1929). He discussed other spiritualist issues in his *Case for Spirit Photography* (1922), *Pheneas Speaks* (1927), and a two-volume *The History of Spiritualism* (1926). Conan Doyle became the world's most renowned proponent of spiritualism, but he faced considerable opposition for his conviction from the magician Harry Houdini and in a 1920 debate with the humanist Joseph McCabe. Even spiritualists joined in criticizing Conan Doyle's article "The Evidence for Fairies," published in *The Strand Magazine* in 1921, and his subsequent book *The Coming of the Fairies* (1922), in which he voiced support for the claim that two young girls, Elsie Wright and Frances Griffiths, had photographed actual fairies that they had seen in the Yorkshire village of Cottingley.

Conan Doyle died in Windlesham, his home in Crowborough, Sussex, and at his funeral his family and members of the spiritualist community celebrated rather than mourned the occasion of his passing beyond the veil. On July 13, 1930, thousands of people filled London's Royal

Albert Hall for a séance during which Estelle Roberts, the spiritualist medium, claimed to have contacted Sir Arthur.

Conan Doyle detailed what he valued most in life in his autobiography, *Memories and Adventures* (1924), and the importance that books held for him in *Through the Magic Door* (1907).

KNUT HAMSUN

(b. August 4, 1859, Lom, Norway—d. February 19, 1952, near Grimstad)

The Norwegian novelist, dramatist, poet, and Nobel Prize winner Knut Hamsun was christened Knut Pedersen. Of peasant origin, he spent most of his childhood in remote Hamarøy, Nordland county, and had almost no formal education. He started to write at age 19, when he was a shoemaker's apprentice in Bodø, in northern Norway. During the next 10 years, he worked as a casual labourer. Twice he visited the United States, where he held a variety of mostly menial jobs in Chicago, North Dakota, and Minneapolis, Minnesota.

His first publication was the novel *Sult* (1890; *Hunger*), the story of a starving young writer in Norway. *Sult* marked a clear departure from the social realism of the typical Norwegian novel of the period. Its refreshing viewpoint and impulsive, lyrical style had an electrifying effect on European writers. Hamsun followed his first success with a series of lectures that revealed his obsession with August Strindberg and attacked such idols as Henrik Ibsen and Leo Tolstoy, and he produced a flow of works that continued until his death.

Like the asocial heroes of his early works—e.g., *Mysterier* (1892; *Mysteries*), *Pan* (1894; Eng. trans. *Pan*), and

Victoria (1898; Eng. trans. *Victoria*)—Hamsun either was indifferent to or took an irreverent view of progress. In a work of his mature style, *Markens grøde* (1917; *Growth of the Soil*), he expresses a back-to-nature philosophy. It was almost universally considered a masterpiece, and it won Hamsun the Nobel Prize in Literature for 1920. Though it was a breakthrough for him in style, the book retains his message of fierce individualism, influenced by Friedrich Nietzsche and Strindberg.

Consistent to the end in his antipathy to modern Anglo-American culture, Hamsun supported the Germans during their occupation of Norway in World War II. After the war he was imprisoned as a traitor, but charges against him were dropped in view of his age. He was, however, convicted of economic collaboration and had to pay a fine that ruined him financially.

Hamsun's collaboration with the Nazis seriously damaged his reputation, but after his death critical interest in his works was renewed and new translations made them again accessible to an international readership. Already in 1949, at age 90, he had made a remarkable literary comeback with *Paa gjengrodde stier* (*On Overgrown Paths*), which was in part memoir, in part self-defense, but first and foremost a treasure trove of vibrant impressions of nature and the seasons. As a leader of the Neoromantic revolt at the turn of the century, he had rescued the novel from a tendency toward excessive naturalism. His deliberate irrationalism and his wayward, spontaneous, impressionistic style had wide influence throughout Europe, and such writers as Maksim Gorky, Thomas Mann, and Isaac Bashevis Singer acknowledged him as a master.

A six-volume comprehensive edition of Hamsun's letters, *Knut Hamsuns brev*, was published in Norwegian (1994–2001), with two volumes of *Selected Letters* (1990–98) appearing in English translation.

ANTON CHEKHOV

(b. January 29 [January 17, Old Style], 1860, Taganrog, Russia—d. July 14/15 [July 1/2], 1904, Badenweiler, Germany)

Anton Pavlovich Chekhov was a major Russian playwright and master of the modern short story. A literary artist of laconic precision, he probed below the surface of life, laying bare the secret motives of his characters. Chekhov's best plays and short stories lack complex plots and neat solutions. Concentrating on apparent trivialities, they create a special kind of atmosphere, sometimes termed haunting or lyrical. Chekhov described the Russian life of his time using a deceptively simple technique devoid of obtrusive literary devices, and he is regarded as the outstanding representative of the late 19th-century Russian realist school.

Boyhood and Youth

Chekhov's father was a struggling grocer and pious martinet who had been born a serf. He compelled his son to serve in his shop, also conscripting him into a church choir, which he himself conducted. Despite the kindness of his mother, childhood

Anton Chekhov, 1902. **David Magarshack**

remained a painful memory to Chekhov, although it later proved to be a vivid and absorbing experience that he often invoked in his works.

After briefly attending a local school for Greek boys, Chekhov entered the town *gimnaziya* (high school), where he remained for 10 years. There he received the best standard education then available—thorough but unimaginative and based on the Greek and Latin classics. During his last three years at school Chekhov lived alone and supported himself by tutoring younger boys; his father, having gone bankrupt, had moved with the rest of his family to Moscow to make a fresh start.

In the autumn of 1879 Chekhov joined his family in Moscow, which was to be his main base until 1892. He at once enrolled in the university's medical faculty, graduating in 1884 as a doctor. By this time he was already the economic mainstay of his family, for his father could obtain only poorly paid employment. As unofficial head of the family Anton showed great reserves of responsibility and energy, cheerfully supporting his mother and his younger siblings through his freelance earnings as a journalist and writer of comic sketches—work that he combined with arduous medical studies and a busy social life.

Chekhov began his writing career as the author of anecdotes for humorous journals, signing his early work pseudonymously. By 1888 he had become widely popular with a "lowbrow" public and had already produced a body of work more voluminous than all his later writings put together. And he had, in the process, turned the short comic sketch of about 1,000 words into a minor art form. He had also experimented in serious writing, providing studies of human misery and despair strangely at variance with the frenzied facetiousness of his comic work. Gradually this serious vein absorbed him and soon predominated over the comic.

Literary Maturity

Chekhov's literary progress during his early 20s may be charted by the first appearance of his work in a sequence of publications in the capital, St. Petersburg, each successive vehicle being more serious and respected than its predecessor. Finally, in 1888, Chekhov published his first work in a leading literary review, *Severny vestnik* ("Northern Herald"). With the work in question—a long story entitled "Steppe"—he at last turned his back on comic fiction. "Steppe," an autobiographical work describing a journey in the Ukraine as seen through the eyes of a child, is the first among more than 50 stories published in a variety of journals and selections between 1888 and his death in 1904. It is on this corpus of later stories, but also on his mature dramas of the same period, that Chekhov's main reputation rests.

Although the year 1888 first saw Chekhov concentrating almost exclusively on short stories that were serious in conception, humour—now underlying—nearly always remained an important ingredient. There was also a concentration on quality at the expense of quantity, the number of publications dropping suddenly from over a hundred items a year in the peak years 1886 and 1887 to only 10 short stories in 1888. Besides "Steppe," Chekhov also wrote several profoundly tragic studies at this time, the most notable of which was "A Dreary Story" (1889), a penetrating study into the mind of an elderly and dying professor of medicine. The ingenuity and insight displayed in this tour de force was especially remarkable, coming from an author so young. The play *Ivanov* (1887–89) culminates in the suicide of a young man nearer to the author's own age. Together with "A Dreary Story," this belongs to a group among Chekhov's works that have been called clinical studies. They explore the experiences of the mentally or physically ill in a spirit that reminds one that the author was himself a qualified—and remained a sporadically practicing—doctor.

By the late 1880s many critics had begun to reprimand Chekhov, now that he was sufficiently well known to attract their attention, for holding no firm political and social views and for failing to endow his works with a sense of direction. Such expectations irked Chekhov, who was unpolitical and philosophically uncommitted. In early 1890 he suddenly sought relief from the irritations of urban intellectual life by undertaking a one-man sociological expedition to the remote island of Sakhalin. Situated nearly 6,000 miles (9,650 km) east of Moscow, on the other side of Siberia, it was notorious as an imperial Russian penal settlement. Chekhov's journey there was a long and hazardous ordeal by carriage and riverboat. After arriving unscathed, studying local conditions, and conducting a census of the islanders, he returned to publish his findings as a research thesis, which retains an honoured place in the annals of Russian penology: *The Island of Sakhalin* (1893–94).

Chekhov paid his first visit to western Europe in the company of A.S. Suvorin, a wealthy newspaper proprietor and the publisher of much of Chekhov's own work. Their long and close friendship caused Chekhov some unpopularity, owing to the politically reactionary character of Suvorin's newspaper, *Novoye vremya* ("New Time"). Eventually Chekhov broke with Suvorin over the attitude taken by the paper toward the notorious Alfred Dreyfus affair in France, with Chekhov championing Dreyfus.

During the years just before and after his Sakhalin expedition, Chekhov had continued his experiments as a dramatist. His *Leshy* (1888–89; *The Wood Demon*) is a long-winded and ineptly facetious four-act play, which somehow, by a miracle of art, became converted—largely by cutting—into *Dyadya Vanya* (*Uncle Vanya*), one of his greatest stage masterpieces. The conversion—to a superb study of aimlessness in a rural manor house—took place some time between 1890 and 1896; the play was published in 1897. Other dramatic efforts of the period include several of the uproarious one-act farces known as vaudevilles: *Medved* (*The Bear*), *Predlozheniye* (*The Proposal*), *Svadba* (*The Wedding*), *Yubiley* (*The Anniversary*), and others.

Melikhovo Period: 1892–98

After helping, both as doctor and as medical administrator, to relieve the disastrous famine of 1891–92, Chekhov bought a country estate in the village of Melikhovo, about 50 miles (80 km) south of Moscow. This was his main residence for about six years, providing a home for his aging parents, as well as for his sister Mariya, who acted as his housekeeper and remained unmarried in order to look after her brother. The Melikhovo period was the most creatively effective of Chekhov's life so far as short stories were concerned, for it was during these six years that he wrote "The Butterfly," "Neighbours" (1892), "An Anonymous Story" (1893), "The Black Monk" (1894), "Murder," and "Ariadne" (1895), among many other masterpieces. Village life now became a leading theme in his work, most notably in "Peasants" (1897). Undistinguished by plot, this short sequence of brilliant sketches created more stir in Russia than any other single work of Chekhov's, partly owing to his rejection of the convention whereby writers commonly presented the Russian peasantry in sentimentalized and debrutalized form.

Continuing to provide many portraits of the intelligentsia, Chekhov also described the commercial and factory-owning world in such stories as "A Woman's Kingdom," (1894) and "Three Years" (1895). As has often been recognized, Chekhov's work provides a panoramic study of the Russia of his day, and one so accurate that it could even be used as a sociological source.

In some of his stories of the Melikhovo period, Chekhov attacked by implication the teachings of Leo Tolstoy, the well-known novelist and thinker, and Chekhov's revered elder contemporary. Himself once (in the late 1880s) a tentative disciple of the Tolstoyan simple life, and also of nonresistance to evil as advocated by Tolstoy, Chekhov had now rejected these doctrines. He illustrated his new view in one particularly outstanding story: "Ward Number Six" (1892). Here an elderly doctor shows himself nonresistant to evil by refraining from remedying the appalling conditions in the mental ward of which he has charge—only to be incarcerated as a patient himself through the intrigues of a subordinate. In "My Life" (1896) the young hero, son of a provincial architect, insists on defying middle-class convention by becoming a house painter, a cultivation of the Tolstoyan simple life that Chekhov portrays as misconceived. In a later trio of linked stories, "The Man in a Case," "Gooseberries," and "About Love" (1898), Chekhov further develops the same theme, showing various figures who similarly fail to realize their full potentialities. As these pleas in favour of personal freedom illustrate, Chekhov's stories frequently contain some kind of submerged moral.

Chayka (*The Seagull*) is Chekhov's only dramatic work dating with certainty from the Melikhovo period. First performed in St. Petersburg on October 17, 1896 (Old Style), this four-act drama, misnamed a comedy, was badly received; indeed, it was almost hissed off the stage. Chekhov was greatly distressed and left the auditorium during the second act, having suffered one of the most traumatic experiences of his life and vowing never to write for the stage again. Two years later, however, the play was revived by the newly created Moscow Art Theatre, enjoying considerable success and helping to reestablish Chekhov as a dramatist. *The Seagull* is a study of the clash between the older and younger generations as it affects two actresses and two writers, some of the details having been suggested by episodes in the lives of Chekhov's friends.

Yalta Period: 1899–1904

In March 1897 Chekhov had suffered a lung hemorrhage caused by tuberculosis, symptoms of which had become apparent considerably earlier. Now forced to acknowledge himself a semi-invalid, Chekhov sold his Melikhovo estate and built a villa in Yalta, the Crimean coastal resort. From then on he spent most of his winters there or on the French Riviera, cut off from the intellectual life of Moscow and St. Petersburg. This was all the more galling since his plays were beginning to attract serious attention. Moreover, Chekhov had become attracted by a young actress, Olga Knipper, who was appearing in his plays, and whom he eventually married in 1901; the marriage probably marked the only profound love affair of his life. But since Knipper continued to pursue her acting career, husband and wife lived apart during most of the winter months, and there were no children of the marriage.

Never a successful financial manager, Chekhov attempted to regularize his literary affairs in 1899 by selling the copyright of all his existing works, excluding plays, to the publisher A.F. Marx for 75,000 rubles, an unduly low sum. In 1899–1901 Marx issued the first comprehensive edition of Chekhov's works, in 10 volumes, after the author had himself rejected many of his juvenilia. Even so, this publication, reprinted in 1903 with supplementary material, was unsatisfactory in many ways.

Chekhov's Yalta period saw a decline in the production of short stories and a greater emphasis on drama. His two last plays—*Tri sestry* (1901; *Three Sisters*) and *Vishnyovy sad* (1904; *The Cherry Orchard*)—were both written for the Moscow Art Theatre. But much as Chekhov owed to the theatre's two founders, Vladimir Nemirovich-Danchenko and Konstanin Stanislavsky, he remained dissatisfied with such rehearsals and performances of his plays as he was able to witness. Repeatedly insisting that his mature drama was comedy rather than tragedy, Chekhov grew distressed when producers insisted on a heavy treatment, overemphasizing the—admittedly frequent—occasions on which the characters inveigh against the boredom and futility of their lives. Despite Stanislavsky's reputation as an innovator who had brought a natural, nondeclamatory style to the hitherto overhistrionic Russian stage, his productions were never natural and nondeclamatory enough for Chekhov, who wished his work to be acted with the lightest possible touch. And though Chekhov's mature plays have since become established in repertoires all over the world, it remains doubtful whether his craving for the light touch has been satisfied except on the rarest of occasions. Yet oversolemnity can be the ruin of *Three Sisters*, for example—the play in which Chekhov so sensitively portrays the longings of a trio of provincial young women. Insisting that his *The Cherry Orchard* was "a comedy, in places even a farce," Chekhov offered in this last play a poignant picture of the Russian landowning class in decline, portraying characters who remain comic despite their very poignancy. This play was first performed in Moscow on January 17, 1904 (Old Style), and less than six months later Chekhov died of tuberculosis.

Though already celebrated by the Russian literary public at the time of his death, Chekhov did not become internationally famous until the years after World War I, by which time the translations by Constance Garnett (into English) and others had helped to publicize his work.

Yet his elusive, superficially guileless style of writing—in which what is left unsaid often seems so much more important than what is said—has defied effective analysis by literary critics, as well as effective imitation by creative writers.

It was not until 40 years after his death, with the issue of the 20-volume *Polnoye sobraniye sochineny i pisem A.P. Chekhova* ("Complete Works and Letters of A.P. Chekhov") of 1944–51, that Chekhov was at last presented in Russian on a level of scholarship worthy—though with certain reservations—of his achievement. Eight volumes of this edition contain his correspondence, amounting to several thousand letters. Outstandingly witty and lively, they belie the legend—commonly believed during the author's lifetime—that he was hopelessly pessimistic in outlook. Although Chekhov is still chiefly known for his plays, critical opinion shows signs of establishing the stories—and particularly those that were written after 1888—as an even more significant and creative literary achievement.

RABINDRANATH TAGORE

(b. May 7, 1861, Calcutta [now Kolkata],
India—d. August 7, 1941, Calcutta)

Bengali poet, short-story writer, song composer, playwright, essayist, and painter Rabindranath Tagore introduced new prose and verse forms and the use of colloquial language into Bengali literature, thereby freeing it from traditional models based on classical Sanskrit. He was highly influential in introducing the best of Indian culture to the West and vice versa, and he is generally regarded as the outstanding creative artist of modern India.

The son of the religious reformer Debendranath Tagore, he early began to write verses, and after incomplete studies in England in the late 1870s, he returned to India. There he published several books of poetry in the 1880s and completed *Manasi* (1890), a collection that marks the maturing of his genius. It contains some of his best-known poems, including many in verse forms new to Bengali, as well as some social and political satire that was critical of his fellow Bengalis.

In 1891 Tagore went to East Bengal (now in Bangladesh) to manage his family's estates at Shilaidah and Shazadpur for 10 years. There he often stayed in a houseboat on the Padma River (i.e., the Ganges River), in close contact with village folk, and his sympathy for their poverty and respect for tradition became the keynote of much of his later writing. Most of his finest short stories, which examine "humble lives and their small miseries," date from the 1890s and have a poignancy, laced with gentle irony, that is unique to him, though admirably captured by the Indian director Satyajit Ray in later film adaptations. Tagore came to love the Bengali countryside, most of all the Padma River, an often-repeated image in his verse. During these years he published several poetry collections, notably *Sonar Tari* (1894; *The Golden Boat*), and plays, notably *Chitrangada* (1892; *Chitra*). Tagore's poems are virtually untranslatable, as are his more than 2,000 songs, which remain extremely popular among all classes of Bengali society.

In 1901 Tagore founded an experimental school in rural West Bengal at Shantiniketan ("Abode of Peace"), where he sought to blend the best in the Indian and Western traditions. He settled permanently at the school, which became Vishva-Bharati University in 1921. Years of sadness arising from the deaths of his wife and two children between 1902 and 1907 are reflected in his later poetry, which was introduced to the West in *Gitanjali, Song Offerings* (1912). This

Rabindranath Tagore in his study at Shantiniketan ("Abode of Peace"; later Vishva-Bharati University), West Bengal , India. Encyclopædia Britannica, Inc.

book, containing Tagore's English prose translations of religious poems from several of his Bengali verse collections, including *Gitanjali* (1910), was hailed by Irish poet W.B. Yeats and French writer André Gide and won him the Nobel Prize in 1913. Tagore was awarded a knighthood in 1915, but he repudiated it in 1919 as a protest against the Amritsar Massacre, in which British troops fired on unarmed Indian protesters, killing a large number of people.

From 1912 Tagore spent long periods out of India, lecturing and reading from his work in Europe, the Americas, and East Asia and becoming an eloquent spokesperson for the cause of Indian independence. Tagore's novels, though less outstanding than his poems and short stories, are also worthy of attention; the best known are *Gora* (1910) and *Ghare-Baire* (1916; *The Home and the World*). In the late 1920s, at nearly 70 years of age, Tagore took up painting and produced works that won him a place among India's foremost contemporary artists.

EDITH WHARTON

(b. January 24, 1862, New York, New York, U.S. — d. August 11, 1937, St.-Brice-sous-Forêt, near Paris, France)

Edith Newbold Jones came of a distinguished and long-established New York family. She was educated by private tutors and governesses at home and in Europe, where the family resided for six years after the American Civil War, and she read voraciously. She made her debut in society in 1879 and married Edward Wharton, a wealthy Boston banker, in 1885 (divorced 1913).

Although she had had a book of her own poems privately printed when she was 16, it was not until after several years of married life that Wharton began to write in earnest. Her major literary model was Henry James, whom she knew, and her work reveals James's concern for artistic form and ethical issues. She contributed a few poems and stories to *Harper's*, *Scribner's*, and other magazines in the 1890s, and in 1897, after overseeing the remodeling of a house in Newport, Rhode Island, she collaborated with the architect Ogden Codman, Jr., on *The Decoration of Houses*. Her next books, *The Greater Inclination* (1899) and *Crucial Instances* (1901), were collections of stories.

Wharton's first novel, *The Valley of Decision*, was published in 1902. *The House of Mirth* (1905) was a novel of manners that analyzed the stratified upper-class society in which she had been reared and its reaction to social change. The book won her critical acclaim and a wide audience. In the next two decades—before the quality of her work began to decline under the demands of writing for women's magazines—she wrote such novels as *The Reef* (1912), *The Custom of the Country* (1913), *Summer* (1917), and *The Age of Innocence* (1920), which won a Pulitzer Prize.

The Age of Innocence presents a picture of upper-class New York society in the 1870s. In the story, Newland Archer is engaged to May Welland, a beautiful but proper fellow member of elite society, but he falls deeply in love with Ellen Olenska, a former member of their circle who has returned to New York to escape her disastrous marriage to a Polish nobleman. Both lovers prove too obedient to conventional taboos to break with their upper-class social surroundings, however, and Newland feels compelled to renounce Ellen and marry May.

Perhaps Wharton's best-known work is the long tale *Ethan Frome* (1911), which exploits the grimmer possibilities of the New England farm life she observed from her home in Lenox, Massachusetts. The protagonist, the farmer Ethan Frome, is married to a whining hypochondriac but falls in love with her cousin, Mattie. As she is forced to leave his household, Frome tries to end their dilemma by steering their bobsled into a tree, but he ends up only crippling Mattie for life. They spend the rest of their miserable lives together with his wife on the farm.

Wharton's short stories, which appeared in numerous collections, among them *Xingu and Other Stories* (1916), demonstrate her gifts for social satire and comedy, as do the four novelettes collected in *Old New York* (1924). In her manual *The Writing of Fiction* (1925) she acknowledged her debt to Henry James. Among her later novels are *Twilight Sleep* (1927), *Hudson River Bracketed* (1929), and its sequel, *The Gods Arrive* (1932). Her autobiography, *A Backward Glance*, appeared in 1934. In all Wharton published more than 50 books, including fiction, short stories, travel books, historical novels, and criticism.

She lived in France after 1907, visiting the United States only at rare intervals. She was a close friend of novelist James in his later years.

MAURICE MAETERLINCK

(b. August 29, 1862, Ghent, Belgium — d. May 6, 1949, Nice, France)

Belgian poet, playwright, and essayist Maurice Polydore-Marie-Bernard Maeterlinck studied law at the University of Ghent and was admitted to the bar in that city in 1886. In Paris in 1885–86 he met Auguste Villiers de L'Isle-Adam and the leaders of the Symbolist movement, and he soon abandoned law for literature. His first verse collection, *Serres chaudes* ("Hothouses"), and his first play, *La Princesse Maleine*, were published in 1889. Maeterlinck made a dramatic breakthrough in 1890 with two one-act plays, *L'Intruse* (*The Intruder*) and *Les Aveugles* (*The Blind*). His *Pelléas et Mélisande* (1892), produced in Paris at the avant-garde Théâtre de l'Oeuvre by the director Aurélien Lugné-Poë, is the unquestioned masterpiece of Symbolist drama and provided the basis for an opera (1902) by Claude Debussy. Set in a nebulous, fairy-tale past, the play conveys a mood of hopeless melancholy and doom in its story of the destructive passion of Princess Mélisande, who falls in love with her husband's younger brother, Pelléas. Though written in prose, *Pelléas et Mélisande* may be considered the most accomplished of all 19th-century attempts at poetic drama.

Maeterlinck wrote many other plays, including historical dramas such as *Monna Vanna* (1902). Gradually, his Symbolism was tempered by his interest in English drama, especially William Shakespeare and the Jacobeans. Only *L'Oiseau bleu* (1908; *The Blue Bird*) rivaled *Pelléas et Mélisande* in popularity. An allegorical fantasy conceived as a play for children, it portrays a search for happiness in the world. First performed by the Moscow Art Theatre in 1908, this somewhat sentimental dramatic parable was highly regarded for a time, but its charm has largely evaporated, and the optimism of the play now seems almost facile. After he won the Nobel Prize for Literature (1911), however, his reputation declined, although his *Le Bourgmestre de Stilmonde* (1917; *The Burgomaster of Stilmonde*), a patriotic play in which he explores the problems of Flanders under the wartime rule of an unprincipled German officer, briefly enjoyed great success.

In his Symbolist plays, Maeterlinck uses poetic speech, gesture, lighting, setting, and ritual to create images that reflect his protagonists' moods and dilemmas. Often the protagonists are waiting for something mysterious and fearful that will destroy them. The profound and moving atmosphere of the plays, though lacking in intellectual complexity, is augmented by tentative dialogue, based on half-formed suggestions, at times naively repetitious, and occasionally sentimental, but sometimes possessed of great subtlety and power. As a dramatist, Maeterlinck influenced Hugo von Hofmannsthal, W.B. Yeats, John Millington Synge, and Eugene O'Neill. Maeterlinck's plays have been widely translated, and no Belgian dramatist had greater effect on worldwide audiences.

Maeterlinck's prose writings are remarkable blends of mysticism, occultism, and interest in the world of nature. They represent the common Symbolist reaction against materialism, science, and mechanization and are concerned with such questions as the immortality of the soul, the nature of death, and the attainment of wisdom. Maeterlinck presented his mystical speculations in *Le Trésor des humbles* (1896; *The Treasure of the Humble*) and *La Sagesse et la destinée* (1898; "Wisdom and Destiny"). His most widely read prose writings, however, are two extended essays, *La Vie des abeilles* (1901; *The Life of the Bee*) and *L'Intelligence des fleurs* (1907; *The Intelligence of Flowers*), in which Maeterlinck sets out his philosophy of the human condition. King Albert I made Maeterlinck a count in 1932.

O. HENRY

(b. September 11, 1862, Greensboro, North Carolina, U.S.—d. June 5, 1910, New York, New York)

O. Henry is the pseudonym of American short-story writer William Sidney Porter, who later spelled his middle name Sydney. He is known for tales that romanticized the commonplace—in particular the life of ordinary people in New York City. His stories expressed the effect of coincidence on character through humour, grim or ironic, and often had surprise endings, a device that became identified with his name and cost him critical favour when its vogue had passed.

Porter attended a school taught by his aunt, then clerked in his uncle's drugstore. In 1882 he went to Texas, where he worked on a ranch, in a general land office, and later as teller in the First National Bank in Austin. He began writing sketches at about the time of his marriage to Athol Estes in 1887, and in 1894 he started a humorous weekly, *The Rolling Stone*. When that venture failed, Porter joined the *Houston Post* as reporter, columnist, and occasional cartoonist.

In February 1896 he was indicted for embezzlement of bank funds. Friends aided his flight to Honduras. News of his wife's fatal illness, however, took him back to Austin, and lenient authorities did not press his case until after her death. When convicted, Porter received the lightest sentence possible, and in 1898 he entered the penitentiary at Columbus, Ohio; his sentence was shortened to three years and three months for good behaviour. As night druggist in the prison hospital, he could write to earn money for support of his daughter Margaret. His stories of adventure in the Southwest U.S. and Central America were immediately popular with magazine readers, and when he emerged from prison W.S. Porter had become O. Henry.

In 1902 O. Henry arrived in New York—his "Bagdad on the Subway." From December 1903 to January 1906 he produced a story a week for the New York *World*, writing also for magazines. His first book, *Cabbages and Kings* (1904), depicted fantastic characters against exotic Honduran backgrounds. Both *The Four Million* (1906) and *The Trimmed Lamp* (1907) explored the lives of the multitude of New York in their daily routines and searchings for romance and adventure. *Heart of the West* (1907) presented accurate and fascinating tales of the Texas range.

Then in rapid succession came *The Voice of the City* (1908), *The Gentle Grafter* (1908), *Roads of Destiny* (1909), *Options* (1909), *Strictly Business* (1910), and *Whirligigs* (1910). *Whirligigs* contains perhaps Porter's funniest story, "The Ransom of Red Chief." In the story, two kidnappers make off with the young son of a prominent man only to find that the child is more trouble than he is worth; in the end, they agree to pay the boy's father to take him back.

Despite his popularity, O. Henry's final years were marred by ill health, a desperate financial struggle, and alcoholism. A second marriage in 1907 was unhappy. After his death three more collected volumes appeared: *Sixes and Sevens* (1911), *Rolling Stones* (1912), and *Waifs and Strays* (1917). Later seven fugitive stories and poems, *O. Henryana* (1920), *Letters to Lithopolis* (1922), and two collections of his early work on the *Houston Post, Postscripts* (1923) and *O. Henry Encore* (1939), were published. Foreign translations and adaptations for other art forms, including films and television, attest his universal application and appeal.

GERHART HAUPTMANN

(b. November 15, 1862, Bad Salzbrunn, Silesia, Prussia [Germany]—d. June 6, 1946, Agnetendorf, Germany [now Jagniątków, Poland])

Gerhart Johann Robert Hauptmann was born in a then-fashionable Silesian resort town, where his father owned the main hotel. He studied sculpture from 1880 to 1882 at the Breslau Art Institute and then studied science and philosophy at the university in Jena (1882–83). He worked as a sculptor in Rome (1883–84) and studied further in Berlin (1884–85). It was at this time that he decided to make his career as a poet and dramatist. Having married the well-to-do Marie Thienemann in 1885, Hauptmann settled down in Erkner, a suburb of Berlin, taking lessons in acting and associating with a group of scientists, philosophers, and avant-garde writers who were interested in naturalist and socialist ideas. Hauptmann began writing novellas, most notably *Fasching* (1887; "Carnival"), but his membership in the literary club Durch ("Through") and his reading of the works of such writers as Émile Zola and Ivan Turgenev led him to start writing plays.

In October 1889 the performance of Hauptmann's social drama *Vor Sonnenaufgang* (*Before Dawn*) made him famous overnight, though it shocked the theatregoing public. This starkly realistic tragedy, dealing with contemporary social problems, signaled the end of the rhetorical and highly stylized German drama of the 19th century. Encouraged by the controversy, Hauptmann wrote in rapid succession a number of outstanding dramas on naturalistic themes (heredity, the plight of the poor, the clash of personal needs with societal restrictions) in which he artistically reproduced social reality and common speech. Most gripping and humane, as well as most objectionable to the political authorities at the time of its publication, is *Die Weber* (1892; *The Weavers*), a compassionate dramatization of the Silesian weavers' revolt of 1844. *Das Friedensfest* (1890; "The Peace Festival") is an analysis of the troubled relations within a neurotic family, while *Einsame Menschen* (1891; *Lonely Lives*) describes the tragic end of an unhappy intellectual torn between his wife and a young woman (patterned after the writer Lou Andreas-Salomé) with whom he can share his thoughts.

Hauptmann resumed his treatment of proletarian tragedy with *Fuhrmann Henschel* (1898; *Drayman Henschel*), a claustrophobic study of a workman's personal deterioration from the stresses of his domestic life. However, critics felt that the playwright had abandoned naturalistic tenets in *Hanneles Himmelfahrt* (1894; *The Assumption of Hannele*), a poetic evocation of the dreams an abused workhouse girl has shortly before she dies. *Der Biberpelz* (1893; *The Beaver Coat*) is a successful comedy, written in a Berlin dialect, that centres on a cunning female thief and her successful confrontation with pompous, stupid Prussian officials.

Hauptmann's longtime estrangement from his wife resulted in their divorce in 1904, and in the same year he married the violinist Margarete Marschalk, with whom he had moved in 1901 to a house in Agnetendorf in Silesia. Hauptmann spent the rest of his life there, though he traveled frequently.

Although Hauptmann helped to establish naturalism in Germany, he later abandoned naturalistic principles in his plays. In his later plays, fairy-tale and saga elements mingle with mystical religiosity and mythical symbolism. The portrayal of the primordial forces of the human personality in a historical setting (*Kaiser Karls Geisel*, 1908; *Charlemagne's Hostage*) stands beside naturalistic studies of the destinies of contemporary people (*Dorothea Angermann*, 1926). The culmination of the final phase in Hauptmann's dramatic work is the Atrides cycle, *Die Atriden-Tetralogie* (1941–48), which expresses through tragic Greek myths Hauptmann's horror of the cruelty of his own time.

Hauptmann's stories, novels, and epic poems are as varied as his dramatic works and are often thematically interwoven with them. The novel *Der Narr in Christo, Emanuel Quint* (1910; *The Fool in Christ, Emanuel Quint*) depicts, in a modern parallel to the life of Christ, the passion of a Silesian carpenter's son, possessed by pietistic ecstasy. A contrasted figure is the apostate priest in his most famous story, *Der Ketzer von Soana* (1918; *The Heretic of Soana*), who surrenders himself to a pagan cult of Eros.

In his early career Hauptmann found sustained effort difficult; later his literary production became more prolific, but it also became more uneven in quality. For example, the ambitious and visionary epic poems *Till Eulenspiegel* (1928) and *Der grosse Traum* (1942; "The Great Dream") successfully synthesize his scholarly pursuits with his philosophical and religious thinking, but are of uncertain literary value. The cosmological speculations of Hauptmann's later decades distracted him from his spontaneous talent for creating characters that come alive on the stage and in the imagination of the reader. Nevertheless, Hauptmann's literary reputation in Germany was unequaled until the ascendancy of Nazism, when he was barely tolerated by the regime and at the same time was denounced by émigrés for staying in Germany. Though privately out of tune with the Nazi ideology, he was politically naive and tended to be indecisive. He remained in Germany throughout World War II and died a year after his Silesian environs had been occupied by the Soviet Red Army.

Hauptmann was the most prominent German dramatist of the early 20th century. The unifying element of his vast and varied literary output is his sympathetic concern for human suffering, as expressed through characters who are generally passive victims of social and other elementary forces. His plays, the early naturalistic ones especially, are still frequently performed.

*C*ONSTANTINE *C*AVAFY

(b. April 17, 1863, Alexandria, Egypt—d. April 29, 1933, Alexandria)

The Greek poet Konstantínos Pétrou Kaváfis (better known as Constantine Cavafy) became one of the most important figures not only in Greek poetry but in Western poetry as well. He lived most of his life in Alexandria, Egypt.

He loved English and French literature and generally spoke English; even his Greek had a British accent.

Cavafy's parents were both from Constantinople (now Istanbul). His father, a merchant in the import-export business, worked in Constantinople and England, eventually establishing a firm with his brother George. After living for some years in England, the family eventually settled in Alexandria, where Constantine, the youngest of seven boys, was born. Cavafy's father died suddenly in 1870, and two years later his widow moved with her sons to England. The branch offices that had been established in Liverpool and London declined and failed and after some seven years most of the family returned to Alexandria. They were once again uprooted in 1882, when the British bombarded the city and then occupied it.

The years Cavafy spent in England during his youth were instrumental in the formation of his cosmopolitan character. Although he wrote much, he was his own harshest critic, publishing only about 200 poems in his lifetime. His most important poetry was written after his 40th year, and with some justification he called himself a "poet of old age." A skeptic, he denied or ridiculed traditional values of Christianity, patriotism, and heterosexuality, though he was ill at ease with his own nonconformity. His language is a mixture of the refined and stilted Greek called Katharevusa, inherited from the Byzantines, and the Demotic, or spoken, tongue. His style and tone are intimate and realistic. The lyric treatment he gave to familiar historical themes made him popular and influential after his death.

He became known to English readers from the many references to his work in Lawrence Durrell's *The Alexandria Quartet* (four interconnected novels published between 1957 and 1960). Cavafy's poems were first published without date before World War II and reprinted in 1949. English translations of his work are numerous and include

The Poems of C.P. Cavafy (1951), *The Complete Poems of Cavafy* (1961, expanded ed. 1976), and *The Collected Poems of C.P. Cavafy* (2006). *Collected Poems* (2009) and *The Unfinished Poems* (2009), both translated by Daniel Mendelsohn, are together a definitive collection in English of Cavafy's published and unpublished works.

FRANK WEDEKIND

(b. July 24, 1864, Hannover, Hanover [Germany] — d. March 9, 1918, Munich)

The son of a German American father and a Swiss mother, Benjamin Franklin Wedekind lived in Switzerland from 1872 to 1884, when he moved to Munich, where he remained until his death. He was successively an advertising manager, the secretary of a circus, a journalist for the satirical weekly *Simplicissimus*, a cabaret performer, and the producer of his own plays. The electric quality of his personality has been attested by his contemporaries.

Wedekind's characteristic theme in his dramas was the antagonism of the elemental force of sex to the philistinism of society. In 1891 the publication of his tragedy *Frühlings Erwachen* (*The Awakening of Spring*, also published as *Spring Awakening*) created a scandal. Successfully produced by Max Reinhardt in 1905, the play is a series of brief scenes, some poetic and tender, others harsh and frank, dealing with the awakening of sexuality in three adolescents. In the Lulu plays, *Erdgeist* (1895; *Earth Spirit*) and *Die Büchse der Pandora* (1904; *Pandora's Box*), he extended the theme of sex to the underworld of society and introduced the eternal, amoral femme fatale Lulu, who is destroyed in the tragic conflict of sexual freedom with hypocritical bourgeois morality. These two tragedies inspired Alban Berg's opera *Lulu*. The character of Lulu is most identified with actress Louise Brooks, who portrayed her in G.W. Pabst's masterful silent film version of *Die Büchse der Pandora* (1929).

Wedekind wrote a number of other, less remembered plays as well as poetry, novels, songs, and essays. His diary was posthumously published as *Die Tagebücher: ein erotisches Leben* (1986; *Diary of an Erotic Life*). He was a direct forebear of the modern Theatre of the Absurd. He employed episodic scenes, fragmented dialogue, distortion, and caricature in his dramas, which helped transform the emphasis in theatre from the realism of his own age to the Expressionism of the following generation.

WILLIAM BUTLER YEATS

(b. June 13, 1865, Sandymount, Dublin, Ireland — d. January 28, 1939, Roquebrune-Cap-Martin, France)

William Butler Yeats's father, John Butler Yeats, was a barrister who eventually became a portrait painter. His mother, formerly Susan Pollexfen, was the daughter of a prosperous merchant in Sligo, in western Ireland. Through both parents Yeats claimed kinship with various Anglo-Irish Protestant families who are mentioned in his work. Normally, Yeats would have been expected to identify with his Protestant tradition—which represented a powerful minority among Ireland's predominantly Roman Catholic population—but he did not. Indeed, he was separated from both historical traditions available to him in Ireland—from the Roman Catholics, because he could not share their faith, and from the Protestants, because he felt repelled by their concern for material success. Yeats's best hope, he felt, was to cultivate the tradition of a hidden Ireland that existed largely in the anthropological evidence of its surviving customs, beliefs, and holy places, more pagan than Christian.

Youth and Early Writings

In 1867, when Yeats was only two, his family moved to London, but he spent much of his boyhood and school holidays in Sligo with his grandparents. This county—its scenery, folklore, and supernatural legend—would colour Yeats's work and form the setting of many of his poems. In 1880 his family moved back to Dublin, where he attended the high school. In 1883 he attended the Metropolitan School of Art in Dublin, where the most important part of his education was in meeting other poets and artists.

Meanwhile, Yeats was beginning to write: his first publication, two brief lyrics, appeared in the *Dublin University Review* in 1885. When the family moved back to London in 1887, Yeats took up the life of a professional writer. He joined the Theosophical Society, whose mysticism appealed to him because it was a form of imaginative life far removed from the workaday world. The age of science was repellent to Yeats; he was a visionary, and he insisted upon surrounding himself with poetic images. He began a study of the prophetic books of William Blake, and this enterprise brought him into contact with other visionary traditions, such as the Platonic, the Neoplatonic, the Swedenborgian, and the alchemical.

Yeats was already a proud young man, and his pride required him to rely on his own taste and his sense of artistic style. He was not boastful, but spiritual arrogance came easily to him. His early poems, collected in *The Wanderings of Oisin, and Other Poems* (1889), are the work of an aesthete, often beautiful but always rarefied, a soul's cry for release from circumstance.

Yeats quickly became involved in the literary life of London. He became friends with William Morris and W.E. Henley, and he was a cofounder of the Rhymers' Club, whose members included his friends Lionel Johnson and Arthur Symons. In 1889 Yeats met Maud Gonne, an Irish beauty, ardent and brilliant. From that moment, as he wrote, "the troubling of my life began." He fell in love with her, but his love was hopeless. Maud Gonne liked and admired him, but she was not in love with him. Her passion was lavished upon Ireland; she was an Irish patriot, a rebel, and a rhetorician, commanding in voice and in person. When Yeats joined in the Irish nationalist cause, he did so partly from conviction, but mostly for love of Maud. When Yeats's play *Cathleen ni Houlihan* was first performed in Dublin in 1902, she played the title role. It was during this period that Yeats came under the influence of John O'Leary, a charismatic leader of the Fenians, a secret society of Irish nationalists.

Development as a Writer

After the rapid decline and death of the controversial Irish leader Charles Stewart Parnell in 1891, Yeats felt that Irish political life lost its significance. The vacuum left by politics might be filled, he felt, by literature, art, poetry, drama, and legend. *The Celtic Twilight* (1893), a volume of essays, was Yeats's first effort toward this end, but progress was slow until 1898, when he met Augusta Lady Gregory, an aristocrat who was to become a playwright and his close friend. She was already collecting old stories, the lore of the west of Ireland. Yeats found that this lore chimed with his feeling for ancient ritual, for pagan beliefs never entirely destroyed by Christianity. He felt that if he could treat it in a strict and high style, he would create a genuine poetry while, in personal terms, moving toward his own identity. From 1898, Yeats spent his summers at Lady Gregory's home, Coole Park, County Galway, and he eventually purchased a ruined Norman castle called Thoor Ballylee in the neighbourhood. Under the name of the Tower, this structure would become a dominant symbol in many of his latest and best poems.

In 1899 Yeats asked Maud Gonne to marry him, but she declined. Four years later she married Major John MacBride, an Irish soldier who shared her feeling for Ireland and her hatred of English oppression: he was one of the rebels later executed by the British government for their part in the Easter Rising of 1916. Meanwhile, Yeats devoted himself to literature and drama, believing that poems and plays would engender a national unity

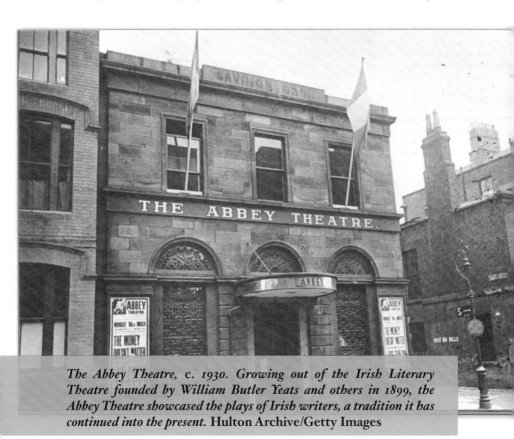

The Abbey Theatre, c. 1930. Growing out of the Irish Literary Theatre founded by William Butler Yeats and others in 1899, the Abbey Theatre showcased the plays of Irish writers, a tradition it has continued into the present. Hulton Archive/Getty Images

capable of transfiguring the Irish nation. He (along with Lady Gregory and others) was one of the originators of the Irish Literary Theatre, which gave its first performance in Dublin in 1899 with Yeats's play *The Countess Cathleen*. To the end of his life Yeats remained a director of this theatre, which became the Abbey Theatre in 1904. In the crucial period from 1899 to 1907, he managed the theatre's affairs, encouraged its playwrights (notably John Millington Synge), and contributed many of his own plays. Among the latter that became part of the Abbey Theatre's repertoire are *The Land of Heart's Desire* (1894), *Cathleen ni Houlihan* (1902), *The Hour Glass* (1903), *The King's Threshold* (1904), *On Baile's Strand* (1905), and *Deirdre* (1907).

Yeats published several volumes of poetry during this period, notably *Poems* (1895) and *The Wind Among the Reeds* (1899), which are typical of his early verse in their dreamlike atmosphere and their use of Irish folklore and legend. But in the collections *In the Seven Woods* (1903) and *The Green Helmet* (1910), Yeats slowly discarded the Pre-Raphaelite colours and rhythms of his early verse and purged it of certain Celtic and esoteric influences. The years from 1909 to 1914 mark a decisive change in his poetry. The otherworldly, ecstatic atmosphere of the early lyrics has cleared, and the poems in *Responsibilities: Poems and a Play* (1914) show a tightening and hardening of his verse line, a more sparse and resonant imagery, and a new directness with which Yeats confronts reality and its imperfections.

Maturity

In 1917 Yeats published *The Wild Swans at Coole*. From then onward he reached and maintained the height of his achievement—a renewal of inspiration and a perfecting of technique that are almost without parallel in the history of English poetry. *The Tower* (1928), named after the castle he owned and had restored, is the work of a fully accomplished artist; in it, the experience of a lifetime is brought to perfection of form. Still, some of Yeats's greatest verse was written subsequently, appearing in *The Winding Stair* (1929). The poems in both of these works use, as their dominant subjects and symbols, the Easter Rising and the Irish civil war; Yeats's own tower; the Byzantine Empire and its mosaics; Plato, Plotinus, and Porphyry; and the author's interest in contemporary psychical research. Yeats explained his own philosophy in the prose work *A Vision* (1925, revised version 1937); this meditation upon the relation between imagination, history, and the occult remains indispensable to serious students of Yeats despite its obscurities.

In 1913 Yeats spent some months at Stone Cottage, Sussex, with the American poet Ezra Pound acting as his secretary. Pound was then editing translations of the Noh plays of Japan, and Yeats was greatly excited by them. The Noh drama provided a framework of drama designed for a small audience of initiates, a stylized, intimate drama capable of fully using the resources offered by masks, mime, dance, and song and conveying—in contrast to the public theatre—Yeats's own recondite symbolism. Yeats devised what he considered an equivalent of the Noh drama in such plays as *Four Plays for Dancers* (1921), *At the Hawk's Well* (first performed 1916), and several others.

In 1917 Yeats asked Iseult Gonne, Maud Gonne's daughter, to marry him. She refused. Some weeks later he proposed to Miss George Hyde-Lees and was accepted; they were married in 1917. A daughter, Anne Butler Yeats, was born in 1919, and a son, William Michael Yeats, in 1921.

In 1922, on the foundation of the Irish Free State, Yeats accepted an invitation to become a member of the new Irish Senate: he served for six years. In 1923 he was awarded the Nobel Prize for Literature. Now a celebrated figure, he was indisputably one of the most significant modern poets. In 1936 his *Oxford Book of Modern Verse, 1892–1935*, a gathering of the poems he loved, was published. Still working on his last plays, he completed *The Herne's Egg*, his most raucous work, in 1938. Yeats's last two verse collections, *New Poems* and *Last Poems and Two Plays*, appeared in 1938 and 1939 respectively. In these books many of his previous themes are gathered up and rehandled, with an immense technical range; the aged poet was using ballad rhythms and dialogue structure with undiminished energy as he approached his 75th year.

Yeats died in January 1939 while abroad. Final arrangements for his burial in Ireland could not be made, so he was buried at Roquebrune, France. The intention of having his body buried in Sligo was thwarted when World War II began in the autumn of 1939. In 1948 his body was finally taken back to Sligo and buried in a little Protestant churchyard at Drumcliffe, as he specified in "Under Ben Bulben," in his *Last Poems*, under his own epitaph: "Cast a cold eye/On life, on death./Horseman, pass by!"

Assessment

Had Yeats ceased to write at age 40, he would probably now be valued as a minor poet writing in a dying Pre-Raphaelite tradition that had drawn renewed beauty and poignancy for a time from the Celtic revival. There is no precedent in literary history for a poet who produces his greatest work between the ages of 50 and 75. Yeats's work of this period takes its strength from his long and dedicated apprenticeship to poetry; from his experiments in a wide range of forms of poetry, drama, and prose; and from his spiritual growth and his gradual acquisition of personal wisdom, which he incorporated into the framework of his own mythology.

Yeats's mythology, from which arises the distilled symbolism of his great period, is not always easy to understand, nor did Yeats intend its full meaning to be immediately apparent to those unfamiliar with his thought and the tradition in which he worked. His own cyclic view of history suggested to him a recurrence and convergence of images, so that they become multiplied and enriched; and this progressive enrichment may be traced throughout his work. Among Yeats's dominant images are Leda and the Swan; Helen and the burning of Troy; the Tower in its many forms; the sun and moon; the burning house; cave, thorn tree, and well; eagle, heron, sea gull, and hawk; blind man, lame man, and beggar; unicorn and phoenix; and horse, hound, and boar. Yet these traditional images are continually validated by their alignment with Yeats's own personal experience, and it is this that gives them their peculiarly vital quality. In Yeats's verse they are often shaped into a strong and proud rhetoric and into the many poetic tones of which he was the master. All are informed by the two qualities that Yeats valued and that he retained into old age—passion and joy.

RUDYARD KIPLING

(b. December 30, 1865, Bombay, India—d. January 18, 1936, London, England)

English short-story writer, poet, and novelist Joseph Rudyard Kipling is chiefly remembered for his celebration of British imperialism, his tales and poems of British soldiers in India, and his tales for children. Kipling's father, John Lockwood Kipling, was an artist and scholar who had considerable influence on his son's work, became curator of the Lahore museum, and is described presiding over this "wonder house" in the first chapter of *Kim*, Rudyard's most famous novel. His mother was Alice Macdonald, two of whose sisters married the highly successful 19th-century painters Sir Edward Burne-Jones and Sir Edward Poynter, while a third married Alfred Baldwin and became the mother of Stanley Baldwin, later prime minister. These connections were of lifelong importance to Kipling.

Life

Much of his childhood was unhappy. Kipling was taken to England by his parents at age six and was left for five years at a foster home at Southsea, the horrors of which he described in the story *Baa, Baa, Black Sheep* (1888). He then went on to the United Services College at Westward Ho, north Devon, a new, inexpensive, and inferior board-ing school. It haunted Kipling for the rest of his life—but always as the glorious place celebrated in *Stalky & Co.* (1899) and related stories: an unruly paradise in which the highest goals of English education are met amid a tumult of teasing, bullying, and beating. The Stalky saga is one of Kipling's great imaginative achievements. Readers repelled by a strain of brutality—even of cruelty—in his writings should remember the sensitive and shortsighted boy who was brought to terms with the ethos of this deplorable estab-lishment through the demands of self-preservation.

Kipling returned to India in 1882 and worked for seven years as a journalist. His parents, although not officially important, belonged to the highest Anglo-Indian society, and Rudyard thus had opportunities for exploring the whole range of that life. All the while he had remained keenly obser-vant of the thronging spectacle of native India, which had engaged his interest and affection from earliest childhood. He was quickly filling the journals he worked for with prose sketches and light verse. He published the verse collection

Departmental Ditties in 1886, the short-story collection *Plain Tales from the Hills* in 1888, and between 1887 and 1889 he brought out six paper-covered volumes of short stories. Among the latter were *Soldiers Three, The Phantom Rickshaw* (containing the story "The Man Who Would Be King"), and *Wee Willie Winkie* (containing "Baa, Baa, Black Sheep"). When Kipling returned to England in 1889, his reputation had preceded him, and within a year he was acclaimed as one of the most brilliant prose writers of his time. His fame was redoubled upon the publication in 1892 of the verse collection *Barrack-Room Ballads*, which contained such popular poems as "Mandalay", "Gunga Din," and "Danny Deever." Not since the English poet Lord Byron had such a reputation been achieved so rapidly. When the poet laureate Alfred, Lord Tennyson died in 1892, it may be said that Kipling took his place in popular estimation.

In 1892 Kipling married Caroline Balestier, the sister of Wolcott Balestier, an American publisher and writer with whom he had collaborated in *The Naulahka* (1892), a facile and unsuccessful romance. That year the young couple moved to the United States and settled on Mrs. Kipling's property in Vermont, but their manners and attitudes were considered objectionable by their neighbours. Unable or unwilling to adjust to life in America, the Kiplings returned to England in 1896. Ever after Kipling remained very aware that Americans were "foreigners," and he extended to them, as to the French, no more than a semiexemption from his proposition that only "lesser breeds" are born beyond the English Channel.

Besides numerous short-story collections and poetry collections such as *The Seven Seas* (1896), Kipling published his best-known novels in the 1890s and immediately thereafter. His novel *The Light That Failed* (1890) is the story of a painter going blind and spurned by the woman he loves. *Captains Courageous* (1897), in spite of its sense of adventure, is often considered a poor novel because of the excessive descriptive writing. *Kim* (1901), although essentially a children's book, must be considered a classic. *The Jungle Books* (1894 and 1895) is a stylistically superb collection of stories linked by poems for children. These books give further proof that Kipling excelled at telling a story but was inconsistent in producing balanced, cohesive novels.

In 1902 Kipling bought a house at Burwash, Sussex, which remained his home until his death. Sussex was the background of much of his later writing—especially in *Puck of Pook's Hill* (1906) and *Rewards and Fairies* (1910), two volumes that, although devoted to simple dramatic presentations of English history, embodied some of his deepest intuitions. In 1907 he received the Nobel Prize for Literature, the first Englishman to be so honoured. In South Africa, where he spent much time, he was given a house by Cecil Rhodes, the diamond magnate and South African statesman. This association fostered Kipling's imperialist persuasions, which were to grow stronger with the years. These convictions are not to be dismissed in a word; they were bound up with a genuine sense of a civilizing mission that required every Englishman, or, more broadly, every white man, to bring European culture to those they viewed as heathen natives of the uncivilized world. Kipling's ideas were not in accord with much that was liberal in the thought of the age, and as he became older he was an increasingly isolated figure. When he died, two days before King George V, he must have seemed to many a far less representative Englishman than his sovereign.

Assessment

Kipling's poems and stories were extraordinarily popular in the late 19th and early 20th century, but after World War I his reputation as a serious writer suffered through his being widely viewed as a jingoistic imperialist. As a poet he scarcely ranks high, although his rehabilitation was attempted by so distinguished a critic as T.S. Eliot. His verse is indeed vigorous, and in dealing with the lives and colloquial speech of common soldiers and sailors it broke new ground. But balladry, music-hall song, and popular hymnology provide its unassuming basis; and even at its most serious—as in *Recessional* (1897) and similar pieces in which Kipling addressed himself to his fellow countrymen in times of crisis—the effect is rhetorical rather than imaginative.

But it is otherwise with Kipling's prose. In the whole sweep of his adult storytelling, he displays a steadily developing art, from the early volumes of short stories set in India through the collections *Life's Handicap* (1891), *Many Inventions* (1893), *The Day's Work* (1898), *Traffics and Discoveries* (1904), *Actions and Reactions* (1909), *Debits and Credits* (1926), and *Limits and Renewals* (1932). While his later stories cannot exactly be called better than the earlier ones, they are as good—and they bring a subtler if less dazzling technical proficiency to the exploration of deeper though sometimes more perplexing themes. It is a far cry from the broadly effective eruption of the supernatural in *The Phantom Rickshaw* (1888) to its subtle exploitation in *The Wish House* or *A Madonna of the Trenches* (1924), or from the innocent chauvinism of the bravura *The Man Who Was* (1890) to the depth of implication beneath the seemingly insensate xenophobia of *Mary Postgate* (1915). There is much in Kipling's later art to curtail its popular appeal. It is compressed and elliptical in manner and sombre in many of its themes. The author's critical reputation declined steadily during his lifetime—a decline that can scarcely be accounted for except in terms of political prejudice. Paradoxically, postcolonial critics later rekindled an intense interest in his work, viewing it as both symptomatic and critical of imperialist attitudes.

Rudyard Kipling's illustration for "The Elephant's Child" from Just
So Stories *(1902).*

Kipling, it should be noted, wrote much and successfully for children; for the very young in *Just So Stories*
(1902), and for others in *The Jungle Books* and in *Puck of
Pook's Hill* and *Rewards and Fairies.*

BEATRIX POTTER

(b. July 28, 1866, South Kensington, Middlesex [now in Greater
London], England—d. December 22, 1943, Sawrey, Lancashire
[now in Cumbria])

Helen Beatrix Potter was the only daughter of heirs to cotton fortunes. She spent a solitary childhood, enlivened by long holidays in Scotland or the English Lake District, which inspired her love of animals and stimulated her imaginative watercolour drawings. On one of these holidays in Scotland, at age 27, she sent an illustrated animal story to a sick child of a former governess, about four bunnies named Flopsy, Mopsy, Cotton-tail, and Peter. The illustrated letter was so well received that she decided to privately publish it as *The Tale of Peter Rabbit* (1900). In 1902 it was published commercially with great success by Frederick Warne & Company, which in the next 20 years brought out 22 additional books, beginning with *The Tailor of Gloucester* (1903), *The Tale of Squirrel Nutkin* (1903), and *The Tale of Benjamin Bunny* (1904). Among the many additional animal characters she created are Jeremy Fisher, Jemima Puddle-Duck, and Mrs. Tiggy-Winkle. She took the significant step of designing her books in a tiny format so that even the smallest children could hold them. Her stories combined a deceptively simple prose, concealing dry North Country humour, with illustrations in the best English watercolour tradition. (In old age, as her sight deteriorated, she lost much of her freshness of vision, and her last few stories, written for publication in the United States, did not match her earlier work in style or draftsmanship.)

During her summer trips with her parents, Potter also closely studied fungi, of which she made detailed drawings; she wrote a paper on spore germination that was read before the Linnean Society in 1897. Despite strong parental opposition, she became engaged in 1905 to Norman Warne, the son of her publisher, and after his sudden death a few months later she spent much of her time alone at Hill Top, a small farm in the village of Sawrey in the Lake District, bought with the proceeds of a legacy and the royalties from her books. In 1913 she married her solicitor, William Heelis, and spent the last 30 years of her life extending her farm property and breeding Herdwick sheep. She bequeathed her land to the National Trust, which maintains the Hill Top farmhouse as it was when she lived in it.

H.G. WELLS

(b. September 21, 1866, Bromley, Kent, England—d. August 13, 1946, London)

The English novelist, journalist, sociologist, and historian Herbert George Wells is best known for such science fiction novels as *The Time Machine* and *The War of the Worlds* and such comic novels as *Tono-Bungay* and *The History of Mr. Polly*. In his lifetime, he was regarded as the chief literary spokesman of the liberal optimism that preceded World War I.

Early Life

Wells was the son of domestic servants turned small shopkeepers. He grew up under the continual threat of poverty, and at age 14, after a very inadequate education supplemented by his inexhaustible love of reading, he was apprenticed to a draper (cloth dealer) in Windsor. His employer soon dismissed him; and he became assistant to a chemist, then to another draper, and finally, in 1883, an usher (assistant teacher) at Midhurst Grammar School. At 18 he won a scholarship to study biology at the Normal School (later the Royal College) of Science, in South Kensington, London, where British biologist T.H. Huxley was one of his teachers. He graduated from

London University in 1888, becoming a science teacher and undergoing a period of ill health and financial worries, the latter aggravated by his marriage, in 1891, to his cousin, Isabel Mary Wells. The marriage was not a success, and in 1894 Wells ran off with Amy Catherine Robbins (d. 1927), a former pupil, who in 1895 became his second wife.

Early Writings

Wells's first published book was a *Textbook of Biology* (1893). With his first novel, *The Time Machine* (1895), which was immediately successful, he began a series of science fiction novels that revealed him as a writer of marked originality and an immense fecundity of ideas: *The Wonderful Visit* (1895), *The Island of Doctor Moreau* (1896), *The Invisible Man* (1897), *The War of the Worlds* (1898), *The First Men in the Moon* (1901), and *The Food of the Gods* (1904). He also wrote many short stories, which were collected in *The Stolen Bacillus* (1895), *The Plattner Story* (1897), and *Tales of Space and Time* (1899). For a time he acquired a reputation as a prophet of the future, and indeed, in *The War in the Air* (1908), he foresaw certain developments in the military use of aircraft. But his imagination flourished at its best not in the manner of the comparatively mechanical anticipations of Jules Verne but in the astronomical fantasies of *The First Men in the Moon* and *The War of the Worlds*, the latter of which introduced the image of the Martian that has passed into popular mythology.

Behind his inventiveness lay a passionate concern for humanity and society, which increasingly broke into the fantasy of his science fiction, often diverting it into satire and sometimes, as in *The Food of the Gods*, destroying its credibility. Eventually, Wells decided to abandon science fiction for comic novels of lower middle-class life, most notably in *Love and Mr. Lewisham* (1900), *Kipps: The Story of a Simple Soul* (1905), and *The History of Mr. Polly* (1910). In these novels, and in *Tono-Bungay* (1909), he drew on memories of his own earlier life, and, through the thoughts of inarticulate yet often ambitious heroes, revealed the hopes and frustrations of clerks, shop assistants, and underpaid teachers, who had rarely before been treated in fiction with such sympathetic understanding. In these novels, too, he made his liveliest, most persuasive comment on the problems of Western society that were soon to become his main preoccupation. The sombre vision of a dying world in *The Time Machine* shows that, in his long-term view of humanity's prospects, Wells felt much of the pessimism prevalent in the 1890s. In his short-term view, however, his study of biology led him to hope that human society would evolve into higher forms, and with *Anticipations* (1901), *Mankind in the Making* (1903), and *A Modern Utopia* (1905), he took his place in the British public's mind as a leading preacher of the doctrine of social progress. About this time, too, he became an active socialist, and in 1903 joined the Fabian Society, a middle-class socialist group, though he soon began to criticize its methods. The bitter quarrel he precipitated by his unsuccessful attempt to wrest control of the Fabian Society from George Bernard Shaw and Sidney and Beatrice Webb in 1906–07 is retold in his novel *The New Machiavelli* (1911), in which the Webbs are parodied as the Baileys.

Middle and Late Works

After about 1906 the pamphleteer and the novelist were in conflict in Wells, and only *The History of Mr. Polly* and the lighthearted *Bealby* (1915) can be considered primarily as fiction. His later novels are mainly discussions of social or political themes that show little concern for the novel as a literary form. Wells himself affected not to care about the literary merit of his work, and he rejected the tutelage of the American novelist Henry James, saying, "I would rather be called a journalist than an artist." Indeed, his novel *Boon* (1915) included a spiteful parody of James. His next novel, *Mr. Britling Sees It Through* (1916), though touched by the prejudice and shortsightedness of wartime, gives a brilliant picture of the English people in World War I.

World War I shook Wells's faith in even short-term human progress, and in subsequent works he modified his conception of social evolution, putting forward the view that humans could only progress if they adapted to changing circumstances through knowledge and education. To help bring about this process of adaptation Wells began an ambitious work of popular education, of which the main products were *The Outline of History* (1920; revised 1931), *The Science of Life* (1931), cowritten with biologist and educator Julian Huxley and G.P. Wells (his elder son by his second wife), and *The Work, Wealth, and Happiness of Mankind* (1932). At the same time he continued to publish works of fiction, in which his gifts of narrative and dialogue give way almost entirely to polemics. His sense of humour reappears, however, in the reminiscences of his *Experiment in Autobiography* (1934).

In 1933 Wells published a novelized version of a film script, *The Shape of Things to Come*. (Produced by Alexander Korda, the film *Things to Come* [1936] remains, on account of its special effects, one of the outstanding British films of the 20th century.) Wells's version reverts to the utopianism of some earlier books, but as a whole his outlook grew steadily less optimistic, and some of his later novels contain much that is bitterly satiric. Fear of a tragic wrong turning in the development of the human race, to which he had early given imaginative expression in the grotesque animal mutations of *The Island of Doctor Moreau*, dominates the short novels and fables he wrote in the later 1930s. Wells was now ill and aging. With the outbreak of World War II, he lost all confidence in the future, and in *Mind at the End of Its Tether* (1945) he depicts a bleak vision of a world in which nature has rejected, and is destroying, humankind.

Assessment

No other writer has caught so vividly the energy of the period after World War I, its adventurousness, its feeling of release from the conventions of Victorian thought and propriety. Wells's influence was enormous, both on his own generation and on that which immediately followed it. None of his contemporaries did more to encourage revolt against Christian tenets and accepted codes of behaviour, especially as regards sex, in which, both in his books and in his personal life, he was a persistent advocate of an almost complete freedom. Though in many ways hasty, ill-tempered, and contradictory, Wells was undeviating and fearless in his efforts for social equality, world peace, and what he considered to be the future good of humanity.

As a creative writer his reputation rests on the early science fiction books and on the comic novels. In his science fiction, he took the ideas and fears that haunted the mind of his age and gave them symbolic expression as brilliantly conceived fantasy made credible by the quiet realism of its setting. In the comic novels he shows a fund of humour and a deep sympathy for ordinary people. Wells's prose style is always careless and lacks grace, yet he has his own gift of phrase and a true ear for vernacular speech, especially that of the lower middle class of London and southeastern England. His best work has a vigour, vitality, and exuberance unsurpassed, in its way, by that of any other British writer of the early 20th century.

RUBÉN DARÍO

(b. January 18, 1867, Metapa [now Ciudad Darío],
Nicaragua—d. February 6, 1916, León)

Félix Rubén García Sarmiento, who published under the name of Rubén Darío, was an influential Nicaraguan poet, journalist, and diplomat. As a leader of the Spanish American literary movement known as Modernismo, which flourished at the end of the 19th century, he revivified and modernized poetry in Spanish on both sides of the Atlantic through his experiments with rhythm, metre, and imagery. Darío developed a highly original poetic style that founded a tradition.

Life and Work

Precocious and prolific, from age 14 he signed the name Rubén Darío to his poems and stories of love, heroism, and adventure, which, although imitative in form, showed a strikingly vivid imagination. In 1886 he left Nicaragua, beginning the travels that continued throughout his life. He settled for a time in Chile, where in 1888 he published his first major work, *Azul* ("Blue"), a

Rubén Darío. Universal Images Group/Getty Images

collection of short stories, descriptive sketches, and verse. This volume was soon recognized in Europe and Latin America as the herald of a new era in Spanish American literature. Darío had only recently become acquainted with French Parnassian poetry, and *Azul* represents his attempt to apply to Spanish the tenets of that stylistic movement. (The Parnassians, in contrast to the Romantics, stressed restraint, objectivity, technical perfection, and precise description.) In the prose works in *Azul* he discarded the traditional long and grammatically complex Spanish sentence structure, replacing it with simple and direct language. Both the prose and poetry in this volume are generally concerned with objective description, and both deal with exotic subjects, chiefly classical mythology, France, and Asia. As a whole, the volume exhibits Darío's concern with "art for art's sake," and it reveals little interest in everyday life.

After his return to Central America in 1889 and two brief marriages (the first ended by his wife's death and the other by separation), he left to take up an appointment in 1893 as Colombian consul in Buenos Aires, where he found the cosmopolitan atmosphere stimulating. Young writers there hailed him as their leader, and the Modernist movement organized around him. Darío's next significant work, *Prosas profanas y otros poemas* (1896; "Profane Hymns and Other Poems"), a collection of verse, continued the innovative stylistic trends of *Azul* but treated its exotic scenes and personages in a manner more symbolic than objective, for it was influenced by the contemporary French Symbolist poets.

Darío went to Europe in 1898 as a correspondent for the Buenos Aires newspaper *La Nación*. Based in Paris and Majorca, he traveled extensively on the European continent on journalistic and diplomatic missions. By this time, world events and his own advancing age had brought about a profound change in his outlook on life. He became vitally concerned with the world outside the realm of art: the possible threat of North American imperialism after the defeat of Spain in 1898, the solidarity of Spanish-speaking peoples, the future of Spanish America after the collapse of Spain's empire in the New World, and the age-old problems of human existence. The collection that is generally considered to be his masterpiece, *Cantos de vida y esperanza* (1905; "Songs of Life and Hope"), reflects these concerns and is the culmination of his technical experimentation and his artistic resourcefulness.

On the outbreak of World War I in 1914, Darío left Europe, physically ill and on the brink of poverty. In an attempt to alleviate his financial difficulties, he began a lecture tour of North America, but he developed pneumonia in New York and died shortly after his return to his homeland.

Among the many editions of Darío's work in Spanish is *Obras completas*, 2 vol. (1971), edited by A.M. Plancarte. *Selected Poems*, translated by Lysander Kemp (1965, reissued 1988), contains an introduction by Octavio Paz and a tribute—originally given before the Buenos Aires Pen Club in 1933—by Federico García Lorca and Pablo Neruda. *Songs of Life and Hope/Canto de vida y esperanza* (2004) is a bilingual edition, edited and translated by Will Derusha and Alberto Acereda. They also published *Selected Poems of Rubén Darío: A Bilingual Anthology* (2001).

Assessment

In addition to the three major collections on which his greatest fame rests, Darío wrote approximately 100 short stories and tales, several volumes of poetry and penetrating literary criticism, and the journalistic articles that appeared in *La Nación* and elsewhere.

From the standpoint of artistic resourcefulness and technical perfection, Darío is considered by many to be one of the greatest poets who ever wrote in Spanish. Throughout his career he boldly experimented with many forms of verse, and he probably introduced more metrical innovations than any other Spanish-language poet. Darío's poetry is notable for its remarkable musicality, grace, and sonority, and he had a masterly command of rhyme and metrical structure. His earlier anecdotal and descriptive poems treat faraway places, mythology, and other exotic subjects with a rich lyricism, while the later poems in *Cantos de vida* contain a pronounced philosophical note and exhibit a poignant and powerful sense of the tragic side of life.

ARNOLD BENNETT

(b. May 27, 1867, Hanley, Staffordshire, England—d. March 27, 1931, London)

Enoch Arnold Bennett's father was a self-made man who had managed to qualify as a solicitor, and the family atmosphere was one of sturdy respectability and self-improvement. Arnold, the eldest of nine children, was educated at the Middle School, Newcastle-under-Lyme; he then entered his father's office as a clerk. In 1889 he moved to London, still as a solicitor's clerk, but soon gained a footing in literature by writing popular serial fiction and editing a women's magazine. After the publication of his first novel, *A Man from the North* (1898), he became a professional writer, living first in the Bedfordshire countryside, then, following his father's death, moving to Paris in 1903. In 1907 he married a French actress, Marguerite Soulié; they separated in 1921.

Bennett is best known for his highly detailed novels of the "Five Towns"—the Potteries, since amalgamated to form the city of Stoke-on-Trent, in his native Staffordshire. As a young writer he learned his craft from intensive study of the French realistic novelists, especially Gustave Flaubert and Honoré de Balzac, who emphasized detailed description of people, scenes, and events. He also owes an immediate debt to George Moore, who was influenced by the same writers. Bennett's criticism was of such high calibre that, even if he had never written fiction, he would rank as an important writer. He was less successful in his plays, although *Milestones* (1912), written with Edward Knoblock, and *The Great Adventure* (1913), adapted from his novel of five years earlier, *Buried Alive* (1908), both had long runs and have been revived.

As early as 1893 he had used the "Five Towns" as background for a story, and his major novels—*Anna of the Five Towns* (1902), *The Old Wives' Tale* (1908), and *Clayhanger* (1910; included with its successors, *Hilda Lessways*, 1911, and *These Twain*, 1916, in *The Clayhanger Family*, 1925)—have their setting there, the only exception being *Riceyman Steps* (1923), set in a lower-middle-class district of London.

Paris during Bennett's eight years there was the capital of the arts, and he made full use of his opportunities to study music, art, and literature as well as life. He retained an understanding of provincial life, but he shed the provincial outlook, becoming one of the least insular of Englishmen. At a time when the popular culture and the arcane complacencies of the elite were equally inbred, Bennett was a cosmopolitan who appreciated Impressionist painting, the ballet of Serge Diaghilev, and the music of Igor Stravinsky before they reached London. Later, reviewing a constant stream of new books, he unerringly picked out the important writers of the next generation—James Joyce, D.H. Lawrence, William Faulkner, Ernest Hemingway—and praised them discerningly. When Bennett returned to England, he did not return to the Potteries except on brief visits, but he continued to live there imaginatively, much as Joyce did in Dublin.

Bennett wrote 30 novels, and even many of the lesser ones display the essential Bennettian values, ironic yet kindly, critical yet with a large tolerance. His major works form an important link between the English novel and the mainstream of European realism. *The Journals of Arnold Bennett, 1896–1928* were published in three volumes (1932–33).

LUIGI PIRANDELLO

(b. June 28, 1867, Agrigento, Sicily, Italy—d. December 10, 1936, Rome)

Italian playwright, novelist, and short-story writer Luigi Pirandello was the son of a sulfur merchant who wanted him to enter commerce. Pirandello, however, was not interested in business; he wanted to study. He first went to Palermo, the capital of Sicily, and, in 1887, to the University of Rome. After a quarrel with the professor of classics there, he went in 1888 to the University of Bonn, Germany, where in 1891 he gained his doctorate in philology for a thesis on the dialect of Agrigento.

In 1894 his father arranged his marriage to Antonietta Portulano, the daughter of a business associate, a wealthy sulfur merchant. This marriage gave him financial independence, allowing him to live in Rome and to write. He had already published an early volume of verse, *Mal giocondo*

(1889), which paid tribute to the poetic fashions set by Giosuè Carducci. This was followed by other volumes of verse, including *Pasqua di Gea* (1891; dedicated to Jenny Schulz-Lander, the love he had left behind in Bonn) and a translation of J.W. von Goethe's *Roman Elegies* (1896; *Elegie romane*). But his first significant works were short stories, which he initially contributed to periodicals without payment.

In 1903 a landslide shut down the sulfur mine in which his wife's and his father's capital was invested. Suddenly poor, Pirandello was forced to earn his living not only by writing but also by teaching Italian at a teacher's college in Rome. As a further result of the financial disaster, his wife developed a persecution mania, which manifested itself in a frenzied jealousy of her husband. His torment ended only with her removal to a sanatorium in 1919 (she died in 1959). It was this bitter experience that finally determined the theme of his most characteristic work, already perceptible in his early short stories—the exploration of the tightly closed world of the forever changeable human personality.

Pirandello's early narrative style stems from the *verismo* ("realism") of two Italian novelists of the late 19th century—Luigi Capuana and Giovanni Verga. The titles of Pirandello's early collections of short stories—*Amori senza amore* (1894; "Loves Without Love") and *Beffe della morte e della vita* (1902–03; "The Jests of Life and Death")—suggest the wry nature of his realism that is seen also in his first novels: *L'esclusa* (1901; *The Outcast*) and *Il turno* (1902; Eng. trans. *The Merry-Go-Round of Love*). Success came with his third novel, often acclaimed as his best, *Il fu Mattia Pascal* (1904; *The Late Mattia Pascal*). Although the theme is not typically "Pirandellian," since the obstacles confronting its hero result from external circumstances, it already shows the acute psychological observation that Pirandello would later direct toward his characters' subconscious.

Pirandello's understanding of psychology was sharpened by reading such works as *Les altérations de la personnalité* (1892), by the French experimental psychologist Alfred Binet; and traces of its influence can be seen in the long essay *L'umorismo* (1908; *On Humor*), in which he examines the principles of his art. Common to both books is the theory of the subconscious personality, which postulates that what a person knows, or thinks he knows, is the least part of what he is. Pirandello had begun to focus his writing on the themes of psychology even before he knew of the work of Sigmund Freud, the founder of psychoanalysis. The psychological themes used by Pirandello found their most complete expression in the volumes of short stories *La trappola* (1915; "The Trap") and *E domani, lunedì ...* (1917; "And Tomorrow, Monday..."), and in such individual stories as "Una voce," "Pena di vivere così," and "Con altri occhi."

Meanwhile, he had been writing other novels, notably *I vecchi e i giovani* (1913; *The Old and The Young*) and *Uno, nessuno e centomila* (1925–26; *One, None, and a Hundred Thousand*). Both are more typical than *Il fu Mattia Pascal*. The first, a historical novel reflecting the Sicily of the end of the 19th century and the general bitterness at the loss of the ideals of the Risorgimento (the movement that led to the unification of Italy), suffers from Pirandello's tendency to "discompose" rather than to "compose" (to use his own terms, in *L'umorismo*), so that individual episodes stand out at the expense of the work as a whole. *Uno, nessuno e centomila*, however, is at once the most original and the most typical of his novels. It is a surrealistic description of the consequences of the hero's discovery that his wife (and others) see him with quite different eyes than he does himself. Its exploration of the reality of personality is of a type better known from his plays.

Pirandello wrote more than 50 plays. He had first turned to the theatre in 1898 with *L'epilogo*, but the accidents that prevented its production until 1910 (when it was retitled *La morsa*) kept him from other than sporadic attempts at drama until the success of *Così è (se vi pare)* in 1917. This delay may have been fortunate for the development of his dramatic powers. *L'epilogo* does not greatly differ from other drama of its period, but *Così è (se vi pare)* began the series of plays that were to make him world famous in the 1920s. Its title can be translated as *Right You Are (If You Think You Are)*. A demonstration, in dramatic terms, of the relativity of truth, and a rejection of the idea of any objective reality not at the mercy of individual vision, it anticipates Pirandello's two great plays, *Sei personaggi in cerca d'autore* (1921; *Six Characters in Search of an Author*) and *Enrico IV* (1922; *Henry IV*). *Six Characters* is the most arresting presentation of the typical Pirandellian contrast between art, which is unchanging, and life, which is an inconstant flux. Characters that have been rejected by their author materialize on stage, throbbing with a more intense vitality than the real actors, who, inevitably, distort their drama as they attempt its presentation. With his invention of the "theatre within the theatre" in this play, Pirandello became an important innovator in modern drama. And in *Henry IV* the theme is madness, which lies just under the skin of ordinary life and is, perhaps, superior to ordinary life in its construction of a satisfying reality. The play finds dramatic strength in its hero's choice of retirement into unreality in preference to life in the uncertain world.

The production of *Six Characters* in Paris in 1923 made Pirandello widely known, and his work became one of the central influences on the French theatre. French drama from the existential pessimism of Jean Anouilh and Jean-Paul Sartre to the absurdist comedy of Eugène Ionesco and Samuel Beckett is tinged with "Pirandellianism." His influence can also be detected in the drama of other countries, even in the religious verse dramas of T.S. Eliot.

In 1920 Pirandello said of his own art:

> *I think that life is a very sad piece of buffoonery; because we have in ourselves, without being able to know why, wherefore or whence, the need to deceive ourselves constantly by creating a reality (one for each and never the same for all), which from time to time is discovered to be vain and illusory... My art is full of bitter compassion for all those who deceive themselves; but this compassion cannot fail to be followed by the ferocious derision of destiny which condemns man to deception.*

This despairing outlook attained its most vigorous expression in Pirandello's plays, which were criticized at first for being too "cerebral" but later recognized for their underlying sensitivity and compassion. The plays' main themes are the necessity and the vanity of illusion, and the multifarious appearances, all of them unreal, of what is presumed to be the truth. A human being is not what he thinks he is, but instead is "one, no one and a hundred thousand," according to his appearance to this person or that, which is always different from the image of himself in his own mind. Pirandello's plays reflect the *verismo* of Capuana and Verga in dealing mostly with people in modest circumstances, such as clerks, teachers, and lodging-house keepers, but from whose vicissitudes he draws conclusions of general human significance.

The universal acclaim that followed *Six Characters* and *Henry IV* sent Pirandello touring the world (1925–27) with his own company, the Teatro d'Arte in Rome. It also emboldened him to disfigure some of his later plays (e.g., *Ciascuno a suo modo* [1924]) by calling attention to himself, just as in some of the later short stories it is the surrealistic and fantastic elements that are accentuated.

After the dissolution—because of financial losses—of the Teatro d'Arte in 1928, Pirandello spent his remaining years in frequent and extensive travel, and in 1934 he won the Nobel Prize for Literature. In his will he requested that there should be no public ceremony marking his death— only "a hearse of the poor, the horse and the coachman."

Maksim Gorky

(b. March 16 [March 28, New Style], 1868, Nizhny Novgorod, Russia—d. June 14, 1936)

Russian short-story writer and novelist Maksim (or Maxim) Gorky was born Aleksey Maksimovich Peshkov. Gorky's earliest years were spent in Astrakhan, where his father, a former upholsterer, became a shipping agent. When the boy was five his father died; Gorky returned to Nizhny Novgorod to live with his maternal grandparents, who brought him up after his mother remarried. The grandfather treated Gorky harshly. From his grandmother he received most of what little kindness he experienced as a child.

Childhood and Youth

Gorky knew the Russian working-class background intimately, for his grandfather afforded him only a few months of formal schooling, sending him out into the world to earn his living at age eight. He worked in a great variety of jobs, including assistant in a shoemaker's shop, errand boy for an icon painter, and dishwasher on a Volga steamer, where the cook introduced him to reading—soon to become his main passion in life. Frequently beaten by his employers, nearly always hungry and ill clothed, he came to know the seamy side of Russian life as few other Russian authors before or since. The bitterness of these early experiences later led him to choose the word *gorky* ("bitter") as his pseudonym.

His late adolescence and early manhood were spent in Kazan, where he worked as a baker, docker, and night watchman. There he first learned about Russian revolutionary ideas from representatives of the Populist movement, whose tendency to idealize the Russian peasant he later rejected. Oppressed by the misery of his surroundings, he attempted suicide by shooting himself. Leaving Kazan at age 21, he became a tramp, doing odd jobs of all kinds during extensive wanderings through southern Russia.

First Stories

In Tiflis (now Tbilisi, Georgia) Gorky began to publish stories in the provincial press, of which the first was "Makar Chudra" (1892). With the publication of "Chelkash" (1895) in a leading St. Petersburg journal, he began a success story as spectacular as any in the history of Russian literature. "Chelkash," one of his outstanding works, is the story of a colourful harbour thief in which elements of Romanticism and realism are mingled. It began Gorky's celebrated "tramp period," during which he described the social dregs of Russia. He expressed sympathy and self-identification with the strength and determination of the individual hobo or criminal, characters that had been treated more objectively by other authors. "Dvadtsat shest i odna"

(1899; "Twenty-Six Men and a Girl"), describing the harsh labour conditions in a bakery, is often regarded as his best short story. So great was the success of these works that Gorky began to be spoken of almost as an equal of Leo Tolstoy and Anton Chekhov.

Plays and Novels

Next Gorky wrote a series of plays and novels, all considered inferior to the best of his earlier stories. The first novel, *Foma Gordeyev* (1899), illustrates his admiration for strength of body and will in the masterful barge owner and rising capitalist Ignat Gordeyev, who is contrasted with his relatively feeble and intellectual son Foma, a "seeker after the meaning of life," as are many of Gorky's other characters. From this point, the rise of Russian capitalism became one of Gorky's main fictional interests. The other novels of this series are all to some extent failures because they lack sustained narrative and contain much rumination on the meaning of life. *Mat* (1906; *Mother*) is probably the least successful of the novels, yet it has considerable interest as Gorky's only long work devoted to the Russian revolutionary movement. It was made into a notable silent film by Vsevolod Pudovkin (1926) and dramatized by Bertolt Brecht in *Die Mutter* (1930–31). Gorky also wrote a series of plays, the most famous of which is *Na dne* (1902; *The Lower Depths*). A dramatic rendering of the kind of flophouse character that Gorky had already used so extensively in his stories, it still enjoys great success abroad and in Russia.

Marxist Activity

Between 1899 and 1906 Gorky lived mainly in St. Petersburg, where he became a Marxist, supporting the

Social Democratic Party. After the split in that party in 1903, Gorky went with its Bolshevik wing. But he was often at odds with the Bolshevik leader V.I. Lenin. Nor did Gorky ever, formally, become a member of Lenin's party, though his enormous earnings, which he largely gave to party funds, were one of that organization's main sources of income. In 1902 he was elected a member of the Russian Academy of Sciences, but his election was soon withdrawn for political reasons, an event that led to the resignations of Chekhov and the writer V.G. Korolenko from the academy.

Gorky took a prominent part in the Russian Revolution of 1905, was arrested in the following year, and was quickly released, partly as the result of protests from abroad. He toured America in the company of his mistress, an event that led to his partial ostracism there and to a consequent reaction on his part against the United States as expressed in stories about New York City, *Gorod zhyoltogo dyavola* (1906; "The City of the Yellow Devil").

Exile and Revolution

On leaving Russia in 1906, Gorky spent seven years as a political exile, living mainly in a villa on Capri in Italy. Politically, Gorky was a nuisance to his fellow Marxists because of his insistence on remaining independent, but his great influence was a powerful asset, which from their point of view outweighed such minor defects. He returned to Russia in 1913, and during World War I he agreed with the Bolsheviks in opposing Russia's participation in the war. He opposed the Bolshevik seizure of power during the Russian Revolution of 1917 and went on to attack the victorious Lenin's dictatorial methods in his newspaper *Novaya zhizn* ("New Life") until July 1918, when his protests were silenced by censorship on Lenin's orders.

Living in Petrograd (the renamed St. Petersburg), Gorky often assisted imprisoned scholars and writers, helping them survive hunger and cold. His efforts, however, were thwarted, and in 1921 Lenin sent Gorky into exile under the pretext of Gorky's needing specialized medical treatment abroad.

Last Period

In the decade ending in 1923 Gorky's greatest masterpiece appeared. This is the autobiographical trilogy *Detstvo* (1913–14; *My Childhood*), *V lyudyakh* (1915–16; *In the World*), and *Moi universitety* (1923; *My Universities*). The title of the last volume is sardonic because Gorky's only university had been that of life, and his wish to study at Kazan University had been frustrated. This trilogy is one of the finest autobiographies in Russian. It describes Gorky's childhood and early manhood and reveals him as an acute observer of detail, with a flair for describing his own family, his numerous employers, and a panoply of minor but memorable figures.

Gorky finished his trilogy abroad, where he also wrote the stories published in *Rasskazy 1922–1924* (1925; "Stories 1922–24"), which are among his best work. From 1924 he lived at a villa in Sorrento, Italy, to which he invited many Russian artists and writers who stayed for lengthy periods. Gorky's health was poor, and he was disillusioned by postrevolutionary life in Russia, but in 1928 he yielded to pressures to return, and in the following year he returned to the U.S.S.R. permanently and lived there until his death. His return coincided with the establishment of Stalin's ascendancy, and Gorky became a prop of Stalinist political orthodoxy. He was now more than ever the undisputed leader of Soviet writers, and, when the Soviet Writers' Union was founded in 1934, he became its first president.

At the same time, he helped to found the literary method of Socialist Realism, which was imposed on all Soviet writers and which obliged them—in effect—to become outright political propagandists.

Gorky remained active as a writer, but almost all his later fiction is concerned with the period before 1917. In *Delo Artamonovykh* (1925; *The Artamonov Business*), one of his best novels, he showed his continued interest in the rise and fall of prerevolutionary Russian capitalism. From 1925 until the end of his life, Gorky worked on the novel *Zhizn Klima Samgina* ("The Life of Klim Samgin"), which remained unfinished at his death. There were also more plays, but the most generally admired work is a set of reminiscences of Russian writers—*Vospominaniya o Tolstom* (1919; *Reminiscences of Leo Nikolaevich Tolstoy*) and *O pisatelyakh* (1928; "About Writers"). The memoir of Tolstoy is so lively and free from the hagiographic approach traditional in Russian studies of their leading authors that it has sometimes been acclaimed as Gorky's masterpiece. Almost equally impressive is Gorky's study of Chekhov.

Some mystery attaches to Gorky's death, which occurred suddenly in 1936 while he was under medical treatment. Whether his death was natural or not is unknown, but it came to figure in the trial of Nikolay I. Bukharin and others in 1938, at which it was claimed that Gorky had been the victim of an anti-Soviet plot by the "Bloc of Rightists and Trotskyites."

ANDRÉ GIDE

(b. November 22, 1869, Paris, France—d. February 19, 1951, Paris)

André-Paul-Guillaume Gide was the only child of Paul Gide and his wife, Juliette Rondeaux. His father was of southern Huguenot peasant stock; his mother, a Norman heiress, although Protestant by upbringing, belonged to a northern Roman Catholic family long established at Rouen. When Gide was eight he was sent to the École Alsacienne in Paris, but his education was frequently interrupted by neurotic bouts of ill health. After his father's early death in 1880, his well-being became the chief concern of his devoutly austere mother. Often kept at home, he was taught by indifferent tutors and by his mother's governess. While in Rouen Gide formed a deep attachment for his cousin, Madeleine Rondeaux.

Gide returned to the École Alsacienne to prepare for his *baccalauréat* examination, and after passing it in 1889, he decided to spend his life in writing, music, and travel. His first work was an autobiographical study of youthful unrest entitled *Les Cahiers d'André Walter* (1891; *The Notebooks of André Walter*). Written, like most of his later works, in the first person, it uses the confessional form in which Gide was to achieve his greatest successes.

Symbolist Period

In 1891 a school friend, the writer Pierre Louÿs, introduced Gide into the poet Stéphane Mallarmé's famous "Tuesday evenings," which were the centre of the French Symbolist movement, and for a time Gide was influenced by Symbolist aesthetic theories. His works "Narcissus" (1891), *Le Voyage d'Urien* (1893; *Urien's Voyage*), and "The Lovers' Attempt" (1893) belong to this period.

In 1893 Gide paid his first visit to North Africa, hoping to escape the constraints of his puritanically strict Protestant upbringing. Gide's contact with the Arab world and its radically different culture helped to liberate him from the Victorian social and sexual conventions he felt stifled by. One result of this nascent intellectual revolt against social hypocrisy was his growing awareness of his homosexuality. The lyrical prose poem *Les Nourritures ter-restres* (1897; *Fruits of the Earth*) reflects Gide's evolving notions of sin and his need for self-acceptance. But after he returned to France, Gide's relief at having shed the shackles of convention evaporated in what he called the "stifling atmosphere" of the Paris salons. He satirized his surroundings in *Marshlands* (1894), a brilliant parable of animals who, living always in dark caves, lose their sight because they never use it.

In 1894 Gide returned to North Africa, where he met Oscar Wilde and Lord Alfred Douglas, who encouraged him to embrace his homosexuality. He was recalled to France because of his mother's illness, however, and she died in May 1895.

In October 1895 Gide married his cousin Madeleine, who had earlier refused him. Early in 1896 he was elected mayor of the commune of La Roque. At 27, he was the youngest mayor in France. He took his duties seriously but managed to complete *Fruits of the Earth*. It was published in 1897 and fell completely flat, although after World War I it was to become Gide's most popular and influential work. Its call to each individual to express fully whatever is within struck an immediate chord with the postwar generation.

Great Creative Period

Le Prométhée mal enchaîné (1899; *Prometheus Misbound*), a return to the satirical style of *Urien's Voyage* and *Marshland*, is Gide's last discussion of the human search for individual values. His next tales mark the beginning of his great creative period. *L'Immoraliste* (1902; *The Immoralist*), *La Porte étroite* (1909; *Strait Is the Gate*), and *La Symphonie pastorale* (1919; "The Pastoral Symphony" in *Two Symphonies*) in their treatment of the problems of human relationships reflect Gide's own struggle to achieve harmony in his marriage.

These works mark an important stage in his development: adapting his works' treatment and style to his concern with psychological problems. *The Immoralist* and *Strait Is the Gate* are in the prose form that Gide termed a *récit*, i.e., a studiedly simple but deeply ironic tale in which a first-person narrator reveals the inherent moral ambiguities of life by means of his seemingly innocuous reminiscences. In these works Gide achieves a mastery of classical construction and a pure, simple style.

During most of this period Gide was suffering deep anxiety and distress. Although his love for Madeleine had given his life what he called its "mystic orientation," he found himself unable, in a close, permanent relationship, to reconcile this love with his need for freedom and for experience of every kind. *Les Caves du Vatican* (1914; *The Vatican Swindle*) marks the transition to the second phase of Gide's great creative period. He called it not a tale but a *sotie*, by which he meant a satirical work whose foolish or mad characters are treated farcically within an unconventional narrative structure. This was the first of his works to be violently attacked for anticlericalism.

In the early 1900s Gide had already begun to be widely known as a literary critic, and in 1908 he was foremost among those who founded *La Nouvelle Revue Française*, the literary review that was to unite progressive French writers until World War II. During World War I Gide worked in Paris, first for the Red Cross, then in a soldiers' convalescent home, and finally in providing shelter to war refugees. In 1916 he returned to Cuverville, his home since his marriage, and began to write again.

The war had intensified Gide's anguish, and early in 1916 he had begun to keep a second *Journal* (published in 1926 as *Numquid et tu?*) in which he recorded his search for God. Finally, however, unable to resolve the dilemma (expressed in his statement "Catholicism is inadmissible, Protestantism is intolerable; and I feel profoundly Christian"), he resolved to achieve his own ethic, and by casting off his sense of guilt to become his true self. Now, in a desire to liquidate the past, he began his autobiography, *Si le grain ne meurt* (1926; *If It Die...*), an account of his life from birth to marriage that is among the great works of confessional literature. In 1918 his friendship with the young future filmmaker Marc Allégret caused a serious crisis in his marriage, when his wife in jealous despair destroyed her "dearest possession on earth"—his letters to her.

After the war a great change took place in Gide, and his face began to assume the serene expression of his later years. By the decision involved in beginning his autobiography and the completion in 1918 of *Corydon* (a Socratic dialogue in defense of homosexuality begun earlier), he had achieved at last an inner reconciliation. *Corydon*'s publication in 1924 was disastrous, though, and Gide was violently attacked, even by his closest friends.

Gide called his next work, *Les Faux-Monnayeurs* (1926; *The Counterfeiters*), his only novel. He meant by this that in conception, range, and scope it was on a vaster scale than his tales or his *soties*. It is the most complex and intricately constructed of his works, dealing as it does with the relatives and teachers of a group of schoolboys subject to corrupting influences both in and out of the classroom. *The Counterfeiters* treats all of Gide's favourite themes in a progression of discontinuous scenes and happenings that come close to approximating the texture of daily life itself.

In 1925 Gide set off for French Equatorial Africa. When he returned he published *Voyage au Congo* (1927; *Travels in the Congo*), in which he criticized French colonial policies. The compassionate, objective concern for humanity that marks the final phase of Gide's life found expression in his political activities at this time. He

86

became the champion of society's victims and outcasts, demanding more humane conditions for criminals and equality for women. For a time it seemed to him that he had found a faith in communism. In 1936 he set out on a visit to the Soviet Union, but later expressed his disillusionment with the Soviet system in *Retour de l'U.R.S.S.* (1936; *Return from the U.S.S.R.*) and *Retouches à mon retour de l'U.R.S.S.* (1937; *Afterthoughts on the U.S.S.R.*).

Late Works

In 1938 Gide's wife, Madeleine, died. After a long estrangement they had been brought together by her final illness. To him she was always the great—perhaps the only— love of his life. With the outbreak of World War II, Gide began to realize the value of tradition and to appreciate the past. In a series of imaginary interviews written in 1941 and 1942 for *Le Figaro*, he expressed a new concept of liberty, declaring that absolute freedom destroys both the individual and society: freedom must be linked with the discipline of tradition. From 1942 until the end of the war Gide lived in North Africa. There he wrote "Theseus," whose story symbolizes Gide's realization of the value of the past: Theseus returns to Ariadne only because he has clung to the thread of tradition.

In June 1947 Gide received the first honour of his life: the Doctor of Letters of the University of Oxford. It was followed in November by the Nobel Prize for Literature. In 1950 he published the last volume of his *Journal*, which took the record of his life up to his 80th birthday. All Gide's writings illuminate some aspect of his complex character. He is seen at his most characteristic, however, in the *Journal* he kept from 1889, a unique work of more than a million words in which he records his experiences, impressions, interests, and moral crises during a period of more than 60 years. After its publication he resolved to write no more.

Gide's lifelong emphasis on the self-aware and sincere individual as the touchstone of both collective and individual morality was complemented by the tolerant and enlightened views he expressed on literary, social, and political questions throughout his career. For most of his life a controversial figure, Gide was long regarded as a revolutionary for his open support of the claims of the individual's freedom of action in defiance of conventional morality. Before his death he was widely recognized as an important humanist and moralist in the great 17th-century French tradition. The integrity and nobility of his thought and the purity and harmony of style that characterize his stories, verse, and autobiographical works have ensured his place among the masters of French literature.

*F*RANK *N*ORRIS

(b. March 5, 1870, Chicago, Illinois, U.S.—d. October 25, 1902, San Francisco, California)

American novelist Benjamin Franklin Norris, better known as Frank Norris, studied painting in Paris for two years before deciding that literature was his vocation. He attended the University of California in 1890–94 and then spent another year at Harvard University. He was a news correspondent in South Africa in 1895, an editorial assistant on the *San Francisco Wave* (1896–97), and a war correspondent in Cuba for *McClure's Magazine* in 1898. He joined the New York City publishing firm of Doubleday, Page, and Company in 1899. He died three years later after an operation for appendicitis.

Norris's first important novel, *McTeague* (1899), is a naturalist work set in San Francisco. It tells the story of a stupid and brutal dentist who murders his miserly wife and then meets his own end while fleeing through Death Valley. With this book and those that followed, Norris joined Theodore Dreiser in the front rank of American novelists. Norris's masterpiece, *The Octopus* (1901), was the first novel of a projected trilogy, *The Epic of the Wheat*, dealing with the economic and social forces involved in the production, distribution, and consumption of wheat. *The Octopus* pictures with bold symbolism the raising of wheat in California and the struggle of the wheat growers there against a monopolistic railway corporation. The second novel in the trilogy, *The Pit* (1903), deals with wheat speculation on the Chicago Board of Trade. The third novel, *Wolf*, unwritten at Norris's death, was to have shown the American-grown wheat relieving a famine-stricken village in Europe. *Vandover and the Brute*, posthumously published in 1914, is a study of degeneration. *McTeague* was filmed by Erich von Stroheim in 1924 under the title *Greed* and staged as an opera by composer William Bolcom and director Robert Altman in 1992.

After the example of Émile Zola and the European naturalists, Norris in *McTeague* sought to describe with realistic detail the influence of heredity and environment on human life. From *The Octopus* on he adopted a more humanitarian ideal and began to view the novel as a proper agent for social betterment. In *The Octopus* and other novels he strove to return American fiction, which was then dominated by historical romance, to more serious themes. Despite their romanticizing tendencies, his novels present a vividly authentic and highly readable picture of life in California at the turn of the 20th century. Norris's writings were collected (10 vol.) in 1928 (reissued 1967).

IVAN ALEKSEYEVICH BUNIN

(b. October 10 [October 22, New Style], 1870, Voronezh, Russia—d. November 8, 1953, Paris, France)

The descendant of an old noble family, Ivan Alekseyevich Bunin spent his childhood and youth in the Russian provinces. He attended secondary school in Yelets, in western Russia, but did not graduate; his older brother subsequently tutored him. Bunin began publishing poems and short stories in 1887, and in 1889–92 he worked for the newspaper *Orlovsky Vestnik* ("The Orlovsky Herald"). His first book, *Stikhotvoreniya: 1887–1891* ("Poetry: 1887–1891"), appeared in 1891 as a supplement to that newspaper. In the mid-1890s he was strongly drawn to the ideas of the novelist Leo Tolstoy, whom he met in person. During this period Bunin gradually entered the Moscow and St. Petersburg literary scenes, including the growing Symbolist movement. Bunin's *Listopad* (1901; "Falling Leaves"), a book of poetry, testifies to his association with the Symbolists, primarily Valery Bryusov. However, Bunin's work had more in common with the traditions of classical Russian literature of the 19th century, of which his older contemporaries Tolstoy and Anton Chekhov were models.

By the beginning of the 20th century, Bunin had become one of Russia's most popular writers. His sketches and stories "Antonovskiye yabloki" (1900; "Antonov Apples"), "Grammatika lyubvi" (1929; "Grammar of Love"), "Lyogkoye dykhaniye" (1922; "Light Breathing"), "Sny Changa" (1916; "The Dreams of Chang and Other Stories"), "Sukhodol" (1912; "Dry Valley"), "Derevnya"

(1910; "The Village"), and "Gospodin iz San-Frantsisko" (1916; "The Gentleman from San Francisco") show Bunin's penchant for extreme precision of language, delicate description of nature, detailed psychological analysis, and masterly control of plot. While his democratic views gave rise to criticism in Russia, they did not turn him into a politically engaged writer. Bunin also believed that change was inevitable in Russian life. His urge to keep his independence is evident in his break with the writer Maksim Gorky and other old friends after the Russian Revolution of 1917, which he perceived as the triumph of the basest side of the Russian people.

Bunin's articles and diaries of 1917–20 are a record of Russian life during the years of terror. In May 1918 he left Moscow and settled in Odessa (now in Ukraine), and at the beginning of 1920 he emigrated first to Constantinople (now Istanbul) and then to France, where he lived for the rest of his life. There he became one of the most famous Russian émigré writers. His stories, the novella *Mitina lyubov* (1925; *Mitya's Love*), and the autobiographical novel *Zhizn Arsenyeva* (*The Life of Arsenev*)—which Bunin began writing during the 1920s and of which he published parts in the 1930s and 1950s—were recognized by critics and Russian readers abroad as testimony of the independence of Russian émigré culture.

Bunin lived in the south of France during World War II, refusing all contact with the Nazis and hiding Jews in his villa. *Tyomnye allei* (1943; *Dark Avenues, and Other Stories*), a book of short stories, was one of his last great works. After the end of the war, Bunin was invited to return to the Soviet Union, but he remained in France. His *Vospominaniya* (*Memories and Portraits*) appeared in 1950. An unfinished book, *O Chekhove* (1955; "On Chekhov"; Eng. trans. *About Chekhov: The*

Unfinished Symphony), was published posthumously. His stories continued to enjoy popularity into the 21st century. Many were published in *Night of Denial: Stories and Novellas* (2006), translated by Robert Lee Bowie. Bunin was one of the first Russian émigré writers whose works were published in the Soviet Union after the death of Soviet leader Joseph Stalin.

JOHN MILLINGTON SYNGE

(b. April 16, 1871, Rathfarnham, near Dublin, Ireland—d. March 24, 1909, Dublin)

After studying at Trinity College and at the Royal Irish Academy of Music in Dublin, John Millington Synge pursued further studies from 1893 to 1897 in Germany, Italy, and France. In 1894 he abandoned his plan to become a musician and instead concentrated on languages and literature. He met William Butler Yeats while studying at the Sorbonne in Paris in 1896. Yeats inspired him with enthusiasm for the Irish literary renaissance and advised him to stop writing critical essays and instead to go to the Aran Islands and draw material from life. Already struggling against the progression of a lymphatic sarcoma that was to cause his death, Synge lived in the islands during part of each year (1898–1902), observing the people and learning their language, recording his impressions in *The Aran Islands* (1907) and basing his one-act plays *In the Shadow of the Glen* (first performed 1903) and *Riders to the Sea* (1904) on islanders' stories. In 1905 his first three-act play, *The Well of the Saints*, was produced.

Synge's travels on the Irish west coast inspired his most famous play, *The Playboy of the Western World* (1907).

This morbid comedy deals with the moment of glory of a peasant boy who becomes a hero in a strange village when he boasts of having just killed his father but who loses the villagers' respect when his father turns up alive. In protest against the play's unsentimental treatment of the Irishmen's love for boasting and their tendency to glamorize ruffians, the audience rioted at its opening at Dublin's Abbey Theatre. Riots of Irish Americans accompanied its opening in New York (1911), and there were further riots in Boston and Philadelphia. Synge remained associated with the Abbey Theatre, where his plays gradually won acceptance, until his death. His unfinished *Deirdre of the Sorrows*, a vigorous poetic dramatization of one of the great love stories of Celtic mythology, was performed there in 1910.

In the seven plays he wrote during his comparatively short career as a dramatist, Synge recorded the colourful and outrageous sayings, flights of fancy, eloquent invective, bawdy witticisms, and earthy phrases of the peasantry from Kerry to Donegal. In the process he created a new, musical dramatic idiom, spoken in English but vitalized by Irish syntax, ways of thought, and imagery.

MARCEL PROUST

(b. July 10, 1871, Auteuil, near Paris, France—d. November 18, 1922, Paris)

The French novelist Marcel Proust is known for his novel *À la recherche du temps perdu* (1913–27; *In Search of Lost Time*), a seven-volume work based on his own experiences. His father was Adrien Proust, an eminent physician of provincial French Catholic descent, and his mother, Jeanne, née Weil, was of a wealthy Jewish family.

Marcel Proust. Apic/Hulton Archive/Getty Images

Early Life and Influences

After a first asthma attack in 1880, Proust suffered from asthma throughout his life. His childhood holidays were spent at Illiers and Auteuil (which together became the Combray of his novel) or at seaside resorts in Normandy with his maternal grandmother. At the Lycée Condorcet (1882–89) he wrote for class magazines, fell in love with a little girl named Marie de Benardaky in the Champs-Élysées, made friends whose mothers were society hostesses, and was influenced by his philosophy master Alphonse Darlu.

He enjoyed the discipline and comradeship of military service at Orléans (1889–90) and studied at the School of Political Sciences, taking licences in law (1893) and in literature (1895). During these student days his thought was influenced by the philosophers Henri Bergson (his cousin by marriage) and Paul Desjardins and by the historian Albert Sorel. Meanwhile, via the bourgeois salons of Madames Straus, Arman de Caillavet, Aubernon, and Madeleine Lemaire, he became an observant habitué of the most exclusive drawing rooms of the nobility.

In 1896 he published *Les Plaisirs et les jours* (*Pleasures and Days*), a collection of short stories at once precious and profound, most of which had appeared during 1892–93 in the magazines *Le Banquet* and *La Revue Blanche*. From 1895 to 1899 he wrote *Jean Santeuil*, an autobiographical novel that, though unfinished and ill-constructed, showed awakening genius and foreshadowed *À la recherche*. A gradual disengagement from social life coincided with growing ill health and with his active involvement in the Dreyfus affair of 1897–99, when French politics and society were split by the movement to liberate the Jewish army officer Alfred Dreyfus, who had been unjustly imprisoned on Devil's Island as a spy. Proust helped to organize petitions and assisted Dreyfus's lawyer Labori, courageously defying the risk of social ostracism. (Although Proust was not, in fact, ostracized, the experience helped to crystallize his disillusionment with aristocratic society, which became visible in his novel.)

Proust's discovery of John Ruskin's art criticism in 1899 caused him to abandon *Jean Santeuil* and to seek a new revelation in the beauty of nature and in Gothic architecture, considered as symbols of the human confrontation with eternity: "Suddenly," he wrote, "the universe regained in my eyes an immeasurable value." On this quest he visited Venice (with his mother in May 1900) and the churches of France and translated Ruskin's *Bible of Amiens* and *Sesame and Lilies*, with prefaces in which the note of his mature prose is first heard.

Financial Independence

The death of Proust's father in 1903 and of his mother in 1905 left him grief stricken and alone but financially independent and free to attempt his great novel. At least one early version was written in 1905–06. Another, begun in 1907, was laid aside in October 1908. This had itself been interrupted by a series of brilliant parodies—of Balzac, Flaubert, Renan, Saint-Simon, and others of Proust's favourite French authors—called "L'Affaire Lemoine" (published in *Le Figaro*), through which he endeavoured to purge his style of extraneous influences. Then, realizing the need to establish the philosophical basis that his novel had hitherto lacked, he wrote the essay *Contre Sainte-Beuve* (published 1954), attacking the French critic's view of literature as a pastime of the cultivated intelligence and putting forward his own, in which the artist's task is to release from the buried world of unconscious memory the ever-living reality to which habit makes us blind.

In January 1909 occurred the real-life incident of an involuntary revival of a childhood memory through the taste of tea and a rusk biscuit (which in his novel became madeleine cake); in May the characters of his novel invaded his essay; and, in July of this crucial year, he began *À la recherche du temps perdu*. He thought of marrying "a very young and delightful girl" whom he met at Cabourg, a seaside resort in Normandy that became the Balbec of his novel, where he spent summer holidays from 1907 to 1914. Instead he retired from the world to write his novel, finishing the first draft in September 1912.

The first volume, *Du côté de chez Swann* (*Swann's Way*), was refused by the best-selling publishers Fasquelle and Ollendorff and even by the intellectual *La Nouvelle Revue Française*, under the direction of the novelist André Gide, but was finally issued at the author's expense in November 1913 by the progressive young publisher Bernard Grasset and met with some success. Proust then planned only two further volumes, the premature appearance of which was fortunately thwarted by his anguish at the flight and death of his secretary Alfred Agostinelli and by the outbreak of World War I.

During the war he revised the remainder of his novel, enriching and deepening its feeling, texture, and construction, increasing the realistic and satirical elements, and tripling its length. In this majestic process he transformed a work that in its earlier state was still below the level of his highest powers into one of the greatest achievements of the modern novel.

In March 1914, instigated by the repentant Gide, *La Nouvelle Revue Française* offered to take over his novel, but Proust now rejected them. Further negotiations in May–September 1916 were successful, and in June 1919 *À l'ombre des jeunes filles en fleurs* (*Within a Budding Grove*) was published simultaneously with a reprint of *Swann* and with *Pastiches et mélanges*, a miscellaneous volume containing "L'Affaire Lemoine" and the Ruskin prefaces.

In December 1919, through Léon Daudet's recommendation, *À l'ombre* received the Prix Goncourt, and Proust suddenly became world famous. Three more installments appeared in his lifetime, with the benefit of his final revision, comprising *Le Côté de Guermantes* (1920–21; *The Guermantes Way*) and *Sodome et Gomorrhe* (1921–22; *Sodom and Gomorrah*). He died in Paris of pneumonia, succumbing to a weakness of the lungs that many had mistaken for a form of hypochondria and struggling to the last with the revision of *La Prisonnière* (*The Captive*). The last three parts of *À la recherche* were published posthumously, in an advanced but not final stage of revision: *La Prisonnière* (1923), *Albertine disparue* (1925; *The Fugitive*), and *Le Temps retrouvé* (1927; *Time Regained*).

À la recherche du temps perdu is the story of Proust's own life, told as an allegorical search for truth. At first, the only childhood memory available to the middle-aged narrator is the evening of a visit from the family friend, Swann, when the child forced his mother to give him the goodnight kiss that she had refused. But, through the accidental tasting of tea and a madeleine cake, the narrator retrieves from his unconscious memory the landscape and people of his boyhood holidays in the village of Combray. In an ominous digression on love and jealousy, the reader learns of the unhappy passion of Swann (a Jewish dilettante received in high society) for the courtesan Odette, whom he had met in the bourgeois salon of the Verdurins during the years before the narrator's birth. As an adolescent the narrator falls in love with Gilberte (the daughter of Swann and Odette) in the Champs-Élysées. During a seaside holiday at Balbec, he meets the handsome young nobleman Saint-Loup, Saint-Loup's strange uncle the Baron de Charlus, and a band of young girls led by Albertine. He falls in love with the Duchesse de Guermantes but, after an autumnal visit to Saint-Loup's garrison-town Doncières, is cured when he meets her in society. As he travels through the Guermantes's world, its apparent poetry and intelligence is dispersed and its real vanity and sterility revealed. Charlus is discovered to be homosexual, pursuing the elderly tailor Jupien and the young violinist Morel, and the vices of Sodom and Gomorrah henceforth proliferate through the novel. On a second visit to Balbec the narrator suspects Albertine of loving women, carries her back to Paris, and keeps her captive. He witnesses the tragic betrayal of Charlus by the Verdurins and Morel; his own jealous passion is only intensified by the flight and death of Albertine. When he attains oblivion of his love, time is lost; beauty and meaning have faded from all he ever pursued and won; and he renounces the book he has always hoped to write. A long absence in a sanatorium is interrupted by a wartime visit to Paris, bombarded like Pompeii or Sodom from the skies. Charlus, disintegrated by his vice, is seen in Jupien's infernal brothel, and Saint-Loup, married to Gilberte and turned homosexual, dies heroically in battle. After the war, at the Princesse de Guermantes's afternoon reception, the narrator becomes aware, through a series of incidents of unconscious memory, that all the beauty he has experienced in the past is eternally alive. Time is regained, and he sets to work, racing against death, to write the very novel the reader has just experienced.

Assessment

The entire climate of the 20th-century novel was affected by *À la recherche du temps perdu*, which is one of the supreme achievements of modern fiction. Taking as raw material the author's past life, *À la recherche* is ostensibly about the irrecoverability of time lost, about the forfeiture of innocence through experience, the emptiness of love and friendship, the vanity of human endeavour, and the triumph of sin and despair. Proust's conclusion is that the life of every day is supremely important, full of moral joy and beauty, which, though they may be lost through faults inherent in human nature, are indestructible and recoverable. Proust's style is one of the most original in all literature and is unique in its union of speed and protraction, precision and iridescence, force and enchantment, classicism and symbolism.

THEODORE DREISER

(b. August 27, 1871, Terre Haute, Indiana, U.S.—d. December 28, 1945, Hollywood, California)

The outstanding American practitioner of naturalism Theodore Dreiser was the leading figure in a national literary movement that replaced the observance of Victorian notions of propriety with the unflinching presentation of real-life subject matter.

Life

Dreiser was the ninth of 10 surviving children in a family whose perennial poverty forced frequent moves

Theodore Dreiser. Library of Congress, Washington, D.C.

between small Indiana towns and Chicago in search of a lower cost of living. His father, a German immigrant, was a mostly unemployed millworker who subscribed to a stern and narrow Roman Catholicism. His mother's gentle and compassionate outlook sprang from her Czech Mennonite background. In later life Dreiser would bitterly associate religion with his father's ineffectuality and the family's resulting material deprivation, but he always spoke and wrote of his mother with unswerving affection. Dreiser's own harsh experience of poverty as a youth and his early yearnings for wealth and success would become dominant themes in his novels, and the misadventures of his brothers and sisters in early adult life gave him additional material on which to base his characters.

Dreiser's spotty education in parochial and public schools was capped by a year (1889–90) at Indiana University. He began a career as a newspaper reporter in Chicago in 1892 and worked his way to the East Coast. While writing for a Pittsburgh newspaper in 1894, he read works by the scientists T.H. Huxley and John Tyndall and adopted the speculations of the philosopher Herbert Spencer. Through these readings and his own experience, Dreiser came to believe that human beings are helpless in the grip of instincts and social forces beyond their control, and he judged human society as an unequal contest between the strong and the weak. In 1894 Dreiser arrived in New York City, where he worked for several newspapers and contributed to magazines. He married Sara White in 1898, but his roving affections (and resulting infidelities) doomed their relationship. The couple separated permanently in 1912.

Dreiser began writing his first novel, *Sister Carrie*, in 1899 at the suggestion of a newspaper colleague. Doubleday, Page and Company published it the following year, thanks in large measure to the enthusiasm of that firm's reader, the novelist Frank Norris. But Doubleday's qualms about the book, the story line of which involves a young kept woman whose "immorality" goes unpunished, led the publisher to limit the book's advertising, and consequently it sold fewer than 500 copies. This disappointment and an accumulation of family and marital troubles sent Dreiser into a suicidal depression from which he was rescued in 1901 by his brother, Paul Dresser, a well-known songwriter, who arranged for Theodore's treatment in a sanitarium. Dreiser recovered his spirits, and in the next nine years he achieved notable financial success as an editor in chief of several women's magazines. He was forced to resign in 1910, however, because of an office imbroglio involving his romantic fascination with an assistant's daughter.

Somewhat encouraged by the earlier response to *Sister Carrie* in England and the novel's republication in America, Dreiser returned to writing fiction. The reception accorded his second novel, *Jennie Gerhardt* (1911), the story of a woman who submits sexually to rich and powerful men to help her poverty-stricken family, lent him further encouragement. The first two volumes of a projected trilogy of novels based on the life of the American transportation magnate Charles T. Yerkes, *The Financier* (1912) and *The Titan* (1914), followed. Dreiser recorded his experiences on a trip to Europe in *A Traveler at Forty* (1913). In his next major novel, *The "Genius"* (1915), he transformed his own life and numerous love affairs into a sprawling semiautobiographical chronicle that was censured by the New York Society for the Suppression of Vice. There ensued 10 years of sustained literary activity during which Dreiser produced a short-story collection, *Free and Other Stories* (1918); a book of sketches, *Twelve Men* (1919); philosophical essays, *Hey-Rub-a-Dub-Dub* (1920); a rhapsodic description of New York, *The Color of a Great City* (1923); works of drama, including *Plays of the Natural and Supernatural* (1916) and *The Hand of the Potter* (1918);

and the autobiographical works *A Hoosier Holiday* (1916) and *A Book About Myself* (1922).

In 1925 Dreiser's first novel in a decade, *An American Tragedy*, based on a celebrated murder case, was published. This book brought Dreiser a degree of critical and commercial success he had never before attained and would not thereafter equal. The book's highly critical view of the American legal system also made him the adopted champion of social reformers. He became involved in a variety of causes and slackened his literary production. A visit to the Soviet Union in 1927 produced a skeptical critique of that communist society entitled *Dreiser Looks at Russia* (1928). His only other significant publications in the late 1920s were collections of stories and sketches written earlier, *Chains* (1927) and *A Gallery of Women* (1929), and an unsuccessful collection of poetry, *Moods, Cadenced and Declaimed* (1926).

The Great Depression of the 1930s ended Dreiser's prosperity and intensified his commitment to social causes. He came to reconsider his opposition to communism and wrote the anticapitalist *Tragic America* (1931). His only important literary achievement in this decade was the autobiography of his childhood and teens, *Dawn* (1931), one of the most candid self-revelations by any major writer.

In 1938 Dreiser moved from New York to Los Angeles with Helen Richardson, who had been his mistress since 1920. There he set about marketing the film rights to his earlier works. In 1942 he began belatedly to rewrite *The Bulwark*, a novel begun in 1912. The task was completed in 1944, the same year he married Helen. (Sara White Dreiser had died in 1942.) One of his last acts was to join the American Communist Party. Helen helped him complete most of *The Stoic*, the long-postponed third volume of his Yerkes trilogy, in the weeks before his death. Both *The Bulwark* and *The Stoic* were published posthumously

(1946 and 1947, respectively). A collection of Dreiser's philosophical speculations, *Notes on Life*, appeared in 1974.

Works

Dreiser's first novel, *Sister Carrie* (1900), is a work of pivotal importance in American literature despite its inauspicious launching. It became a beacon to subsequent American writers whose allegiance was to the realistic treatment of any and all subject matter. *Sister Carrie* tells the story of a rudderless but pretty small-town girl who comes to the big city filled with vague ambitions. She is used by men and uses them in turn to become a successful Broadway actress while George Hurstwood, the married man who has run away with her, loses his grip on life and descends into beggary and suicide. *Sister Carrie* was the first masterpiece of the American naturalistic movement in its grittily factual presentation of the vagaries of urban life and in its ingenuous heroine, who goes unpunished for her transgressions against conventional sexual morality. The book's strengths include a brooding but compassionate view of humanity, a memorable cast of characters, and a compelling narrative line. The emotional disintegration of Hurstwood is a much-praised triumph of psychological analysis.

Dreiser's second novel, *Jennie Gerhardt* (1911), is a lesser achievement than *Sister Carrie* owing to its heroine's comparative lack of credibility. Based on Dreiser's remembrance of his beloved mother, Jennie emerges as a plaster saint with whom most modern readers find it difficult to empathize. The novel's strengths include stinging characterizations of social snobs and narrow "religionists," as well as a deep sympathy for the poor.

The Financier (1912) and *The Titan* (1914) are the first two novels of a trilogy dealing with the career of the late-19th-century American financier and traction tycoon

Charles T. Yerkes, who is cast in fictionalized form as Frank Cowperwood. As Cowperwood successfully plots monopolistic business coups first in Philadelphia and then in Chicago, the focus of the novels alternates between his amoral business dealings and his marital and other erotic relations. *The Financier* and *The Titan* are important examples of the business novel and represent probably the most meticulously researched and documented studies of high finance in first-rate fiction. Cowperwood, like all of Dreiser's major characters, remains unfulfilled despite achieving most of his apparent wishes. The third novel in the trilogy, *The Stoic* (1947), is fatally weakened by Dreiser's diminished interest in his protagonist.

Dreiser's longest novel, *An American Tragedy* (1925), is a complex and compassionate account of the life and death of a young antihero named Clyde Griffiths. The novel begins with Clyde's blighted background, recounts his path to success, and culminates in his apprehension, trial, and execution for murder. The book was called by one influential critic "the worst-written great novel in the world," but its questionable grammar and style are transcended by its narrative power. Dreiser's labyrinthine speculations on the extent of Clyde's guilt do not blunt his searing indictment of materialism and the American dream of success.

Dreiser's next-to-last novel, *The Bulwark* (1946), is the story of a Quaker father's unavailing struggle to shield his children from the materialism of modern American life. More intellectually consistent than Dreiser's earlier novels, this book also boasts some of his most polished prose.

eAssessment

Dreiser's considerable stature, beyond his historic importance as a pioneer of unvarnished truth-telling in modern literature, is due almost entirely to his achievements as a novelist. His sprawling imagination and cumbersome style kept him from performing well in the smaller literary forms, and his nonfiction writing, especially his essays, are marred by intellectual inconsistency, a lack of objectivity, and even bitterness. But these latter traits are much less obtrusive in his novels, where his compassion and empathy for human striving make his best work moving and memorable. The long novel gave Dreiser the prime form through which to explore in depth the possibilities of 20th-century American life, with its material profusion and spiritual doubt. Dreiser's characters struggle for self-realization in the face of society's narrow and repressive moral conventions, and they often obtain material success and erotic gratification while a more enduring spiritual satisfaction eludes them. Despite Dreiser's alleged deficiencies as a stylist, his novels succeed in their accumulation of realistic detail and in the power and integrity with which they delineate the tragic aspects of the American pursuit of worldly success. *Sister Carrie* and *An American Tragedy* are certainly enduring works of literature that display a deep understanding of the American experience around the turn of the century, with its expansive desires and pervasive disillusionments.

STEPHEN CRANE

(b. November 1, 1871, Newark, New Jersey, U.S. — d. June 5, 1900, Badenweiler, Baden, Germany)

Stephen Crane's father, Jonathan Crane, was a Methodist minister who died in 1880, leaving Stephen, the youngest of 14 children, to be reared by his devout, strongminded mother. After attending preparatory school at the

Stephen Crane, 1897. Stephen Crane Collection, Syracuse University Library Department of Special Collections

Claverack College (1888–90), Crane spent less than two years at college and then went to New York City to live in a medical students' boardinghouse while freelancing his way to a literary career. While alternating bohemian student life and explorations of the Bowery slums with visits to genteel relatives in the country near Port Jervis, New York, Crane wrote his first book, *Maggie: A Girl of the Streets* (1893), a sympathetic study of an innocent and abused slum girl's descent into prostitution and her eventual suicide.

At that time so shocking that Crane published it under a pseudonym and at his own expense, *Maggie* left him to struggle as a poor and unknown freelance journalist, until he was befriended by Hamlin Garland and the influential critic William Dean Howells. Suddenly in 1895 the publication of *The Red Badge of Courage* and of his first book of poems, *The Black Riders*, brought him international fame. Strikingly different in tone and technique from *Maggie*, *The Red Badge of Courage* is a subtle impressionistic study of a young soldier trying to find reality amid the conflict of fierce warfare. The book's hero, Henry Fleming, survives his own fear, cowardice, and vainglory and goes on to discover courage, humility, and perhaps wisdom in the confused combat of an unnamed Civil War battle. Crane, who had as yet seen no war, was widely praised by veterans for his uncanny power to imagine and reproduce the sense of actual combat.

Crane's few remaining years were chaotic and personally disastrous. His unconventionality and his sympathy for the downtrodden aroused malicious gossip and false charges of drug addiction and Satanism that disgusted the fastidious author. His reputation as a war writer, his desire to see if he had guessed right about the psychology of combat, and his fascination with death and danger sent him to Greece and then to Cuba as a war correspondent.

His first attempt in 1897 to report on the insurrection in Cuba ended in near disaster. The ship *Commodore* on which he was traveling sank with $5,000 worth of ammunition, and Crane—reported drowned—finally rowed into shore in a dinghy with the captain, cook, and oiler, Crane scuttling his money belt of gold before swimming through dangerous surf. The result was one of the world's great short stories, "The Open Boat."

Unable to get to Cuba, Crane went to Greece to report the Greco-Turkish War for the New York *Journal*. He was accompanied by Cora Taylor, a former brothel-house proprietor. At the end of the war they settled in England in a villa at Oxted, Surrey, and in April 1898 Crane departed to report the Spanish-American War in Cuba, first for the New York *World* and then for the New York *Journal*. When the war ended, Crane wrote the first draft of *Active Service*, a novel centred on the Greek war. He finally returned to Cora in England nine months after his departure and settled in a costly 14th-century manor house at Brede Place, Sussex. Here Cora, a silly woman with social and literary pretensions, contributed to Crane's ruin by encouraging his own social ambitions. They ruined themselves financially by entertaining hordes of spongers, as well as close literary friends—including Joseph Conrad, Ford Madox Ford, H.G. Wells, Henry James, and Robert Barr, who completed Crane's Irish romance *The O'Ruddy*.

Crane now fought a desperate battle against time, illness, and debts. Privation and exposure in his Bowery years and as a correspondent, together with an almost deliberate disregard for his health, probably hastened the disease that killed him at an early age. He died of tuberculosis that was compounded by the recurrent malarial fever he had caught in Cuba.

After *The Red Badge of Courage*, Crane's few attempts at the novel were of small importance, but he achieved an extraordinary mastery of the short story. He exploited youthful small-town experiences in *The Monster and Other Stories* (1899) and *Whilomville Stories* (1900); the Bowery again in *George's Mother* (1896); an early trip to the south-west and Mexico in "The Blue Hotel" and "The Bride Comes to Yellow Sky"; the Civil War again in *The Little Regiment* (1896); and war correspondent experiences in *The Open Boat and Other Tales of Adventure* (1898) and *Wounds in the Rain* (1900). In the best of these tales Crane showed a rare ability to shape colourful settings, dramatic action, and perceptive characterization into ironic explorations of human nature and destiny. In even briefer scope, rhymeless, cadenced and "free" in form, his unique, flashing poetry was extended into *War Is Kind* (1899).

Stephen Crane first broke new ground in *Maggie*, which evinced an uncompromising (then considered sordid) realism that initiated the literary trend of the succeeding generations—i.e., the sociological novels of Frank Norris, Theodore Dreiser, and James T. Farrell. Crane intended *The Red Badge of Courage* to be "a psychological portrayal of fear," and reviewers rightly praised its psychological realism. The first nonromantic novel of the Civil War to attain widespread popularity, *The Red Badge of Courage* turned the tide of the prevailing convention about war fiction and established a new, if not unprecedented, one. The secret of Crane's success as war correspondent, journalist, novelist, short-story writer, and poet lay in his achieving tensions between irony and pity, illusion and reality, or the double mood of hope contradicted by despair. Crane was a great stylist and a master of the contradictory effect.

*C*OLETTE

(b. January 28, 1873, Saint-Sauveur-en-Puisaye, France—d. August 3, 1954, Paris)

Colette. Encyclopædia Britannica, Inc.

Sidonie-Gabrielle Colette was reared in a village in Burgundy, where her much-loved mother awakened her to the wonders of the natural world—everything that "germinates, blossoms, or flies." At age 20, though ill-prepared for both married life and the Paris scene, Colette married the writer and critic Henri Gauthier-Villars ("Willy"), 15 years her senior. He introduced her to the world of Parisian salons and the demimonde, and, not long after their marriage, he discovered her talent for writing. Locking her in a room to encourage her to focus on the task at hand, Willy forced her to write—but published as his own work—the four "Claudine" novels, *Claudine à l'école* (1900; *Claudine at School*), *Claudine à Paris* (1901; *Claudine in Paris*), *Claudine en ménage* (1902; republished as

Claudine amoureuse, translated as *The Indulgent Husband*), and *Claudine s'en va: Journal d'Annie* (1903; *The Innocent Wife*). For these novels, Colette drew on her own experiences (both as a girl from the provinces and as a young married woman with a libertine husband) to produce scenes from the life of the young ingénue. Both Claudine and the passive, domestic Annie, who narrates the fourth Claudine book, reappear in Colette's *La Retraite sentimentale* (1907; *Retreat from Love*), which was published under the name Colette Willy.

Colette left Willy in 1906. Though her slightly salacious novels were wildly popular, as were the plays derived from them, she saw none of her earnings, as Willy kept the royalties. Ever resourceful, she took a job as a music-hall performer, working long hours to keep poverty at bay. During these years (roughly 1906–10), she was involved with the marquise de Balbeuf ("Missy"), an independently wealthy lesbian who affected male dress and mocked the masculine manner. This period of her life inspired *La Vagabonde* (1910; *The Vagabond*) and *L'Envers du music-hall* (1913; *Music-Hall Sidelights*). She was finally divorced from Willy in 1910, and in 1912 she married Henry de Jouvenel, editor in chief of the paper *Le Matin*, to which she contributed theatre chronicles and short stories. Their daughter (b. 1913) is the Bel-Gazou of the delightful animal story *La Paix chez les bêtes* (1916; some stories translated as *Dogs, Cats, & I*).

The writings she published up to this point belong to what Colette called her years of apprenticeship; she wrote of them in *Mes Apprentissages* (1936; *My Apprenticeships*). Her best work was produced after 1920 and followed two veins. The first vein followed the lives of the slightly depraved, postwar younger generation. Among these novels are *Chéri* (1920) and *La Fin de Chéri*

(1926; *The Last of Chéri*), dealing with a liaison between a young man (Chéri) and an older woman, and *Le Blé en herbe* (1923; *The Ripening Seed*), which concerns a tender and acid initiation to love. The second vein looked back to the countryside of her enchanted childhood and away from the pleasures and disillusions of shallow love affairs. *La Maison de Claudine* (1922; *My Mother's House*) and *Sido* (1930) are her poetic meditations on these years. In these books and others, her command of sensual description is extraordinary. Indeed, her greatest strength as a writer is an exact sensory evocation of the sounds, smells, tastes, textures, and colours of her world.

After 1930 her life was both productive and serene. In 1935, having divorced de Jouvenel the previous year, she married the writer Maurice Goudeket. The marriage brought much happiness, as Goudeket recorded in his memoirs *Près de Colette* (1955; *Close to Colette*). During her last two decades, Colette wrote on a number of topics. In *Ces Plaisirs* (1932; "Those Pleasures," later published as *Le Pur et l'impur* [1941; *The Pure and the Impure*]), she examined aspects of female sexuality. *La Chatte* (1933; *The Cat*) and *Duo* (1934) are treatments of jealousy. *Gigi* (1944), the story of a girl reared by two elderly sisters to become a courtesan, was adapted for both stage and screen. A charming musical film version of 1958, starring Maurice Chevalier, Louis Jourdan, and a winsome Leslie Caron, enjoyed great popularity.

Colette was made a member of the Belgian Royal Academy (1935) and the French Académie Goncourt (1945) and a grand officer of the Legion of Honour—all honours rarely granted to women.

A delicate and humorous realist, Colette was the annalist of female existence. She wrote chiefly of women in traditional roles, such as husband hunters or discarded, aging, or déclassé mistresses. Her chosen format was the novella, her style a blend of the sophisticated and the natural, laced with all the subtle cadences of sensuous pleasures and intuitive acumen. From 1949 she was increasingly crippled by arthritis. She ended her days, a legendary figure surrounded by her beloved cats, confined to her beautiful Palais-Royal apartment overlooking Paris.

WILLA CATHER

(b. December 7, 1873, near Winchester, Virginia, U.S.—d. April 24, 1947, New York, New York)

At age 9 Wilella Sibert Cather moved with her family from Virginia to frontier Nebraska, where from age 10 she lived in the village of Red Cloud. There she grew up among the immigrants from Europe—Swedes, Bohemians, Russians, and Germans—who were breaking the land on the Great Plains.

At the University of Nebraska she showed a marked talent for journalism and story writing, and on graduating in 1895 she obtained a position in Pittsburgh, Pennsylvania,

Willa Cather. Encyclopædia Britannica, Inc.

on a family magazine. Later she worked as copy editor and music and drama editor of the *Pittsburgh Leader*. She turned to teaching in 1901 and in 1903 published her first book of verses, *April Twilights*. In 1905, after the publication of her first collection of short stories, *The Troll Garden*, she was appointed managing editor of *McClure's*, the New York muckraking monthly. After building up its declining circulation, she left in 1912 to devote herself wholly to writing novels.

Cather's first novel, *Alexander's Bridge* (1912), was a factitious story of cosmopolitan life. Under the influence of writer Sarah Orne Jewett's regionalism, however, she turned to her familiar Nebraska material. With *O Pioneers!* (1913) and *My Ántonia* (1918), which has frequently been adjudged her finest achievement, she found her characteristic themes — the spirit and courage of the frontier she had known in her youth. *One of Ours* (1922), which won a Pulitzer Prize, and *A Lost Lady* (1923) mourned the passing of the pioneer spirit.

In her earlier *Song of the Lark* (1915), as well as in the tales assembled in *Youth and the Bright Medusa* (1920), including the much-anthologized "Paul's Case," and *Lucy Gayheart* (1935), Cather reflected the other side of her experience — the struggle of a talent to emerge from the constricting life of the prairies and the stifling effects of small-town life.

A mature statement of both themes can be found in *Obscure Destinies* (1932). With success and middle age, however, Cather experienced a strong disillusionment, which was reflected in *The Professor's House* (1925) and her essays *Not Under Forty* (1936).

Her solution was to write of the pioneer spirit of another age, that of the French Catholic missionaries in the Southwest in *Death Comes for the Archbishop* (1927) and of the French Canadians at Quebec in *Shadows on the Rock* (1931). For the setting of her last novel, *Sapphira and the Slave Girl* (1940), she used the Virginia of her ancestors and her childhood.

W. SOMERSET MAUGHAM

(b. January 25, 1874, Paris, France — d. December 16, 1965, Nice)

William Somerset Maugham was orphaned at age 10; he was brought up by an uncle and educated at King's School, Canterbury. After a year at Heidelberg, he entered St. Thomas' medical school, London, and qualified as a doctor in 1897. He drew upon his experiences as an obstetrician in his first novel, *Liza of Lambeth* (1897), and its success, though small, encouraged him to abandon medicine. He traveled in Spain and Italy and in 1908 achieved a theatrical triumph— four plays running in London at once—that brought him financial security. During World War I he worked as a secret agent. After the war he resumed his interrupted travels and, in 1928, bought a villa on Cape Ferrat in the south of France, which became his permanent home.

Maugham's reputation as a novelist rests primarily on four books: *Of Human Bondage* (1915), a semi-autobiographical account of a young medical student's painful progress toward maturity; *The Moon and Sixpence* (1919), an account of an unconventional artist, suggested by the life of French painter Paul Gauguin; *Cakes and Ale* (1930), the story of a famous novelist, which is thought to contain caricatures of Thomas Hardy and Hugh Walpole; and *The Razor's Edge* (1944), the story of a young American war veteran's quest for a satisfying way of life. Maugham's plays, mainly Edwardian social comedies, soon became dated, but his short stories have increased in popularity. Many portray the conflict of Europeans in alien surroundings that provoke strong emotions, and Maugham's skill in handling plot, in the manner of Guy de Maupassant, is distinguished by economy and

W. Somerset Maugham. Encyclopædia Britannica, Inc.

suspense. His work is characterized by a clear, unadorned style, cosmopolitan settings, and a shrewd understanding of human nature. In *The Summing Up* (1938) and *A Writer's Notebook* (1949) Maugham explains his philosophy of life as a resigned atheism and a certain skepticism about the purported innate goodness and intelligence of humankind; it is this that gives his work its astringent cynicism.

GERTRUDE STEIN

(b. February 3, 1874, Allegheny City [now in Pittsburgh], Pennsylvania, U.S. — d. July 27, 1946, Neuilly-sur-Seine, France)

American Modernist writer, eccentric, and self-styled genius Gertrude Stein spent her infancy in Vienna and in Passy, France, and her girlhood in Oakland, California. She entered the Society for the Collegiate Instruction of Women (renamed Radcliffe College in 1894), where she studied psychology with the philosopher William James and received her degree in 1898. She studied at Johns Hopkins Medical School from 1897 to 1902 and then, with her older

Gertrude Stein, photographed by Carl Van Vechten, 1934. Carl Van Vechten/Library of Congress, Washington, D.C. (LC-USZ62-103678)

brother Leo, moved first to London and then to Paris, where she was able to live by private means. She lived with Leo, who became an accomplished art critic, until 1909; thereafter she lived with her lifelong companion, Alice B. Toklas (1877–1967).

Stein and her brother were among the first collectors of works by the Cubists and other experimental painters of the period, such as Pablo Picasso (who painted her portrait), Henri Matisse, and Georges Braque, several of whom became her friends. At her weekly salon they mingled with expatriate American writers whom she dubbed the "Lost Generation," including Sherwood Anderson and Ernest Hemingway, and other visitors drawn by her literary reputation. Her literary and artistic judgments were revered, and her chance remarks could make or destroy reputations.

In her own work, she attempted to parallel the theories of Cubism, specifically in her concentration on the illumination of the present moment (for which she often relied on the present perfect tense) and her use of slightly varied repetitions and extreme simplification and fragmentation. The best explanation of her theory of writing is found in the essay *Composition as Explanation*, which is based on lectures that she gave at the Universities of Oxford and Cambridge and was issued as a book in 1926. Among her works that were most thoroughly influenced by Cubism is *Tender Buttons* (1914), which carries fragmentation and abstraction to an extreme.

Her first published book, *Three Lives* (1909), the stories of three working-class women, has been called a minor masterpiece. *The Making of Americans*, a long composition written in 1906–11 but not published until 1925, was too convoluted and obscure for general readers, for whom she remained essentially the author of such lines as "Rose is a rose is a rose is a rose." Her only book to reach a wide public was *The Autobiography of Alice B. Toklas* (1933), actually Stein's own autobiography. The performance in the United States of her *Four Saints in Three Acts* (1934), which the composer Virgil Thomson had made into an opera, led to a triumphal American lecture tour in 1934–35. Thomson also wrote the music for her second opera, *The Mother of Us All* (published 1947), based on the life of feminist Susan B. Anthony. One of Stein's early short stories, "Q.E.D.," was first published in *Things as They Are* (1950).

The eccentric Stein was not modest in her self-estimation: "Einstein was the creative philosophic mind of the century, and I have been the creative literary mind of the century." She became a legend in Paris and befriended the many young American servicemen who visited her. She wrote about these soldiers in *Brewsie and Willie* (1946).

ROBERT FROST

(b. March 26, 1874, San Francisco, California, U.S.—d. January 29, 1963, Boston, Massachusetts)

The American poet Robert Lee Frost was much admired for his depictions of the rural life of New England and his command of American colloquial speech. He wrote realistic verse portraying ordinary people in everyday situations.

Life

Frost's father, William Prescott Frost, Jr., was a journalist with ambitions of establishing a career in California, and in 1873 he and his wife moved to San Francisco. Her husband's untimely death from tuberculosis in 1885 prompted Isabelle Moodie Frost to take her two children, Robert and Jeanie, to Lawrence, Massachusetts, where they were taken in by the children's paternal grandparents. While their mother taught at a variety of schools in New Hampshire and Massachusetts, Robert and Jeanie grew up in Lawrence, and Robert graduated from high school in 1892. A top student in his class, he shared valedictorian honours with Elinor White, with whom he had already fallen in love.

Robert and Elinor shared a deep interest in poetry, but their continued education sent Robert to Dartmouth College and Elinor to St. Lawrence University. Meanwhile, Robert continued to labour on the poetic career he had begun in a small way during high school; he first achieved professional publication in 1894 when *The Independent*, a weekly literary journal, printed his poem "My Butterfly: An Elegy." Impatient with academic routine, Frost left Dartmouth after less than a year. He and Elinor married in 1895 but found life difficult, and the young poet supported them by teaching school and farming, neither with notable success. During the next dozen years, six children were born, two of whom died early, leaving a family of one son and three daughters. Frost resumed his college education at Harvard University in 1897 but left after two years' study there. From 1900 to 1909 the family raised poultry on a farm near Derry, New Hampshire, and for a time Frost also taught at the Pinkerton Academy in Derry. Frost became an enthusiastic botanist and acquired his poetic persona of a New England rural sage during the years he and his family spent at Derry. All this while he was writing poems, but publishing outlets showed little interest in them.

By 1911 Frost was fighting against discouragement. Poetry had always been considered a young person's game, but Frost, who was nearly 40 years old, had not published a single book of poems and had seen just a handful appear in magazines. In 1911 ownership of the Derry farm passed to Frost. A momentous decision was made: to sell the farm and use the proceeds to make a radical new start in London, where publishers were perceived to be more receptive to new talent. Accordingly, in August 1912 the Frost family sailed across the Atlantic to England. Frost carried with him sheaves of verses he had written but not gotten into print. English publishers in London did indeed prove more receptive to innovative verse, and, through his own vigorous efforts and those of the expatriate American poet Ezra Pound, Frost within a year had published *A Boy's Will* (1913). From this first book, such poems as "Storm Fear," "Mowing," and "The Tuft of Flowers" have remained standard anthology pieces.

A Boy's Will was followed in 1914 by a second collection, *North of Boston*, that introduced some of the most popular poems in all of Frost's work, among them "Mending Wall," "The Death of the Hired Man," "Home Burial," and "After Apple-Picking." In London, Frost's name was frequently mentioned by those who followed the course of modern literature, and soon American visitors were returning home with news of this unknown poet who was causing a sensation abroad. The Boston poet Amy Lowell traveled to England in 1914, and in the bookstores there she encountered Frost's work. Taking his books home to America, Lowell then began a campaign to locate an American publisher for them, meanwhile writing her own laudatory review of *North of Boston*.

Without his being fully aware of it, Frost was on his way to fame. The outbreak of World War I brought the Frosts back to the United States in 1915. By then Amy Lowell's review had already appeared in *The New Republic*, and writers and publishers throughout the Northeast were aware that a writer of unusual abilities stood in their midst. The American publishing house of Henry Holt had brought out its edition of *North of Boston* in 1914. It became a best-seller, and, by the time the Frost family landed in Boston, Holt was adding the American edition of *A Boy's Will.* Frost soon found himself besieged by magazines seeking to publish his poems. Never before had an American poet achieved such rapid fame after such a disheartening delay. From this moment his career rose on an ascending curve.

Frost bought a small farm at Franconia, New Hampshire, in 1915, but his income from both poetry and farming proved inadequate to support his family, and so he lectured and taught part-time at Amherst College and at the University of Michigan from 1916 to 1938. Any remaining doubt about his poetic abilities was dispelled by the collection *Mountain Interval* (1916), which continued the high level established by his first books. His reputation was further enhanced by *New Hampshire* (1923), which received the Pulitzer Prize. That prize was also awarded to Frost's *Collected Poems* (1930) and to the collections *A Further Range* (1936) and *A Witness Tree* (1942). His other poetry volumes include *West-Running Brook* (1928), *Steeple Bush* (1947), and *In the Clearing* (1962). Frost served as a poet-in-residence at Harvard (1939–43), Dartmouth (1943–49), and Amherst College (1949–63), and in his old age he gathered honours and awards from every quarter. He was the poetry consultant to the Library of Congress (1958–59; the post is now styled poet laureate consultant in poetry), and his recital of his poem "The Gift Outright" at the inauguration of President John F. Kennedy in 1961 was a memorable occasion.

Works

The poems in Frost's early books, especially *North of Boston*, differ radically from late-19th-century Romantic verse with its ever-benign view of nature, its didactic emphasis, and its slavish conformity to established verse forms and themes. Lowell called *North of Boston* a "sad" book, referring to its portraits of inbred, isolated, and psychologically troubled rural New Englanders. These off-mainstream portraits signaled Frost's departure from the old tradition and his own fresh interest in delineating New England characters and their formative background. Among these psychological investigations are the alienated life of Silas in "The Death of the Hired Man," the inability of Amy in "Home Burial" to walk the difficult path from grief back to normality, the rigid mindset of the neighbour in "Mending Wall," and the paralyzing fear that twists the personality of Doctor Magoon in "A Hundred Collars."

The natural world, for Frost, wore two faces. Early on he overturned the Emersonian concept of nature as healer and mentor in a poem in *A Boy's Will* entitled "Storm Fear," a grim picture of a blizzard as a raging beast that dares the inhabitants of an isolated house to come outside and be killed. In such later poems as "The Hill Wife" and "Stopping by Woods on a Snowy Evening," the benign surface of nature cloaks potential dangers, and death itself lurks behind dark, mysterious trees. Nature's frolicsome aspect predominates in other poems such as "Birches," where a destructive ice storm is recalled as a thing of memorable beauty. Although Frost is known to many as essentially a "happy" poet, the tragic elements in life continued to mark his poems, from "'Out, Out—'" (1916), in which a lad's hand is severed and life ended, to a fine verse entitled "The Fear of Man" from *Steeple Bush*, in which human release from pervading fear is contained in the image of a breathless dash through the nighttime city from the security of one faint street lamp to another just as faint. Even in his final volume, *In the Clearing*, so filled with the stubborn courage of old age, Frost portrays human security as a rather tiny and quite vulnerable opening in a thickly grown forest, a pinpoint of light against which the encroaching trees cast their very real threat of darkness.

Frost demonstrated an enviable versatility of theme, but he most commonly investigated human contacts with the natural world in small encounters that serve as metaphors for larger aspects of the human condition. He often portrayed the human ability to turn even the slightest incident or natural detail to emotional profit, seen at its most economical form in "Dust of Snow":

The way a crow
Shook down on me
The dust of snow
From a hemlock tree
Has given my heart
A change of mood
And saved some part
Of a day I had rued.

Other poems are portraits of the introspective mind possessed by its own private demons, as in "Desert Places," which could serve to illustrate Frost's celebrated definition of poetry as a "momentary stay against confusion":

They cannot scare me with their empty spaces
Between stars—on stars where no human race is.
I have it in me so much nearer home
To scare myself with my own desert places.

Frost was widely admired for his mastery of metrical form, which he often set against the natural rhythms of everyday, unadorned speech. In this way the traditional stanza and metrical line achieved new vigour in his hands. Frost's command of traditional metrics is evident in the tight, older, prescribed patterns of such sonnets as

"Design" and "The Silken Tent." His strongest allegiance probably was to the quatrain with simple rhymes such as *abab* and *abcb*, and within its restrictions he was able to achieve an infinite variety, as in the aforementioned "Dust of Snow" and "Desert Places." Frost was never an enthusiast of free verse and regarded its looseness as something less than ideal, similar to playing tennis without a net. His determination to be "new" but to employ "old ways to be new" set him aside from the radical experimentalism of the advocates of vers libre (free verse) in the early 20th century. On occasion Frost did employ free verse to advantage, one outstanding example being "After Apple-Picking," with its random pattern of long and short lines and its nontraditional use of rhyme. Here he shows his power to stand as a transitional figure between the old and the new in poetry. Frost mastered blank verse (i.e., unrhymed verse in iambic pentameter) for use in such dramatic narratives as "Mending Wall" and "Home Burial," becoming one of the few modern poets to use it both appropriately and well. His chief technical innovation in these dramatic-dialogue poems was to unify the regular pentameter line with the irregular rhythms of conversational speech. Frost's blank verse has the same terseness and concision that mark his poetry in general.

Assessment

Frost was the most widely admired and highly honoured American poet of the 20th century. It is true that certain criticisms of Frost have never been wholly refuted, one being that he was overly interested in the past, another that he was too little concerned with the present and future of American society. Those who criticize Frost's detachment from the "modern" emphasize the undeniable absence in his poems of meaningful references to the modern realities of industrialization, urbanization, and the concentration of wealth, or to such familiar items as radios, motion pictures, automobiles, factories, or sky-scrapers. The poet has been viewed as a singer of sweet nostalgia and a social and political conservative who was content to sigh for the good things of the past.

Such views have failed to gain general acceptance, however, in the face of the universality of Frost's themes, the emotional authenticity of his voice, and the austere technical brilliance of his verse. Frost was often able to endow his rural imagery with a larger symbolic or meta-physical significance, and his best poems transcend the immediate realities of their subject matter to illuminate the unique blend of tragic endurance, stoicism, and tena-cious affirmation that marked his outlook on life. Over his long career Frost succeeded in lodging more than a few poems where, as he put it, they would be "hard to get rid of," and he can be said to have lodged himself just as sol-idly in the affections of his fellow Americans.

G.K. CHESTERTON

(b. May 29, 1874, London, England—d. June 14, 1936, Beaconsfield, Buckinghamshire)

Gilbert Keith Chesterton was educated at St. Paul's School and later studied art at the Slade School and literature at University College, London. His writings to 1910 were of three kinds. First, his social criticism, largely in his voluminous journalism, was gathered in *The Defendant* (1901), *Twelve Types* (1902), and *Heretics* (1905). In it he expressed strongly pro-Boer views in the South African War. Politically, he began as a Liberal but after a brief radical period became, with his Christian and medievalist friend Hilaire Belloc, a Distributist, favouring the distribution of land. This phase of his thinking is exemplified by *What's Wrong with the World* (1910).

His second preoccupation was literary criticism. *Robert Browning* (1903) was followed by *Charles Dickens* (1906) and *Appreciations and Criticisms of the Works of Charles Dickens* (1911), prefaces to the individual novels, which are among his finest contributions to criticism. His *George Bernard Shaw* (1909) and *The Victorian Age in Literature* (1913) together with *William Blake* (1910) and the later monographs *William Cobbett* (1925) and *Robert Louis Stevenson* (1927) have a spontaneity that places them above the works of many academic critics.

Chesterton's third major concern was theology and religious argument. He was converted from Anglicanism to Roman Catholicism in 1922. Although he had written on Christianity earlier, as in his book *Orthodoxy* (1909), his conversion added edge to his controversial writing, notably *The Catholic Church and Conversion* (1926), his writings in *G.K.'s Weekly*, and *Avowals and Denials* (1934). Other works arising from his conversion were *St. Francis of Assisi* (1923), the essay

G.K. Chesterton. Encyclopædia Britannica, Inc

in historical theology *The Everlasting Man* (1925), and *St. Thomas Aquinas* (1933).

In his verse Chesterton was a master of ballad forms, as shown in the stirring "Lepanto" (1911). When it was not uproariously comic, his verse was frankly partisan and didactic. His essays developed his shrewd, paradoxical irreverence to its ultimate point of real seriousness. He is seen at his happiest in such essays as "On Running After One's Hat" (1908) and "A Defence of Nonsense" (1901), in which he says that nonsense and faith are "the two supreme symbolic assertions of truth" and "to draw out the soul of things with a syllogism is as impossible as to draw out Leviathan with a hook."

Many readers value Chesterton's fiction most highly. *The Napoleon of Notting Hill* (1904), a romance of civil war in suburban London, was followed by the loosely knit collection of short stories, *The Club of Queer Trades* (1905), and the popular allegorical novel *The Man Who Was Thursday* (1908). But the most successful association of fiction with social judgment is in Chesterton's series on the priest-sleuth Father Brown: *The Innocence of Father Brown* (1911), followed by *The Wisdom...* (1914), *The Incredulity...* (1926), *The Secret...* (1927), and *The Scandal of Father Brown* (1935).

Chesterton's friendships were with men as diverse as H.G. Wells, Shaw, Belloc, and Max Beerbohm. His *Autobiography* was published in 1936.

THOMAS MANN

(b. June 6, 1875, Lübeck, Germany—d. August 12, 1955, near Zürich, Switzerland)

Thomas Mann's father died in 1891, and Mann moved to Munich, a centre of art and literature, where he lived until 1933. After perfunctory work in an insurance office and on the editorial staff of *Simplicissimus*, a satirical weekly, he devoted himself to writing, as his elder brother Heinrich had already done. His early tales, collected as *Der kleine Herr Friedemann* (1898), reflect the aestheticism of the 1890s but are given depth by the influence of the philosophers Arthur Schopenhauer and Friedrich Nietzsche and the composer Richard Wagner, to all of whom Mann was always to acknowledge a deep, if ambiguous, debt. Most of Mann's first stories centre on the problem of the creative artist, who in his devotion to form contests the meaninglessness of existence, an antithesis that Mann enlarged into that between spirit (*Geist*) and life (*Leben*). But while he showed sympathy for the artistic misfits he described, Mann was also aware that the world of imagination is a world of make-believe, and the closeness of the artist to the charlatan was already becoming a theme. At the same time, a certain nostalgia for ordinary, unproblematical life appeared in his work.

This ambivalence found full expression in his first novel, *Buddenbrooks* (1900), which Mann had at first intended to be a novella in which the experience of the transcendental realities of Wagner's music would extinguish the will to live in the son of a bourgeois family. On this beginning, the novel builds the story of the family and its business house over four generations, showing how an artistic streak not only unfits the family's later members for the practicalities of business life but undermines their vitality as well. But, almost against his will, in *Buddenbrooks* Mann wrote a tender elegy for the old bourgeois virtues.

In 1905 Mann married Katja Pringsheim. There were six children of the marriage, which was a happy one. It was this happiness, perhaps, that led Mann, in *Royal Highness*, to provide a fairy-tale reconciliation of "form" and "life," of degenerate feudal authority and the vigour of modern

American capitalism. In 1912, however, he returned to the tragic dilemma of the artist with *Der Tod in Venedig* (*Death in Venice*), a sombre masterpiece. In this story, the main character, a distinguished writer whose nervous and "decadent" sensibility is controlled by the discipline of style and composition, seeks relaxation from overstrain in Venice, where, as disease creeps over the city, he succumbs to an infatuation and the wish for death. Symbols of eros and death weave a subtle pattern in the sensuous opulence of this tale, which closes an epoch in Mann's work.

World War I and Political Crisis

The outbreak of World War I evoked Mann's ardent patriotism and awoke, too, an awareness of the artist's social commitment. His brother Heinrich was one of the few German writers to question German war aims, and his criticism of German authoritarianism stung Thomas to a bitter attack on cosmopolitan litterateurs. In 1918 he published a large political treatise, *Reflections of an Unpolitical Man*, in which all his ingenuity of mind was summoned to justify the authoritarian state as against democracy, creative irrationalism as against "flat" rationalism, and inward culture as against moralistic civilization. This work belongs to the tradition of "revolutionary conservatism" that leads from the 19th-century German nationalistic and antidemocratic thinkers Paul Anton de Lagarde and Houston Stewart Chamberlain, the apostle of the superiority of the "Germanic" race, toward National Socialism; Mann later was to repudiate these ideas.

With the establishment of the German (Weimar) Republic in 1919, Mann slowly revised his outlook; the essays "Goethe und Tolstoi" and "Von deutscher Republik" ("The German Republic") show his somewhat hesitant espousal of democratic principles. His new position was clarified in the novel *Der Zauberberg* (1924; *The Magic Mountain*). Its theme grows out of an earlier motif: a young engineer, Hans Castorp, visiting a cousin in a sanatorium in Davos, abandons practical life to submit to the rich seductions of disease, inwardness, and death. But the sanatorium comes to be the spiritual reflection of the possibilities and dangers of the actual world. In the end, somewhat skeptically but humanely, Castorp decides for life and service to his people: a decision Mann calls "a leave-taking from many a perilous sympathy, enchantment, and temptation, to which the European soul had been inclined." In this great work Mann formulates with remarkable insight the fateful choices facing Europe.

World War II and Exile

From this time onward Mann's imaginative effort was directed to the novel, scarcely interrupted by the charming personal novella *Early Sorrow* or by *Mario and the Magician*, a novella that, in the person of a seedy illusionist, symbolizes the character of fascism. His literary and cultural essays began to play an ever-growing part in elucidating and communicating his awareness of the fragility of humaneness, tolerance, and reason in the face of political crisis. His essays on Freud (1929) and Wagner (1933) are concerned with this, as are those on Goethe (1932), who more and more became for Mann an exemplary figure in his wisdom and balance. The various essays on Nietzsche document with particular poignancy Mann's struggle against attitudes once dear to him. In 1930 he gave a courageous address in Berlin, "Ein Appell an die Vernunft" ("An Appeal to Reason"), appealing for the formation of a common front of the cultured bourgeoisie and the Socialist working class against the inhuman fanaticism of the National Socialists. In essays and on lecture tours in

Germany, to Paris, Vienna, Warsaw, Amsterdam, and elsewhere during the 1930s, Mann, while steadfastly attacking Nazi policy, often expressed sympathy with socialist and communist principles in the very general sense that they were the guarantee of humanism and freedom.

When Hitler became chancellor early in 1933, Mann and his wife, on holiday in Switzerland, were warned by their son and daughter in Munich not to return. For some years his home was in Switzerland, near Zürich, but he traveled widely, visiting the United States on lecture tours and finally, in 1938, settling there, first at Princeton, and from 1941 to 1952 in southern California. In 1936 he was deprived of his German citizenship; in the same year the University of Bonn took away the honorary doctorate it had bestowed in 1919 (it was restored in 1949). From 1936 to 1944 Mann was a citizen of Czechoslovakia. In 1944 he became a U.S. citizen.

After the war, Mann visited both East Germany and West Germany several times and received many public honours, but he refused to return to Germany to live. In 1952 he settled again near Zürich. His last major essays—on Goethe (1949), Chekhov (1954), and Schiller (1955)—are impressive evocations of the moral and social responsibilities of writers.

Later Novels

The novels on which Mann was working throughout this period reflect variously the cultural crisis of his times. In 1933 he published *The Tales of Jacob* (U.S. title, *Joseph and His Brothers*), the first part of his four-part novel on the biblical Joseph, continued the following year in *The Young Joseph* and two years later with *Joseph in Egypt*, and completed with *Joseph the Provider* in 1943. In the complete work, published as *Joseph and His Brothers*, Mann reinterpreted the biblical story as the emergence of mobile, responsible individuality out of the tribal collective, of history out of myth, and of a human God out of the unknowable. In the first volume a timeless myth seems to be reenacted in the lives of the Hebrews. Joseph, however, though sustained by the belief that his life, too, is the reenactment of a myth, is thrown out of the "timeless collective" into Egypt, the world of change and history, and there learns the management of events, ideas, and himself. Though based on wide and scholarly study of history, the work is not a historical novel, and the "history" is full of irony and humour, of conscious modernization. Mann's concern is to provide a myth for his own times, capable of sustaining and directing his generation and of restoring a belief in the power of humane reason.

Mann took time off from this work to write, in the same spirit, his *Lotte in Weimar* (U.S. title, *The Beloved Returns*). Lotte Kestner, the heroine of Goethe's *The Sorrows of Young Werther*, his semi-autobiographical story of unrequited love and romantic despair, visits Weimar in old age to see once again her old lover, now famous, and to win some acknowledgment from him. But Goethe remains distant and refuses to reenter the past; she learns from him that true reverence for man means also acceptance of and reverence for change, intelligent activity directed to the "demand of the day." In this, as in the Joseph novels, in settings so distant from his own time, Mann was seeking to define the essential principles of humane civilization; their spacious and often humorous serenity of tone implicitly challenges the inhuman irrationalism of the Nazis.

In *Doktor Faustus*, begun in 1943 at the darkest period of the war, Mann wrote the most directly political of his novels. It is the life story of a German composer, Adrian Leverkühn, born in 1885, who dies in 1940 after 10 years of mental alienation. A solitary, estranged figure, he "speaks" the experience of his times in his music, and the story of Leverkühn's compositions is that of German culture in the two decades before 1930—more specifically of the collapse of traditional humanism and the victory of the mixture of sophisticated nihilism and barbaric primitivism that undermine it. With imaginative insight Mann interpreted the new musical forms and themes of Leverkühn's compositions up to the final work, a setting of the lament of Doctor Faustus in the 16th-century version of the Faust legend, who once, in hope, had made a pact with the Devil, but in the end is reduced to hopelessness. The one gleam of hope in this sombre work, however, in which the personal tragedy of Leverkühn is subtly related to Germany's destruction in the war through the comments of the fictitious narrator, Zeitblom, lies in its very grief.

The composition of the novel was fully documented by Mann in 1949 in *The Genesis of a Novel. Doktor Faustus* exhausted him as no other work of his had done, and *The Holy Sinner* and *The Black Swan*, published in 1951 and 1953, respectively, show a relaxation of intensity in spite of their accomplished, even virtuoso style. Mann rounded off his imaginative work in 1954 with *The Confessions of Felix Krull, Confidence Man,* the light, often uproariously funny story of a confidence man who wins the favour and love of others by enacting the roles they desire of him.

Mann's style is finely wrought and full of resources, enriched by humour, irony, and parody. His composition is subtle and many-layered, brilliantly realistic on one level and yet reaching to deeper levels of symbolism. His works lack simplicity, and his tendency to set his characters at a distance by his own ironical view of them has sometimes laid him open to the charge of lack of heart. He was, however, aware that simplicity and sentiment lend themselves to manipulation by ideological and political powers, and the sometimes elaborate sophistication of his works cannot hide from the discerning reader his underlying impassioned and tender solicitude for humankind.

Assessment

Mann was the greatest German novelist of the 20th century, and by the end of his life his works had acquired the status of classics both in and outside of Germany. His subtly structured novels and shorter stories constitute a persistent and imaginative enquiry into the nature of Western bourgeois culture, in which a haunting awareness of its precariousness and threatened disintegration is balanced by an appreciation of and tender concern for its spiritual achievements. Around this central theme cluster a group of related problems that recur in different forms—the relation of thought to reality and of the artist to society, the complexity of reality and of time, the seductions of spirituality, eros, and death. Mann's imaginative and practical involvement in the social and political catastrophes of his time provided him with fresh insights that make his work rich and varied. His finely wrought essays, notably those on Tolstoy, Goethe, Freud, and Nietzsche, record the intellectual struggles through which he reached the ethical commitment that shapes the major imaginative works.

RAINER MARIA RILKE

(b. December 4, 1875, Prague, Bohemia, Austria-Hungary [now in Czech Republic]—d. December 29, 1926, Valmont, Switzerland)

Rainer Maria Rilke, christened René Maria Rilke, was the only son of an unhappy marriage. His father, Josef, a civil servant, was frustrated in his career. His mother, the daughter of an upper-middle-class merchant and imperial councillor, was a difficult woman, who felt that she had married beneath her. She left her husband in 1884 and moved to Vienna so as to be close to the imperial court.

Early Life

Rilke's education was ill planned and fragmentary. It had been decided that he was to become an officer to assure him the social standing barred to his father. Consequently, after some years at a rather select school run by the Piarist brothers of Prague, he was enrolled in the military lower *Realschule* of Sankt Pölten (Austria) and four years later entered the military upper *Realschule* at Mährisch-Weisskirchen (Bohemia). These two schools were completely at variance with the needs of this highly sensitive boy, and he finally was forced to leave the school prematurely because of poor health. In later life he called these years a time of merciless affliction, a "primer of horror." After another futile year spent at the Academy of Business Administration at Linz (1891–92), Rilke, with the energetic help of a paternal uncle, was able to leave this misguided educational path. In the summer of 1895, he completed the course of studies at the German *Gymnasium* (a school designed to prepare for the university) of the Prague suburb of Neustadt.

By the time he left school, Rilke had already published a volume of poetry (1894), and he had no doubt that he would pursue a literary career. Matriculating at Prague's Charles University in 1895, he enrolled in courses in German literature and art history and, to appease his family, read one semester of law. But he could not become really involved in his studies, and so in 1896 he left school and went to Munich, a city whose artistic and cosmopolitan atmosphere held a strong appeal. Thus began his mature life, of the restless travels of a man driven by inner needs, and of the artist who managed to persuade others of the validity of his vision. The European continent in all its breadth and variety—Russia, France, Spain, Austria, Switzerland, and Italy—was to be the physical setting of that life.

Maturity

In May 1897 Rilke met Lou Andreas-Salomé, who shortly became his mistress. Lou, 36 years of age, was from St. Petersburg, the daughter of a Russian general and a German mother. In her youth she had been wooed by, and refused, the philosopher Friedrich Nietzsche; 10 years before her meeting with Rilke she had married a German professor. Rilke's affair with Lou was a turning point in his life. More than mistress, she was surrogate mother, the leading influence in his *éducation sentimentale*, and, above all, the person who introduced Russia to him. Even after their affair ended, Lou remained his close friend and confidante. In late 1897 he followed her to Berlin to take part in her life as far as possible.

His acquaintance with Russia was a milestone in Rilke's life. It was the first and most incisive of a series of "elective homelands," leaving a deeper mark than any of his subsequent discoveries, with the possible exception of Paris. He and Lou visited Russia first in the spring of 1899 and then in the summer of 1900. There he found an external reality that he saw as the ideal symbol of his feelings, his inner reality. Russia for him was imbued with an amorphous, elemental, almost religiously moving quality—a harmonious, powerful constellation of "God," "human community," and "nature"—the distillation of the "cosmic" spirit of being.

Russia evoked in him a poetic response that he later said marked the true beginning of his serious work: a long three-part cycle of poems written between 1899 and 1903, *Das Stunden-Buch* (1905). Here the poetic "I" presents himself to the reader in the guise of a young monk who circles his god with swarms of prayers, a god conceived as the incarnation of "life," as the numinous quality of the inner-worldly diversity of "things." The language and motifs of the work are largely those of Europe of the 1890s: Art Nouveau, moods inspired by the dramas of Henrik Ibsen and Maurice Maeterlinck, the enthusiasm for the art of John Ruskin and Walter Pater, and, above all, the emphasis on "life" of Nietzsche's philosophy. Yet, the self-celebratory fervour of these devotional exercises, with their rhythmic, suggestive power and flowing musicality, contained a completely new element. In them, a poet of unique stature had found his voice.

Soon after his second trip to Russia, Rilke joined the artists' colony of Worpswede, near Bremen, where he hoped to settle down among congenial artists experimenting with developing a new life-style. In April 1901 he married Clara Westhoff, a young sculptor from Bremen who had studied with the French sculptor Auguste Rodin. The couple set up housekeeping in a farm cottage in nearby Westerwede. There Rilke worked on the second part of the *Stunden-Buch* and also wrote a book about the Worpswede colony. In December 1901 Clara gave birth to a daughter, and soon afterward the two decided on a friendly separation so as to be free to pursue their separate careers.

Rilke was commissioned by a German publisher to write a book about Rodin and went to Paris, where the sculptor lived, in 1902. For the next 12 years Paris was the geographic centre of Rilke's life. He frequently left the city for visits to other cities and countries, beginning in the spring of 1903, when, to recover from what seemed to him the indifferent life of Paris, he went to Viareggio, Italy. There he wrote the third part of the *Stunden-Buch*. He also worked in Rome (1903–04), in Sweden (1904), and repeatedly in Capri (1906–08); he traveled to the south of France, Spain, Tunisia, and Egypt and frequently visited friends in Germany and Austria. Yet Paris was his second elective home, no less important than Russia, for both its historic, human, "scenic" qualities and its intellectual challenge.

Rilke's Paris was not the *belle époque* capital steeped in luxury and eroticism. It was a city of abysmal, dehumanizing misery, of the faceless and the dispossessed, and of the aged, sick, and dying. It was the capital of fear, poverty, and death. His preoccupation with these phenomena combined with a second one: his growing awareness of new approaches to art and creativity, an awareness gained through his association with Rodin. Their friendship lasted until the spring of 1906. Rodin taught him his personal art ethic of unremitting work, which stood in sharp contrast to the traditional idea of artistic inspiration. Rodin's method was one of dedication to detail and nuance and of unswerving search for "form" in the sense of concentration and objectivization. Rodin also gave Rilke new insight into the treasures of the Louvre, the Cathedral of Chartres, and the forms and shapes of Paris. Of the literary models, the poet Charles Baudelaire impressed him the most.

During those Paris years Rilke developed a new style of lyrical poetry, the so-called *Ding-Gedicht* ("object poem"), which attempts to capture the plastic essence of a physical object. Some of the most successful of these poems are imaginative verbal translations of certain works of the visual arts. Other poems deal with landscapes, portraits, and biblical and mythological themes as a painter would depict them. These *Neue Gedichte* (1907–08) represented a departure from traditional German lyric poetry. Rilke forced his language to such extremes of subtlety and refinement that it may be characterized as a distinct art among other arts and a language distinct from existing languages. The worldly elegance of these poems cannot obscure their inherent emotional and moral engagement. When Rilke, in letters about Paul Cézanne written in the autumn of 1907, defines the painter's method as a "using up of love in anonymous labour," he doubtless was also speaking of himself. In a letter to Lou Salomé written in July 1903, he had defined his method with this formulation: "making objects out of fear."

Die Aufzeichnungen des Malte Laurids Brigge (1910; *The Notebook of Malte Laurids Brigge*), on which he began work in Rome in 1904, is a prose counterpart to the *Neue Gedichte*. That which hovered in the background in the poems, behind the perfection of style, is in the foreground of the prose work: the subjective, personal problems of the lonely occupant of a Paris hotel room, the "fear" that is the inspiration for the creation of "the objects." If the poems seem like a glorious affirmation of the Symbolists' idea of "pure poetry," the *Aufzeichnungen* reads like a brilliant early example of existentialist writing. It is an artfully assembled suite of descriptive, reminiscent, and meditative parts, supposedly written by Malte, a young Danish expatriate in Paris who refuses to abide by the traditional chronology of narrative exposition but, instead, presents his themes as "simultaneous" occurrences set against a background of an all-encompassing "spatial time." Here are found all of Rilke's major themes: love, death, the fears of childhood, the idolization of woman, and, finally, the matter of "God," which is treated simply as a "tendency of the heart." The work must be seen as the description of the disintegration of a soul—but a disintegration not devoid of a dialectic mental reservation: "Only a step," writes Malte, "and my deepest misery could turn into bliss."

The price Rilke paid for these masterpieces was a writing block and depression so severe that it led him to toy with the idea of giving up writing. Aside from a short poetry cycle, *Das Marienleben* (1913), he did not publish anything for 13 years. The first works in which he transcended even his *Neue Gedichte* were written early in 1912 — two long poems in the style of elegies. He did not undertake their immediate publication, however, because they promised to become part of a new cycle. He wrote these two poems while staying at Duino Castle, near Trieste.

At the outbreak of World War I Rilke was in Munich, where he decided to remain, spending most of the war there. In December 1915 he was called up for military service with the Austrian army at Vienna, but by June 1916 he had returned to civilian life. The social climate of these years was inimical to his way of life and to his poetry, and when the war ended he felt almost completely paralyzed. He had only one relatively productive phase: the fall of 1915, when, in addition to a series of new poems, he wrote the "Fourth Duino Elegy."

Late Life

Rilke spent the next seven years in Switzerland, the last of his series of elective homes. He once more came into full command of his creative gifts. In the summer of 1921 he took up residence at the Château de Muzot, a castle in the Rhône Valley, as the guest of a Swiss patron. In February 1922, within the space of a few days of obsessive productivity, he completed the Duino cycle begun years earlier and, unexpectedly and almost effortlessly, another superb cycle of 55 poems, in mood and theme closely related to the *Elegies*—his *Sonette an Orpheus* (*Sonnets to Orpheus*).

The *Duineser Elegien* (*Duino Elegies*) are the culmination of the development of Rilke's poetry. That which in the *Stunden-Buch* had begun as a naively uncertain celebration of "life," as a devotional exercise of mystical worship of God, and which in *Malte* led him to assert that "this life suspended over an abyss is in fact impossible" in the *Elegies* sounds an affirmative note, in panegyric justification of life as an entity: "The affirmation of life and death prove to be identical in the *Elegies*," wrote Rilke in 1925. These poems can be seen as a new myth that reflects the condition of "modern" humanity, the condition of an emancipated, "disinherited" consciousness maintaining itself as a counterpart to the traditional cosmic image of Christianity. Like Nietzsche, Rilke opposes the Christian dualism of immanence and transcendence. Instead, he speaks out for an emphatic monism of the "cosmic inner space," gathering life and death, earth and space, and all dimensions of time into one all-encompassing unity. This Rilkean myth is articulated in an image-laden cosmology that, analogous to medieval models, sees all of reality—from animal to "angel"—as a hierarchical order. This cosmology in turn results in a systematic, consistent doctrine of life and being in which humans are assigned the task of transforming everything that is visible into the invisible through the power of sensory perceptions: "We are the bees of the invisible." And this ultimate human fate is concretized in the activity that alternately is called "saying," "singing," "extolling," or "praising." Thus the poet is turned into the protagonist of humanity, its representative "before the Angel" (the pseudonym of God), as in the "Ninth Elegy," and even more strikingly in the *Sonnets to Orpheus*.

The triumphant breakthrough of February 1922 was Rilke's last major contribution, yet both thematically and stylistically some of his late poems go beyond even the *Elegies* and the *Sonnets* in their experimentation with forms that no longer seem at all related to the nature of the poetic language of the 1920s. In addition to these late works he also wrote a number of simple, almost songlike poems, some short cycles, and four collections in French, in which he pays homage to the landscape of Valais.

Muzot remained his home, but he continued his travels, mostly within Switzerland, devoting himself to his friends and his vast, superbly articulate correspondence. Early in 1925 he again went to Paris, with whose literary life he had remained in close touch. He was royally received by such old friends as André Gide and Paul Valéry as well as by new admirers; for the first and only time in his life he was at the centre of a literary season in a European metropolis. But the strain of this visit proved too much for his frail health. On August 18, unannounced, he slipped out of Paris. He had been ill since 1923, but the cause of his debility, a rare form of incurable leukemia, was not diagnosed until a few weeks before his death in 1926. He died at a sanatorium above Territet, on Lake Geneva.

JACK LONDON

(b. January 12, 1876, San Francisco, California, U.S.—d. November 22, 1916, Glen Ellen, California)

John Griffith Chaney—who became the American novelist and short-story writer Jack London—was deserted by his father, a roving astrologer. The boy was raised in Oakland, California, by his spiritualist mother and his stepfather, whose surname, London, he took. At 14 he quit school to escape poverty and find adventure. He explored San Francisco Bay in his sloop, alternately stealing oysters or working for the government fish patrol. He went to Japan as a sailor and saw much of the United States as a hobo riding freight trains and as a member of Kelly's industrial army (one of the many protest armies of unemployed workers born of the panic of 1893). He saw Depression conditions, was jailed for vagrancy, and in 1894 became a militant socialist. London educated himself at public libraries with the writings of Charles Darwin, Karl Marx, and Friedrich Nietzsche, usually in popularized forms, and created his own amal-gam of socialism and white superiority. At 19 he crammed a four-year high school course into one year and entered the University of California at Berkeley, but after a year he quit school to seek a fortune in the Klondike gold rush of 1897. Returning the next year, still poor and unable to find work, he decided to earn a living as a writer.

Artist's rendering based on Jack London's classic novel, The Call of the Wild. **Buyenlarge/Archive Photos/Getty Images**

London studied magazines and then set himself a daily schedule of producing sonnets, ballads, jokes, anecdotes, adventure stories, or horror stories, steadily increasing his output. The optimism and energy with which he attacked his task are best conveyed in his autobiographical novel *Martin Eden* (1909), perhaps his most enduring work. Within two years stories of his Alaskan adventures, though often crude, began to win acceptance for their fresh subject matter and virile force. His first book, *The Son of the Wolf* (1900), gained a wide audience. During the remainder of his life he produced steadily, completing 50 books of fiction and nonfiction in 17 years. Although he became the highest-paid writer in the United States, his earnings never matched his expenditures, and he was never freed of the urgency of writing for money. He sailed a ketch to the South Pacific, telling of his adventures in *The Cruise of the Snark* (1911). In 1910 he settled on a ranch near Glen Ellen, California, where he built his grandiose Wolf House.

Jack London's hastily written output is of uneven quality. His Alaskan stories *Call of the Wild* (1903), *White Fang* (1906), and *Burning Daylight* (1910), in which he dramatized in turn atavism, adaptability, and the appeal of the wilderness, are outstanding. In addition to *Martin Eden*, he wrote two other autobiographical novels of considerable interest: *The Road* (1907) and *John Barleycorn* (1913). His other important works are *The Sea Wolf* (1904), which features a Nietzschean superman hero, and *The Iron Heel* (1907), a fantasy of the future that is a terrifying anticipation of fascism. London's reputation declined in the United States in the 1920s when a brilliant new generation of postwar writers made the prewar writers seem lacking in sophistication, but his popularity has remained high throughout the world. A three-volume set of his letters, edited by Earle Labor et al., was published in 1988.

SHERWOOD ANDERSON

(b. September 13, 1876, Camden, Ohio, U.S.—d. March 8, 1941, Colon, Panama)

Sherwood Anderson strongly influenced American writing between World Wars I and II, particularly the technique of the short story. His writing had an impact on such notable writers as Ernest Hemingway and William Faulkner, both of whom owe the first publication of their books to his efforts. His prose style, based on everyday speech and derived from the experimental writing of Gertrude Stein, was markedly influential on the early Hemingway—who parodied it cruelly in *Torrents of Spring* (1926) to make a clean break and become his own man.

One of seven children of a day labourer, Anderson attended school intermittently as a youth in Clyde, Ohio, and worked as a newsboy, house painter, farmhand, and racetrack helper. After a year at Wittenberg Academy, a preparatory school in Springfield, Ohio, he worked as an advertising writer in Chicago until 1906, when he went back to Ohio and for the next six years sought—without success—to prosper as a businessman while writing fiction in his spare time. A paint manufacturer in Elyria, Ohio, he left his office abruptly one day in 1912 and wandered off, turning up four days later in Cleveland, disheveled and mentally distraught. He later said he staged this episode to get away from the business world and devote himself to literature.

Anderson went back to his advertising job in Chicago and remained there until he began to earn enough from his published work to quit. Encouraged by Theodore Dreiser,

Floyd Dell, Carl Sandburg, and Ben Hecht—leaders of the Chicago literary movement—he began to contribute experimental verse and short fiction to *The Little Review*, *The Masses*, the *Seven Arts*, and *Poetry*. Dell and Dreiser arranged the publication of his first two novels, *Windy McPherson's Son* (1916; rev. 1921) and *Marching Men* (1917), both written while he was still a manufacturer. *Winesburg, Ohio* (1919) was his first mature book and made his reputation as an author. Its interrelated short sketches and tales are told by a newspaper reporter-narrator who is as emotionally stunted in some ways as the people he describes. Anderson's novels include *Many Marriages* (1923), which stresses the need for sexual fulfillment; *Dark Laughter* (1925), which values the "primitive" over the civilized; and *Beyond Desire* (1932), a novel of Southern textile mill labour struggles.

His best work is generally thought to be in his short stories, collected in *Winesburg, Ohio, The Triumph of the Egg* (1921), *Horses and Men* (1923), and *Death in the Woods* (1933). Also valued are the autobiographical sketches *A Story Teller's Story* (1924), *Tar: A Midwest Childhood* (1926), and the posthumous *Memoirs* (1942; critical edition 1969). A selection of his *Letters* appeared in 1953.

HERMANN HESSE

(b. July 2, 1877, Calw, Germany—d. August 9, 1962, Montagnola, Switzerland)

At the behest of his father, Hermann Hesse entered the Maulbronn seminary. Though a model student, he was unable to adapt, so he was apprenticed in a Calw tower-clock factory and later in a Tübingen bookstore.

His disgust with conventional schooling was expressed in the novel *Unterm Rad* (1906; *Beneath the Wheel*), in which an overly diligent student is driven to self-destruction.

Hesse remained in the bookselling business until 1904, when he became a freelance writer and brought out his first novel, *Peter Camenzind,* about a failed and dissipated writer. The inward and outward search of the artist is further explored in *Gertrud* (1910) and *Rosshalde* (1914). A visit to India in these years was later reflected in *Siddhartha* (1922), a poetic novel, set in India at the time of the Buddha, about the search for enlightenment.

During World War I, Hesse lived in neutral Switzerland, wrote denunciations of militarism and nationalism, and edited a journal for German war prisoners and internees. He became a permanent resident of Switzerland in 1919 and a citizen in 1923, settling in Montagnola.

A deepening sense of personal crisis led Hesse to psychoanalysis with J.B. Lang, a disciple of Carl Gustav Jung. The influence of analysis appears in *Demian* (1919), an examination of the achievement of self-awareness by a troubled adolescent. This novel had a pervasive effect on a troubled Germany and made its author famous. Hesse's later work shows his interest in Jungian concepts of introversion and extraversion, the collective unconscious, idealism, and symbols. The duality of human nature preoccupied Hesse throughout the rest of his career.

Der Steppenwolf (1927; *Steppenwolf*) describes the conflict between bourgeois acceptance and spiritual self-realization in a middle-aged man. In *Narziss und Goldmund* (1930; *Narcissus and Goldmund*), an intellectual ascetic who is content with established religious faith is contrasted with an artistic sensualist pursuing his own form of salvation. In his last and longest novel, *Das Glasperlenspiel* (1943; English titles *The Glass Bead Game* and *Magister Ludi*), Hesse again explores the dualism of the contemplative and the active life, this time through the figure of a supremely gifted intellectual. In 1946 he was awarded the Nobel Prize for Literature.

Hesse's main theme deals with the necessity of breaking out of the established modes of civilization to find one's essential spirit. It is little wonder that with this emphasis on self-realization and his celebration of Eastern mysticism, Hesse posthumously became a cult figure to young people in the English-speaking world.

CARL SANDBURG

(b. January 6, 1878, Galesburg, Illinois, U.S. — d. July 22, 1967, Flat Rock, North Carolina)

From age 11, Carl Sandburg worked in various occupations—as a barbershop porter, a milk truck driver, a brickyard hand, and a harvester in the Kansas wheat fields. When the Spanish-American War broke out in 1898, he enlisted in the 6th Illinois Infantry. These early years he later described in his autobiography *Always the Young Strangers* (1953).

From 1910 to 1912 he acted as an organizer for the Social Democratic Party and secretary to the mayor of Milwaukee. Moving to Chicago in 1913, he became an editor of *System*, a business magazine, and later joined the staff of the *Chicago Daily News*.

In 1914 a group of his *Chicago Poems* appeared in *Poetry* magazine (issued in book form in 1916). In his most famous poem, "Chicago," he depicted the city as the laughing, lusty, heedless "Hog Butcher, Tool Maker, Stacker of Wheat, Player with Railroads and Freight Handler to the Nation." Sandburg's poetry made an instant and

Carl Sandburg. Encyclopædia Britannica, Inc.

favourable impression. In Whitmanesque free verse, he eulogized workers: "Pittsburgh, Youngstown, Gary, they make their steel with men" (*Smoke and Steel,* 1920).

In *Good Morning, America* (1928) Sandburg seemed to have lost some of his faith in democracy, but from the depths of the Great Depression he wrote *The People, Yes* (1936), a poetic testament to the power of the people to go forward. The folk songs he sang before delighted audiences were issued in two collections, *The American Songbag* (1927) and *New American Songbag* (1950). He wrote the popular biography *Abraham Lincoln: The Prairie Years*, 2 vol. (1926), and *Abraham Lincoln: The War Years*, 4 vol. (1939), which won the 1940 Pulitzer Prize in history.

Another biography, *Steichen the Photographer,* the life of his famous brother-in-law, Edward Steichen, appeared in 1929. In 1948 Sandburg published a long novel, *Remembrance Rock*, which recapitulates the American experience from Plymouth Rock to World War II. *Complete Poems* appeared in 1950. He also wrote four books for children—*Rootabaga Stories* (1922); *Rootabaga Pigeons* (1923); *Rootabaga Country* (1929); and *Potato Face* (1930).

ALFRED DÖBLIN

(b. August 10, 1878, Stettin, Germany—d. June 26, 1957, Emmendingen, near Freiburg im Breisgau, West Germany)

Alfred Döblin studied medicine and became a doctor, practicing psychiatry in the workers' district of the Alexanderplatz in Berlin. His Jewish ancestry and socialist views obliged him to leave Germany for France in 1933 after the Nazi takeover, and in 1940 he escaped to the United States, where he converted to Roman Catholicism in 1941. He returned to Germany in 1945 at the war's end to work for the Allied occupying powers, but he resettled in Paris in the early 1950s. He was seeking medical treatment in Germany when he died.

Although Döblin's technique and style vary, two of his constant preoccupations were the urge to expose the hollowness of a civilization heading toward its own destruction and a quasi-religious urge to provide a means of salvation for suffering humanity. His first successful novel, *Die drei Sprünge des Wang-lun* (1915; *The Three Leaps of Wang-lun*), is set in China and describes a rebellion that is crushed by the tyrannical power of the state. *Wallenstein* (1920) is a historical novel, and *Berge, Meere und Giganten* (1924; "Mountains, Seas, and Giants"; republished as *Giganten* in 1932) is a merciless anti-utopian satire.

Döblin's best-known and most Expressionistic novel, *Berlin Alexanderplatz* (1929; *Alexanderplatz, Berlin*), tells the story of Franz Biberkopf, a Berlin proletarian who tries to rehabilitate himself after his release from jail but undergoes a series of vicissitudes, many of them violent and squalid, before he can finally attain a normal life. The book combines interior monologue (in colloquial language and Berlin slang) with a somewhat cinematic technique to create a compelling rhythm that dramatizes the human condition in a disintegrating social order. It was immediately appealing to filmmakers; the story was filmed twice, once by the German Expressionist cinematographer and director Piel Jutzi (1931) and again by Rainer Werner Fassbinder (1980).

Döblin's subsequent books, which continue to focus on individuals destroyed by opposing social forces, include *Babylonische Wandrung* (1934; "Babylonian Wandering"), sometimes described as a late masterwork of German Surrealism; *Pardon wird nicht gegeben* (1935; *Men Without Mercy*); and two unsuccessful trilogies of historical novels.

He also wrote essays on political and literary topics, and his *Reise in Polen* (1926; *Journey to Poland*) is a stimulating travel account. Döblin recounted his flight from France in 1940 and his observations of postwar Germany in the book *Schicksalsreise* (1949; *Destiny's Journey*).

UPTON SINCLAIR

b. September 20, 1878, Baltimore, Maryland, U.S.—d. November 25, 1968, Bound Brook, New Jersey)

Upton Beall Sinclair graduated from the College of the City of New York in 1897 and did graduate work at Columbia University, supporting himself by journalistic writing. *The Jungle* (1906), his sixth novel and first popular success, was written when he was sent by the socialist weekly newspaper *Appeal to Reason* to Chicago to investigate conditions in the stockyards. Though intended to create sympathy for the exploited and poorly treated immigrant workers in the meat-packing industry, *The Jungle* instead aroused widespread public indignation at the quality of and impurities in processed meats and thus helped bring about the passage of federal food-inspection laws. Sinclair ironically commented at the time, "I aimed at the public's heart and by accident I hit it in the stomach." *The Jungle* is the most enduring of the works of the "muckrakers" (investigative journalists). Published at Sinclair's own expense after several publishers rejected it, it became a best-seller, and Sinclair used the proceeds to open Helicon Hall, a cooperative-living venture in Englewood, New Jersey. The building was destroyed by fire in 1907 and the project abandoned.

A long series of other topical novels followed, none as popular as *The Jungle*; among them were *Oil!* (1927), based on the Teapot Dome Scandal (regarding the secret leasing of federal oil reserve lands), and *Boston* (1928), based on the Sacco-Vanzetti case (a controversial murder trial and execution involving two anarchists). Sinclair's works were highly popular in Russia both before and immediately after the Revolution of 1917. Later his active opposition to the communist regime caused a decline in his reputation there, but it was revived temporarily in the late 1930s and '40s by his antifascist writings. Sinclair again reached a wide audience with the Lanny Budd series, 11 contemporary historical novels beginning with *World's End* (1940) that were constructed around an implausible antifascist hero who happens to be on hand for all the momentous events of the day.

During the economic crisis of the 1930s, Sinclair organized the EPIC (End Poverty in California) socialist reform movement. In 1934 he was defeated as Democratic candidate for governor. Of his autobiographical writings, *American Outpost: A Book of Reminiscences* (1932; also published as *Candid Reminiscences: My First Thirty Years*) was reworked and extended in *The Autobiography of Upton Sinclair* (1962).

E. M. Forster

(b. January 1, 1879, London, England—d. June 7, 1970, Coventry, Warwickshire)

Edward Morgan Forster's father, an architect, died when his son was a baby, and the child was brought up by his mother and paternal aunts. The difference between the two families—his father's being strongly evangelical with a high sense of moral responsibility, his mother's more feckless and generous-minded—gave him an enduring insight into the nature of domestic tensions, while his education as a dayboy (day student) at Tonbridge School, Kent, was responsible for many of his later criticisms of the English public school (private) system. At King's College, Cambridge, he enjoyed a sense of liberation. For the first time he was free to follow his own intellectual inclinations; and he gained a sense of the uniqueness of the individual, of the healthiness of moderate skepticism, and of the importance of Mediterranean civilization as a counterbalance to the more straitlaced attitudes of northern European countries.

On leaving Cambridge, Forster decided to devote his life to writing. His first novels and short stories were redolent of an age that was shaking off the shackles of Victorianism. While adopting certain themes (the importance of women in their own right, for example) from earlier English novelists such as George Meredith, he broke with the elaborations and intricacies favoured in the late 19th century and wrote in a freer, more colloquial style. From the first his novels included a strong strain of social comment, based on acute observation of middle-class life. There was also a deeper concern, however, a belief, associated with Forster's interest in Mediterranean "paganism," that, if men and women were to achieve a satisfactory life, they needed to keep contact with the earth and to cultivate their imaginations. In an early novel, *The Longest Journey* (1907), he suggested that cultivation of either in isolation is not enough, reliance on the earth alone leading to a genial brutishness and exaggerated development of imagination undermining the individual's sense of reality.

The same theme runs through *Howards End* (1910), a more ambitious novel that brought Forster his first major success. The novel is conceived in terms of an alliance between the Schlegel sisters, Margaret and Helen, who embody the liberal imagination at its best, and Ruth Wilcox, the owner of the house Howards End, which has remained close to the earth for generations; spiritually they recognize a kinship against the values of Henry Wilcox and his children, who conceive life mainly in terms of commerce. In a symbolic ending, Margaret Schlegel marries Henry Wilcox and brings him back, a broken man, to Howards End, reestablishing there a link (however heavily threatened by the forces of progress around it) between the imagination and the earth.

The resolution is a precarious one, and World War I was to undermine it still further. Forster spent three wartime years in Alexandria, doing civilian war work, and visited India twice, in 1912–13 and 1921. When he returned to former themes in his postwar novel *A Passage to India* (1924), they presented themselves in a negative form: against the vaster scale of India, in which the earth itself seems alien, a resolution between it and the imagination could appear as almost impossible to achieve. Only Adela Quested, the young girl who is most open to experience, can glimpse their possible concord, and then only momentarily, in the courtroom during the trial at which she is the central witness. Much of the novel is devoted to less spectacular values: those of seriousness and truthfulness (represented here by the administrator Fielding) and of an outgoing and benevolent sensibility (embodied in the English visitor Mrs. Moore). Neither Fielding nor Mrs. Moore is totally successful; neither totally fails. The novel ends in an uneasy equilibrium. Immediate reconciliation between Indians and British is ruled out, but the further possibilities inherent in Adela's experience, along with the surrounding uncertainties, are echoed in the ritual birth of the God of Love amid scenes of confusion at a Hindu festival.

The values of truthfulness and kindness dominate Forster's later thinking. A reconciliation of humanity to the earth and its own imagination may be the ultimate ideal, but Forster sees it receding in a civilization devoting itself more and more to technological progress. The values of common sense, goodwill, and regard for the individual, on the other hand, can still be cultivated, and these underlie Forster's later pleas for more liberal attitudes. During World War II he acquired a position of particular respect as a man who had never been seduced by totalitarianisms of any kind and whose belief in personal relationships and the simple decencies seemed to embody some of the common values behind the fight against Nazism and fascism. In 1946 his old college gave him an honorary fellowship, which enabled him to make his home in Cambridge and to keep in communication with both old and young until his death.

Although the later Forster is an important figure in mid-20th-century culture, his emphasis on a kindly, uncommitted, and understated morality being congenial to many of his contemporaries, it is by his novels that he is more likely to be remembered, and these are best seen in the context of the preceding Romantic tradition. The novels sustain the cult of the heart's affections that was central to that tradition, but they also share with the first Romantics a concern for the status of man in nature and for his imaginative life, a concern that remains important to an age that has turned against other aspects of Romanticism.

In addition to essays, short stories, and novels, Forster wrote a biography of his great-aunt, *Marianne Thornton* (1956); a documentary account of his Indian experiences,

The Hill of Devi (1953); and *Alexandria: A History and a Guide* (1922; new ed., 1961). *Maurice*, a novel with a homosexual theme, was published posthumously in 1971 but written many years earlier.

WALLACE STEVENS

(b. October 2, 1879, Reading, Pennsylvania, U.S.—d. August 2, 1955, Hartford, Connecticut)

Wallace Stevens attended Harvard for three years, worked briefly for the New York *Herald Tribune*, and then won a degree (1904) at the New York Law School and practiced law in New York City. His first published poems, aside from college verse, appeared in 1914 in *Poetry*, and thereafter he was a frequent contributor to literary magazines. In 1916 he joined an insurance firm in Hartford, Connecticut, rising in 1934 to vice president, a position he held until his death.

Harmonium (1923), his first book, sold fewer than 100 copies but received some favourable critical notices; it was reissued in 1931 and in 1947. In it he introduced the imagination–reality theme that occupied his creative life-time, making his work so unified that he considered three decades later calling his collected poems "The Whole of Harmonium."

He displayed his most dazzling verbal brilliance in his first book; he later tended to relinquish surface lustre for philosophical rigour. In *Harmonium* appeared such poems as "Le Monocle de Mon Oncle," "Sunday Morning," "Peter Quince at the Clavier," and Stevens's own favourites, "Domination of Black" and "The Emperor of Ice-Cream"; all were frequently republished in anthologies. *Harmonium* also contained "Sea Surface Full of Clouds," in which waves are described in terms of such unlikely equivalents as umbrellas, French phrases, and varieties of chocolate, and "The Comedian as the Letter C," in which he examines the relation of the poet, or man of imagination, to society.

In the 1930s and early '40s, this theme was to reappear, although not to the exclusion of others, in Stevens's *Ideas of Order* (1935), *The Man with the Blue Guitar* (1937), and *Parts of a World* (1942). *Transport to Summer* (1947) incorporated two long sequences that had appeared earlier: "Notes Towards a Supreme Fiction" and "Esthétique du Mal" ("Aesthetic of Evil"), in which he argues that beauty is inextricably linked with evil. *The Auroras of Autumn* (1950) was followed by his *Collected Poems* (1954), which earned him the Pulitzer Prize for Poetry. A volume of critical essays, *The Necessary Angel*, appeared in 1951.

Stevens was not read at all widely or recognized as a major poet by more than a few contemporaries until late in life. After his death, Samuel French Morse edited *Opus Posthumous* (1957), including poems, plays, and prose omitted from the earlier collection. His *Collected Poetry and Prose* was published by the Library of America in 1997.

RADCLYFFE HALL

(b. August 12, 1880, Bournemouth, Hampshire, England—
d. October 7, 1943, London)

Marguerite Radclyffe-Hall was educated at King's College, London, and then attended school in Germany. She began her literary career by writing verses, which were later collected into five volumes of poetry. *The Blind Ploughman,* one of her best-known poems, was set to music by Conigsby Clarke. It was recorded by the likes of Feodor Chaliapin, Paul Robeson, and Nelson Eddy. By 1924 she had written her first two novels, *The Forge* and *The Unlit Lamp*. The latter book was her first to treat lesbian love. *Adam's Breed* (1926), a sensitive novel about the life of a restaurant keeper, won the coveted Prix Fémina and the 1927 James Tait Black Memorial Prize for fiction.

Hall's fame turned to notoriety with the publication of *The Well of Loneliness*, in which she explored in detail the attachment between a young girl and an older woman. The intense and earnest love story was condemned by the British, and a London magistrate, Sir Chartres Biron, ruled that although the book was dignified and restrained, it presented an appeal to "decent people" to not only recognize lesbianism but also understand that the person so afflicted was not at fault. He judged the book an "obscene libel" and ordered all copies of it destroyed. Later, a decree handed down in a U.S. court disagreed with Biron, finding that discussion of homosexuality was not in itself obscene. The British ban on *The Well of Loneliness* was eventually overturned on appeal after Hall's death.

Although Hall had been vindicated by the American verdict, she did not write any other controversial novels. Among her following works are *Twixt Earth and Stars: Poems* (1906), *Songs of Three Counties and Other Poems* (1913), *The Master of the House* (1932), and *The Sixth Beatitude* (1936). A novel on which she was working in her declining years was destroyed, at her request, after her death.

GUILLAUME APOLLINAIRE

(b. August 26, 1880, Rome?, Italy—d. November 9, 1918, Paris, France)

Guillelmus (or Wilhelm) Apollinaris de Kostrowitzki, who would be known to the world as Guillaume Apollinaire, was the son of a Polish *émigrée* and an Italian officer. Further information about his origins he kept secret. Left more or less to himself, he went at age 20 to Paris, where he led a bohemian life. Several months spent in Germany in 1901 had a profound effect on him and helped to awaken him to his poetic vocation. He fell under the spell of the Rhineland and later recaptured the beauty of its forests and its legends in his poetry. He fell in love with a young Englishwoman, whom he pursued, unsuccessfully, as far as London. That romantic disappointment inspired him to write his famous *Chanson du mal-aimé* ("Song of the Poorly Loved").

After his return to Paris, Apollinaire became well known as a writer and a fixture of the cafés patronized by literary men. He also made friends with some young painters who were to become famous—Maurice de Vlaminck, André Derain, Raoul Dufy, and Pablo Picasso. He introduced his contemporaries to Henri Rousseau's paintings and to African sculpture. With Picasso and Gertrude Stein, he applied himself to the task of defining the principles of a Cubist aesthetic in literature as well as in painting. His *Peintures cubistes* appeared in 1913 (*Cubist Painters*).

Apollinaire's first volume, *L'Enchanteur pourrissant* (1909; "The Rotting Magician"), is a strange dialogue in poetic prose between the magician Merlin and the nymph Viviane. In the following year a collection of vivid stories, some whimsical and some wildly fantastic, appeared under the title *L'Hérésiarque et Cie* (1910; "The Heresiarch and Co."). Then came *Le Bestiaire* (1911), in mannered quatrains. But his poetic masterpiece was *Alcools* (1913; Eng. trans., 1964). In these poems he relived all his experiences and expressed them sometimes in alexandrines and regular stanzas, sometimes in short unrhymed lines, and always without punctuation.

In 1914 Apollinaire enlisted, became a second lieutenant in the infantry, and received a head wound in 1916. Discharged from the army, he returned to Paris and published a symbolic story, *Le Poète assassiné* (1916; *The Poet Assassinated*), and more significantly, a new collection of poems, *Calligrammes* (1918), dominated by images of war and his obsession with a new love affair. Weakened by war wounds, he died of Spanish influenza in 1918.

His play *Les Mamelles de Tirésias* was staged the year before he died (1917). He called it surrealist, believed to be the first use of the term. Francis Poulenc turned the play into a light opera (first produced in 1947).

In his poetry Apollinaire made daring, even outrageous, technical experiments. His *calligrammes*, thanks to an ingenious typographical arrangement, are images as well as poems. More generally, Apollinaire set out to create an effect of surprise or even astonishment by means of unusual verbal associations, and, because of this, he can be considered a forebear of Surrealism.

SHOLEM ASCH

(b. November 1, 1880, Kutno, Poland, Russian Empire — d. July 10, 1957, London, England)

The youngest of the 10 surviving children of a poor Hasidic family, Sholem Asch was educated at Kutno's Hebrew school. In 1899 he went to Warsaw, and in 1900 he published his highly praised first story—written, as was a cycle that followed, in Hebrew. On the advice of the Yiddish writer I.L. Peretz, he subsequently decided to write only in Yiddish, and with *A Shtetl* (1905; *The Little Town*) he began a career outstanding for both output and impact. His tales, novels, and plays filled 29 volumes in a collected Yiddish edition published in 1929–38. By their vitality and vigorous naturalism, his works attracted sizable reading publics in Europe and the United States and were soon widely translated. Unlike his great Yiddish predecessors, Asch was fortunate in having several inspired translators—among them Edwin and Willa Muir and Maurice Samuel—through whom his work could enter the literary mainstream.

Asch's work falls into three periods. In his first, he described the tragicomedy of life in the small eastern European Jewish towns torn between devotion to traditional Jewishness and the urge toward emancipation. To this period belong two novels—*Kidush ha-shem* (1919; "Sanctification of [God's] Name"), a historical novel about the pogroms instigated by the Cossack leader Bohdan Khmelnytsky in 1648, and *Motke ganef* (1916; *Mottke, the Thief*)—and the play *Got fun nekome* (1907; *God of Vengeance* in *The Great Jewish Plays*), about a Jewish brothel owner whose daughter has a lesbian relationship with one of her father's prostitutes. The play was produced in Berlin by Max Reinhardt in 1910 but banned elsewhere.

Asch visited the United States in 1910, returned there in 1914, and became a naturalized U.S. citizen in 1920. To this period belong *Onkl Mozes* (1918; *Uncle Moses*), *Toyt urteyl* (1924; "Death Sentence"; Eng. trans. *Judge Not—*), and *Khaym Lederers tsurikumen* (1927; *Chaim Lederer's Return*). These novels describe the cultural and economic conflicts experienced by eastern European Jewish immigrants in America.

Throughout his career Asch spent much time in Europe and made long visits to Palestine. In his last, most controversial period he attempted to unite Judaism and Christianity through emphasis upon their historical and theologico-ethical connections: *Der man fun Natseres* (1943; *The Nazarene*), a reconstruction of Christ's life as expressive of essential Judaism; *The Apostle* (1943), a study of St. Paul; *Mary* (1949), the mother of Jesus seen as the Jewish "handmaid of the Lord"; and *The Prophet* (1955), on the Second (Deutero-) Isaiah, whose message of comfort and hope replaces the earlier prophecies of doom. In the presentation of this unknown prophet, conjectures based on archaeology and theology are blended by Asch's depth of psychological insight.

But these last years, devoted to asserting a belief formulated when Asch visited Palestine in 1906—that Christianity is essentially a Jewish phenomenon, "one culture and civilization"—were tragic years. A number of his fellow Jews criticized him as an apostate for his fictional presentations of New Testament personages. He lived the last years of his life in Bat Yam, a suburb of Tel Aviv, and his house there is now the Sholem Asch Museum.

ROBERT MUSIL

(b. November 6, 1880, Klagenfurt, Austria—d. April 15, 1942, Geneva, Switzerland)

Robert Musil—also called Robert, Edler ("Nobleman") von Musil—received a doctorate from the University of Berlin in 1908 and then held jobs as a librarian and an editor before serving in the Austrian army in World War I (1914–18). (He inherited the *Edler* title, awarded his father in 1917, but did not use it as an author.) From 1918 to 1922 Musil was a civil servant in Vienna and thereafter worked randomly as a writer and journalist. He lived in Berlin (1932–33) but returned to Vienna until the Nazi Anschluss (annexation of Austria) of 1938, when he fled to Switzerland, where he lived first in Zurich and then in Geneva.

Musil began writing as a student and attracted some notice in the 1920s writing various fiction and two plays, *Die Schwärmer* (1920; *The Enthusiasts*) and *Vinzenz und die Freundin bedeutender Männer* (1924; "Vincent and the Lady Friend of Important Men"), both of which were performed in Berlin and Vienna. In 1924 he began the work for which he is best known, the monumental unfinished novel *Der Mann ohne Eigenschaften* (1930–43; *The Man Without Qualities*). A witty and urbane portrait of life in the glittering world of the Austro-Hungarian empire, the novel is also a farce that gives an account of the slow collapse of a society into anarchy and chaos. The story is told from the viewpoint of Ulrich, a fictionalized Musil. The First Book was published in 1930, and part of the Second Book in 1933; a remaining portion was published posthumously in 1943.

ALEKSANDR ALEKSANDROVICH BLOK

(b. November 28 [November 16, Old Style], 1880, St. Petersburg, Russia—d. August 7, 1921, Petrograd [now St. Petersburg])

Aleksandr Aleksandrovich Blok was born into a sheltered, intellectual environment. After his father, a law professor, and his mother, the cultured daughter of the rector of St. Petersburg University, separated, Blok was reared from age three in an atmosphere of artistic refinement at the manor of his aristocratic maternal grandparents. In 1903 Blok married Lyubov Mendeleyeva, daughter of the famous chemist D.I. Mendeleyev. To Blok, who had begun to write at age five, poetic expression came naturally. In 1903 he published for the first time, and his early verse communicates the exaltation and spiritual fulfillment his marriage brought.

The early 19th-century Romantic poetry of Aleksandr Pushkin and the apocalyptic philosophy of the poet and mystic Vladimir Solovyov exerted a strong influence on Blok. Using innovative poetic rhythms, he drew on their concepts to develop an original style of expression. For Blok, sound was paramount, and musicality is the primary characteristic of his verse.

His first collection of poems, the cycle *Stikhi o prekrasnoy dame* (1904; "Verses About the Lady Beautiful"), focuses on personal, intimate themes that are presented on a mystical plane and lack any contemporaneity. The heroine of the poems is not only the beloved whom the poet treats with knightly chivalry but is also the epitome of eternal femininity. In a three-volume anthology of his poetry that he compiled shortly before his death, Blok placed *Verses About the Lady Beautiful* in the first volume, a decision that made clear his belief that it represented the first, mystical phase in his career.

Blok's next poetry collections differed significantly from his first. *Nechayannaya radost* (1907; "Inadvertent Joy"), *Snezhnaya maska* (1907; "Mask of Snow"), and *Zemlya v snegu* (1908; "Earth in Snow") treated themes of contemporary city life, including revolutionary events, deeply felt love, and complex psychology. Many critics, among them Blok's close friend Andrey Bely, saw these poems as a betrayal of the ideal expressed in his first collection, where reality was subjected to mystic transformation.

Blok's thinking during these years was also reflected in plays—*Neznakomka* (written 1907; "The Stranger") and *Pesnya sudby* (written 1909; "The Song of Fate")—and a number of essays. In these he repeatedly returned to the ideals of the old Russian intelligentsia and the traditions of social radicalism.

Blok's standing as lyric poet culminates in the third volume of his anthology, traditionally seen as the pinnacle of his poetic work. This volume contains the poems previously collected in the books *Nochnye chasy* (1911; "Night Hours") and *Stikhi o Rossii* (1915; "Poems About Russia") as well as uncollected poems. Together they draw on a historical and mystical perspective to depict Russia as Blok saw it during the 1910s. World War I (during which Blok was drafted into the army and served in an engineering and construction detail but did not participate in combat) and the Russian Revolution of 1917 forged his view. Blok understood the events affecting not only Russia but the whole world as a critical, tragic, and threatening catastrophe. But underlying this view was faith in the future of humankind.

In 1917 Blok worked for the commission that investigated the crimes of the imperial government, and after the last phase of the revolution he began working for the Bolsheviks, whom he felt represented the will of the people. His state of mind in late 1917 and in 1918 is best expressed in a line of his poetry: "Terrible, sweet, inescapable, imperative." He could see in Russia and elsewhere "the downfall of humanism"—a phrase he used in an article he wrote in 1918—but he felt that it was an inescapable stage in history. Blok expressed this outlook in the novel in verse *Dvenadtsat* (1918; *The Twelve*) and the poem *Skify* (1918; "The Scythians"). Many early readers of *The Twelve* regarded its depiction of Christ in revolutionary Petrograd as blasphemous, but through it Blok expressed vividly the mood of the time. He quickly became disillusioned with the Bolshevik government, however, and all but stopped writing poetry thereafter.

Lu Xun

(b. September 25, 1881, Shaoxing, Zhejiang province, China — d. October 19, 1936, Shanghai)

The Chinese writer Zhou Shuren, who wrote under the pen name Lu Xun (Lu Hsün), is commonly considered the greatest 20th-century writer of Chinese literature. He was also an important critic known for his sharp and unique essays on the historical traditions and modern conditions of China.

Youth

Born to a family that was traditional, wealthy, and esteemed (his grandfather had been a government official in Beijing), Zhou Shuren had a happy childhood. In 1893, however, his grandfather was sentenced to prison for examination fraud, and his father became bedridden. The family's reputation declined, and they were treated with disdain by their community and relatives. This experience is thought to have had a great influence on his writing, which was marked by sensitivity and pessimism.

Zhou Shuren left his hometown in 1899 and attended a mining school in Nanjing. There he developed an interest in Darwin's theory of evolution, which became an important influence in his work. Chinese intellectuals of the time understood Darwin's theory to encourage the struggle for social reform, to privilege the new and fresh over the old and traditional. In 1902 he traveled to Japan to study Japanese and medical science, and while there he became a supporter of the Chinese revolutionaries who gathered there. In 1903 he began to write articles for radical magazines edited by Chinese students in Japan. In 1905 he entered an arranged marriage against his will. In 1909 he published, with his younger brother Zhou Zuoren, a two-volume translation of 19th-century European stories, in the hope that it would inspire readers to revolution, but the project failed to attract interest. Disillusioned, Lu Xun returned to China later that year.

Literary Career

After working for several years as a teacher in his hometown and then as a low-level government official in Beijing, Lu Xun returned to writing and became associated with the nascent Chinese literary movement in 1918. That year, at the urging of friends, he published his now-famous short story *Kuangren riji* ("Diary of a Madman"). Modeled on the Russian realist Nikolay Gogol's tale of the same title, the story is a condemnation of traditional Confucian culture, which the madman narrator sees as a "man-eating" society. The first published Western-style story written wholly in vernacular Chinese, it was a tour de force that attracted immediate attention and helped gain acceptance for the short-story form as an effective literary vehicle. Another representative work is the novelette *A-Q zhengzhuan* (1921; *The True Story of Ah Q*). A mixture of humour and pathos, it is a repudiation of the old order; it added "Ah Q-ism" to the modern Chinese language as a term characterizing the Chinese penchant for rationalizing defeat as a "spiritual victory." These stories, which were collected in *Nahan* (1923; *Call to Arms*), established Lu Xun's reputation as the leading Chinese writer. Three years later the collection *Panghuang* (1926; *Wandering*) was published. His various symbolic prose poems, which were published in the collection *Yecao* (1927; *Wild Grass*), as well as his reminiscences and retold classical tales, all reveal a modern sensibility informed by sardonic humour and biting satire.

In the 1920s Lu Xun worked at various universities in Beijing as a part-time professor of Chinese script and literature. His academic study *Zhongguo xiaoshuo shilue* (1923–24; *A Brief History of Chinese Fiction*) and companion compilations of classical fiction remain standard works. His translations, especially those of Russian works, are also considered significant.

Despite his success, Lu Xun continued to struggle with his increasingly pessimistic view of Chinese society, which was aggravated by conflicts in his personal and professional life. In addition to marital troubles and mounting pressures from the government, his disagreements with Zhou Zuoren (who had also become one of the leading intellectuals in Beijing) led to a rift between the two brothers in 1926. Such depressing conditions led Lu Xun to formulate the idea that one could resist social darkness only when he was pessimistic about the society. His famous phrase "resistance of despair" is commonly considered a core concept of his thought.

Shanghai Years

Forced by these political and personal circumstances to flee Beijing in 1926, Lu Xun traveled to Xiamen and Guangzhou, finally settling in Shanghai in 1927. There he began to live with Xu Guangping, his former student;

they had a son in 1929. Lu Xun stopped writing fiction and devoted himself to writing satiric critical essays (*zawen*), which he used as a form of political protest. In 1930 he became the nominal leader of the League of Left-Wing Writers. During the following decade he began to see the Chinese communists as the only salvation for his country. Although he himself refused to join the Chinese Communist Party, he considered himself a *tongluren* (fellow traveler), recruiting many writers and countrymen to the communist cause through his Chinese translations of Marxist literary theories, as well as through his own political writing.

During the last several years of Lu Xun's life, the government prohibited the publication of most of his work, so he published the majority of his new articles under various pseudonyms. He criticized the Shanghai communist literary circles for their embrace of propaganda, and he was politically attacked by many of their members. In 1934 he described his political position as *hengzhan* ("horizontal stand"), meaning he was struggling simultaneously against both the right and the left, against both cultural conservatism and mechanical evolution. *Hengzhan*, the most important idea in Lu Xun's later thought, indicates the complex and tragic predicament of an intellectual in modern society.

The Chinese communist movement adopted Lu Xun posthumously as the exemplar of Socialist Realism. Many of his fiction and prose works have been incorporated into school textbooks. In 1951 the Lu Xun Museum opened in Shanghai; it contains letters, manuscripts, photographs, and other memorabilia. English translations of Lu Xun's works include *Silent China: Selected Writings of Lu Xun* (1973), *Lu Hsun: Complete Poems* (1988), and *Diary of a Madman and Other Stories* (1990).

P.G. WODEHOUSE

(b. October 15, 1881, Guildford, Surrey, England—d. February 14, 1975, Southampton, New York, U.S.)

Pelham Grenville Wodehouse was educated at Dulwich College, London, and, after a period in a bank, took a job as a humorous columnist at the London *Globe* (1902) and wrote freelance for many other publications. After 1909 he lived and worked for long periods in the United States and in France. He was captured in France by the Germans in 1940 and spent much of the war interned in Berlin. In 1941 he made five radio broadcasts from there to the United States in which he humorously described his experiences as a prisoner and subtly ridiculed his captors. His use of enemy broadcasting facilities evoked deep and lasting resentment in Britain, however, which was then practically under siege by Germany. After the war Wodehouse settled in the United States, becoming a citizen in 1955. He was knighted in 1975.

Wodehouse began by writing public-school stories and then light romances. It was not until 1913 (in *Something New*; published in England as *Something Fresh*, 1915) that he turned to farce, which became his special strength. He had a scholar's command of the English sentence. He delighted in vivid, far-fetched imagery and in slang. His plots are highly complicated and carefully planned. Whatever the dates of publication of his books, Wodehouse's English social atmosphere is of the late Edwardian era. His best known stories concern the young bachelor Bertie Wooster and his effortlessly superior manservant (or "gentleman's gentleman"), Jeeves. These two were still together, their ages unadvanced, in *Much Obliged, Jeeves* (1971), though they first appeared in a story in *The Man with Two Left Feet* (1917). Wodehouse wrote more than 90 books and more than 20 film scripts and collaborated on more than 30 plays and musical comedies.

A.A. Milne

(b. January 18, 1882, London, England — d. January 31, 1956, Hartfield, Sussex)

Alan Alexander Milne's father ran a private school, where one of his son's teachers was a young H.G. Wells. Milne went on to attend Westminster School, London, and Trinity College, Cambridge, the latter on a mathematics scholarship. While at Cambridge, he edited and wrote for *Granta* magazine (then called *The Granta*, for Cambridge's other river). He took a degree in mathematics in 1903 and thereafter moved to London to make a living as a freelance writer. In 1906 he joined the staff of *Punch* (where he worked until 1914), writing humorous verse and whimsical essays. He was married in 1913, and in 1915, though a pacifist, he joined the service during World War I as a signalling officer. He served briefly in France, but he became ill and was sent home. He was discharged in 1919.

When he was not rehired by *Punch*, Milne turned his attention to writing plays. He achieved considerable success with a series of light comedies including *Mr. Pim Passes By* (1921) and *Michael and Mary* (1930). Milne also wrote one memorable detective novel, *The Red House Mystery* (1922); and a children's play, *Make-Believe* (1918), before stumbling upon his true literary forte with some verses written for his son Christopher Robin. These grew into the collections *When We Were Very Young* (1924) and *Now We Are Six* (1927), which remain classics of light verse for children.

Despite Milne's success as a playwright, only these verses and his two sets of stories about the adventures of Christopher Robin and his toy animals—Pooh, Piglet, Tigger, Kanga, Roo, Rabbit, Owl, and Eeyore—as told in *Winnie-the-Pooh* (1926) and *The House at Pooh Corner* (1928) endured into the 21st century. Illustrations by Ernest Shepard added to their considerable charm. In 1929 Milne adapted another children's classic, *The Wind in the Willows*, by Kenneth Grahame, for the stage as *Toad of Toad Hall*. A decade later he wrote his autobiography, *It's Too Late Now*.

VIRGINIA WOOLF

(b. January 25, 1882, London, England—d. March 28, 1941, near Rodmell, Sussex)

English writer Virginia Woolf is known for a number of novels whose nonlinear narratives exerted a major influence on the genre. While she is best known for her novels, especially *Mrs. Dalloway* (1925) and *To the Lighthouse* (1927), Woolf also wrote pioneering essays on artistic theory, literary history, women's writing, and the politics of power. A fine stylist, she experimented with several forms of biographical writing, composed painterly short fictions, and sent to her friends and family a lifetime of brilliant letters.

Virginia Woolf. New York World-Telegram & Sun Collection/ Library of Congress, Washington, D.C. (neg. no. LC-USZ62-111438)

Early Life and Influences

Born Adeline Virginia Stephen, she was the child of ideal Victorian parents. Her father, Leslie Stephen, was an eminent literary figure and the first editor (1882–91) of the *Dictionary of National Biography*. Her mother, Julia Jackson, possessed great beauty and a reputation for saintly self-sacrifice; she also had prominent social and artistic connections, which included Julia Margaret Cameron, her aunt and one of the greatest portrait photographers of the 19th century. Both Julia Jackson's first husband, Herbert Duckworth, and Leslie's first wife, a daughter of the novelist William Makepeace Thackeray, had died unexpectedly, leaving her three children and him one.

Julia Jackson Duckworth and Leslie Stephen married in 1878, and four children followed: Vanessa (born 1879), Thoby (born 1880), Virginia (born 1882), and Adrian (born 1883). The Stephen family made summer migrations from their London town house near Kensington Gardens to the rather disheveled Talland House on the rugged Cornwall coast. That annual relocation structured Virginia's childhood world in terms of opposites: city and country, winter and summer, repression and freedom, fragmentation and wholeness. Her neatly divided, predictable world ended, however, when her mother died in 1895 at age 49. Virginia, at 13, ceased writing amusing accounts of family news, which she had begun doing at age nine. Almost a year passed before she wrote a cheerful letter to her brother Thoby. She was just emerging from depression when, in 1897, her half sister Stella Duckworth died at age 28, an event Virginia noted in her diary as "impossible to write of." Then in 1904, after her father died, Virginia had a nervous breakdown.

While Virginia was recovering, Vanessa supervised the Stephen children's move to the bohemian Bloomsbury section of London. There the siblings lived independent of their Duckworth half brothers, free to pursue studies, to paint or write, and to entertain. Leonard Woolf dined with them in November 1904, just before sailing to Ceylon (now Sri Lanka) to become a colonial administrator. Soon the Stephens hosted weekly gatherings of radical young people, including Clive Bell, Lytton Strachey, and John Maynard Keynes, all later to achieve fame as, respectively, an art critic, a biographer, and an economist. Then, after a family excursion to Greece in 1906, Thoby died of typhoid fever. He was 26. Virginia grieved but did not slip into depression. She overcame the loss of Thoby and the "loss" of Vanessa, who became engaged to Bell just after Thoby's death, through writing. Vanessa's marriage (and perhaps Thoby's absence) helped transform conversation at the avant-garde gatherings of what came to be known as the Bloomsbury group into irreverent, sometimes bawdy repartee that inspired Virginia to exercise her wit publicly, even while privately she was writing her poignant *Reminiscences*—about her childhood and her lost mother—which was published in 1908.

Early Fiction

Virginia Stephen determined in 1908 to "re-form" the novel by creating a holistic form embracing aspects of life that were "fugitive" from the Victorian novel. While writing anonymous reviews for the *Times Literary Supplement* and other journals, she experimented with such a novel, which she called *Melymbrosia*. In November 1910, Roger Fry, a new friend of the Bells, launched the exhibit "Manet and the Post-Impressionists," which introduced radical European art to the London bourgeoisie. As Clive Bell was unfaithful, Vanessa began an affair with Fry, and Fry began a lifelong debate with Virginia about the visual and verbal arts. In the summer of 1911, Leonard Woolf returned from the East. After he resigned from the colonial service, Leonard and Virginia married in August 1912.

Between 1910 and 1915, Virginia's mental health was precarious. Nevertheless, she completely recast *Melymbrosia* as *The Voyage Out* in 1913. She based many of her novel's characters on real-life prototypes: Lytton Strachey, Leslie Stephen, her half brother George Duckworth, Clive and Vanessa Bell, and herself. Rachel Vinrace, the novel's central character, is a sheltered young woman who, on an excursion to South America, is introduced to freedom and sexuality (though from the novel's inception she was to die before marrying). Woolf first made Terence, Rachel's suitor, rather Clive-like; as she revised, Terence became a more sensitive, Leonard-like character. After an excursion up the Amazon, Rachel contracts a terrible illness that plunges her into delirium and then death. Woolf's characters suggest everything from poorly washed vegetables to jungle disease to a malevolent universe as possible causes for this disaster, but the book endorses no explanation. That indeterminacy, at odds with the certainties of the Victorian era, is echoed in descriptions that distort perception: while the narrative often describes people, buildings, and natural objects as featureless forms, Rachel, in dreams and then delirium, journeys into surrealistic worlds. Rachel's voyage into the unknown began Woolf's voyage beyond the conventions of realism.

Woolf's manic-depressive worries (that she was a failure as a writer and a woman, that she was despised by Vanessa and unloved by Leonard) provoked a suicide attempt in September 1913. Publication of *The Voyage Out* was delayed until early 1915; then, that April, she sank into a distressed state in which she was often delirious. Later that year she overcame the "vile imaginations" that had threatened her sanity. She kept the demons of mania and depression mostly at bay for the rest of her life.

In 1917 the Woolfs bought a printing press and founded the Hogarth Press, named for Hogarth House, their home in the London suburbs. The Woolfs themselves (she was the compositor while he worked the press) published their own *Two Stories* in the summer of 1917. It consisted of Leonard's *Three Jews* and Virginia's *The Mark on the Wall*, the latter about contemplation itself.

Since 1910, Virginia had kept (sometimes with Vanessa) a country house in Sussex, and in 1916 Vanessa settled into a Sussex farmhouse called Charleston. She had ended her affair with Fry to take up with the painter Duncan Grant, who moved to Charleston with Vanessa and her children, Julian and Quentin Bell; a daughter, Angelica, would be born to Vanessa and Grant at the end of 1918. Charleston soon became an extravagantly decorated, unorthodox retreat for artists and writers, especially Clive Bell, who continued on friendly terms with Vanessa, and Fry, Vanessa's lifelong devotee.

Virginia had kept a diary, off and on, since 1897. In 1919 she envisioned "the shadow of some kind of form which a diary might attain to," organized not by a mechanical recording of events but by the interplay between the objective and the subjective. Her diary, as she wrote in 1924, would reveal people as "splinters & mosaics; not, as they used to hold, immaculate, monolithic, consistent wholes." Such terms later inspired critical distinctions, based on anatomy and culture, between the feminine and the masculine, the feminine being a varied but all-embracing way of experiencing the world and the masculine a monolithic or linear way. Critics using these distinctions have credited Woolf with evolving a distinctly feminine diary form, one that explores, with perception, honesty, and humour, her own ever-changing, mosaic self.

Proving that she could master the traditional form of the novel before breaking it, she plotted her next novel in two romantic triangles, with its protagonist Katharine in both. *Night and Day* (1919) answers Leonard's *The Wise Virgins*, in which he had his Leonard-like protagonist lose the Virginia-like beloved and end up in a conventional marriage. In *Night and Day*, the Leonard-like Ralph learns to value Katharine for herself, not as some superior being. And Katharine overcomes (as Virginia had) class and familial prejudices to marry the good and intelligent Ralph. This novel focuses on the very sort of details that Woolf had deleted from *The Voyage Out*: credible dialogue, realistic descriptions of early 20th-century settings, and investigations of issues such as class, politics, and suffrage.

Woolf was writing nearly a review a week for the *Times Literary Supplement* in 1918. Her essay *Modern Novels* (1919; revised in 1925 as *Modern Fiction*) attacked the "materialists" who wrote about superficial rather than spiritual or "luminous" experiences. The Woolfs also printed by hand, with Vanessa Bell's illustrations, Virginia's *Kew Gardens* (1919), a story organized, like a Post-Impressionistic painting, by pattern. With the Hogarth Press's emergence as a major publishing house, the Woolfs gradually ceased being their own printers.

In 1919 they bought a cottage in Rodmell village called Monk's House, which looked out over the Sussex Downs and the meadows where the River Ouse wound down to the English Channel. Virginia could walk or bicycle to visit Vanessa, her children, and a changing cast of guests at the bohemian Charleston and then retreat to Monk's House to write. She envisioned a new book that would apply the theories of *Modern Novels* and the achievements of her short stories to the novel form.

In 1921 Woolf's minimally plotted short fictions were gathered in *Monday or Tuesday*. In *Jacob's Room* (1922) she transformed personal grief over the death of Thoby Stephen into a "spiritual shape." Though she takes Jacob from childhood to his early death in war, she leaves out plot, conflict, even character. The emptiness of Jacob's room and the irrelevance of his belongings convey in their minimalism the profound emptiness of loss.

Major Period

At the beginning of 1924, the Woolfs moved their city residence from the suburbs back to Bloomsbury, where they were less isolated from London society. Soon the aristocratic Vita Sackville-West began to court Virginia, a relationship that would blossom into a lesbian affair. Having already written a story about a Mrs. Dalloway, Woolf thought of a foiling device that would pair that highly sensitive woman with a shell-shocked war victim, a Mr. Smith, so that "the sane and the insane" would exist "side by side." Her aim was to "tunnel" into these two characters until Clarissa Dalloway's affirmations meet Septimus Smith's negations. Also in 1924 Woolf gave a talk at Cambridge called *Character in Fiction,* revised later that year as the Hogarth Press pamphlet *Mr. Bennett and Mrs. Brown.* In it she celebrated the breakdown in patriarchal values that had occurred "in or about December, 1910"—during Fry's exhibit "Manet and the Post-Impressionists"—and she attacked "materialist" novelists for omitting the essence of character.

In *Mrs. Dalloway* (1925), the boorish doctors presume to understand personality, but its essence evades them. This novel is as patterned as a Post-Impressionist painting but is also so accurately representational that the reader can trace Clarissa's and Septimus's movements through the streets of London on a single day in June 1923. At the end of the day, Clarissa gives a grand party and Septimus commits suicide. Their lives come together when the doctor who was treating (or, rather, mistreating) Septimus arrives at Clarissa's party with news of the death. The main characters are connected by motifs and, finally, by Clarissa's intuiting why Septimus threw his life away.

Woolf wished to build on her achievement in *Mrs. Dalloway* by merging the novelistic and elegiac forms. As an elegy, *To the Lighthouse*—published on May 5, 1927, the 32nd anniversary of Julia Stephen's death—evoked childhood summers at Talland House. As a novel, it broke narrative continuity into a tripartite structure. The first section, "The Window," begins as Mrs. Ramsay and James, her youngest son—like Julia and Adrian Stephen—sit in the French window of the Ramsays' summer home while a houseguest named Lily Briscoe paints them and James begs to go to a nearby lighthouse. Mr. Ramsay, like Leslie Stephen, sees poetry as didacticism, conversation as winning points, and life as a tally of accomplishments. He uses logic to deflate hopes for a trip to the lighthouse, but he needs sympathy from his wife. She is more attuned to emotions than reason. In the climactic dinner-party scene, she inspires such harmony and composure that the moment "partook, she felt,...of eternity." The novel's middle "Time Passes" section focuses on the empty house during a 10-year hiatus and the last-minute housecleaning for the returning Ramsays. Woolf describes the progress of weeds, mold, dust, and gusts of wind, but she merely announces such major events as the deaths of Mrs. Ramsay and a son and daughter. In the novel's third section, "The Lighthouse," Woolf brings Mr. Ramsay, his youngest children (James and Cam), Lily Briscoe, and others from "The Window" back to the house. As Mr. Ramsay and the now-teenage children reach the lighthouse and achieve a moment of reconciliation, Lily completes her painting. *To the Lighthouse* melds into its structure questions about creativity and the nature and function of art.

In two 1927 essays, *The Art of Fiction* and *The New Biography,* she wrote that fiction writers should be less concerned with naive notions of reality and more with language and design. However restricted by fact, she argued, biographers should yoke truth with imagination, "granite-like solidity" with "rainbow-like intangibility." Their relationship having cooled by 1927, Woolf sought to reclaim Sackville-West through a "biography" that would include Sackville family history. Woolf solved biographical, historical, and personal dilemmas with the story of Orlando, who lives from Elizabethan times through the entire 18th century; he then becomes female, experiences debilitating gender constraints, and lives into the 20th century. Orlando begins writing poetry during the Renaissance, using history and mythology as models, and over the ensuing centuries returns to the poem *The Oak Tree,* revising it according to shifting poetic conventions. Woolf herself writes in mock-heroic imitation of biographical styles that change over the same period of time. Thus, *Orlando: A Biography* (1928) exposes the artificiality of both gender and genre prescriptions. However fantastic, *Orlando* also argues for a novelistic approach to biography.

In *A Room of One's Own* (1929), Woolf blamed women's absence from history not on their lack of brains and talent but on their poverty. For her 1931 talk *Professions for Women,* Woolf studied the history of women's education and employment and argued that unequal opportunities for women negatively affect all of society. She urged women to destroy the "angel in the house," a reference to Coventry Patmore's poem of that title, the quintessential Victorian paean to women who sacrifice themselves to men.

Having praised a 1930 exhibit of Vanessa Bell's paintings for their wordlessness, Woolf planned a mystical novel that would be similarly impersonal and abstract. In *The Waves* (1931), poetic interludes describe the sea and sky from dawn to dusk. Between the interludes, the voices of six named characters appear in sections that move from their childhood to old age. In the middle section, when the six friends meet at a farewell dinner for another friend leaving for India, the single flower at the centre of the dinner table becomes a "seven-sided flower...a whole flower to which every eye brings its own contribution." *The Waves* offers a six-sided shape that illustrates how each individual experiences events—including their friend's death—uniquely. Bernard, the writer in the group, narrates the final section, defying death and a world "without a self." Unique though they are (and their prototypes can be identified in the Bloomsbury group), the characters become one, just as the sea and sky become indistinguishable in the interludes. This oneness with all creation was the primal

Dust jacket designed by Vanessa Bell for the first edition of Virginia Woolf's The Waves, *published by the Hogarth Press in 1931*. **Between the Covers Rare Books, Merchantville, NJ**

experience Woolf had felt as a child in Cornwall. In this her most experimental novel, she achieved its poetic equivalent. Through *To the Lighthouse* and *The Waves*, Woolf became, with James Joyce and William Faulkner, one of the three major English-language Modernist experimenters in stream-of-consciousness writing.

Late Work

Even before finishing *The Waves*, she began compiling a scrapbook of clippings illustrating the horrors of war, the threat of fascism, and the oppression of women. The discrimination against women that Woolf had discussed in *A Room of One's Own* and *Professions for Women* inspired her to plan a book that would trace the story of a fictional family named Pargiter and explain the social conditions affecting family members over a period of time. In *The Pargiters: A Novel-Essay* she would alternate between sections of fiction and of fact, a daunting challenge she set for herself.

Woolf took a holiday from *The Pargiters* to write a mock biography of Flush, the dog of poet Elizabeth Barrett Browning. Lytton Strachey having recently died, Woolf muted her spoof of his biographical method; nevertheless, *Flush* (1933) remains both a biographical satire and a lighthearted exploration of perception, in this case a dog's. In 1935 Woolf completed *Freshwater*, an absurdist drama based on the life of her great-aunt Julia Margaret Cameron. Featuring such other eminences as the poet Alfred, Lord Tennyson, and the painter George Frederick Watts, this riotous play satirizes high-minded Victorian notions of art.

Meanwhile, Woolf feared she would never finish *The Pargiters*. Alternating between types of prose was proving cumbersome, and the book was becoming too long. She solved this dilemma by jettisoning the essay sections, keeping the family narrative, and renaming her book *The Years*. She narrated 50 years of family history through the decline of class and patriarchal systems, the rise of feminism, and the threat of another war. Desperate to finish, Woolf lightened the book with poetic echoes of gestures, objects, colours, and sounds and with wholesale deletions, cutting epiphanies for Eleanor Pargiter and explicit references to women's bodies. The novel illustrates the damage done to women and society over the years by sexual repression, ignorance, and discrimination. Though (or perhaps because) Woolf's trimming muted the book's radicalism, *The Years* (1937) became a best seller.

When Fry died in 1934, Virginia was distressed; Vanessa was devastated. Then in July 1937 Vanessa's elder son, Julian Bell, was killed in the Spanish Civil War while driving an ambulance for the Republican army. Vanessa was so disconsolate that Virginia put aside her writing for a time to try to comfort her sister. Privately a lament over Julian's death and publicly a diatribe against war, *Three Guineas* (1938) proposes answers to the question of how to prevent war. Woolf connected masculine symbols of authority with militarism and misogyny, an argument buttressed by notes from her clippings about aggression, fascism, and war.

She determined to test her theories about experimental novelistic biography in a life of Fry. As she acknowledged in *The Art of Biography* (1939), the recalcitrance of evidence brought her near despair over the possibility of writing an imaginative biography. Against the "grind" of finishing the Fry biography, Woolf wrote a verse play about the history of English literature. Her next novel, *Pointz Hall* (later retitled *Between the Acts*), would include the play as a pageant performed by villagers and would convey the gentry's varied reactions to it. As another holiday from Fry's biography, Woolf returned to her own childhood with *A Sketch of the Past,* a memoir about her mixed feelings toward her parents and her past and about memoir writing itself. (Here surfaced for the first time in writing a memory of the teenage Gerald Duckworth, her other half brother, touching her inappropriately when she was a girl of perhaps four or five.) Through last-minute borrowing from the letters between Fry and Vanessa, Woolf finished her biography. Though convinced that *Roger Fry* (1940) was more granite than rainbow, Virginia congratulated herself on at least giving back to Vanessa "her Roger."

Woolf's chief anodyne against Adolf Hitler, World War II, and her own despair was writing. During the bombing of London in 1940 and 1941, she worked on her memoir and *Between the Acts.* In her novel, war threatens art and humanity itself, and, in the interplay between the pageant—performed on a June day in 1939—and the audience, Woolf raises questions about perception and response. Despite *Between the Acts*'s affirmation of the value of art, Woolf worried that this novel was "too slight" and indeed that all writing was irrelevant when England seemed on the verge of invasion and civilization about to slide over a precipice. Facing such horrors, a depressed Woolf found herself unable to write. The demons of self-doubt that she had kept at bay for so long returned to haunt her. On March 28, 1941, fearing that she now lacked the resilience to battle them, she walked behind Monk's House and down to the River Ouse, put stones in her pockets, and drowned herself. *Between the Acts* was published posthumously later that year.

Assessment

Woolf's experiments with point of view confirm that, as Bernard thinks in *The Waves,* "we are not single." Being neither single nor fixed, perception in her novels is fluid, as is the world she presents. While fellow Modernists Joyce and Faulkner separate one character's interior monologues from another's, Woolf's narratives move between inner and outer and between characters without clear demarcations. Furthermore, she avoids the self-absorption of many of her contemporaries and implies a brutal society without the explicit details some of her contemporaries felt obligatory. Her nonlinear forms invite reading not for neat solutions but for an aesthetic resolution of "shivering fragments," as she wrote in 1908. While Woolf's fragmented style is distinctly Modernist, her indeterminacy anticipates a postmodern awareness of the evanescence of boundaries and categories.

Woolf's many essays about the art of writing and about reading itself today retain their appeal to a range of, in Samuel Johnson's words, "common" (unspecialized) readers. Woolf's collection of essays *The Common Reader* (1925) was followed by *The Common Reader: Second Series* (1932; also published as *The Second Common Reader*). She continued writing essays on reading and writing, women and history, and class and politics for the rest of her life. Many were collected after her death in volumes edited by Leonard Woolf.

Woolf's haunting language, her prescient insights into wide-ranging historical, political, feminist, and artistic issues, and her revisionist experiments with novelistic form during a remarkably productive career altered the course of Modernist and postmodernist letters.

JAMES JOYCE

(b. February 2, 1882, Dublin, Ireland — d. January 13, 1941, Zürich, Switzerland)

James Augustine Aloysius Joyce, the eldest of 10 children in his family to survive infancy, was sent at age six to Clongowes Wood College, a Jesuit boarding school that has been described as "the Eton of Ireland." But his father was not the man to stay affluent for long; he drank, neglected his affairs, and borrowed money from his office, and his family sank deeper and deeper into poverty, the children becoming accustomed to conditions of increasing sordidness. Joyce did not return to Clongowes in 1891; instead he stayed at home for the next two years and tried to educate himself, asking his mother to check his work. In April 1893 he and his brother Stanislaus were admitted, without fees, to Belvedere College, a Jesuit grammar school in Dublin. Joyce did well there academically and was twice elected president of the Marian Society, a position virtually that of head boy. He left, however, under a cloud, as it was thought (correctly) that he had lost his Roman Catholic faith.

The Emerging Writer

He entered University College, Dublin, which was then staffed by Jesuit priests. There he studied languages and reserved his energies for extracurricular activities, reading widely—particularly in books not recommended by the Jesuits—and taking an active part in the college's Literary and Historical Society. Greatly admiring Henrik Ibsen, he learned Dano-Norwegian to read the original and had an article, *Ibsen's New Drama*—a review of the play *When We Dead Awaken*—published in the London *Fortnightly Review* in 1900 just after his 18th birthday. This early success confirmed Joyce in his resolution to become a writer and persuaded his family, friends, and teachers that the resolution was justified. In October 1901 he published an essay, "The Day of the Rabblement," attacking the Irish

Literary Theatre (later the Dublin Abbey Theatre) for catering to popular taste.

Joyce was leading a dissolute life at this time but worked sufficiently hard to pass his final examinations, matriculating with "second-class honours in Latin" and obtaining the degree of B.A. on October 31, 1902. Never did he relax his efforts to master the art of writing. He wrote verses and experimented with short prose passages that he called "epiphanies," a word that Joyce used to describe his accounts of moments when the real truth about some person or object was revealed. To support himself while writing, he decided to become a doctor, but, after attending a few lectures in Dublin, he borrowed what money he could and went to Paris, where he abandoned the idea of medical studies, wrote some book reviews, and studied in the Sainte-Geneviève Library.

Recalled home in April 1903 because his mother was dying, he tried various occupations, including teaching, and lived at various addresses, including the Martello Tower at Sandycove, now Ireland's Joyce Museum. He had begun writing a lengthy naturalistic novel, *Stephen Hero*, based on the events of his own life, when in 1904 George Russell offered £1 each for some simple short stories with an Irish background to appear in a farmers' magazine, *The Irish Homestead*. In response Joyce began writing the stories published as *Dubliners* (1914). Three stories, "The Sisters," "Eveline," and "After the Race," had appeared under the pseudonym Stephen Dedalus before the editor decided that Joyce's work was not suitable for his readers. Meanwhile Joyce had met a girl named Nora Barnacle, with whom he fell in love on June 16, the day that he chose as what is known as "Bloomsday" (the day of his novel *Ulysses*). Eventually he persuaded her to leave Ireland with him, although he refused, on principle, to go through a ceremony of marriage.

Early Travels and Works

Joyce and Nora left Dublin together in October 1904. Joyce obtained a position in the Berlitz School, Pola, Austria-Hungary, working in his spare time at his novel and short stories. In 1905 they moved to Trieste, where James's brother Stanislaus joined them and where their children, George and Lucia, were born. In 1906–07, for eight months, he worked at a bank in Rome, disliking almost everything he saw. Ireland seemed pleasant by contrast; he wrote to Stanislaus that he had not given credit in his stories to the Irish virtue of hospitality and began to plan a new story, "The Dead." The early stories were meant, he said, to show the stultifying inertia and social conformity from which Dublin suffered, but they are written with a vividness that arises from his success in making every word and every detail significant. His studies in European literature had interested him in both the Symbolists and the Realists; his work began to show a synthesis of these two rival movements. He decided that *Stephen Hero* lacked artistic control and form and rewrote it as "a work in five chapters" under a title—*A Portrait of the Artist as a Young Man*—intended to direct attention to its focus upon the central figure.

In 1909 he visited Ireland twice to try to publish *Dubliners* and set up a chain of Irish cinemas. Neither effort succeeded, and he was distressed when a former friend told him that he had shared Nora's affections in the summer of 1904. Another old friend proved this to be a lie. Joyce always felt that he had been betrayed, however, and the theme of betrayal runs through much of his later writings.

When Italy declared war in 1915 Stanislaus was interned, but James and his family were allowed to go to Zürich. At first, while he gave private lessons in English and worked on the early chapters of *Ulysses*—which he had first thought of as another short story about a "Mr. Hunter"—his financial difficulties were great. He was helped by a large grant from Edith Rockefeller McCormick and finally by a series of grants from Harriet Shaw Weaver, editor of the *Egoist* magazine, which by 1930 had amounted to more than £23,000. Her generosity resulted partly from her admiration for his work and partly from her sympathy with his difficulties, for, as well as poverty, he had to contend with eye diseases that never really left him. From February 1917 until 1930 he endured a series of 25 operations for iritis, glaucoma, and cataracts, sometimes being for short intervals totally blind. Despite this he kept up his spirits and continued working, some of his most joyful passages being composed when his health was at its worst.

Unable to find an English printer willing to set up *A Portrait of the Artist as a Young Man* for book publication, Weaver published it herself, having the sheets printed in the United States, where it was also published, on December 29, 1916, by B.W. Huebsch, in advance of the English Egoist Press edition. Encouraged by the acclaim given to this, in March 1918, the American *Little Review* began to publish episodes from *Ulysses*, continuing until the work was banned in December 1920. An autobiographical novel, *A Portrait of the Artist* traces the intellectual and emotional development of a young man named Stephen Dedalus and ends with his decision to leave Dublin for Paris to devote his life to art. The last words of Stephen prior to his departure are thought to express the author's feelings upon the same occasion in his own life: "Welcome, O life! I go to encounter for the millionth time the reality of my experience and to forge in the smithy of my soul the uncreated conscience of my race."

James Joyce (left) *sitting in the Shakespeare and Company book-store in Paris with Sylvia Beach* (centre), *the store's owner, and her companion, Adrienne Monnier. Beach was the first to publish Joyce's novel,* Ulysses, *now widely regarded as one of the finest literary works in the world.* Gisele Freund/Time & Life Pictures/Getty Images

Ulysses

After World War I Joyce returned for a few months to Trieste, and then—at the invitation of Ezra Pound—in July 1920 he went to Paris. His novel *Ulysses* was published there on February 2, 1922, by Sylvia Beach, proprietor of a bookshop called "Shakespeare and Company." *Ulysses* is constructed as a modern parallel to Homer's *Odyssey*. All of the action of the novel takes place in Dublin on a single day (June 16, 1904). The three central characters— Stephen Dedalus (the hero of Joyce's earlier *Portrait of the Artist*), Leopold Bloom, a Jewish advertising canvasser, and his wife, Molly Bloom—are intended to be modern counterparts of Telemachus, Ulysses, and Penelope. By the use of interior monologue Joyce reveals the innermost thoughts and feelings of these characters as they live hour by hour, passing from a public bath to a funeral, library, maternity hospital, and brothel.

The main strength of *Ulysses* lies in its depth of character portrayal and its breadth of humour. Yet the book is most famous for its use of a variant of the interior monologue known as the "stream-of-consciousness" technique. Joyce claimed to have taken this technique from a forgotten French writer, Édouard Dujardin (1861–1949), who had used interior monologues in his novel *Les Lauriers sont coupés* (1888; *We'll to the Woods No More*), but many critics have pointed out that it is at least as old as the novel, though no one before Joyce had used it so continuously. Joyce's major innovation was to carry the interior monologue one step further by rendering, for the first time in literature, the myriad flow of impressions, half thoughts, associations, lapses and hesitations, incidental worries, and sudden impulses that form part of the individual's conscious awareness along with the trend of his rational thoughts.

Sometimes the abundant technical and stylistic devices in *Ulysses* become too prominent, particularly in the much-praised "Oxen of the Sun" chapter (Episode 14), in which the language goes through every stage in the development of English prose from Anglo-Saxon to the present day to symbolize the growth of a fetus in the womb. The execution is brilliant, but the process itself seems ill-advised. More often the effect is to add intensity and depth, as, for example, in the "Aeolus" chapter (Episode 7) set in a newspaper office, with rhetoric as the theme. Joyce inserted into it hundreds of rhetorical figures and many references to winds—something "blows up" instead of happening, people "raise the wind" when they are getting money—and the reader becomes aware of an unusual liveliness in the very texture of the prose. The famous last chapter of the novel, in which we follow the stream of consciousness of Molly Bloom as she lies in bed, gains much of its effect from being written in eight huge unpunctuated paragraphs.

Ulysses, which was already well known because of the censorship troubles, became immediately famous upon publication. Joyce had prepared for its critical reception by having a lecture given by Valery Larbaud, who pointed out the Homeric correspondences in it and that "each episode deals with a particular art or science, contains a particular symbol, represents a special organ of the human body, has its particular colour...proper technique, and takes place at a particular time." Joyce never published this scheme; indeed, he even deleted the chapter titles in the book as printed. It may be that this scheme was more useful to Joyce when he was writing than it is to the reader.

Finnegans Wake

In Paris Joyce worked on *Finnegans Wake*, the title of which was kept secret, the novel being known simply as "Work in Progress" until it was published in its entirety in May 1939. In addition to his chronic eye troubles, Joyce suffered great and prolonged anxiety over his daughter's mental health. What had seemed her slight eccentricity grew into unmistakable and sometimes violent mental disorder that Joyce tried by every possible means to cure, but it became necessary finally to place her in a mental hospital near Paris. In 1931 he and Nora visited London, where they were married, his scruples on this point having yielded to his daughter's complaints.

Meanwhile he wrote and rewrote sections of *Finnegans Wake*; often a passage was revised more than a dozen times before he was satisfied. Basically the book is, in one sense, the story of a publican in Chapelizod, near Dublin, his wife, and their three children; but Mr. Humphrey Chimpden Earwicker (often designated by variations on his initials, HCE, one form of which is "Here Comes Everybody"), Mrs. Anna Livia Plurabelle, Kevin, Jerry, and Isabel are every family of mankind, the archetypal family about whom all humanity is dreaming. The 18th-century Italian Giambattista Vico provides the basic theory that history is cyclic; to demonstrate this the book begins with the end of a sentence left unfinished on the last page. It is thousands of dreams in one. Languages merge: Anna Livia has "vlossyhair"—*włosy* being Polish for "hair"; "a bad of wind" blows, *bâd* being Turkish for "wind." Characters from literature and history appear and merge and disappear as "the intermisunderstanding minds of the anticollaborators" dream on. On another level, the protagonists are the city of Dublin and the River Liffey— which flows enchantingly through the pages, "leaning with the sloothering slide of her, giddygaddy, grannyma, gossipaceous Anna Livia"—standing as representatives of the history of Ireland and, by extension, of all human history. And throughout the book Joyce himself is present, joking, mocking his critics, defending his theories, remembering his father, enjoying himself.

After the fall of France in World War II (1940), Joyce took his family back to Zürich, where he died, still disappointed with the reception given to his last book.

Assessment

James Joyce's subtle yet frank portrayal of human nature, coupled with his mastery of language and brilliant development of new literary forms, made him one of the most commanding influences on novelists of the 20th century. *Ulysses* has come to be accepted as a major masterpiece, two of its characters, Leopold Bloom and his wife, Molly, being portrayed with a fullness and warmth of humanity unsurpassed in fiction. Joyce's *A Portrait of the Artist as a Young Man* is also remarkable for the intimacy of the reader's contact with the central figure and contains some astonishingly vivid passages. The 15 short stories collected in *Dubliners* mainly focused upon Dublin life's sordidness, but "The Dead" is one of the world's great short stories. Critical opinion remains divided over Joyce's last work, *Finnegans Wake*, a universal dream about an Irish family, composed in a multilingual style on many levels and aiming at a multiplicity of meanings; but, although seemingly unintelligible at first reading, the book is full of poetry and wit, containing passages of great beauty.

FRANZ KAFKA

(b. July 3, 1883, Prague, Bohemia, Austria-Hungary [now in Czech Republic] — d. June 3, 1924, Kierling, near Vienna, Austria)

Franz Kafka was a writer of visionary fiction whose posthumously published novels — especially *Der Prozess* (1925; *The Trial*) and *Das Schloss* (1926; *The Castle*) — express the anxieties and alienation of 20th-century humanity. His language of composition was German.

Life

Kafka was born into a prosperous middle-class Jewish family. After two brothers died in infancy, he became the oldest child, remaining forever conscious of his role as older brother. Ottla, the youngest of his three sisters, became the family member closest to him. Kafka strongly identified with his maternal ancestors because of their spirituality, intellectual distinction, piety, rabbinical learning, eccentricity, melancholy disposition, and delicate physical and mental constitution. He was not, however, particularly close to his mother, a simple woman devoted to her children. Subservient to her overwhelming, ill-tempered husband and his exacting business, she shared with her spouse a lack of comprehension of their son's unprofitable and possibly unhealthy dedication to the literary "recording of [his]...dreamlike inner life."

The figure of Kafka's father overshadowed his work as well as his existence; the figure is, in fact, one of his most impressive creations. For, in his imagination, this coarse, practical, and domineering shopkeeper and patriarch, who worshiped nothing but material success and social advancement, belonged to a race of giants and was an awesome, admirable, but repulsive tyrant. In Kafka's most important attempt at autobiography, *Brief an den Vater* (written 1919; *Letter to Father*), a letter that never reached the addressee, Kafka attributed his failure to live—to cut loose from parental ties and establish himself in marriage and fatherhood—as well as his escape into literature, to the prohibitive father figure, which instilled in him the sense of his own impotence. He felt his will had been broken by his father. The conflict with the father is reflected directly in Kafka's story *Das Urteil* (1913; *The Judgment*). It is projected on a grander scale in Kafka's novels, which portray in lucid, deceptively simple prose a man's desperate struggle with an overwhelming power, one that may persecute its victim (as in *The Trial*) or one that may be sought after and begged in vain for approval (as in *The Castle*). Yet the roots of Kafka's anxiety and despair go deeper than his relationship to his father and family, with whom he chose to live in close and cramped proximity for the major part of his adult life. The source of Kafka's despair lies in a sense of ultimate isolation from true communion with all human beings—the friends he cherished, the women he loved, the job he detested, the society he lived in—and with God, or, as he put it, with true indestructible Being.

The son of an assimilated Jew who held only perfunctorily to the religious practices and social formalities of the Jewish community, Kafka was German both in language and culture. He was a timid, guilt-ridden, and obedient child who did well in school. He was respected and liked by his teachers. Inwardly, however, he rebelled against the authoritarian institution and the dehumanized humanistic curriculum, with its emphasis on rote learning and classical languages. Kafka's opposition to established society became apparent when, as an adolescent, he declared himself a socialist as well as an atheist. Throughout his adult life he expressed qualified sympathies for the socialists, he attended meetings of the Czech Anarchists (before World War I), and in his later years he showed marked interest and sympathy for a socialized Zionism. Even then he was essentially passive and politically unengaged. As a Jew, Kafka was isolated from the German community in Prague, but, as a modern intellectual, he was also alienated from his own Jewish heritage. He was sympathetic to Czech political and cultural aspirations, but his identification with German culture kept even these sympathies subdued. Thus, social isolation and rootlessness contributed to Kafka's lifelong personal unhappiness. Kafka did, however, become friendly with some German-Jewish intellectuals and literati in Prague, and in 1902 he met Max Brod; this minor literary artist became the most intimate and solicitous of Kafka's friends, and eventually he emerged as the promoter, saviour, and interpreter of Kafka's writings and as his most influential biographer.

The two men became acquainted while Kafka was studying law at the University of Prague. He received his doctorate in 1906, and in 1907 he took up regular employment with Assicurazioni Generali, an insurance company. The long hours and exacting requirements of his job, however, did not permit Kafka to devote himself to writing. In 1908 he found in Prague a job in the seminationalized Workers' Accident Insurance Institute for the Kingdom of Bohemia. There he remained until 1917, when tuberculosis forced him to take intermittent sick leaves and, finally, to retire (with a pension) in 1922, about two years before he died. In his job he was considered tireless and ambitious; he soon became the right hand of his boss, and he was esteemed and liked by all who worked with him.

In fact, generally speaking, Kafka was a charming, intelligent, and humorous individual, but he found his routine office job and the exhausting double life into which it forced him (for his nights were frequently consumed in writing) to be excruciating torture, and his deeper personal relationships were neurotically disturbed. The conflicting inclinations of his complex and ambivalent personality found expression in his sexual relationships. Inhibition painfully disturbed his relations with Felice Bauer, to whom he was twice engaged before their final rupture in 1917. Later his love for Milena Jesenská Pollak was also thwarted. His health was poor and office work exhausted him. In 1917 he was diagnosed as having tuberculosis, and from then onward he spent frequent periods in sanatoriums.

In 1923 Kafka went to Berlin to devote himself to writing. During a vacation on the Baltic coast later that year, he met Dora Dymant (Diamant), a young Jewish socialist. The couple lived in Berlin until Kafka's health significantly worsened during the spring of 1924. After a brief final stay in Prague, where Dymant joined him, he died of tuberculosis in a clinic near Vienna.

Works

Sought out by leading avant-garde publishers, Kafka reluctantly published a few of his writings during his lifetime. These publications include two sections (1909) from *Beschreibung eines Kampfes* (1936; *Description of a Struggle*); *Betrachtung* (1913; *Meditation*), a collection of short prose pieces; and other works representative of Kafka's maturity as an artist—*The Judgment*, a long story written in 1912; two further long stories, *Die Verwandlung* (1915; *Metamorphosis*) and *In der Strafkolonie* (1919; *In the Penal Colony*); and a collection of short prose, *Ein Landarzt* (1919; *A Country Doctor*). *Ein Hungerkünstler* (1924; *A Hunger Artist*), four stories exhibiting the concision and lucidity characteristic of Kafka's late style, had been prepared by the author but did not appear until after his death.

In fact, misgivings about his work caused Kafka before his death to request that all of his unpublished manuscripts be destroyed; his literary executor, Max Brod, disregarded his instructions. Brod published the novels *The Trial*, *The Castle*, and *Amerika* in 1925, 1926, and 1927, respectively, and a collection of shorter pieces, *Beim Bau der chinesischen Mauer* (*The Great Wall of China*), in 1931. Such early works by Kafka as *Description of a Struggle* (begun about 1904) and *Meditation*, though their style is more concretely imaged and their structure more incoherent than that of the later works, are already original in a characteristic way. The characters in these works fail to establish communication with others; they follow a hidden logic that flouts normal, everyday logic; their world erupts in grotesque incidents and violence. Each character is only an anguished voice, vainly questing for information and understanding of the world and for a way to believe in his own identity and purpose.

Many of Kafka's fables contain an inscrutable, baffling mixture of the normal and the fantastic, though occasionally the strangeness may be understood as the outcome of a literary or verbal device, as when the delusions of a pathological state are given the status of reality or when the metaphor of a common figure of speech is taken literally. Thus in *The Judgment* a son unquestioningly commits suicide at the behest of his aged father. In *The Metamorphosis* the son wakes up to find himself transformed into a monstrous and repulsive insect; he slowly dies, not only because of his family's shame and its neglect of him but because of his own guilty despair.

Many of the tales are even more unfathomable. *In the Penal Colony* presents an officer who demonstrates his devotion to duty by submitting himself to the appalling (and clinically described) mutilations of his own instrument of torture. This theme, the ambiguity of a task's value and the horror of devotion to it—one of Kafka's constant preoccupations—appears again in *A Hunger Artist*. The fable "Vor dem Gesetz" (1914; "Before the Law," later incorporated into *The Trial*) presents both the inaccessibility of meaning (the "law") and man's tenacious longing for it. A group of fables written in 1923–24, the last year of Kafka's life, all centre on the individual's vain but undaunted struggle for understanding and security.

Many of the motifs in the short fables recur in the novels. In *Amerika*, for example, the boy Karl Rossmann has been sent by his family to America. There he seeks shelter with a number of father figures. His innocence and simplicity are everywhere exploited, and a last chapter describes his admission to a dreamworld, the "nature-theatre of Oklahoma"; Kafka made a note that Rossmann was ultimately to perish. In *The Trial*, Joseph K., an able and conscientious bank official and a bachelor, is awakened by bailiffs, who arrest him. The investigation in the magistrate's court turns into a squalid farce, the charge against him is never defined, and from this point the courts take no further initiative. But Joseph K. consumes himself in a search for inaccessible courts and for an acquittal from his unknown offense. He appeals to intermediaries whose advice and explanations produce new bewilderment; he adopts absurd stratagems; squalor, darkness, and lewdness attend his search. Resting in a cathedral, he is told by a priest that his protestations of innocence are themselves a sign of guilt and that the justice he is forced to seek must forever be barred to him. A last chapter describes his execution as—still looking around desperately for help—he protests to the last. This is Kafka's blackest work: evil is everywhere, acquittal or redemption is inaccessible, frenzied effort only indicates man's real impotence.

In *The Castle*, one of Kafka's last works, the setting is a village dominated by a castle. Time seems to have stopped in this wintry landscape, and nearly all the scenes occur in the dark. K. arrives at the village claiming to be a land surveyor appointed by the castle authorities. His claim is rejected by the village officials, and the novel recounts K.'s efforts to gain recognition from an authority that is as elusive as Joseph K.'s courts. But K. is not a victim; he is an aggressor, challenging both the petty, arrogant officials and the villagers who accept their authority. All of his stratagems fail. Like Joseph K., he makes love to a servant, the barmaid Frieda, but she leaves him when she discovers that he is simply using her. Brod observes that Kafka intended that K. should die exhausted by his efforts but that on his deathbed he was to receive a permit to stay. There are new elements in this novel; it is tragic, not desolate. While the majority of Kafka's characters are mere functions, Frieda is a resolute person, calm and matter-of-fact. K. gains through her personality some insight into a possible solution of his quest, and, when he speaks of her with affection, he seems himself to be breaking through his sense of isolation.

Kafka's stories and novels have provoked a wealth of interpretations. Brod and Kafka's foremost English translators, Willa and Edwin Muir, viewed the novels as allegories of divine grace. Existentialists have seen Kafka's environment of guilt and despair as the ground upon which to construct an authentic existence. Some have seen his neurotic involvement with his father as the heart of his work; others have emphasized the social criticism, the inhumanity of the powerful and their agents, the violence and barbarity that lurk beneath normal routine. Some have found an imaginative anticipation of totalitarianism in the random and faceless bureaucratic terror of *The Trial*. The Surrealists delighted in the persistent intrusions of the absurd. There is evidence in both the works and the diaries for each of these interpretations, but Kafka's work as a whole transcends them all. One critic may have put it most accurately when he wrote of the works as "open parables" whose final meanings can never be rounded off.

But Kafka's oeuvre is also limited. Each of his works bears the marks of a man suffering in spirit and body, searching desperately, but always inwardly, for meaning, security, self-worth, and a sense of purpose. Kafka himself looked upon his writing and the creative act it signified as a means of "redemption," as a "form of prayer" through which he might be reconciled to the world or might transcend his negative experience of it. The lucidly described but inexplicable darkness of his works reveal Kafka's own frustrated personal struggles, but through his powerless characters and the strange incidents that befall them the author achieved a compelling symbolism that more broadly signifies the anxiety and alienation of the 20th-century world itself.

At the time of his death, Kafka was appreciated only by a small literary coterie. His name and work would not have survived if Max Brod had honoured Kafka's testament—two notes requiring his friend to destroy all unpublished manuscripts and to refrain from republishing the works that had already appeared in print. Brod took the opposite course, and thus the name and work of Kafka gained worldwide posthumous fame. This development took place first during the regime of Adolf Hitler, in France and the English-speaking countries—at the very time when Kafka's three sisters were deported and killed in concentration camps. After 1945 Kafka was rediscovered and began to greatly influence Western literature.

WILLIAM CARLOS WILLIAMS

(b. September 17, 1883, Rutherford, New Jersey, U.S.—d. March 4, 1963, Rutherford)

After receiving an M.D. from the University of Pennsylvania in 1906 and after internship in New York and graduate study in pediatrics in Leipzig, William Carlos Williams returned in 1910 to a lifetime of poetry and medical practice in his hometown.

In *Al Que Quiere!* (1917; "To Him Who Wants It!") his style was distinctly his own. Characteristic poems that proffer Williams's fresh, direct impression of the sensuous world are the frequently anthologized "Lighthearted William," "By the Road to the Contagious Hospital," and "Red Wheelbarrow."

In the 1930s during the Depression, his images became less a celebration of the world and more a catalog of its wrongs. Such poems as "Proletarian Portrait" and "The

Yachts" reveal his skill in conveying attitudes by presentation rather than explanation.

In *Paterson* (5 vol., 1946–58), Williams expressed the idea of the city, which in its complexity also represents human complexity. The poem is based on the industrial city in New Jersey on the Passaic River and evokes a complex vision of America and modern individuals.

Williams was also a prolific writer of prose. His *In the American Grain* (1925) analyzed the American character and culture through essays on historical figures. Three novels form a trilogy about a family — *White Mule* (1937), *In the Money* (1940), and *The Build-Up* (1952). Among his notable short stories are "Jean Beicke," "A Face of Stone," and "The Farmers' Daughters." His play *A Dream of Love* (published 1948) was produced in off-Broadway and academic theatres. Williams's *Autobiography* appeared in 1951, and in 1963 he was posthumously awarded the Pulitzer Prize in poetry for his *Pictures from Brueghel, and Other Poems* (1962).

WILL CUPPY

(b. August 23, 1884, Auburn, Indiana, U.S. — d. September 19, 1949, Greenwich Village, New York)

William Jacob Cuppy earned a degree in philosophy at the University of Chicago in 1907 and remained there as a graduate student until 1914. He supported himself by writing for several Chicago newspapers. A university editor's request that he write about traditions at the young campus resulted in his first book, *Maroon Tales*, published in 1910. In 1914 he moved to New York City and worked as a journalist.

During World War I, Cuppy was a publicist for the Motor Transport Corps in Washington, D.C. In 1921 he started writing his first weekly column, a book-review feature for the *New York Herald Tribune* entitled "Light Reading" (renamed "Mystery and Adventure" in 1926). For this column Cuppy read four to six books every week, mostly detective and crime novels.

In 1921 Cuppy moved to a small house on Jones Island, New York, where he lived by himself. His solitary life provided him with material for his first popular success, *How to Be a Hermit* (1929). In 1929 he moved to Greenwich Village in New York City, where he packed thousands of note cards and books into a small apartment. For his best-selling books *How to Tell Your Friends from the Apes* (1931), *How to Become Extinct* (1941), and *How to Attract the Wombat* (1949), Cuppy combined extensive research with a longtime interest in the natural world to expound on his cynical view of human behaviour.

Cuppy took his own life by taking an overdose of pills; he was found unconscious in his home. A friend pieced together the final chapters of Cuppy's last work, *The Decline and Fall of Practically Everybody* (1950), which treated figures from history humorously and unsentimentally and became the most popular of all his books. Selected clips from Cuppy's note cards provided the material for *How to Get from January to December* (1951).

SINCLAIR LEWIS

(b. February 7, 1885, Sauk Centre, Minnesota, U.S.—d. January 10, 1951, near Rome, Italy)

American novelist and social critic Harry Sinclair Lewis punctured American complacency with his broadly drawn, widely popular satirical novels. He won the Nobel Prize for Literature in 1930, the first given to an American.

Lewis graduated from Yale University (1907) and was for a time a reporter and also worked as an editor for several publishers. His first novel, *Our Mr. Wrenn* (1914), attracted favourable criticism but few readers. At the same time he was writing with ever-increasing success for such popular magazines as *The Saturday Evening Post* and *Cosmopolitan*, but he never lost sight of his ambition to become a serious novelist. He undertook the writing of *Main Street* as a major effort, assuming that it would not bring him the ready rewards of magazine fiction. Yet its publication in 1920 made his literary reputation. *Main Street* is seen through the eyes of Carol Kennicott, an Eastern girl married to a Midwestern doctor who settles in Gopher Prairie, Minnesota (modeled on Lewis's hometown of Sauk Centre). The power of

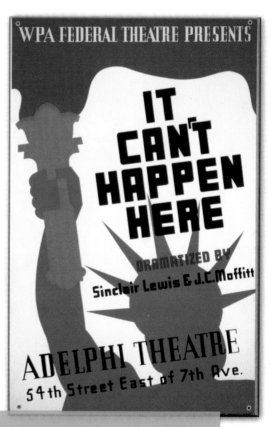

Poster for the Federal Theatre's 1936 staging of It Can't Happen Here *by Sinclair Lewis.* Work Projects Administration Poster Collection/Library of Congress, Washington, D.C. (digital. id. cph 3b48562)

the book derives from Lewis's careful rendering of local speech, customs, and social amenities. The satire is double-edged—directed against both the townspeople and the superficial intellectualism that despises them. In the years following its publication, *Main Street* became not just a novel but the textbook on American provincialism.

In 1922 Lewis published *Babbitt*, a study of the complacent American whose individuality has been sucked out of him by Rotary clubs, business ideals, and general conformity. The name Babbitt passed into general usage to represent the optimistic, self-congratulatory, middle-aged businessman whose horizons were bounded by his village limits.

He followed this success with *Arrowsmith* (1925), a satiric study of the medical profession, with emphasis on the frustration of fine scientific ideals. His next important book, *Elmer Gantry* (1927), was an attack on the ignorant, gross, and predatory leaders who had crept into the Protestant church. *Dodsworth* (1929), concerning the experiences of a retired big businessman and his wife on a European tour, offered Lewis a chance to contrast American and European values and the very different temperaments of the man and his wife.

Lewis's later books did not achieve the popular or critical success of his work in the 1920s. *It Can't Happen Here* (1935) dramatized the possibilities of a fascist takeover of the United States. It was produced as a play by the Federal Theatre with 21 companies in 1936. *Kingsblood Royal* (1947) is a novel of race relations.

In his final years Lewis lived much of the time abroad. His reputation declined steadily after 1930. His two marriages (the second was to the political columnist Dorothy Thompson) ended in divorce, and he drank excessively.

ISAK DINESEN

(b. April 17, 1885, Rungsted, Denmark—d. September 7, 1962, Rungsted)

Isak Dinesen is the pseudonym of the Danish writer Karen Christence Dinesen, Baroness Blixen-Finecke. Dinesen wrote finely crafted stories set in the past and pervaded with an aura of supernaturalism. They incorporate the themes of eros and dreams.

Educated privately and at the Academy of Fine Arts, Copenhagen, Dinesen married her cousin, Baron Bror Blixen-Finecke, in 1914 and went with him to Africa. There they owned and directed a coffee plantation in Kenya and became big-game hunters. After her divorce in 1921 she continued to operate the plantation for 10 years until mismanagement, drought, and the falling price of coffee forced her return to Denmark.

Her years in Kenya are recorded in a nonfiction book, *Out of Africa* (1937; *Den afrikanske farm*). These highly regarded memoirs of her years in Kenya reveal an almost mystical love of Africa and its people. The book is a poetic reminiscence of her triumphs and her sorrows on the loss of her farm, the death of her companion, the English hunter Denys Finch Hatton, and the disappearance of the simple African way of life she admired. In 1944 she produced her only novel *Gengældelsens veje* (*The Angelic Avengers*) under the pseudonym Pierre Andrézel. It is a melodramatic tale of innocents who defeat their apparently benevolent but actually evil captor, but Danish readers saw in it a clever satire of Nazi-occupied Denmark.

She initially wrote first in English and then rewrote her books in Danish, but her later books usually appeared simultaneously in both languages. Dinesen's characteristic writings were in the form of tales—highly polished narratives in the Romantic tradition. Collections include *Seven Gothic Tales* (1934; *Syv fantastiske fortællinger*), *Winter's Tales* (1942; *Vinter-eventyr*), and *Last Tales* (1957; *Sidste fortællinger*). *Carnival: Entertainments and Posthumous Tales* (1977) includes uncollected or hitherto unpublished stories. Her other posthumously published works include *Daguerreotypes, and Other Essays* (1979) and *Letters from Africa, 1914–31* (1981).

D.H. LAWRENCE

(b. September 11, 1885, Eastwood, Nottinghamshire, England—d. March 2, 1930, Vence, France)

David Herbert Lawrence was the fourth child of a north Midlands coal miner who had worked from age 10, was a dialect speaker, a drinker, and virtually illiterate. Lawrence's mother, who came from the south of England, was educated, refined, and pious. Lawrence won a scholarship to Nottingham High School (1898–1901) and left at 16 to earn a living as clerk in a factory, but he had to give up work after a first attack of pneumonia. While convalescing, he began visiting the Haggs Farm nearby and began an intense friendship (1902–10) with Jessie Chambers. He became a pupil-teacher in Eastwood in 1902 and performed brilliantly in the national examination. Encouraged by Chambers, he began to write in 1905. His first story was published in a local newspaper in 1907. He studied at University College, Nottingham, from

1906 to 1908, earning a teacher's certificate, and went on writing poems and stories and drafting his first novel, *The White Peacock*.

Early Career

The Eastwood setting, especially the contrast between mining town and unspoiled countryside, the life and

D.H. Lawrence. © Photos.com/Thinkstock

culture of the miners, the strife between his parents, and its effect on his tortured relationship with Jessie all became themes of Lawrence's early short stories and novels. He kept on returning to Eastwood in imagination long after he had left it in fact.

In 1908 Lawrence went to teach in Croydon, a London suburb. Jessie Chambers sent some of his poems to Ford Madox Hueffer (Ford Madox Ford), editor of the influential *English Review*. Hueffer recognized his genius, the *Review* began to publish his work, and Lawrence was able to meet such rising young writers as Ezra Pound. Hueffer recommended *The White Peacock* to the publisher William Heinemann, who published it in 1911, just after the death of Lawrence's mother, his break with Jessie, and his engagement to Louie Burrows. His second novel, *The Trespasser* (1912), gained the interest of the influential editor Edward Garnett, who secured the third novel, *Sons and Lovers*, for his own firm, Duckworth. In the crucial year of 1911–12 Lawrence had another attack of pneumonia. He broke his engagement to Louie and decided to give up teaching and live by writing, preferably abroad. Most importantly, he fell in love and eloped with Frieda Weekley (née von Richthofen), the aristocratic German wife of a professor at Nottingham. The couple went first to Germany and then to Italy, where Lawrence completed *Sons and Lovers*. They were married in England in 1914 after Frieda's divorce.

Sons and Lovers

Lawrence's first two novels, first play, and most of his early short stories, including such masterpieces as *Odour of Chrysanthemums* and *Daughters of the Vicar* (collected in *The Prussian Officer, and Other Stories*, 1914), use early experience as a departure point. *Sons and Lovers* carries this process to the point of quasi-autobiography. The book depicts Eastwood and the Haggs Farm, the twin poles of Lawrence's early life, with vivid realism. The central character, Paul Morel, is naturally identified as Lawrence; the miner-father who drinks and the powerful mother who resists him are clearly modeled on his parents; and the painful devotion of Miriam Leivers resembles that of Jessie Chambers. An older brother, William, who dies young, parallels Lawrence's brother Ernest, who met an early death. In the novel, the mother turns to her elder son William for emotional fulfillment in place of his father. This section of the original manuscript was much reduced by Garnett before publication. Garnett's editing not only eliminated some passages of sexual outspokenness but also removed as repetitive structural elements that constitute the establishment of a pattern in the mother's behaviour and that explain the plural nouns of the title. When William dies, his younger brother Paul becomes the mother's mission and, ultimately, her victim. Paul's adolescent love for Miriam is undermined by his mother's dominance; though fatally attracted to Miriam, Paul cannot be sexually involved with anyone so like his mother, and the sexual relationship he forces on her proves a disaster. He then, in reaction, has a passionate affair with a married woman, Clara Dawes, in what is the only purely imaginary part of the novel. Clara's husband is a drunken workingman whom she has undermined by her social and intellectual superiority, so their situation mirrors that of the Morels. Though Clara wants more from him, Paul can manage sexual passion only when it is split off from commitment; their affair ends after Paul and Dawes have a murderous fight, and Clara returns to her husband. Paul, for all his intelligence, cannot fully grasp his own unconscious motivations, but Lawrence silently conveys them in the pattern of the plot. Paul can only be released by his mother's death, and at the end of the book, he is at last free to take up his own life, though it remains uncertain whether he can finally overcome her influence. The whole narrative can be seen as Lawrence's psychoanalytic study of his own case, a young man's struggle to gain detachment from his mother.

The Rainbow and Women in Love

During World War I Lawrence and his wife were trapped in England and living in poverty. At this time he was engaged in two related projects. The first was a vein of philosophical writing that he had initiated in the "Foreword" to *Sons and Lovers* and continued in "Study of Thomas Hardy" (1914) and later works. The other, more important project was an ambitious novel of provincial life that Lawrence rewrote and revised until it split into two major novels: *The Rainbow*, which was immediately suppressed in Britain as obscene; and *Women in Love*, which was not published until 1920. In the meantime the Lawrences, living in a cottage in remote Cornwall, had to endure growing suspicion and hostility from their rural neighbours on account of Lawrence's pacifism and Frieda's German origins. They were expelled from the county in 1917 on suspicion of signaling to German submarines and spent the rest of the war in London and Derbyshire. Though threatened with military conscription, Lawrence wrote some of his finest work during the war.

It was also a period of personal crisis. Lawrence and Frieda fought often; Frieda had always felt free to have lovers. Following a 1915 visit to Cambridge, where he met Bertrand Russell, Maynard Keynes, and other members of the Cambridge secret society known as the Apostles, Lawrence began to question his own sexual orientation. This internal conflict, which was resolved a few years later, is evident in the abandoned first chapter of *Women in Love*.

In *The Rainbow*, the first of the novels of this period, Lawrence extends the scope of *Sons and Lovers* by following the Brangwen family (who live near Eastwood) over three generations, so that social and spiritual change are woven into the chronicle. The Brangwens begin as farmers so attached to the land and the seasons as to represent a premodern unconsciousness, and succeeding generations in the novel evolve toward modern consciousness, self-consciousness, and even alienation. The book's early part, which is poetic and mythical, records the love and marriage of Tom Brangwen with the widowed Polish exile Lydia in the 1860s. Lydia's child Anna marries a Brangwen cousin, Will, in the 1880s. These two initially have a stormy relationship but subside into conventional domesticity anchored by work, home, and children. Expanding consciousness is transmitted to the next generation, Lawrence's own, in the person of their daughter Ursula. The last third of the novel describes Ursula's childhood relationship with her father and her passionate but unsuccessful romantic involvement with the soldier Anton Skrebensky. Ursula's attraction toward Skrebensky is negated by his social conventionality, and her rejection of him is symbolized by a sexual relationship in which she becomes dominant. Ursula miscarries their child, and at the novel's end she is left on her own in a convalescence like Paul Morel's, facing a difficult future before World War I. There was an element of war hysteria in the legal suppression of the book in 1915, but the specific ground was a homoerotic episode between Ursula and a female teacher. Lawrence was marked as a subversive writer.

Women in Love takes up the story, but across the gap of changed consciousness created by World War I. The women of the title are Ursula, picking up her life, still at home, and doubtful of her role as teacher and her social and intellectual status; and her sister Gudrun, who is also a teacher but an artist and a free spirit as well. They are modern women, educated, free from stereotyped assumptions about their role, and sexually autonomous. Though unsure of what to do with their lives, they are unwilling to settle for an ordinary marriage as a solution to the problem. The sisters' aspirations crystallize in their romantic relationships: Ursula's with Rupert Birkin, a university graduate and school inspector (and also a Lawrence-figure), Gudrun's with Gerald Crich, the handsome, ruthless, seemingly dominant industrialist who runs his family's mines. Birkin and Gerald themselves are deeply if inarticulately attached to each other. The novel follows the growth of the two relationships: one (Ursula and Birkin) is productive and hopeful, if difficult to maintain as an equilibrium of free partners. The other (Gudrun and Gerald) tips over into dominance and dependence, violence and death. The account is characterized by the extreme consciousness of the protagonists: the inarticulate struggles of earlier generations are now succeeded at the verbal level by earnest or bitter debate. Birkin's intellectual force is met by Ursula's mixture of warmth and skepticism and her emotional stability. The Gerald-Gudrun relationship shows his male dominance to be a shell overlying a crippling inner emptiness and lack of self-awareness, which eventually inspire revulsion in Gudrun. The final conflict between them is played out in the high bareness of an Alpine ski resort; after a brutal assault on Gudrun, Gerald wanders off into the snow and dies. Birkin, grieving, leaves with Ursula for a new life in the warm symbolic south, in Italy.

The search for a fulfilling sexual love and for a form of marriage that will satisfy a modern consciousness is the goal of Lawrence's early novels and yet becomes increasingly problematic. None of his novels ends happily: at best, they conclude with an open question.

Later Life and Works

After World War I Lawrence and his wife went to Italy (1919), and he never again lived in England. He soon embarked on a group of novels consisting of *The Lost Girl* (1920), *Aaron's Rod* (1922), and the uncompleted *Mr. Noon* (published in its entirety only in 1984). All three novels are in two parts: one set in Eastwood and sardonic about local mores, especially the tribal ritual of finding a mate, the other set in Europe, where the central figure breaks out of the tribal setting and finds what may be a true partnership. All three novels also end with an open future; in *Mr. Noon*, however, Lawrence gives his protagonist Lawrence's own experience of 1912 with Frieda in Germany, thus continuing in a light-hearted manner the quasi-autobiographical treatment he had begun in *Sons and Lovers*. In 1921 the Lawrences decided to leave Europe and go to the United States, but eastward, via Ceylon (now Sri Lanka) and Australia.

Since 1917 Lawrence had been working on *Studies in Classic American Literature* (1923), which grew out of his sense that the American West was an uncorrupted natural home. His other nonfiction works at this time include *Movements in European History* (1921) and two treatises on his psychological theories, *Psychoanalysis and the Unconscious* (1921) and *Fantasia of the Unconscious* (1922).

Lawrence wrote *Kangaroo* in six weeks while visiting Australia in 1922. This novel is a serious summary of his own position at the time. The main character and his wife move to Australia after World War I and face in the new country a range of political action: his literary talents are courted alike by socialists and by a nationalist quasi-fascist party. He cannot embrace either political movement, however, and an autobiographical chapter on his experiences in England during World War I reveals that the persecution he endured for his antiwar sentiments killed his desire to participate actively in society. In the end he leaves Australia for America.

Finally reaching Taos, New Mexico, where he settled for a time, Lawrence visited Mexico in 1923 and 1924 and embarked on the ambitious novel *The Plumed Serpent* (1926). In this novel Lawrence maintains that the regeneration of Europe's crumbling postwar society must come from a religious root, and if Christianity is dead, each region must return to its own indigenous religious tradition. *The Plumed Serpent*'s prophet-hero, a Mexican general, revives Aztec rites as the basis of a new theocratic state in Mexico whose authoritarian leaders are worshiped as gods. The Lawrence-representative in the story, a European woman, in the end marries one of the leader-gods but remains half-repelled by his violence and irrationality. After pursuing this theme to its logical conclusion in *The Plumed Serpent*, however, Lawrence abandoned it, and he was reduced to his old ideal of a community where he could begin a new life with a few like-minded people. Taos was the most suitable place he had found, but he was now beginning to die; a bout of illness in 1925 produced bronchial hemorrhage, and tuberculosis was diagnosed.

Lawrence returned to Italy in 1925, and in 1926 he embarked on the first versions of *Lady Chatterley's Lover* and wrote *Sketches of Etruscan Places*, a "travel" book that projects Lawrence's ideal personal and social life upon the Etruscans. Privately published in 1928, *Lady Chatterley's Lover* led an underground life until legal decisions in New York (1959) and London (1960) made it freely available— and a model for countless literary descriptions of sexual acts. The London verdict allowing publication capped a trial at which the book was defended by many eminent English writers. In the novel Lawrence returns for the last time to Eastwood and portrays the tender sexual love, across barriers of class and marriage, of two damaged moderns. Lawrence had always seen the need to relate sexuality to feeling, and his fiction had always extended the borders of the permissible—and had been censored in detail. In *Lady Chatterley's Lover* he now fully described sexual acts as expressing aspects or moods of love, and he also used the colloquial four-letter words that naturally occur in free speech.

The dying Lawrence moved to the south of France, where in 1929 he wrote *Apocalypse* (published 1931), a commentary on the biblical Book of Revelation that is his final religious statement. He was buried in Vence, and his ashes were removed to Taos in 1935.

Poetry and Nonfiction

The fascination of Lawrence's personality is attested by all who knew him, and it abundantly survives in his fiction, his poetry, his numerous prose writings, and his letters. Lawrence's poetry deserves special mention. In his early poems his touch is often unsure, he is too "literary," and he is often constrained by rhyme. But by a remarkable triumph of development, he evolved a highly spontaneous mode of free verse that allowed him to express an unrivaled mixture of observation and symbolism. His poetry can be of great biographical interest, as in *Look! We Have Come Through!* (1917), and some of the verse in *Pansies* (1929) and *Nettles* (1930) is brilliantly sardonic. But his most original contribution is *Birds, Beasts and Flowers* (1923), in which he creates an unprecedented poetry of nature, based on his experiences of the Mediterranean scene and the American Southwest. In his *Last Poems* (1932) he contemplates death.

No account of Lawrence's work can omit his unsurpassable letters. In their variety of tone, vivacity, and range of interest, they convey a full and splendid picture of himself, his relation to his correspondents, and the exhilarations, depressions, and prophetic broodings of his wandering life. Lawrence's short stories were collected in *The Prussian Officer, England My England, and Other Stories* (1922), *The Woman Who Rode Away, and Other Stories* (1928), and *Love Among the Haystacks and Other Pieces* (1930), among other volumes. His early plays, *The Widowing of Mrs. Holroyd* (1914) and *The Daughter-in-Law* (performed 1936), have proved effective on stage and television. Of his travel books, *Sea and Sardinia* (1921) is the most spontaneous; the others involve parallel journeys to Lawrence's interior.

Assessment

D.H. Lawrence was first recognized as a working-class novelist showing the reality of English provincial family life and—in the first days of psychoanalysis—as the author-subject of a classic case history of the Oedipus complex. In subsequent works, Lawrence's frank handling of sexuality cast him as a pioneer of a "liberation" he would not himself have approved. From the beginning readers have been won over by the poetic vividness of his writing and his efforts to describe subjective states of emotion, sensation, and intuition. This spontaneity and immediacy of feeling coexists with a continual, slightly modified repetition of themes, characters, and symbols that express Lawrence's own evolving artistic vision and thought. His great novels remain difficult because their realism is underlain by obsessive personal metaphors, by elements of mythology, and above all by his attempt to express in words what is normally wordless because it exists below consciousness. Lawrence tried to go beyond the "old, stable ego" of the characters familiar to readers of more conventional fiction. His characters are continually experiencing transformations driven by unconscious processes rather than by conscious intent, thought, or ideas.

Lawrence was ultimately a religious writer who did not so much reject Christianity as try to create a new religious and moral basis for modern life by continual resurrections and transformations of the self. These changes are never limited to the social self, nor are they ever fully under the eye of consciousness. Lawrence called for a new openness to what he called the "dark gods" of nature, feeling, instinct, and sexuality; a renewed contact with these forces was, for him, the beginning of wisdom.

EZRA POUND

(b. October 30, 1885, Hailey, Idaho, U.S.—d. November 1, 1972, Venice, Italy)

American poet and critic Ezra Loomis Pound was a supremely discerning and energetic entrepreneur of the arts who did more than any other single figure to advance a "modern" movement in English and American literature. Pound promoted, and also occasionally helped to shape, the work of such widely different poets and novelists as William Butler Yeats, James Joyce, Ernest Hemingway, Robert Frost, D.H. Lawrence, and T.S. Eliot. His pro-fascist broadcasts in Italy during World War II led to his postwar arrest and confinement until 1958.

Early Life and Career

Pound was born in a small mining town in Idaho, the only child of a Federal Land Office official, Homer Loomis

Pound of Wisconsin, and Isabel Weston of New York City. About 1887 the family moved to the eastern states, and in June 1889, following Homer Pound's appointment to the U.S. Mint in Philadelphia, they settled in nearby Wyncote, where Pound lived a normal middle-class childhood.

After two years at Cheltenham Military Academy, which he left without graduating, he attended a local high school. From there he went for two years (1901–03) to the University of Pennsylvania, where he met his lifelong friend, the poet William Carlos Williams. He took a Ph.B. (bachelor of philosophy) degree at Hamilton College, Clinton, New York, in 1905 and returned to the University of Pennsylvania for graduate work. He received an M.A. in June 1906 but withdrew from the university after working one more year toward a doctorate. He left with a knowledge of Latin, Greek, French, Italian, German, Spanish, Provençal, and Anglo-Saxon, as well as of English literature and grammar.

In the autumn of 1907, Pound became professor of Romance languages at Wabash Presbyterian College, Crawfordsville, Ind. Although his general behaviour fairly reflected his Presbyterian upbringing, he was already writing poetry and was affecting a bohemian manner. His career came quickly to an end, and in February 1908, with light luggage and the manuscript of a book of poems that had been rejected by at least one American publisher, he set sail for Europe.

He had been to Europe three times before, the third time alone in the summer of 1906, when he had gathered the material for his first three published articles: *Raphaelite Latin,* concerning the Latin poets of the Renaissance, and *Interesting French Publications,* concerning the troubadours (both published in the *Book News Monthly*, Philadelphia, September 1906), and *Burgos, a Dream City of Old Castile* (October issue).

Now, with little money, he sailed to Gibraltar and southern Spain, then on to Venice, where in June 1908 he published, at his own expense, his first book of poems, *A lume spento*. About September 1908 he went to London, where he was befriended by the writer and editor Ford Madox Ford (who published him in his *English Review*), entered William Butler Yeats's circle, and joined the "school of images," a modern group presided over by the philosopher T.E. Hulme.

Success Abroad

In England, success came quickly to Pound. A book of poems, *Personae*, was published in April 1909; a second book, *Exultations*, followed in October; and a third book, *The Spirit of Romance*, based on lectures delivered in London (1909–10), was published in 1910.

After a trip home—a last desperate and unsuccessful attempt to make a literary life for himself in Philadelphia or New York City—he returned to Europe in February 1911, visiting Italy, Germany, and France. Toward the end of 1911 he met an English journalist, Alfred R. Orage, editor of the socialist weekly *New Age*, who opened its pages to him and provided him with a small but regular income during the next nine years.

In 1912 Pound became London correspondent for the small magazine *Poetry* (Chicago); he did much to enhance the magazine's importance and was soon a dominant figure in Anglo-American verse. He was among the first to recognize and review the poetry of Robert Frost and D.H. Lawrence and to praise the sculpture of the Modernists Jacob Epstein and Henri Gaudier-Brzeska. As leader of the Imagist movement of 1912–14, successor of the "school of images," he drew up the first Imagist manifesto, with its emphasis on direct and sparse language and precise images in poetry, and he edited the first Imagist anthology, *Des Imagistes* (1914).

A Shaper of Modern Literature

Though his friend Yeats had already become famous, Pound succeeded in persuading him to adopt a new, leaner style of poetic composition. In 1914, the year of his marriage to Dorothy Shakespear, daughter of Yeats's friend Olivia Shakespear, he began a collaboration with the then-unknown James Joyce. As unofficial editor of *The Egoist* (London) and later as London editor of *The Little Review* (New York City), he saw to the publication of Joyce's novels *Portrait of the Artist as a Young Man* and *Ulysses*, thus spreading Joyce's name and securing financial assistance for him. In that same year he gave T.S. Eliot a similar start in his career as poet and critic.

He continued to publish his own poetry (*Ripostes*, 1912; *Lustra*, 1916) and prose criticism (*Pavannes and Divisions*, 1918). From the literary remains of the great Orientalist Ernest Fenollosa, which had been presented to Pound in 1913, he succeeded in publishing highly acclaimed English versions of early Chinese poetry, *Cathay* (1915), and two volumes of Japanese Noh plays (1916–17) as well.

Development as a Poet

Unsettled by the slaughter of World War I and the spirit of hopelessness he felt was pervading England after its conclusion, Pound decided to move to Paris, publishing before he left two of his most important poetical works, "Homage to Sextus Propertius," in the book *Quia Pauper Amavi* (1919), and *Hugh Selwyn Mauberley* (1920). "Propertius" is a comment on the British Empire in 1917, by way of Propertius and the Roman Empire. *Mauberley*, a finely chiseled "portrait" of one aspect of British literary culture in 1919, was one of the most praised poems of the 20th century.

During his 12 years in London, Pound had completely transformed himself as a poet. He arrived a Late Victorian for whom love was a matter of "lute strings," "crushed lips," and "Dim tales that blind me." Within five or six years he was writing a new, adult poetry that spoke calmly of current concerns in common speech. In this drier intellectual air, "as clear as metal," Pound's verse took on new qualities of economy, brevity, and clarity as he used concrete details and exact visual images to capture concentrated moments of experience. Pound's search for laconic precision owed much to his constant reading of past literature, including Anglo-Saxon poetry, Greek and Latin classics, Dante, and such 19th-century French works as Théophile Gautier's *Émaux et camées* and Gustave Flaubert's novel *Madame Bovary*. Like his friend T.S. Eliot, Pound wanted a Modernism that brought back to life the highest standards of the past. Modernism for its own sake, untested against the past, drew anathemas from him. His progress may be seen in attempts at informality (1911):

> *Have tea, damn the Caesars,*
> *Talk of the latest success...*

in the gathering strength of his 1911 version of the Anglo-Saxon poem "Seafarer":

> *Storms, on the stone-cliffs beaten,*
> *fell on the stern*
> *In icy feathers...*

and in the confident free verse of "The Return" (1912):

> *See, they return; ah, see the tentative*
> *Movements, and the slow feet...*

From this struggle there emerged the short, perfectly worded free-verse poems in *Lustra*. In his poetry Pound was now able to deal efficiently with a whole range of human activities and emotions, without raising his voice. The movement of the words and the images they create are no longer the secondhand borrowings of youth or apprenticeship but seem to belong to the observing intelligence that conjures up the particular work in hand. Many of the *Lustra* poems are remarkable for perfectly paced endings:

Nor has life in it aught better
Than this hour of clear coolness,
the hour of waking together.

But the culmination of Pound's years in London was his 18-part long poem *Hugh Selwyn Mauberley*, which ranged from close observation of the artist and society to the horrors of mass production and World War I; from brilliant echo of the past:

When our two dusts with Waller's shall be laid,
Siftings on siftings in oblivion,
Till change hath broken down
All things save Beauty alone.

to the syncopation of

With a placid and uneducated mistress
He exercises his talents
And the soil meets his distress.

The Cantos

During his stay in Paris (1921–24) Pound met and helped the young American novelist Ernest Hemingway; wrote an opera, *Le Testament*, based on poems of François Villon; assisted T.S. Eliot with the editing of his long poem *The Waste Land*; and acted as correspondent for the New York literary journal *The Dial*.

In 1924 Pound tired of Paris and moved to Rapallo, Italy, which was to be his home for the next 20 years. In 1925 he had a daughter, Maria, by the expatriate American violinist Olga Rudge, and in 1926 his wife, Dorothy, gave birth to a son, Omar. The daughter was brought up by a peasant woman in the Italian Tirol, the son by relatives in England. In 1927–28 Pound edited his own magazine, *Exile*, and in 1930 he brought together, under the title *A Draft of XXX Cantos*, various segments of his ambitious long poem *The Cantos*, which he had begun in 1915.

The 1930s saw the publication of further volumes of *The Cantos* (*Eleven New Cantos*, 1934; *The Fifth Decad of Cantos*, 1937; *Cantos LII–LXXI*, 1940) and a collection of some of his best prose (*Make It New*, 1934). A growing interest in music caused him to arrange a long series of concerts in Rapallo during the 1930s, and, with the assistance of Olga Rudge, he played a large part in the rediscovery of the 18th-century Italian composer Antonio Vivaldi. The results of his continuing investigation in the areas of culture and history were published in his brilliant but fragmentary prose work *Guide to Kulchur* (1938).

Following the Great Depression of the 1930s, he turned more and more to history, especially economic history, a subject in which he had been interested since his meeting in London in 1918 with Clifford Douglas, the founder of Social Credit, an economic theory stating that maldistribution of wealth due to insufficient purchasing power is the cause of economic depressions. Pound had come to believe that a misunderstanding of money and banking by governments and the public, as well as the manipulation of money by international bankers, had led the world into a long series of wars. He became obsessed with monetary reform (*ABC of Economics*, 1933; *Social Credit*, 1935; *What Is Money For?*, 1939), involved himself in politics, and declared his admiration for the Italian dictator Benito Mussolini (*Jefferson and/or Mussolini*, 1935). The obsession affected his *Cantos*, which even earlier had shown evidence of becoming an uncontrolled series of personal and historical episodes.

Anti-American Broadcasts

As war in Europe drew near, Pound returned home (1939) in the hope that he could help keep the peace between Italy and the United States. He went back to Italy a disappointed man, and between 1941 and 1943, after Italy and the United States were at war, he made several hundred broadcasts over Rome Radio on subjects ranging from James Joyce to the control of money and the U.S. government by Jewish bankers and often openly condemned the American war effort. He was arrested by U.S. forces in 1945 and spent six months in a prison camp for army criminals near Pisa. Despite harsh conditions there, he translated Confucius into English (*The Great Digest & Unwobbling Pivot*, 1951) and wrote *The Pisan Cantos* (1948), the most moving section of his long poem-in-progress.

Returned to the United States to face trial for treason, he was pronounced "insane and mentally unfit for trial" by a panel of doctors and spent 12 years (1946–58) in Saint Elizabeth's Hospital for the criminally insane in Washington, D.C. During this time he continued to write *The Cantos* (*Section: Rock-Drill*, 1955; *Thrones*, 1959), translated ancient Chinese poetry (*The Classic Anthology*, 1954) and Sophocles' *Trachiniai* (*Women of Trachis*, 1956), received visitors regularly, and kept up a voluminous and worldwide correspondence. Controversy surrounding him burst out anew when, in 1949, he was awarded the important Bollingen Prize for his *Pisan Cantos*. When on April 18, 1958, he was declared unfit to stand trial and the charges against him were dropped, he was released from Saint Elizabeth's. He returned to Italy, dividing the year between Rapallo and Venice.

Pound lapsed into silence in 1960, leaving *The Cantos* unfinished. More than 800 pages long, they are fragmentary and formless despite recurring themes and ideas. *The Cantos* are the logbook of Pound's own private voyage through Greek mythology, ancient China and Egypt, Byzantium, Renaissance Italy, the works of John Adams and Thomas Jefferson, and many other periods and subjects, including economics and banking and the nooks and crannies of his own memory and experience. Pound even convinced himself that the poem's faults and weaknesses, inevitable from the nature of the undertaking, were part of an underlying method. Yet there are numerous passages such as only he could have written that are among the best of the century.

Pound died in Venice in 1972. Out of his 60 years of publishing activity came 70 books of his own, contributions to about 70 others, and more than 1,500 articles.

TANIZAKI JUN'ICHIRŌ

(b. July 24, 1886, Tokyo, Japan—d. July 30, 1965, Yugawara)

Tanizaki Jun'ichirō's earliest short stories, of which "Shisei" (1910; "The Tattooer") is an example, have affinities with those of Edgar Allan Poe and the French Decadents. After moving from Tokyo to the more conservative Ōsaka area in 1923, however, he seemed to turn toward the exploration of more traditional Japanese ideals of beauty. *Tade kuu mushi* (1929; *Some Prefer Nettles*), one of his finest novels, reflects the change in his own system of values; it tells of marital unhappiness that is in fact a conflict between the new and the old, with the implication that the old will win. Tanizaki began in 1932 to render into modern Japanese one of the monuments of classical Japanese literature, *Genji monogatari* (*The Tale of Genji*) of Murasaki Shikibu. This work undoubtedly had a deep influence on his style, for during the 1930s he produced a number of discursive lyrical works that echo the prose of the Heian period, in which *Genji monogatari* is set. *The Tale of Genji* continued to hold a deep fascination for him, and through the years he produced several revisions of his original rendition. Another of his major novels, *Sasame-yuki* (1943–48; *The Makioka Sisters*), describes—in the leisurely style of classical Japanese literature—the harsh inroads of the modern world on aristocratic traditional society. His postwar writings, including *Kagi* (1956; *The Key*) and *Fūten rōjin nikki* (1961–62; *Diary of a Mad Old Man*), show an eroticism that suggests a return to his youth. His *Bunshō Tokuhon* (1934; "A Style Reader") is a minor masterpiece of criticism. Tanizaki's work has been characterized as a literary quest for "the eternal female."

Hilda Doolittle

(b. September 10, 1886, Bethlehem, Pennsylvania, U.S.—d. September 27, 1961, Zürich, Switzerland)

American poet Hilda Doolittle (called "H.D.") was known initially as an Imagist. She was also a translator, novelist-playwright, and self-proclaimed "pagan mystic."

Doolittle's father was an astronomer, and her mother was a pianist. She was reared in the strict Moravian tradition of her mother's family. (The Moravians, descended in part from the German Pietists, stressed spirituality and belief in God's grace.) From her parents she gained, on her father's side, an intellectual inheritance, and, on her mother's, an artistic and mystical one. She entered Bryn Mawr College in 1904 and, while a student there, formed friendships with Marianne Moore, a fellow student, and with Ezra Pound (to whom she was briefly engaged) and William Carlos Williams, who were at the nearby University of Pennsylvania. Ill health forced her to leave college in 1906. Five years later she traveled to Europe for what was to have been a vacation but became a permanent stay, mainly in England and Switzerland. Her first published poems, sent to *Poetry* magazine by Pound, appeared under the initials H.D., which remained thereafter her nom de plume. Other poems appeared in Pound's anthology *Des Imagistes* (1914) and in the London journal *The Egoist*, edited by Richard Aldington, to whom she was married from 1913 to 1938. Doolittle was closely associated for much of her adult life with the British novelist Bryher.

H.D.'s first volume of verse, *Sea Garden* (1916), established her as an important voice among the radical young Imagist poets. Her subsequent volumes included *Hymen* (1921), *Heliodora and Other Poems* (1924), *Red Roses for Bronze* (1931), and a trilogy comprising *The Walls Do Not Fall* (1944), *Tribute to the Angels* (1945), and *Flowering of the Rod* (1946).

The *Collected Poems of H.D.* (1925 and 1940), *Selected Poems of H.D.* (1957), and *Collected Poems 1912–1944* (1983) secured her position as a major 20th-century poet. She won additional acclaim for her translations (*Choruses from the Iphigeneia in Aulis and the Hippolytus of Euripides* [1919] and *Euripides' Ion* [1937]), for her verse drama (*Hippolytus Temporizes* [1927]), and for prose works such as *Palimpsest*

(1926), *Hedylus* (1928), and, posthumously, *The Gift* (1982). Several of her books are autobiographical—including *Tribute to Freud* (1956); *Bid Me to Live* (1960); and the posthumously published *End to Torment* (1979), a memoir of Pound, and *Hermione* (1981), a semiautobiographical bildungsroman, or perhaps more accurately a *Künstlerroman* (portrait of the artist's development). *Helen in Egypt* (1961), a volume of verse, appeared shortly after her death.

Over the years H.D.'s sharp, spare, classical, and rather passionless style took on rich mythological and mystic overtones. Analyzed by Sigmund Freud, she was preoccupied with the interior journey. She was directly concerned with the woman's role as artist, and she used myth not only to illuminate individual, personal experience but also, it has been pointed out, to reconstruct a mythic past for women. H.D. is sometimes considered first among the Imagists, the seminal 20th-century poetic movement in the United States, though her work goes far beyond Imagism. She also helped define what came to be called free verse and was among the early users of a stream-of-consciousness narrative. Ezra Pound and other important 20th-century poets considered themselves artistically indebted to her.

HERMANN BROCH

(b. November 1, 1886, Vienna, Austria—d. May 30, 1951, New Haven, Connecticut, U.S.)

In 1927 Hermann Broch renounced his inheritance by selling his family's textile mill and enrolling in the University of Vienna in order to pursue studies in physics, mathematics, and philosophy. His first major work was the trilogy *Die Schlafwandler* (1931–32; *The Sleepwalkers*), which traces the disintegration of European society between 1888 and 1918, depicting the triumph of the realist over the romanticist and the anarchist. Paralleling the historical process, the novel moves from a subtle parody of 19th-century realism through expressionism to a juxtaposition of many different forms, including poetry, drama, narrative, and essay.

Between 1934 and 1936 Broch worked on a novel that was published posthumously in 1953 as *Der Versucher*; three versions of it were later published together as *Bergroman*, 4 vol. (1969), and it has also appeared as *Die Verzauberung* (1976; Eng. trans. *The Spell*). This complex novel exemplifies his theory of mass hysteria in its portrayal of a Hitlerian stranger's domination of a mountain village.

In 1938 Broch spent several weeks in a Nazi prison. His release was obtained through the international efforts of friends and fellow artists, including James Joyce. Later that year he emigrated to the United States.

One of Broch's later works, *Der Tod des Vergil* (1945; *The Death of Virgil*), presents the last 18 hours of Virgil's life, in which he reflects on his times, an age of transition that Broch considered similar to his own. Broch later turned from literature to devote himself to political theory and attempts to aid European refugees.

RUPERT BROOKE

(b. August 3, 1887, Rugby, Warwickshire, England—d. April 23, 1915, Skyros, Greece)

At school at Rugby, where his father was a master, Rupert Brooke distinguished himself as a cricket and football (soccer) player as well as a scholar. He was a gifted, handsome youth. At King's College, Cambridge, where he matriculated in 1906, he was prominent in the Fabian (Socialist) Society and attracted innumerable friends. He studied in Germany and traveled in Italy, but his favourite pastime was rambling in the countryside around the village of Grantchester, which he celebrated in a charming and wildly irrational panegyric, "The Old Vicarage, Grantchester" (1912). In 1911 his volume *Poems* was published. He spent a year (1913–14) wandering in the United States, Canada, and the South Seas. With the outbreak of World War I, he received a commission in the Royal Navy. After taking part in a disastrous expedition to Antwerp that ended in a harrowing retreat, he sailed for the Dardanelles, which he never reached. He died of septicemia on a hospital ship off Skyros and was buried in an olive grove on that island. His early death in World War I contributed to his idealized image.

Brooke's wartime sonnets, *1914* (1915), brought him immediate fame. They express an idealism in the face of death that is in strong contrast to the later poetry of trench warfare. One of his most popular sonnets, "The Soldier," begins with the familiar lines:

> *If I should die, think only this of me:*
> *That there's some corner of a foreign field*
> *That is for ever England.*

FERNANDO PESSOA

(b. June 13, 1888, Lisbon, Portugal—d. November 30, 1935, Lisbon)

Fernando António Nogueira Pessoa was one of the greatest of Portuguese poets, whose Modernist work gave Portuguese literature a broader European audience and significance.

From the age of seven Pessoa lived in Durban, South Africa, where his stepfather was Portuguese consul. He became a fluent reader and writer of English. With the hope of becoming a great poet in that language, Pessoa wrote his early verse in English. In 1905 he returned to Lisbon, where he remained, working as a commercial translator while contributing to avant-garde reviews, especially *Orpheu* (1915), the organ of the Modernist movement. Meanwhile he read widely not only in poetry but in philosophy and aesthetics. He published his first book of poetry in English, *Antinous*, in 1918 and subsequently published two others. Yet it was not until 1934 that his first book in Portuguese, *Mensagem* (*Message*), appeared. It attracted little attention, and Pessoa died the next year a virtual unknown.

Fame came to Pessoa posthumously, when his extraordinarily imaginative poems first attracted attention in both Portugal and Brazil in the 1940s. His oeuvre is remarkable for the innovation of what Pessoa called *heteronyms*, or alternative personae. Rather than alter egos—alternative identities that serve as counterparts to or foils for an author's own ideas—Pessoa's heteronyms were presented as distinct authors, each of whom differed from the others in terms of poetic style, aesthetic, philosophy, personality, and even gender and language (Pessoa wrote in Portuguese, English, and French). Under their names were published not only poems but also criticism on the poetry of some of the others, essays on the state of Portuguese literature, and philosophical writings.

Although he also published poems under his own name, Pessoa employed more than 70 heteronyms, some of which were only discovered in the early 21st century. Four particular heteronyms stand out. Three were "masters" of modern poetics and participated in lively dialogue through publications in critical journals about each other's work: Alberto Caeiro, whose poems celebrate the creative process of nature; Álvaro de Campos, whose work was similar in both style and substance to the work of the American poet Walt Whitman; and Ricardo Reis, a Greek and Roman Classicist concerned with fate and destiny. Another heteronym, Bernardo Soares, was the reputed author of *Livro do desassossego* (*The Book of Disquiet*), a diary-like work of poetic fragments that Pessoa worked on through the last two decades of his life and that remained unfinished at his death. It was published together for the first time in 1982 and brought him worldwide attention; a full English translation appeared in 2001.

Pessoa's most important works in addition to *Livro do desassossego* are posthumously edited collections including *Poesias de Fernando Pessoa* (1942), *Poesias de Álvaro de Campos* (1944), *Poemas de Alberto Caeiro* (1946), *Odes de Ricardo Reis* (1946), *Poesia, Alexander Search* (1999), *Quadras* (2002), *Poesia, 1918–1930* (2005), and *Poesia, 1930–1935* (2006). Collections of his work in English translation include *The Selected Prose of Fernando Pessoa* (2001) and *A Little Larger Than the Entire Universe: Selected Poems* (2006), both edited and translated by Richard Zenith, and *A Centenary Pessoa* (1995).

RAYMOND CHANDLER

(b. July 23, 1888, Chicago, Illinois, U.S.—d. March 26, 1959, La Jolla, California)

From 1896 to 1912 Raymond Thornton Chandler lived in England with his mother, a British subject of Irish birth. Although he was an American citizen and a resident of California when World War I began in 1914, he served in the Canadian army and then in the Royal Flying Corps (afterward the Royal Air Force). Having returned to California in 1919, he prospered as a petroleum company executive until the Great Depression of the 1930s, when he turned to writing for a living. His first published short story appeared in the "pulp" magazine *Black Mask* in 1933. From 1943 he was a Hollywood screenwriter. Among his best-known scripts were for the films *Double Indemnity* (1944), *The Blue Dahlia* (1946), and *Strangers on a Train* (1951), the last written in collaboration with Czenzi Ormonde.

Chandler completed seven novels—*The Big Sleep* (1939), *Farewell, My Lovely* (1940), *The High Window* (1942), *The Lady in the Lake* (1943), *The Little Sister* (1949), *The Long Goodbye* (1953), and *Playback* (1958)—all of which were set in Los Angeles. All had the private detective Philip Marlowe as protagonist. Chandler characterized his hero as a poor but honest upholder of ideals in an opportunistic and often brutal world. Among his numerous short-story collections are *Five Murderers* (1944) and *The Midnight Raymond Chandler* (1971). The most popular film versions of Chandler's work were *Murder, My Sweet* (1944; also distributed as *Farewell, My Lovely*), starring Dick Powell and *The Big Sleep* (1946), starring Humphrey Bogart, both film noir classics.

T.S. ELIOT

(b. September 26, 1888, St. Louis, Missouri, U.S.—d. January 4, 1965, London, England)

The American-English poet, playwright, literary critic, and editor Thomas Stearns Eliot was a leader of the

T.S. Eliot. Encyclopædia Britannica, Inc.

Modernist movement in poetry. He exercised a strong influence on Anglo-American culture from the 1920s until late in the century. His experiments in diction, style, and versification revitalized English poetry, and in a series of critical essays he shattered old orthodoxies and erected new ones. The publication of *Four Quartets* led to his recognition as the greatest living English poet and man of letters.

Early Years

Eliot was descended from a distinguished New England family that had relocated to St. Louis, Missouri. His family allowed him the widest education available in his time, with no influence from his father to be "practical" and to go into business. From Smith Academy in St. Louis he went to Milton, in Massachusetts; from Milton he entered Harvard, where he received a B.A. in 1909, after three instead of the usual four years. The men who influenced him at Harvard were George Santayana, the philosopher and poet, and the critic Irving Babbitt. From Babbitt he derived an anti-Romantic attitude that, amplified by his later reading of British philosophers F.H. Bradley and T.E. Hulme, lasted through his life. In the academic year 1909–10 he was an assistant in philosophy at Harvard.

He spent the year 1910–11 in France, attending Henri Bergson's lectures in philosophy at the Sorbonne and reading poetry. Eliot's study of the poetry of Dante, of the English writers John Webster and John Donne, and of the French Symbolist Jules Laforgue helped him to find his own style. From 1911 to 1914 he was back at Harvard reading Indian philosophy and studying Sanskrit. In 1913 he read Bradley's *Appearance and Reality*; by 1916 he had finished, in Europe, a dissertation entitled *Knowledge and*

Experience in the Philosophy of F.H. Bradley. But World War I had intervened, and he never returned to Harvard to take the final oral examination for the Ph.D. degree. In 1914 Eliot met and began a close association with the American poet Ezra Pound.

Early Publications

Eliot was to pursue four careers: editor, dramatist, literary critic, and philosophical poet. He was probably the most erudite poet of his time in the English language. His undergraduate poems were "literary" and conventional. His first important publication, and the first masterpiece of Modernism in English, was *The Love Song of J. Alfred Prufrock*:

> *Let us go then, you and I,*
> *When the evening is spread out against the sky*
> *Like a patient etherized upon a table....*

Although Pound had printed privately a small book, *A lume spento*, as early as 1908, *Prufrock* was the first poem by either of these literary revolutionists to go beyond experiment to achieve perfection. It represented a break with the immediate past as radical as that of Samuel Taylor Coleridge and William Wordsworth in *Lyrical Ballads* (1798). From the appearance of Eliot's first volume, *Prufrock and Other Observations*, in 1917, one may conveniently date the maturity of the 20th-century poetic revolution. The significance of the revolution is still disputed, but the striking similarity to the Romantic revolution of Coleridge and Wordsworth is obvious: Eliot and Pound, like their 18th-century counterparts, set about reforming poetic diction. Eliot struggled to create new verse rhythms based on the rhythms of contemporary speech. He sought a poetic diction that might be spoken by an educated person, being "neither pedantic nor vulgar."

For a year Eliot taught French and Latin at the Highgate School. In 1917 he began his brief career as a bank clerk in Lloyds Bank Ltd. Meanwhile, he was also a prolific reviewer and essayist in both literary criticism and technical philosophy. In 1919 he published *Poems*, which contained the poem *Gerontion,* a meditative interior monologue in blank verse; nothing like this poem had appeared in English.

The Waste Land and Criticism

With the publication in 1922 of his poem *The Waste Land*, Eliot won an international reputation. *The Waste Land* expresses with great power the disenchantment, disillusionment, and disgust of the period after World War I. In a series of vignettes, loosely linked by the legend of the search for the Grail, it portrays a sterile world of panicky fears and barren lusts, and of human beings waiting for some sign or promise of redemption. The poem's style is highly complex, erudite, and allusive, and the poet provided notes and references to explain the work's many quotations and allusions. This scholarly supplement distracted some readers and critics from perceiving the true originality of the poem, which lay rather in its rendering of the universal human predicament of man desiring salvation, and in its manipulation of language, than in its range of literary references. In his earlier poems Eliot had shown himself to be a master of the poetic phrase. *The Waste Land* showed him to be, in addition, a metrist of great virtuosity, capable of astonishing modulations ranging from the sublime to the conversational.

The Waste Land consists of five sections and proceeds on a principle of "rhetorical discontinuity" that reflects the fragmented experience of the 20th-century sensibility of the great modern cities of the West. Eliot expresses the hopelessness and confusion of purpose of life in the secularized city, the decay of *urbs aeterna* (the "eternal city"). This is the ultimate theme of *The Waste Land*, concretized by the poem's constant rhetorical shifts and its juxtapositions of contrasting styles. But *The Waste Land* is not a simple contrast of the heroic past with the degraded present; it is, rather, a timeless simultaneous awareness of moral grandeur and moral evil. The poem's original manuscript of about 800 lines was cut down to 433 at the suggestion of Ezra Pound. *The Waste Land* is not Eliot's greatest poem, though it is his most famous.

Eliot said that the poet-critic must write "programmatic criticism"—that is, criticism that expresses the poet's own interests as a poet, quite different from historical scholarship, which stops at placing the poet in his background. Consciously intended or not, Eliot's criticism created an atmosphere in which his own poetry could be better understood and appreciated than if it had to appear in a literary milieu dominated by the standards of the preceding age. In the essay *Tradition and the Individual Talent*, appearing in his first critical volume, *The Sacred Wood* (1920), Eliot asserts that tradition, as used by the poet, is not a mere repetition of the work of the immediate past ("novelty is better than repetition," he said); rather, it comprises the whole of European literature, from Homer to the present. The poet writing in English may therefore make his own tradition by using materials from any past period, in any language. This point of view is "programmatic" in the sense that it disposes the reader to accept the revolutionary novelty of Eliot's polyglot quotations and serious parodies of other poets' styles in *The Waste Land*.

Also in *The Sacred Wood, Hamlet and His Problems* sets forth Eliot's theory of the objective correlative:

The only way of expressing emotion in the form of art is by finding an "objective correlative"; in other words, a set of objects, a situation, a chain of events which shall be the formula for that particular emotion; such that, when the external facts, which must terminate in sensory experience, are given, the emotion is immediately evoked.

Eliot used the phrase "objective correlative" in the context of his own impersonal theory of poetry; it thus had an immense influence toward correcting the vagueness of late Victorian rhetoric by insisting on a correspondence of word and object. Two other essays, first published the year after *The Sacred Wood*, almost complete the Eliot critical canon: *The Metaphysical Poets* and *Andrew Marvell*, published in *Selected Essays, 1917–32* (1932). In these essays he effects a new historical perspective on the hierarchy of English poetry, putting at the top Donne and other Metaphysical poets of the 17th century and lowering poets of the 18th and 19th centuries. Eliot's second famous phrase appears here — "dissociation of sensibility," invented to explain the change that came over English poetry after Donne and Andrew Marvell. This change seems to him to consist in a loss of the union of thought and feeling. The phrase has been attacked, yet the historical fact that gave rise to it cannot be denied, and with the poetry of Eliot and Pound it had a strong influence in reviving interest in certain 17th-century poets.

The first, or programmatic, phase of Eliot's criticism ended with *The Use of Poetry and the Use of Criticism* (1933) — his Charles Eliot Norton lectures at Harvard. Shortly before this his interests had broadened into theology and sociology; three short books, or long essays, were the result: *Thoughts After Lambeth* (1931), *The Idea of a Christian Society* (1939), and *Notes Towards the Definition of Culture* (1948). These book-essays, along with his *Dante* (1929), an indubitable masterpiece, broadened the base of literature into theology and philosophy: whether a work is poetry must be decided by literary standards; whether it is great poetry must be decided by standards higher than the literary.

Eliot's criticism and poetry are so interwoven that it is difficult to discuss them separately. The great essay on Dante appeared two years after Eliot was confirmed in the Church of England (1927); in that year he also became a British subject. The first long poem after his conversion

T.S. Eliot (right) *receiving the Nobel Prize for Literature, December 1948.* Encyclopædia Britannica, Inc.

was *Ash Wednesday* (1930), a religious meditation in a style entirely different from that of any of the earlier poems. *Ash Wednesday* expresses the pangs and the strain involved in the acceptance of religious belief and religious discipline. This and subsequent poems were written in a more relaxed, musical, and meditative style than his earlier works, in which the dramatic element had been stronger than the lyrical.

Later Poetry and Plays

Eliot's masterpiece is *Four Quartets*, which was issued as a book in 1943, though each "quartet" is a complete poem. The first of the quartets, *Burnt Norton,* had appeared in the *Collected Poems* of 1936. It is a subtle meditation on the nature of time and its relation to eternity. On the model of this, Eliot wrote three more poems—*East Coker* (1940), *The Dry Salvages* (1941), and *Little Gidding* (1942)— in which he explored through images of great beauty and haunting power his own past, the past of the human race, and the meaning of human history. Each of the poems was self-subsistent, but when published together they were seen to make up a single work, in which themes and images recurred and were developed in a musical manner and brought to a final resolution. This work made a deep impression on the reading public, and even those who were unable to accept the poems' Christian beliefs recognized the intellectual integrity with which Eliot pursued his high theme, the originality of the form he had devised, and the technical mastery of his verse. This work led to the award to Eliot, in 1948, of the Nobel Prize for Literature.

Eliot's plays, which begin with *Sweeney Agonistes* (published 1926; first performed in 1934) and end with *The Elder Statesman* (first performed 1958; published 1959), are, with the exception of *Murder in the Cathedral* (published and performed 1935), inferior to the lyric and meditative poetry. After World War II, Eliot returned to writing plays with *The Cocktail Party* in 1949, *The Confidential Clerk* in 1953, and *The Elder Statesman* in 1958. These plays are comedies in which the plots are derived from Greek drama. In them Eliot accepted current theatrical conventions at their most conventional, subduing his style to a conversational level and eschewing the lyrical passages that gave beauty to his earlier plays. Only *The Cocktail Party*, which is based upon the *Alcestis* of Euripides, achieved a popular success.

Eliot's career as editor was ancillary to his main interests, but his quarterly review, *The Criterion* (1922–39), was the most distinguished international critical journal of the period. He was a "director," or working editor, of the publishing firm of Faber & Faber Ltd. from the early 1920s until his death and as such was a generous and discriminating patron of young poets. Eliot rigorously kept his private life in the background. In 1915 he married Vivien Haigh-Wood. After 1933 she was mentally ill, and they lived apart; she died in 1947. In January 1957 he married Valerie Fletcher, with whom he lived happily until his death.

From the 1920s onward, Eliot's influence as a poet and as a critic—in both Great Britain and the United States—was immense, not least among those establishing the study of English literature as an autonomous academic discipline. He also had his detractors, ranging from avant-garde American poets who believed that he had abandoned the attempt to write about contemporary America to traditional English poets who maintained that he had broken the links between poetry and a large popular audience. During his lifetime, however, his work was the subject of much sympathetic exegesis. Since his death (and coinciding with a wider challenge to the academic study of English literature that his critical precepts did much to establish), interpreters have been markedly more critical, focusing on his complex relationship to his American origins, his elitist cultural and social views, and his exclusivist notions of tradition and of race.

KATHERINE MANSFIELD

(b. October 14, 1888, Wellington, New Zealand—d. January 9, 1923, Gurdjieff Institute, near Fontainebleau, France)

After her education (in Wellington and London), Kathleen Mansfield Beauchamp, who would write under the pen name Katherine Mansfield, left New Zealand at age 19 to establish herself in England as a writer. Her initial disillusion appears in the ill-humoured stories collected in *In a German Pension* (1911). Until 1914 she published stories in *Rhythm* and *The Blue Review*, edited by the critic and essayist John Middleton Murry, whom she married in 1918 after her divorce from George Bowden. The death of her soldier brother in 1915 shocked her into a recognition that she owed what she termed a sacred debt to him and to the remembered places of her native country. *Prelude* (1918) was a series of short stories beautifully evocative of her family memories of New Zealand. These, with others, were collected in *Bliss* (1920), which secured her reputation and is typical of her art.

In the next two years Mansfield did her best work, achieving the height of her powers in *The Garden Party* (1922), which includes "At the Bay," "The Voyage," "The Stranger" (with New Zealand settings), and the classic "Daughters of the Late Colonel," a subtle account of genteel frustration. The last five years of her life were shadowed by tuberculosis. Her final work (apart from unfinished material) was published posthumously in *The Dove's Nest* (1923) and *Something Childish* (1924).

From her papers, Murry edited the *Journal* (1927, rev. ed. 1954), and he also published with annotations her letters to him (1928, rev. ed. 1951). Her collected letters were edited by Vincent O'Sullivan and Margaret Scott (1984–2008); Scott also edited Mansfield's notebooks (1997).

Mansfield evolved a distinctive prose style with many overtones of poetry. Her delicate stories, focused upon psychological conflicts, have an obliqueness of narration and a subtlety of observation that reveal the influence of Anton Chekhov. She, in turn, had much influence on the development of the short story as a form of literature.

EUGENE O'NEILL

(b. October 16, 1888, New York, New York, U.S.—d. November 27, 1953, Boston, Massachusetts)

Eugene Gladstone O'Neill was a foremost American dramatist and the winner of the Nobel Prize for Literature in 1936. His masterpiece, *Long Day's Journey into Night* (produced posthumously 1956), is at the apex of a long string of great plays.

Early Life

O'Neill was born into the theatre. His father, James O'Neill, was a successful touring actor in the last quarter of the 19th century whose most famous role was that of the Count of Monte Cristo in a stage adaptation of the Alexandre Dumas *père* novel. His mother, Ella, accompanied her husband back and forth across the country, settling down only briefly for the birth of her first son, James, Jr., and of Eugene.

Eugene, who was born in a hotel, spent his early childhood in hotel rooms, on trains, and backstage. Although he later deplored the nightmare insecurity of his early years and blamed his father for the difficult, rough-and-tumble life the family led—a life that resulted in his mother's drug addiction—Eugene had the theatre in his blood. He was also, as a child, steeped in the peasant Irish Catholicism of his father and the more genteel, mystical piety of his mother, two influences, often in dramatic conflict, which account for the high sense of drama and the struggle with God and religion that distinguish O'Neill's plays.

O'Neill was educated at boarding schools—Mt. St. Vincent in the Bronx and Betts Academy in Stamford, Connecticut. His summers were spent at the family's only permanent home, a modest house overlooking the Thames River in New London, Connecticut. He attended Princeton University for one year (1906–07), after which he left school to begin what he later regarded as his real education in "life experience." The next six years very nearly ended his life. He shipped to sea, lived a derelict's existence on the waterfronts of Buenos Aires, Liverpool, and New York City, submerged himself in alcohol, and attempted suicide. Recovering briefly at age 24, he held a job for a few months as a reporter and contributor to the poetry column of the *New London Telegraph* but soon came down with tuberculosis. Confined to the Gaylord Farm Sanitarium in Wallingford, Connecticut, for six months (1912–13), he confronted himself soberly and nakedly for the first time and seized the chance for what he later called his "rebirth." He began to write plays.

Entry into Theatre

O'Neill's first efforts were awkward melodramas, but they were about people and subjects—prostitutes, derelicts, lonely sailors, God's injustice to humankind—that had, up to that time, been in the province of serious novels and were not considered fit subjects for presentation on the American stage. A theatre critic persuaded his father to send him to Harvard to study with George Pierce Baker in his famous playwriting course. Although what O'Neill produced during that year (1914–15) owed little to Baker's academic instruction, the chance to work steadily at writing set him firmly on his chosen path.

O'Neill's first appearance as a playwright came in the summer of 1916, in the quiet fishing village of Provincetown, Massachusetts, where a group of young writers and painters had launched an experimental theatre. In their tiny, ramshackle playhouse on a wharf, they produced his one-act sea play *Bound East for Cardiff.* The talent inherent in the play was immediately evident to the group, which that fall formed the Playwrights' Theater in Greenwich Village. Their first bill, on November 3, 1916, included *Bound East for Cardiff*—O'Neill's New York debut. Although he was only one of several writers whose plays were produced by the Playwrights' Theater, his contribution within the next few years made the group's reputation. Between 1916 and 1920, the group produced all of O'Neill's one-act sea plays, along with a number of his lesser efforts. By the time his first full-length play, *Beyond the Horizon*, was produced on Broadway, February 2, 1920, at the Morosco Theater, the young playwright already had a small reputation.

Beyond the Horizon impressed the critics with its tragic realism, won for O'Neill the first of four Pulitzer prizes in drama—others were for *Anna Christie, Strange Interlude*, and *Long Day's Journey into Night*—and brought him to the attention of a wider theatre public. For the next 20 years his reputation grew steadily, both in the United States and abroad; after Shakespeare and Shaw, O'Neill became the most widely translated and produced dramatist.

Period of the Major Works

O'Neill's capacity for and commitment to work were staggering. Between 1920 and 1943 he completed 20 long plays—several of them double and triple length—and a number of shorter ones. He wrote and rewrote many of his manuscripts half a dozen times before he was satisfied, and he filled shelves of notebooks with research notes, outlines, play ideas, and other memoranda. His most-distinguished short plays include the four early sea plays, *Bound East for Cardiff, In the Zone, The Long Voyage Home*, and *The Moon of the Caribbees*, which were written between 1913 and 1917 and produced in 1924 under the overall title *S.S. Glencairn*; *The Emperor Jones* (about the disintegration of a Pullman porter turned tropical-island dictator); and *The Hairy Ape* (about the disintegration of a displaced steamship coal stoker).

O'Neill's plays were written from an intensely personal point of view, deriving directly from the scarring effects of his family's tragic relationships—his mother and father, who loved and tormented each other; his older brother, who loved and corrupted him and died of alcoholism in middle age; and O'Neill himself, caught and torn between love for and rage at all three.

Among his most-celebrated long plays is *Anna Christie,* perhaps the classic American example of the ancient "harlot with a heart of gold" theme; it became an instant popular success. O'Neill's serious, almost solemn treatment of the struggle of a poor Swedish-American girl to live down her early, enforced life of prostitution and to find happiness with a likable but unimaginative young sailor is his least-complicated tragedy. He himself disliked it from the moment he finished it, for, in his words, it had been "too easy."

The first full-length play in which O'Neill successfully evoked the starkness and inevitability of Greek tragedy that he felt in his own life was *Desire Under the Elms* (1924). Drawing on Greek themes of incest, infanticide, and fateful retribution, he framed his story in the context of his own family's conflicts. This story of a lustful father, a weak son, and an adulterous wife who murders her infant son was told with a fine disregard for the conventions of the contemporary Broadway theatre. Because of the sparseness of its style, its avoidance of melodrama, and its total honesty of emotion, the play was acclaimed immediately as a powerful tragedy and has continued to rank among the great American plays of the 20th century.

In *The Great God Brown*, O'Neill dealt with a major theme that he expressed more effectively in later plays—the conflict between idealism and materialism. Although the play was too metaphysically intricate to be staged successfully when it was first produced, in 1926, it was significant for its symbolic use of masks and for the experimentation with expressionistic dialogue and action—devices that since have become commonly accepted both on the stage and in motion pictures. In spite of its confusing structure, the play is rich in symbolism and poetry, as well as in daring technique, and it became a forerunner of avant-garde movements in American theatre.

O'Neill's innovative writing continued with *Strange Interlude*. This play was revolutionary in style and length: when first produced, it opened in late afternoon, broke for a dinner intermission, and ended at the conventional hour. Techniques new to the modern theatre included spoken asides or soliloquies to express the characters' hidden

Actor Leo Penn (centre) *starring in a Broadway production of Eugene O'Neill's tragedy,* The Iceman Cometh. Gjon Mili/Time & Life Pictures/Getty Images

thoughts. The play is the saga of Everywoman, who ritualistically acts out her roles as daughter, wife, mistress, mother, and platonic friend. Although it was innovative and startling in 1928, its obvious Freudian overtones have rapidly dated the work.

One of O'Neill's enduring masterpieces, *Mourning Becomes Electra* (1931), represents the playwright's most complete use of Greek forms, themes, and characters. Based on the *Oresteia* trilogy by Aeschylus, it was itself three plays in one. To give the story contemporary credibility, O'Neill set the play in the New England of the Civil War period, yet he retained the forms and the conflicts of the Greek characters: the heroic leader returning from war; his adulterous wife, who murders him; his jealous, repressed daughter, who avenges him through the murder of her mother; and his weak, incestuous son, who is goaded by his sister first to matricide and then to suicide.

Following a long succession of tragic visions, O'Neill's only comedy, *Ah, Wilderness!,* appeared on Broadway in 1933. Written in a lighthearted, nostalgic mood, the work was inspired in part by the playwright's mischievous desire to demonstrate that he could portray the comic as well as the tragic side of life. Significantly, the play is set in the same place and period, a small New England town in the early 1900s, as his later tragic masterpiece, *Long Day's Journey into Night.* Dealing with the growing pains of a sensitive, adolescent boy, *Ah, Wilderness!* was characterized by O'Neill as "the other side of the coin," meaning that it represented his fantasy of what his own youth might have been, rather than what he believed it to have been (as dramatized later in *Long Day's Journey into Night*).

The Iceman Cometh, the most complex and perhaps the finest of the O'Neill tragedies, followed in 1939, although it did not appear on Broadway until 1946. Laced with subtle religious symbolism, the play is a study of man's need to cling to his hope for a better life, even if he must delude himself to do so.

Even in his last writings, O'Neill's youth continued to absorb his attention. The posthumous production of *Long Day's Journey into Night* brought to light an agonizingly autobiographical play, one of O'Neill's greatest. It is straightforward in style but shattering in its depiction of the agonized relations between father, mother, and two sons. Spanning one day in the life of a family, the play strips away layer after layer from each of the four central figures, revealing the mother as a defeated drug addict, the father as a man frustrated in his career and failed as a husband and father, the older son as a bitter alcoholic, and the younger son as a tubercular, disillusioned youth with only the slenderest chance for physical and spiritual survival.

O'Neill's tragic view of life was perpetuated in his relationships with the three women he married—two of whom he divorced—and with his three children. His elder son, Eugene O'Neill, Jr. (by his first wife, Kathleen Jenkins), committed suicide at 40, while his younger son, Shane (by his second wife, Agnes Boulton), drifted into a life of emotional instability. His daughter, Oona (also by Agnes Boulton), was cut out of his life when, at 18, she infuriated him by marrying Charlie Chaplin, who was O'Neill's age.

Until some years after his death in 1953, O'Neill, although respected in the United States, was more highly regarded abroad. Sweden, in particular, always held him in high esteem, partly because of his publicly acknowledged debt to the influence of the Swedish playwright August Strindberg, whose tragic themes often echo in O'Neill's plays. In 1936 the Swedish Academy gave O'Neill the Nobel Prize for Literature, the first time the award had been conferred on an American playwright.

O'Neill's most ambitious project for the theatre was one that he never completed. In the late 1930s he conceived of a cycle of 11 plays, to be performed on 11 consecutive nights, tracing the lives of an American family from the early 1800s to modern times. He wrote scenarios and outlines for several of the plays and drafts of others but completed only one in the cycle—*A Touch of the Poet*—before a crippling illness ended his ability to hold a pencil. An unfinished rough draft of another of the cycle plays, *More Stately Mansions,* was published in 1964 and produced three years later on Broadway, in spite of written instructions left by O'Neill that the incomplete manuscript be destroyed after his death.

O'Neill's final years were spent in grim frustration. Unable to work, he longed for his death and sat waiting for it in a Boston hotel, seeing no one except his doctor, a nurse, and his third wife, Carlotta Monterey. O'Neill died as broken and tragic a figure as any he had created for the stage.

Assessment

O'Neill was the first American dramatist to regard the stage as a literary medium. Through his efforts, the American theatre grew up during the 1920s, developing into a cultural medium that could take its place with the best in American fiction, painting, and music. Until his *Beyond the Horizon* was produced, in 1920, Broadway theatrical fare, apart from musicals and an occasional European import of quality, had consisted largely of contrived melodrama and farce. O'Neill saw the theatre as a valid forum for the presentation of serious ideas. Imbued with the tragic sense of life, he aimed for a contemporary drama that had its roots in the most powerful of ancient Greek tragedies—a drama that could rise to the emotional heights of Shakespeare. He set the pace for other playwrights for more than 20 years.

GABRIELA MISTRAL

(b. April 7, 1889, Vicuña, Chile—d. January 10, 1957, Hempstead, New York, U.S.)

Of Spanish, Basque, and Indian descent, Lucila Godoy Alcayaga (better known by her pseudonym, Gabriela Mistral) grew up in a village of northern Chile. She became a schoolteacher at age 15, advancing later to the rank of college professor. Throughout her life she combined writing with a career as an educator, cultural minister, and diplomat. Her diplomatic assignments included posts in Madrid, Lisbon, Genoa, and Nice.

Mistral's reputation as a poet was established in 1914 when she won a Chilean prize for three *Sonetos de la muerte* ("Sonnets of Death"). They were signed with the name by which she has since been known, which she coined from those of two of her favourite poets, Gabriele D'Annunzio and Frédéric Mistral. A collection of her early works, *Desolación* (1922; "Desolation"), includes the poem "Dolor," detailing the aftermath of a love affair that was ended by the suicide of her lover. Because of this tragedy, she never married, and a haunting, wistful strain of thwarted maternal tenderness informs her work. *Ternura* (1924, enlarged 1945; "Tenderness"), *Tala* (1938; "Destruction"), and *Lagar* (1954; "The Wine Press") evidence a broader interest in humanity, but love of children and of the downtrodden remained her principal themes.

Mistral's extraordinarily passionate verse, which is frequently coloured by figures and words peculiarly her own, is marked by warmth of feeling and emotional power. Selections of her poetry have been translated into English by the American writer Langston Hughes (1957; reissued 1972), by Mistral's secretary and companion Doris Dana (1957; reissued 1971), by American writer Ursula K. Le Guin (2003), and by Paul Burns and Salvador Ortiz-Carboneres (2005). *A Gabriela Mistral Reader* (1993; reissued in 1997) was translated by Maria Giachetti and edited by Marjorie Agosín. *Selected Prose and Prose-Poems* (2002) was translated by Stephen Tapscott. In 1945 Mistral became the first Latin American to win the Nobel Prize for Literature.

Anna Akhmatova

(b. June 11 [June 23, New Style], 1889, Bolshoy Fontan, near Odessa, Ukraine, Russian Empire—d. March 5, 1966, Domodedovo, near Moscow, Russia, U.S.S.R.)

Anna Akhmatova, whose original name was Anna Andreyevna Gorenko, began writing verse at age 11 and at 21 joined a group of St. Petersburg poets, the Acmeists, whose leader, Nikolay Gumilyov, she married in 1910. They soon traveled to Paris, immersing themselves for months in its cultural life. Their son, Lev, was born in 1912, but their marriage did not last (they divorced in 1918). The Acmeists, who included notably Osip Mandelshtam, were associated with the new St. Petersburg journal *Apollon* (1909–17; "Apollo") and such poets of the older generation as Innokenty Annensky and Mikhail Kuzmin, who stood apart from the dominant Symbolist poets of the day. Partly in response to the manifestos of the Russian Futurists (1912–13), the young poets founded Acmeism, a school that affirmed "beautiful clarity" (Kuzmin's term) in place of the vagueness and abstractness of Russian Symbolism. Codifying their own

poetic practice, Acmeists demanded concrete represen-
tation and precise form and meaning—combined with a
broad-ranging erudition (Classical antiquity, European
history and culture, including art and religion). To these
Akhmatova added her own stamp of elegant colloquialism
and the psychological sophistication of a young cosmopolitan woman, fully in control of the subtle verbal and
gestural vocabulary of modern intimacies and romance. A
small detail could evoke a whole gamut of emotions ("You
are drawing on my soul like a drink through a straw").
Her first collections, *Vecher* (1912; "Evening") and *Chyotki*
(1914; "Rosary"), especially the latter, brought her fame
and made her poetic voice emblematic of the experience
of her generation. Her appeal stemmed from the artistic
and emotional integrity of her poetic voice as well as from
her poetic persona, further amplified by her own striking
appearance. Akhmatova's principal motif is frustrated and
tragic love expressed with an intensely feminine accent
and inflection entirely her own.

During World War I and following the Revolution of
1917, she added to her main theme some civic, patriotic,
and religious motifs but did not sacrifice her personal
intensity or artistic conscience. Her artistry and increasing control of her medium were particularly prominent
in her next collections: *Belaya staya* (1917; "The White
Flock"), *Podorozhnik* (1921; "Plantain"), and *Anno Domini
MCMXXI* (1921). The broadening of her thematic range,
however, did not prevent the communist cultural watch-
dogs from proclaiming her "bourgeois and aristocratic"
and condemning her poetry for its narrow preoccupation with love and God, even as her standing as a premier
poetic voice of the generation was being affirmed by major
critical authorities of the 1920s (e.g., Korney Chukovsky
and Boris Eikhenbaum, who in 1922 coined the definition of Akhmatova's poetic persona as a blend of "a harlot

and a nun"). The execution in 1921 of her former husband, Gumilyov, on trumped-up charges of participation in an anti-Soviet conspiracy (the Tagantsev affair) further complicated her position. In 1923 she entered a period of almost complete poetic silence and literary ostracism, and no volume of her poetry appeared in the Soviet Union until 1940. Her public life was now limited to her studies of Aleksandr Pushkin.

The 1930s were especially hard for Akhmatova. Her son, Lev Gumilyov (1912–92), and her third husband (she was married from 1918 to 1928 to the Assyriologist Vladimir Shileiko), art historian and critic Nikolay Punin (1888–1953), were arrested for political deviance in 1935. Both were soon released, but her son was arrested again in 1938 and subsequently served a five-year sentence in the Gulag. Her friend Mandelshtam was arrested in her presence in 1934 and died in a concentration camp in 1938.

In 1940, however, several of her poems were published in the literary monthly *Zvezda* ("The Star"), and a volume of selections from her earlier work appeared under the title *Iz shesti knig* ("From Six Books")—only to be abruptly withdrawn from sale and libraries. Nevertheless, in September 1941, following the German invasion, Akhmatova was permitted to deliver an inspiring radio address to the women of Leningrad (St. Petersburg). Evacuated to Tashkent, Uzbekistan, soon thereafter, she read her poems to hospitalized soldiers and published a number of war-inspired poems; a small volume of selected poetry appeared in Tashkent in 1943. At the end of the war she returned to Leningrad, where her poems began to appear in local magazines and newspapers. She gave poetic readings, and plans were made for publication of a large edition of her works.

In August 1946, however, she was harshly denounced by the Central Committee of the Communist Party for her "eroticism, mysticism, and political indifference." Her poetry was castigated as "alien to the Soviet people," and she herself was publicly insulted as a "harlot-nun" by none other than Andrey Zhdanov, a Politburo member and the director of Stalin's program of cultural repression. She was expelled from the Union of Soviet Writers; an unreleased book of her poems, already in print, was destroyed; and none of her work appeared in print for three years.

Then, in 1950, a number of her poems eulogizing Stalin and Soviet communism were printed in several issues of the illustrated weekly magazine *Ogonyok* ("The Little Light") under the title *Iz tsikla "Slava miru"* ("From the Cycle 'Glory to Peace'"). This uncharacteristic capitulation to the Soviet dictator—in one of the poems Akhmatova declares: "Where Stalin is, there is Freedom, Peace, and the grandeur of the earth"—was motivated by Akhmatova's desire to propitiate Stalin and win the freedom of her son, who again had been arrested in 1949 and exiled to Siberia. The tone of these poems (those glorifying Stalin were omitted from Soviet editions of Akhmatova's works published after his death) is far different from the moving and universalized lyrical cycle, *Rekviem* ("Requiem"), composed between 1935 and 1940 and occasioned by Akhmatova's grief over the earlier arrest and imprisonment of her son in 1938. This masterpiece—a poetic monument to the sufferings of the Soviet people during Stalin's terror—was published in Russia for the first time in 1989.

In the cultural thaw following Stalin's death, Akhmatova was slowly and ambivalently rehabilitated, and a slender volume of her poetry, including some of her translations, was published in 1958. After 1958 a number of editions of her works, including some of her brilliant essays on Pushkin, were published in the Soviet Union (1961, 1965, two in 1976, 1977); none of these, however, contains the complete corpus of her literary productivity.

Akhmatova's longest work and perhaps her masterpiece, *Poema bez geroya* ("Poem Without a Hero"), on which she worked from 1940 to 1962, was not published in the Soviet Union until 1976. This difficult and complex work, in which the life of St. Petersburg bohemia in pre-World War I years is "double-exposed" onto the tragedies and suffering of the post-1917 decades, is a powerful lyric summation of Akhmatova's philosophy and her own definitive statement on the meaning of her life and poetic achievement.

Akhmatova executed a number of superb translations of the works of other poets, including Victor Hugo, Rabindranath Tagore, Giacomo Leopardi, and various Armenian and Korean poets. She also wrote sensitive personal memoirs on Symbolist writer Aleksandr Blok, the artist Amedeo Modigliani, and fellow Acmeist Mandelshtam.

In 1964 she was awarded the Etna-Taormina prize, an international poetry prize awarded in Italy, and in 1965 she received an honorary doctoral degree from the University of Oxford. Her journeys to Sicily and England to receive these honours were her first travel outside her homeland since 1912. Akhmatova's works were widely translated, and her international stature continued to grow after her death. A two-volume edition of Akhmatova's collected works was published in Moscow in 1986, and *The Complete Poems of Anna Akhmatova*, also in two volumes, appeared in 1990 and was updated and expanded in 1992.

BORIS LEONIDOVICH PASTERNAK

(b. February 10 [January 29, Old Style], 1890, Moscow, Russia—d. May 30, 1960, Peredelkino, near Moscow)

The Russian poet Boris Pasternak's novel *Doctor Zhivago* aroused so much opposition in the Soviet Union that he declined the Nobel Prize for Literature—which the novel had helped him win—in 1958. An epic of wandering, spiritual isolation, and love amid the harshness of the Russian Revolution and its aftermath, the novel became an international best-seller but circulated only in secrecy and translation in his own land.

Pasternak grew up in a cultured Jewish household. His father, Leonid, was an art professor and a portraitist of novelist Leo Tolstoy, poet Rainer Maria Rilke, and composer Sergey Rachmaninoff, all frequent guests at his home, and of Lenin. His mother was the pianist Rosa Kaufman.

Young Pasternak himself planned a musical career, though he was a precocious poet. He studied musical theory and composition for six years, then abruptly switched to philosophy courses at Moscow University and the University of Marburg (Germany). Physically disqualified for military service, he worked in a chemical factory in the Urals during World War I. After the Revolution he worked in the library of the Soviet commissariat of education.

His first volume of poetry was published in 1913. In 1917 he brought out a striking second volume, *Poverkh baryerov* ("Over the Barriers"), and with the publication of *Sestra moya zhizn* (1922; "My Sister Life") he was recognized as a major new lyrical voice. His poems of that period reflected Symbolist influences. Though avant-garde and esoteric by Russian standards, they were successful. From 1933 to 1943, however, the gap between his work and the official modes (such as Socialist Realism) was too wide to permit him to publish, and he feared for his safety during the purges of the late 1930s. One theory is that Stalin spared him because Pasternak had translated poets of Stalin's native Georgia. His translations, which were his main livelihood, included renderings of William Shakespeare, Johann Wolfgang von Goethe, English Romantic poets, Paul Verlaine, and Rainer Maria Rilke.

Although Pasternak hoped for the best when he submitted *Doctor Zhivago* to a leading Moscow monthly in 1956, it was rejected with the accusation that "it represented in a libelous manner the October Revolution, the people who made it, and social construction in the Soviet Union." The book reached the West in 1957 through an Italian publishing house that had bought rights to it from Pasternak and refused to return it "for revisions." By 1958, the year of its English edition, the book had been translated into 18 languages.

In the Soviet Union, the Nobel Prize brought a campaign of abuse. Pasternak was ejected from the Union of Soviet Writers and thus deprived of his livelihood. Public meetings called for his deportation; he wrote Premier Nikita S. Khrushchev, "Leaving the motherland will equal death for me." Suffering from cancer and heart trouble, he spent his last years in his home at Peredelkino.

In 1987 the Union of Soviet Writers posthumously reinstated Pasternak, a move that gave his works a legitimacy they had lacked in the Soviet Union since his expulsion from the writers' union in 1958 and that finally made possible the publication of *Doctor Zhivago* in the Soviet Union. In addition Pasternak's home in Peredelkino was made a museum.

KATHERINE ANNE PORTER

(b. May 15, 1890, Indian Creek, Texas, U.S.—d. September 18, 1980, Silver Spring, Maryland)

Katherine Anne Porter was educated at private and convent schools in the South. She worked as a newspaperwoman in Chicago and in Denver, Colorado, before leaving in 1920 for Mexico, the scene of several of her stories. "Maria Concepcion," her first published story (1922), was included in her first book of stories, *Flowering Judas* (1930), which was enlarged in 1935 with other stories.

The title story of her next collection, *Pale Horse, Pale Rider* (1939), is a poignant tale of youthful romance brutally thwarted by the young man's death in the influenza epidemic of 1919. In it and the two other stories of the volume, "Noon Wine" and "Old Mortality," appears for the first time her semiautobiographical heroine, Miranda, a spirited and independent woman.

Porter's reputation was firmly established, but none of her books sold widely, and she supported herself primarily through fellowships, by working occasionally as an uncredited screenwriter in Hollywood, and by serving as writer-in-residence at a succession of colleges and universities. *The Leaning Tower* (1944) won an O. Henry Award for her 1962 story, "Holiday." In this and her other long short stories, she revealed that she was a master stylist whose stories have a richness of texture and complexity of character delineation usually achieved only in the novel. Thus it was that the literary world awaited with great anticipation the appearance of Porter's only full-length novel, on which she had been working since 1941.

With the publication of *Ship of Fools* in 1962, Porter won a large readership for the first time. A best-seller that became a major film in 1965, it tells of the ocean voyage of a group of Germans back to their homeland from Mexico in 1931, on the eve of Hitler's ascendency. Porter's carefully crafted, ironic style is perfectly suited to the allegorical exploration of the collusion of good and evil that is her theme, and the penetrating psychological insight that had always marked her work is evident in the book.

Porter's *Collected Short Stories* (1965) won the National Book Award and the Pulitzer Prize for fiction. Her essays, articles, and book reviews were collected in *The Days Before* (1952; augmented 1970). Her last work, published in 1977, when she suffered a disabling stroke, was *The Never-Ending Wrong*, dealing with the Sacco-Vanzetti case of the 1920s.

AGATHA CHRISTIE

(b. September 15, 1890, Torquay, Devon, England—d. January 12, 1976, Wallingford, Oxfordshire)

Agatha Christie, 1946. UPI/Bettmann Archive

Agatha Christie was christened Agatha Mary Clarissa Miller. Educated at home by her mother, she began writing detective fiction while working as a nurse during World War I. Her first novel, *The Mysterious Affair at Styles* (1920), introduced Hercule Poirot, her eccentric and egotistic Belgian detective; Poirot reappeared in about 25 novels and many short stories before returning to Styles, where, in *Curtain* (1975), he died. The elderly spinster Miss Jane Marple, her other principal detective figure, first appeared in *Murder at the Vicarage* (1930). Christie's first major recognition came with *The Murder of Roger Ackroyd* (1926), which was followed by some 75 novels that usually made best-seller lists and were serialized in popular magazines in England and the United States. Her plays include *The Mousetrap* (1952), which set a world record for the longest continuous run at one theatre (8,862 performances—more than 21 years—at the Ambassadors Theatre, London) and then moved to another theatre, and *Witness for the Prosecution* (1953), which, like many of her works, was adapted into a successful film (1957). Other notable film adaptations include *Murder on the Orient Express* (1933; film, 1974) and *Death on the Nile* (1937; film, 1978). Her works were also adapted for television.

In 1926 Christie's mother died, and her husband, Colonel Archibald Christie, requested a divorce. In a move she never fully explained, Christie disappeared and, after several highly publicized days, was discovered registered in a hotel under the name of the woman her husband wished to marry. In 1930 Christie married the archaeologist Sir Max Mallowan; thereafter she spent several months each year on expeditions in Iraq and Syria with him. She also wrote romantic nondetective novels, such as *Absent in the Spring* (1944), under the pseudonym Mary Westmacott. Her *Autobiography* (1977) appeared posthumously. She was created a Dame of the British Empire in 1971.

OSIP EMILYEVICH MANDELSHTAM

(b. January 3 [January 15, New Style], 1891, Warsaw, Poland, Russian
Empire [now in Poland]—d. December 27, 1938?, Vtoraya Rechka,
near Vladivostok, Russia, U.S.S.R. [now in Russia])

O sip Mandelshtam (Mandelstam) grew up in St.
Petersburg in a cultured Jewish household. After
graduating from the elite Tenishev School in 1907, he
studied at the University of St. Petersburg as well as in
France at the Sorbonne and in Germany at the University
of Heidelberg.

His first poems appeared in the avant-garde journal *Apollon* ("Apollo") in 1910. Together with Nikolay
Gumilyov and Anna Akhmatova, Mandelshtam founded
the Acmeist school of poetry, which rejected the mysticism and abstraction of Russian Symbolism and demanded
clarity and compactness of form. Mandelshtam summed
up his poetic credo in his manifesto *Utro Akmeizma* ("The
Morning of Acmeism"). In 1913 his first slim volume of
verse, *Kamen* ("Stone"), was published. During the Russian
Civil War (1918–20), Mandelshtam spent time in the
Crimea and Georgia. In 1922 he moved to Moscow, where
his second volume of poetry, *Tristia,* appeared. He married
Nadezhda Yakovlevna Khazina in 1922.

Mandelshtam's poetry, which was apolitical and intellectually demanding, distanced him from the official Soviet
literary establishment. His poetry having been withdrawn
from publication, he wrote children's tales and a collection of autobiographical stories, *Shum vremeni* (1925; "The
Noise of Time"). A second edition of this work, augmented

by the tale "Yegipetskaya marka" ("The Egyptian Stamp"), was published in 1928. That year, a volume of his collected poetry, *Stikhotvoreniya* ("Poems"), and a collection of literary criticism, *O poezii* ("On Poetry"), appeared. These were his last books published in the Soviet Union during his lifetime.

In May 1934 he was arrested for an epigram on Joseph Stalin he had written and read to a small circle of friends. In addition to describing Stalin's fingers as "worms" and his moustache as that of a cockroach, the draft that fell into the hands of the police called Stalin "the murderer and peasant slayer."

Shattered by a fierce interrogation, Mandelshtam was exiled with his wife to the provincial town of Cherdyn. After hospitalization and a suicide attempt, he won permission to move to Voronezh. Though suffering from periodic bouts of mental illness, he composed a long cycle of poems, the *Voronezhskiye tetradi* ("Voronezh Notebooks"), which contain some of his finest lyrics.

In May 1937, having served his sentence, Mandelshtam returned with his wife to Moscow. But the following year he was arrested during a stay at a rest home. In a letter to his wife that autumn, Mandelshtam reported that he was ill in a transit camp near Vladivostok. Nothing further was ever heard from him. Soviet authorities officially gave his death date as December 27, 1938, although he was also reported by government sources to have died "at the beginning of 1939." It was primarily through the efforts of his widow, who died in 1980, that little of the poetry of Osip Mandelshtam was lost. She kept his works alive during the repression by memorizing them and by collecting copies.

After Stalin's death the publication in Russian of Mandelshtam's works was resumed.

ZORA NEALE HURSTON

(b. January 7, 1891, Notasulga, Alabama, U.S.—d. January 28, 1960,
Fort Pierce, Florida)

Although Zora Neale Hurston claimed to have been born in 1901 in Eatonville, Florida, she was, in fact, 10 years older and had moved with her family to Eatonville only as a small child. There, in the first incorporated all-black town in the country, she attended school until age 13. After the death of her mother (1904), Hurston's home life became increasingly difficult, and at 16 she joined a travel-ing theatrical company, ending up in New York City during the Harlem Renaissance. She attended Howard University from 1921 to 1924 and in 1925 won a scholarship to Barnard College, where she stud-ied anthropology under Franz Boas. She gradu-ated from Barnard in 1928 and for two years pursued graduate stud-ies in anthropology at

Zora Neale Hurston. **Fotosearch/Archive Photos/Getty Images**

Columbia University. She also conducted field studies in folklore among African Americans in the South. Her trips were funded by folklorist Charlotte Mason, who was a patron to both Hurston and Langston Hughes. For a short time Hurston was an amanuensis (one who takes dictation or copies manuscript) to novelist Fannie Hurst.

In 1930 Hurston collaborated with Hughes on a play (never finished) titled *Mule Bone: A Comedy of Negro Life in Three Acts* (published posthumously 1991). In 1934 she published her first novel, *Jonah's Gourd Vine*, which was well received by critics for its portrayal of African American life uncluttered by stock figures or sentimentality. *Mules and Men*, a study of folkways among the African American population of Florida, followed in 1935. *Their Eyes Were Watching God* (1937), a novel, *Tell My Horse* (1938), a blend of travel writing and anthropology based on her investigations of voodoo in Haiti, and *Moses, Man of the Mountain* (1939), a novel, firmly established her as a major author.

For a number of years Hurston was on the faculty of North Carolina College for Negroes (now North Carolina Central University) in Durham. She also was on the staff of the Library of Congress. *Dust Tracks on a Road* (1942), an autobiography, is highly regarded. Her last book, *Seraph on the Suwanee*, a novel, appeared in 1948. Despite her early promise, by the time of her death Hurston was little remembered by the general reading public, but there was a resurgence of interest in her work in the late 20th century. In addition to *Mule Bone*, several other collections were also published posthumously; these include *Spunk: The Selected Stories* (1985), *The Complete Stories* (1995), and *Every Tongue Got to Confess* (2001), a collection of folktales from the South. In 1995 the Library of America published a two-volume set of her work in its series.

MIKHAIL AFANASYEVICH BULGAKOV

(b. May 15 [May 3, Old Style], 1891, Kiev, Ukraine, Russian Empire—d. March 10, 1940, Moscow, Russia, U.S.S.R.)

Soviet playwright, novelist, and short-story writer Mikhail Bulgakov began his adult life as a doctor, but he gave up medicine for writing. His first major work was the novel *Belaya gvardiya* (*The White Guard*), serialized in 1925 but never published in book form. A realistic and sympathetic portrayal of the motives and behaviour of a group of anti-Bolshevik White officers during the civil war, it was met by a storm of official criticism for its lack of a communist hero. Bulgakov reworked it into a play, *Dni Turbinykh* ("The Days of the Turbins"), which was staged with great success in 1926 but was subsequently banned. In 1925 he published a book of satirical fantasies, *Dyavoliada* ("Deviltries"; *Diaboliad*), implicitly critical of Soviet communist society. This work, too, was officially denounced. In the same year he wrote *Sobachye serdtse* (*Heart of a Dog*), a scathing comic satire on pseudoscience.

Because of their realism and humour, Bulgakov's works enjoyed great popularity, but their trenchant criticism of Soviet mores was increasingly unacceptable to the authorities. By 1930 he was, in effect, prohibited from publishing. His plea for permission to emigrate was rejected by Joseph Stalin. During the subsequent period of literary ostracism, which continued until his death, Bulgakov created his masterpieces. In 1932, as literary consultant to the Moscow Art Theatre staff, he wrote a tragedy on the death of Molière, *Molière*. A revised version was finally staged in 1936 and had a run of seven nights before it was banned because of its thinly disguised attack on Stalin and the Communist Party.

Bulgakov produced two more masterpieces during the 1930s. The first was his unfinished *Teatralny roman* (*Black Snow: A Theatrical Novel*, originally titled *Zapiski pokoynika* ["Notes of a Dead Man"]), an autobiographical novel, which includes a merciless satire on Konstantin Stanislavsky and the backstage life of the Moscow Art Theatre. The second was his dazzling Gogolesque fantasy, *Master i Margarita* (*The Master and Margarita*). Witty and ribald, and at the same time a penetrating philosophical novel wrestling with profound and eternal problems of good and evil, it juxtaposes two planes of action—one set in contemporary Moscow and the other in Pontius Pilate's Judea. The central character is the Devil—disguised as Professor Woland—who descends upon Moscow with his purgative pranks that expose the corruption and hypocrisy of the Soviet cultural elite. His counterpart is the "Master," a repressed novelist who goes into a psychiatric ward for seeking to present the story of Jesus. The work oscillates between grotesque and often ribald scenes of trenchant satiric humour and powerful and moving moments of pathos and tragedy. It was published in the Soviet Union only in 1966–67, and then in an egregiously censored form. The publication came more than 25 years after Bulgakov's death from a kidney disease.

Bulgakov's works were slow to benefit from the limited "thaw" that characterized the Soviet literary milieu following the death of Stalin. His posthumous rehabilitation began slowly in the late 1950s, and starting in 1962 several volumes of his works, including plays, novels, short stories, and his biography of Molière, were published. The three culminating masterpieces of this artist, however, were not published in the Soviet Union during his lifetime.

HENRY MILLER

(b. December 26, 1891, New York City—d. June 7, 1980, Pacific
Palisades, California, U.S.)

Henry Valentine Miller was brought up in Brooklyn, and he wrote about his childhood experiences there in *Black Spring* (1936). In 1924 he left his job with Western Union in New York to devote himself to writing. In 1930 he went to France. *Tropic of Cancer* (published in France in 1934, in the United States in 1961) is based on his hand-to-mouth existence in Depression-ridden Paris. *Tropic of Capricorn* (France, 1939; U.S., 1961) draws on the earlier New York phase.

Miller's visit to Greece in 1939 inspired *The Colossus of Maroussi* (1941), a meditation on the significance of that country. In 1940–41 he toured the United States extensively and wrote a sharply critical account of it, *The Air-Conditioned Nightmare* (1945), which dwelt on the cost in human terms of mechanization and commercialization.

After settling in Big Sur on the California coast, Miller became the centre of a colony of admirers. Many of them were writers of the Beat generation who saw parallels to their own beliefs in Miller's whole-hearted acceptance of the degrading along with the sublime. At Big Sur, Miller produced his *Rosy Crucifixion* trilogy, made up of *Sexus, Plexus*, and *Nexus* (U.S. edition published as a whole in 1965). It covers much the same period of Miller's life as *Tropic of Capricorn* and, together with that book, traces the stages by which the hero-narrator becomes a writer. The publication of the "Tropics" in the United States provoked a series of obscenity trials that culminated in 1964 in a Supreme Court decision rejecting state court findings that the book was obscene.

Other important books by Miller are the collections of essays *The Cosmological Eye* (1939) and *The Wisdom of the Heart* (1941). Also a watercolourist, he exhibited internationally and wrote about art in *To Paint Is To Love Again* (1960). Various volumes of his correspondence have been published: with Lawrence Durrell (1963), to Anaïs Nin (1965), and with Wallace Fowlie (1975).

Miller was a perennial bohemian whose autobiographical novels achieve a candour—particularly about sex—that made them a liberating influence in mid-20th-century literature. He is also notable for a free and easy American style and a gift for comedy that springs from his willingness to admit to feelings others conceal and an almost eager acceptance of the bad along with the good. Because of their sexual frankness, his major works were banned in Britain and the United States until the 1960s, but they were widely known earlier from copies smuggled in from France.

J.R.R. TOLKIEN

(b. January 3, 1892, Bloemfontein, South Africa—d. September 2, 1973, Bournemouth, Hampshire, England)

A t age four John Ronald Reuel Tolkien, with his mother and younger brother, settled near Birmingham, England, after his father, a bank manager, died in South Africa. In 1900 his mother converted to Roman Catholicism, a faith her elder son also practiced devoutly. On her death in 1904, her boys became wards of a Catholic priest. Four years later Tolkien fell in love with another orphan, Edith Bratt, who would inspire his fictional character Lúthien Tinúviel. His guardian, however, disapproved, and not until his 21st birthday could Tolkien ask Edith to marry him. In the meantime, he attended King Edward's School in Birmingham and Exeter College, Oxford (B.A., 1915; M.A., 1919). During World War I he saw action in the Somme. After the Armistice he was briefly on the staff of *The Oxford English Dictionary* (then called *The New English Dictionary*). For most of his adult life, he taught English language and literature, specializing in Old and Middle English, at the universities of Leeds (1920–25) and Oxford (1925–59). Often busy with academic duties and also acting as an examiner for other universities, he produced few but influential scholarly publications, notably a standard edition of *Sir Gawain and the Green Knight* (1925; with E.V. Gordon), a landmark lecture on *Beowulf* (*Beowulf: The Monsters and the Critics*, 1936), and an edition of the *Ancrene Wisse* (1962).

In private, Tolkien amused himself by writing an elaborate series of fantasy tales, often dark and sorrowful, set in a world of his own creation. He made this "legendarium," which eventually became *The Silmarillion*, partly to provide a setting in which "Elvish" languages he had invented could exist. But his tales of Arda and Middle-earth also grew from a desire to tell stories, influenced by a love of myths and legends. To entertain his four children, he devised lighter fare, lively and often humorous. The longest and most important of these stories, begun about 1930, was *The Hobbit*, a coming-of-age fantasy about a comfort-loving "hobbit" (a smaller relative of Man) who joins a quest for a dragon's treasure. In 1937 *The Hobbit* was published, with pictures by the author (an accomplished amateur artist), and was so popular that its publisher asked for a sequel. The result, 17 years later, was Tolkien's masterpiece, *The Lord of the Rings*, a modern version of the heroic epic. A few elements from *The Hobbit* were carried over, in particular a magic ring, now revealed to be the One Ring, which must be destroyed before it can be used by the terrible Dark Lord, Sauron, to rule the world. But *The Lord of the Rings* is also an extension of Tolkien's Silmarillion tales, which gave the new book a "history" in which Elves, Dwarves, Orcs, and Men were already established. Contrary to statements often made by critics, it was not written specifically for children, nor is it a trilogy, though it is often published in three parts: *The Fellowship of the Ring*, *The Two Towers*, and *The Return of the King*. It was divided originally because of its bulk and to reduce the risk to its publisher should it fail to sell. In fact it proved immensely popular. On its publication in paperback in the United States in 1965, it attained cult status on college campuses. Although some critics disparage it, several polls since 1996 have named *The Lord of the Rings* the best book of the 20th century, and its success made it possible for other authors to thrive by writing fantasy fiction. It had sold more than 50 million copies in some 30 languages by the turn of the 21st century. A film version of *The Lord of the Rings* by New Zealand director Peter Jackson, released in three installments in 2001–03, achieved worldwide critical and financial success; the first part of Jackson's adaptation of *The Hobbit* followed in 2012. In 2004 the text of *The Lord of the Rings* was carefully corrected for a 50th-anniversary edition.

Several shorter works by Tolkien appeared during his lifetime. These include a mock-medieval story, *Farmer Giles of Ham* (1949); *The Adventures of Tom Bombadil and Other Verses from the Red Book* (1962), poetry related to *The Lord of the Rings*; *Tree and Leaf* (1964), with the seminal lecture "On Fairy-Stories" and the tale "Leaf by Niggle"; and the fantasy *Smith of Wootton Major* (1967). Tolkien in his old age failed to complete *The Silmarillion*, the "prequel" to *The Lord of the Rings*, and left it to his youngest son, Christopher, to edit and publish (1977). Subsequent study of his father's papers led Christopher to produce *Unfinished Tales of Númenor and Middle-earth* (1980); *The History of Middle-earth*, 12 vol. (1983–96), which traces the writing of the legendarium, including *The Lord of the Rings*, through its various stages; and *The Children of Húrin* (*Narn I Chin Hurin: The Tale of the Children of Hurin*), published in 2007, one of the three "Great Tales" of *The Silmarillion* in longer form.

Among other posthumous works by Tolkien are *The Father Christmas Letters* (1976; also published as *Letters from Father Christmas*), *The Letters of J.R.R. Tolkien* (1981), the children's stories *Mr. Bliss* (1982) and *Roverandom* (1998), and *The Legend of Sigurd and Gudrún* (2009), two narrative poems drawn from northern legend and written in the style of the *Poetic Edda*.

AKUTAGAWA RYŪNOSUKE

(b. March 1, 1892, Tokyo, Japan—d. July 24, 1927, Tokyo)

As a boy Akutagawa Ryūnosuke was sickly and hypersensitive, but he excelled at school and was a voracious reader. He began his literary career while attending Tokyo Imperial University (now the University of Tokyo), where he studied English literature from 1913 to 1916.

The publication in 1915 of his short story "Rashōmon" led to his introduction to Natsume Sōseki, the outstanding Japanese novelist of the day. With Sōseki's encouragement he began to write a series of stories derived largely from 12th- and 13th-century collections of Japanese tales but retold in the light of modern psychology and in a highly individual style. He ranged wide in his choice of material, drawing inspiration from such disparate sources as China, Japan's 16th-century Christian community in Nagasaki, and European contacts with 19th-century Japan. Many of his stories have a feverish intensity that is well-suited to their often macabre themes.

In 1922 he turned toward autobiographical fiction, but Akutagawa's stories of modern life lack the exotic and sometimes lurid glow of the older tales, perhaps accounting for their comparative unpopularity. His last important work, "Kappa" (1927), although a satiric fable about elflike creatures (*kappa*), is written in the mirthless vein of his last period and reflects his depressed state at the time. His suicide nevertheless came as a shock to the literary world.

Akutagawa is one of the most widely translated of all Japanese writers, and a number of his stories have been made into films. The film classic *Rashomon* (1950), directed by Kurosawa Akira, is based on a combination of Akutagawa's story by that title and another story of his, "Yabu no naka" (1921; "In a Grove").

PEARL BUCK

(b. June 26, 1892, Hillsboro, West Virginia, U.S.—d. March 6, 1973, Danby, Vermont)

Pearl Comfort Sydenstricker was raised in Zhenjiang in eastern China by her Presbyterian missionary parents. Initially educated by her mother and a Chinese tutor, she was sent at 15 to a boarding school in Shanghai. Two years later she entered Randolph-Macon Woman's College in Lynchburg, Virginia. She graduated in 1914 and remained for a semester as an instructor in psychology.

Pearl Buck with her daughter, Carol, undated photograph.
Encyclopædia Britannica, Inc.

In May 1917 she married missionary John L. Buck; although later divorced and remarried, she retained the name Buck professionally. She returned to China and taught English literature in Chinese universities between 1925 and 1930. During that time she briefly resumed studying in the United States at Cornell University, where she took an M.A. in 1926. She began contributing articles on Chinese life to American magazines in 1922.

Buck's first published novel, *East Wind, West Wind* (1930), was written aboard a ship headed for America. *The Good Earth* (1931), a poignant tale of a Chinese peasant and his slave-wife and their struggle upward, was a best-seller. The book, which won a Pulitzer Prize (1932), established Buck as an interpreter of the East to the West and was adapted for stage and screen. *The Good Earth*, widely translated, was followed by *Sons* (1932) and *A House Divided* (1935); the trilogy was published as *The House of Earth* (1935). Buck was awarded the Nobel Prize for Literature in 1938. From 1935 Buck lived in the United States. After World War II, in a move to aid children fathered by U.S. servicemen in Asian countries, she instituted the Pearl S. Buck Foundation (in 1967 she turned over to the foundation most of her earnings—more than $7 million).

Buck turned next to biography with lives of her father, Absalom Sydenstricker, *Fighting Angel* (1936), and her mother, Caroline, *The Exile* (1936). Her later novels include *Dragon Seed* (1942) and *Imperial Woman* (1956). She also published short stories, such as *The First Wife and Other Stories* (1933), *Far and Near* (1947), and *The Good Deed* (1969); a nonfictional work, *The Child Who Never Grew* (1950), about her mentally disabled daughter; and three works of autobiography, notably *My Several Worlds* (1954). She also wrote a number of children's books. Under the name John Sedges she published five novels unlike her others, including a best-seller, *The Townsman* (1945).

Marina Ivanovna Tsvetayeva

(b. September 26 [October 8, New Style], 1892, Moscow, Russia—d.
August 31, 1941, Yelabuga)

The Russian poet Marina Tsvetayeva wrote verse that is distinctive for its staccato rhythms, originality, and directness. Though she is not well known outside Russia, she is considered one of the finest 20th-century poets in the Russian language.

Tsvetayeva spent her youth predominantly in Moscow, where her father was a professor at the university and director of a museum and her mother was a talented pianist. The family traveled abroad extensively, and at age 16 she began studies at the Sorbonne. Her first collection of poetry, *Vecherny albom* ("Evening Album"), appeared in 1910. Many of her best and most typical poetical qualities are displayed in the long verse fairy tale *Tsar-devitsa* (1922; "Tsar-Maiden").

Tsvetayeva met the Russian Revolution with hostility (her husband, Sergei Efron, was an officer in the White counterrevolutionary army), and many of her verses written at this time glorify the anti-Bolshevik resistance. Among these is the remarkable cycle *Lebediny stan* ("The Swans' Camp," composed 1917–21, but not published until 1957 in Munich), a moving lyrical chronicle of the Civil War viewed through the eyes and emotions of the wife of a White officer.

Tsvetayeva left the Soviet Union in 1922, going to Berlin and Prague, and finally, in 1925, settling in Paris. There she published several volumes of poetry, including *Stikhi k Bloku* (1922; "Verses to Blok") and *Posle Rossii*

(1928; "After Russia"), the last book of her poetry to be published during her lifetime. She also composed two poetical tragedies on Classical themes, *Ariadne* (1924) and *Phaedra* (1927), several essays on the creative process, and works of literary criticism, including the monograph *Moy Pushkin* (1937; "My Pushkin"). Her last cycle of poems, *Stikhi k Chekhii* (1938–39; "Verses to the Czech Land"), was an impassioned reaction to Nazi Germany's occupation of Czechoslovakia (now the Czech Republic and Slovakia).

In the 1930s Tsvetayeva's poetry increasingly reflected alienation from her émigré existence and a deepening nostalgia for Russia, as in the poems "Toska po rodine" (1935; "Homesick for the Motherland") and "Rodina" (1936; "Motherland"). At the end of the '30s her husband—who had begun to cooperate with the communists—returned to the Soviet Union, taking their daughter with him (both of them were later to become victims of Joseph Stalin's terror). In 1939 Tsvetayeva followed them, settling in Moscow, where she worked on poetic translations. The evacuation of Moscow during World War II sent her to a remote town where she had no friends or support. She committed suicide in 1941.

GUO MORUO

(b. November 1892, Shawan, Leshan county, Sichuan province, China—d. June 12, 1978, Beijing)

The son of a wealthy merchant, Guo Moruo (Kuo Mo-jo) was originally named Guo Kaizhen. He early manifested a stormy, unbridled temperament. After receiving a traditional education, he in 1913 abandoned his Chinese wife from an arranged marriage and went to Japan to study medicine. There he fell in love with a Japanese woman who became his common-law wife. He began to devote himself to the study of foreign languages and literature, reading works by Spinoza, Goethe, the Bengali poet Rabindranath Tagore, and Walt Whitman. His own early poetry was highly emotional free verse reminiscent of Whitman and Percy Bysshe Shelley. The new-style poems that Guo published in *Shishi xinbao* ("New Journal on Current Affairs") were later compiled into the anthology *Nü shen* (1921; "Goddess"). Its publication laid the first cornerstone for the development of new verse in China. In the same year, Guo, together with Cheng Fangwu, Yu Dafu, and Zhang Ziping, gave impetus to the establishment of the Creation Society, one of the most important literary societies during the May Fourth period in China (1917–24). Guo's translation of Goethe's *Sorrows of Young Werther* gained enormous popularity among Chinese youth soon after its publication in 1922. He became interested in the philosophy of the Japanese Marxist Kawakami Hajime, one of whose books he translated in 1924, and Guo soon embraced Marxism. Although his own writing remained tinged with Romanticism, he declared his rejection of individualistic literature, calling for a "socialist literature that is sympathetic toward the proletariat."

Guo returned to China with his wife in 1923. In 1926 he acted as a political commissar in the Northern Expedition, in which Chiang Kai-shek (Jiang Jieshi) attempted to crush the warlords and unify China. But when Chiang purged the communists from his Kuomintang (Nationalist Party) in 1927, Guo participated in the communist Nanchang uprising. After its failure he fled to Japan, where for 10 years he pursued scholarly research on Chinese antiquities. In 1937 he returned to China to take part in the resistance against Japan and was given important government posts.

As a writer, Guo was enormously prolific in every genre. Besides his poetry and fiction, his works include plays, nine autobiographical volumes, and numerous translations of the works of Goethe, Friedrich von Schiller, Ivan Turgenev, Tolstoy, Upton Sinclair, and other Western authors. He also produced historical and philosophical treatises, including his monumental study of inscriptions on oracle bones and bronze vessels, *Liangzhou jinwenci daxi tulu kaoshi* (1935; new ed. 1957; "Corpus of Inscriptions on Bronzes from the Two Zhou Dynasties"). In this work he attempted to demonstrate, according to communist doctrine, the "slave society" nature of ancient China.

After 1949 Guo held many important positions in the People's Republic of China, including the presidency of the Chinese Academy of Sciences. In 1966 he was one of the first to be attacked in the Cultural Revolution. He confessed that he had failed to understand properly the thought of Chinese Communist Party leader Mao Zedong and stated that all his own work should be burned. Strangely, however, Guo was not, as were many of his colleagues, stripped of all official positions. His vast body of work was compiled into *Guo Moruo quanji*, 38 vol. (1982–2002; "The Complete Works of Guo Moruo"). It is divided into three parts: literature, history, and archaeology.

REBECCA WEST

(b. December 21, 1892, London, England—d. March 15, 1983, London)

Cicily Isabel Fairfield, to be known to readers as Rebecca West, was the daughter of an army officer.

She was educated in Edinburgh after her father's death in 1902. She later trained in London as an actress (taking her pseudonym from a role that she had played in Henrik Ibsen's play *Rosmersholm*).

From 1911 West became involved in journalism, contributing frequently to the left-wing press and making a name for herself as a fighter for woman suffrage. In 1916 she published a critical biography of Henry James that revealed something of her lively intellectual curiosity, and she then embarked on a career as a novelist with an outstanding—and Jamesian—novel, *The Return of the Soldier* (1918). Describing the return of a shell-shocked soldier from World War I, the novel subtly explores questions of gender and class, identity and memory. Her other novels include *The Judge* (1922), *Harriet Hume* (1929), *The Thinking Reed* (1936), *The Fountain Overflows* (1957), and *The Birds Fall Down* (1966). In 1937 West visited Yugoslavia and later wrote *Black Lamb and Grey Falcon*, 2 vol. (1942), an examination of Balkan politics, culture, and history. In 1946 she reported on the trial for treason of William Joyce ("Lord Haw-Haw") for *The New Yorker* magazine. Published as *The Meaning of Treason* (1949; rev. ed., 1965). It examined not only the traitor's role in modern society but also that of the intellectual and of the scientist. Later she published a similar collection, *The New Meaning of Treason* (1964). Her brilliant reports on the Nürnberg trials of former Nazi leaders were collected in *A Train of Powder* (1955). West was created a Dame Commander of the Order of the British Empire in 1959. During West's lifetime, her novels attracted much less attention than did her social and cultural writings, but, at the end of the 20th century, feminist critics argued persuasively that her fiction was formally as inventive as that of her female Modernist contemporaries.

Rebecca West: A Celebration, a selection of her works, was published in 1977, and her personal reflection on the turn of the 20th century, *1900*, was published in 1982. *Selected Letters of Rebecca West*, edited by Bonnie Kime Scott, was published in 2000. The critic and author Anthony West was the son of Dame Rebecca and the English novelist H.G. Wells.

VLADIMIR VLADIMIROVICH MAYAKOVSKY

(b. July 7 [July 19, New Style], 1893, Bagdadi, Georgia, Russian Empire—d. April 14, 1930, Moscow, Russia, U.S.S.R.)

Vladimir Mayakovsky's father died while Mayakovsky was young, and his mother moved the family to Moscow in 1906. At age 15 he joined the Russian Social-Democratic Workers' Party and was repeatedly jailed for subversive activity. He started to write poetry during solitary confinement in 1909. On his release he attended the Moscow Art School and joined, with David Burlyuk and a few others, the Russian Futurist group and soon became its leading spokesman. In 1912 the group published a manifesto, *Poshchochina obshchestvennomu vkusu* ("A Slap in the Face of Public Taste"), and Mayakovsky's poetry became conspicuously self-assertive and defiant in form and content. His poetic monodrama *Vladimir Mayakovsky* was performed in St. Petersburg in 1913.

Between 1914 and 1916 Mayakovsky completed two major poems, "Oblako v shtanakh" (1915; "A Cloud in Trousers") and "Fleyta pozvonochnik" (written 1915, published 1916; "The Backbone Flute"). Both record a tragedy of unrequited love and express the author's discontent with the world in which he lived. Mayakovsky sought to "depoetize" poetry, adopting the language of the streets and using daring technical innovations. Above all, his poetry is declamatory, for mass audiences.

When the Russian Revolution of 1917 broke out, Mayakovsky was wholeheartedly for the Bolsheviks. Such poems as "Oda revolutsi" (1918; "Ode to Revolution") and "Levy marsh" (1919; "Left March") became very popular. So, too, did his *Misteriya buff* (first performed 1921; *Mystery Bouffe*), a drama representing a universal flood and the subsequent joyful triumph of the "Unclean" (the proletarians) over the "Clean" (the bourgeoisie).

As a vigorous spokesman for the Communist Party, Mayakovsky expressed himself in many ways. From 1919 to 1921 he worked in the Russian Telegraph Agency as a painter of posters and cartoons, which he provided with apt rhymes and slogans. He poured out topical poems of propaganda and wrote didactic booklets for children while lecturing and reciting all over Russia. In 1924 he composed a 3,000-line elegy on the death of Vladimir Ilich Lenin. After 1925 he traveled in Europe, the United States, Mexico, and Cuba, recording his impressions in poems and in a booklet of caustic sketches, *Moye otkrytiye Ameriki* (1926; "My Discovery of America"). In the poem "Khorosho!" (1927; "Good!") he sought to unite heroic pathos with lyricism and irony. He also wrote sharply satirical verse.

The immensely productive Mayakovsky found time to write scripts for motion pictures, in some of which he acted. In his last three years he completed two satirical plays: *Klop* (performed 1929; *The Bedbug*), lampooning the type of philistine that emerged with the New Economic Policy in the Soviet Union, and *Banya* (performed in Leningrad on January 30, 1930; *The*

Bathhouse), a satire of bureaucratic stupidity and oppor-tunism under Joseph Stalin.

Mayakovsky's poetry was saturated with politics, but no amount of social propaganda could stifle his personal need for love, which burst out again and again because of repeated romantic frustrations. After his early lyrics this need came out particularly strongly in two poems, "Lyublyu" (1922; "I Love") and "Pro eto" (1923; "About This"). Both of these poems were dedicated to Lilya Brik, the wife of the writer Osip Maksimovich Brik. Mayakovsky's love for her and his friendship with her husband had a strong influence on his poetry. Even after Mayakovsky's relationship with Lilya Brik ended, he con-sidered her one of the people closest to him and a member of his family. During a stay in Paris in 1928, he fell in love with a refugee, Tatyana Yakovleva, whom he wanted to marry but who refused him. At the same time, he had mis-understandings with the dogmatic Russian Association of Proletarian Writers and with Soviet authorities. Nor was the production of his *Banya* a success. Disappointed in love, increasingly alienated from Soviet reality, and denied a visa to travel abroad, he committed suicide in Moscow.

Mayakovsky was, in his lifetime, the most dynamic fig-ure of the Soviet literary scene. His predominantly lyrical poems and his technical innovations influenced a number of Soviet poets, and outside Russia his impress was strong, especially in the 1930s, after Stalin declared him the "best and most talented poet of our Soviet epoch." In the 1960s, young poets, drawn to avant-garde art and activism that often clashed with communist dogma, organized poetry readings under Mayakovsky's statue in Moscow. In the Soviet Union's final years there was a strong tendency to view Mayakovsky's work as dated and insignificant, yet, on the basis of his best works, his reputation was later revived.

Dorothy Parker, 1939. Culver Pictures

DOROTHY PARKER

(b. August 22, 1893, West End, near Long Beach, New Jersey, U.S.—d. June 7, 1967, New York, New York)

Dorothy Rothschild was educated at Miss Dana's School in Morristown, New Jersey, and the Blessed Sacrament Convent School, New York City. She joined the editorial staff of *Vogue* magazine in 1916 and the next year moved to *Vanity Fair* as a drama critic. In 1917 she married Edwin Pond Parker II, whom she divorced in 1928 but whose surname she retained in her professional career.

Discharged from *Vanity Fair* in 1920 for the acerbity of her drama reviews, she became a freelance writer. Her first book of light, witty, and sometimes cynical verse, *Enough Rope*, was a best-seller when it appeared in 1926. Two other books of verse, *Sunset Gun* (1928) and *Death and Taxes* (1931), were collected with it in *Collected Poems: Not So Deep as a Well* (1936). In 1927 Parker became book reviewer, known as "Constant Reader," for *The New Yorker*, and she was associated with that magazine as a staff writer or contributor for much of the rest of her career.

Early in the 1920s she had been one of the founders of the famous Algonquin Round Table at the Algonquin Hotel in Manhattan and was by no means the least of a group of dazzling wits that included Robert Benchley, Robert E. Sherwood, and James Thurber. It was there, in conversations that frequently spilled over from the offices of *The New Yorker*, that Parker established her reputation as one of the most brilliant conversationalists in New York. Her rapier wit became so widely renowned that quips and mots were frequently attributed to her on the strength of her reputation alone. She came to epitomize the liberated woman of the 1920s.

In 1929 Parker won the O. Henry Award for the best short story of the year with "Big Blonde," a compassionate account of an aging party girl. *Laments for the Living* (1930) and *After Such Pleasures* (1933) are collections of her short stories, combined and augmented in 1939 as *Here Lies*. Characteristic of both the stories and Parker's verses is a view of the human situation as simultaneously tragic and funny.

In 1933, newly married, she and her second husband, Alan Campbell, went to Hollywood to collaborate as film writers, receiving screen credits for more than 15 films, including *A Star Is Born* (1937), for which they were nominated for an Academy Award. She became active in left-wing politics, disdained her former role as a smart woman about town, reported from the Spanish Civil War, and discovered that her beliefs counted against her employment by the studios in the fervour of anticommunism that seized Hollywood after World War II. She wrote book reviews for *Esquire* magazine and collaborated on two plays: *The Coast of Illyria* (first performance 1949), about the English essayist Charles Lamb, and *The Ladies of the Corridor* (1953), about lonely widows in side-street New York hotels.

Parker's witty remarks are legendary. When told of the death of the taciturn U.S. president Calvin Coolidge, she is said to have asked, "How can they tell?" Of Katharine Hepburn's performance in a 1934 play, Parker said she "ran the gamut of emotions from A to B." She also is responsible for the couplet "Men seldom make passes / at girls who wear glasses." She lived in Hollywood until Campbell's death in 1963 and then returned to New York City.

ISAAK EMMANUILOVICH BABEL

(b. July 13 [July 1, Old Style], 1894, Odessa, Ukraine, Russian
Empire—d. January 27, 1940, Moscow, Russia, U.S.S.R.)

B orn into a Jewish family, Isaak Babel grew up in
an atmosphere of persecution that is reflected in
the sensitivity, pessimism, and morbidity of his stories.
His first works, later included in his *Odesskiye rasskazy*
("Odessa Tales"), were published in 1916 in St. Petersburg
in a monthly edited by Maksim Gorky; but the tsarist censors considered them crude and obscene. Gorky praised
the young author's terse,
naturalistic style, at the
same time advising him
to "see the world." Babel
proceeded to do so, serv-
ing in the Cossack First
Cavalry Army and in the
political police (Babel's
daughter denied this),
working for newspapers,
and holding a number of
other jobs over the next
seven years. Perhaps his
most significant experi-
ence was as a soldier in the
war with Poland. Out of
that campaign came the

Isaak Emmanuilovich Babel. Encyclopædia Britannica, Inc.

group of stories known as *Konarmiya* (1926; *Red Cavalry*). These stories present different aspects of war through the eyes of an inexperienced, intellectual young Jew who reports everything graphically and with naive precision. Though senseless cruelty often pervades the stories, they are lightened by a belief that joy and happiness must exist somewhere, if only in the imagination.

The "Odessa Tales" were published in book form in 1931. This cycle of realistic and humorous sketches of the Moldavanka—the ghetto suburb of Odessa—vividly portrays the lifestyle and jargon of a group of Jewish bandits and gangsters, led by their "king," the legendary Benya Krik.

Babel wrote other short stories, as well as two plays (*Zakat*, 1928; *Mariya*, 1935). In the early 1930s his literary reputation in the Soviet Union was high, but, in the atmosphere of increasing Stalinist cultural regimentation, Communist critics began to question whether his works were compatible with official literary doctrine. After the mid-1930s Babel lived in silence and obscurity. His last published work in the Soviet Union was a short tribute to Gorky in 1938. His powerful patron had died in 1936; in May 1939 Babel was arrested, and he was executed some eight months later. After Stalin's death in 1953, Babel was rehabilitated, and his stories were again published in the Soviet Union.

Aldous Huxley

(b. July 26, 1894, Godalming, Surrey, England—d. November 22, 1963, Los Angeles)

Aldous Leonard Huxley was a grandson of the prominent biologist T.H. Huxley and was the third child of the biographer and man of letters Leonard Huxley. He was educated at Eton, during which time he became partially blind owing to keratitis. He retained enough eyesight to read with difficulty, and he graduated from Balliol College, Oxford, in 1916. He published his first book in 1916 and worked on the periodical *Athenaeum* from 1919 to 1921. Thereafter he devoted himself largely to his own writing and spent much of his time in Italy until the late 1930s, when he settled in California.

Huxley established himself as a major author in his first two published novels, *Crome Yellow* (1921) and *Antic Hay* (1923); these are witty and malicious satires on the pretensions of the English literary and intellectual coteries of his day. *Those Barren Leaves* (1925) and *Point Counter Point* (1928) are works in a similar vein. Huxley's deep distrust of 20th-century trends in both politics and technology found expression in *Brave New World* (1932), a nightmarish vision of a future society in which psychological conditioning forms the basis for a scientifically determined and immutable caste system. The novel *Eyeless in Gaza* (1936) continues to shoot barbs at the emptiness and aimlessness of contemporary society, but it also shows Huxley's growing interest in Hindu philosophy and mysticism as a viable alternative. Many of his subsequent works reflect this preoccupation, notably *The Perennial Philosophy* (1946).

Huxley's most important later works are *The Devils of Loudun* (1952), a brilliantly detailed psychological study of a historical incident in which a group of 17th-century French nuns were allegedly the victims of demonic possession; and *The Doors of Perception* (1954), a book about Huxley's experiences with the hallucinogenic drug mescaline. The author's lifelong preoccupation with the negative and positive impacts of science and technology on 20th-century life make him one of the representative writers and intellectuals of that century. He had an acute and far-ranging intelligence. His works were notable for their elegance, wit, and pessimistic satire.

Ɛ.Ɛ. *CUMMINGS*

(b. October 14, 1894, Cambridge, Massachusetts, U.S.—d. September 3, 1962, North Conway, New Hampshire)

Edward Estlin Cummings first attracted attention, in an age of literary experimentation, for his unconventional punctuation and phrasing. Cummings's name is often styled "e.e. cummings" in the mistaken belief that the poet legally changed his name to lowercase letters only. Cummings used capital letters only irregularly in his verse and did not object when publishers began lowercasing his name, but he himself capitalized his name in his signature and in the title pages of original editions of his books.

Cummings received a B.A. degree from Harvard University in 1915 and was awarded an M.A. in 1916. During World War I he served with an ambulance corps in France, where he was interned for a time in a detention camp because of his friendship with an American who had written letters home that the French censors thought critical of the war effort. This experience deepened Cummings's distrust of officialdom and was symbolically recounted in his first book, *The Enormous Room* (1922).

In the 1920s and '30s he divided his time between Paris, where he studied art, and New York City. His first book of verse was *Tulips and Chimneys* (1923); it was followed by *XLI Poems* and *&* (1925), and in that year he received the Dial Award for distinguished service to American letters.

In 1927 his play *him* was produced by the Provincetown Players in New York City. During those years he exhibited his paintings and drawings, but they failed to attract as much critical interest as his writings. *Eimi* (1933) recorded, in 432 pages of experimental prose, a 36-day visit to the Soviet Union, which confirmed his individualist repugnance for collectivism. He published his discussions as the Charles Eliot Norton lecturer on poetry at Harvard University (1952–53) under the title *i: six nonlectures* (1953).

In all he wrote 12 volumes of verse, assembled in his two-volume *Complete Poems* (1968). Cummings's linguistic experiments ranged from newly invented compound words to inverted syntax. He varied text alignments, spaced lines irregularly, and used nontraditional capitalization to emphasize particular words and phrases. In many instances his distinct typography mimicked the energy or tone of his subject matter. Cummings's moods were alternately satirical and tough or tender and whimsical. He frequently used colloquial language and material from burlesque and the circus. His erotic poetry and love lyrics had a childlike candour and freshness and were often vividly infused with images of nature.

JAMES THURBER

(b. December 8, 1894, Columbus, Ohio, U.S.—d. November 2, 1961, New York, New York)

American writer and cartoonist James Grover Thurber produced a number of well-known and highly acclaimed writings and drawings that picture the urban man as one who escapes into fantasy because he is befuddled and beset by a world that he neither created nor understands. Walter Mitty, the henpecked, daydreaming hero in the short story "The Secret Life of Walter Mitty" (from *My World—and Welcome to It*, 1942), is Thurber's quintessential urban man.

Thurber attended Ohio State University from 1913 to 1918 and left without taking a degree. He held several newspaper jobs before going in 1926 to New York City, where he was a reporter for the *Evening Post*. In 1927 he joined Harold Ross's newly established magazine, *The New Yorker,* as managing editor and staff writer, making a substantial contribution to setting its urbane tone. He was later to write an account of his associates there in *The Years with Ross* (1959).

His first published drawing in the magazine appeared in 1931. He considered himself primarily a writer and had been offhand about his sketches. But his friend, the essayist E.B. White, noticed their worth and had them used as illustrations for their jointly written *Is Sex Necessary?* (1929), a spoof on the then-popular earnest, pseudoscientific approach to sex. Thurber's stock characters—the snarling wife, her timid, hapless husband, and a roster of serene, silently observing animals—have become classics of urban mythology.

After Thurber left *The New Yorker* staff in 1933, he remained a leading contributor. In 1940, failing eyesight, the result of a boyhood accident (he had lost use of his left eye at age 6), forced him to curtail his drawing, and by 1952 he had to give it up altogether as his blindness became nearly total.

My Life and Hard Times (1933) is a whimsical group of autobiographical pieces; a similar collection of family sketches appeared later in *The Thurber Album* (1952). His *Fables for Our Time* (1940) are deceptively simple and charming in style, yet unflinchingly clear-sighted in their appraisal of human foibles. A play, *The Male Animal* (1941), written with Elliott Nugent, is a plea for academic freedom as well as a comedy. His fantasies for children, *The*

13 Clocks (1950) and *The Wonderful O* (1957), are among the most successful fairy tales of modern times. *The Thurber Carnival* (1945), a collection of his writings and drawings, was adapted for the stage in 1960, with Thurber playing himself. A further collection, *Credos and Curios*, was published posthumously in 1962.

ROBERT GRAVES

(b. July 24, 1895, London, England—d. December 7, 1985, Deyá, Majorca, Spain)

As a student at Charterhouse School, London, Robert von Ranke Graves began to write poetry. He continued to do so while serving as a British officer at the western front during World War I, writing three books of verse during 1916–17. The horror of trench warfare was a crucial experience in his life. He was severely wounded in 1916 and remained deeply troubled by his war experiences for at least a decade. Graves's mental conflicts during the 1920s were exacerbated by an increasingly unhappy marriage that ended in divorce. A new acceptance of his own nature, in which sexual love and dread seemed to exist in close proximity, appeared in his verse after he met Laura Riding, an American poet, who accompanied him to the island of Majorca, Spain, in 1929 and with whom he was associated for 13 years.

The success of Graves's autobiographical classic of World War I, *Good-Bye to All That* (1929; rev. ed. 1957), war memoirs notable for their unadorned grimness, enabled him to make his permanent home on Majorca, an island whose simplicity had not yet been altered by tourism. Graves's notable historical novel *I, Claudius* is an engaging first-person narrative purportedly written by the Roman emperor Claudius as he chronicles the personalities and machinations of the Julio-Claudian line during the reigns of Augustus, Tiberius, and Caligula. This work was followed by other historical novels dealing with ancient Mediterranean civilizations and including *Claudius the God* (1934), which extends Claudius's narrative to his own reign as emperor; *Count Belisarius* (1938), a sympathetic study of the great and martyred general of the Byzantine Empire; and *The Golden Fleece* (1944; U.S. title *Hercules, My Shipmate*). Graves's researches for *The Golden Fleece* led him into a wide-ranging study of myths and to what was his most controversial scholarly work, *The White Goddess: A Historical Grammar of Poetic Myth* (1948). In it the author argues the existence of an all-important religion, rooted in the remote past but continuing into the Christian Era, based on the worship of a goddess.

Graves began before 1914 as a typical Georgian poet, but his war experiences and the difficulties of his personal life gave his later poetry a much deeper and more painful note. He remained a traditionalist rather than a modernist, however, in his emphasis on metre and clear meaning in his verse. Graves's sad love poems are regarded as the finest produced in the English language during the 20th century, along with those of W.B. Yeats.

Graves was elected professor of poetry at the University of Oxford in 1961 and served there until 1966. He wrote more than 120 books. His *Collected Poems* appeared in 1948, with revisions in 1955, 1959, 1961, and 1975. His controversial translation of *The Rubáiyát of Omar Khayyàm*, with Omar Ali-Shah, appeared in 1967. His own later views on poetry can be found in *The Crowning Privilege* (1955) and *Oxford Addresses on Poetry* (1962).

JOHN DOS PASSOS

(b. January 14, 1896, Chicago, Illinois, U.S.—d. September 28, 1970, Baltimore, Maryland)

The son of a wealthy lawyer of Portuguese descent, John Roderigo Dos Passos graduated from Harvard University (1916) and volunteered as an ambulance driver in World War I. His early works were basically portraits of the artist recoiling from the shock of his encounter with a brutal world. Among these was the bitter antiwar novel *Three Soldiers* (1921).

Extensive travel in Spain and other countries while working as a newspaper correspondent in the postwar years enlarged his sense of history, sharpened his social perception, and confirmed his radical sympathies. Gradually, his early subjectivism was subordinated to a larger and tougher objective realism. His novel *Manhattan Transfer* (1925) is a rapid-transit rider's view of the metropolis. The narrative shuttles back and forth between the lives of more than a dozen characters in nervous, jerky, impressionistic flashes.

The execution of the anarchists Nicola Sacco and Bartolomeo Vanzetti in 1927 profoundly affected Dos Passos, who had participated in the losing battle to win their pardon. The crisis crystallized his image of the United States as "two nations"—one of the rich and privileged and one of the poor and powerless. *U.S.A.*, Dos Passos's masterpiece, is the portrait of these two nations. It consists of *The 42nd Parallel* (1930), covering the period from 1900 up to the war; *1919* (1932), dealing with the war and the critical year of the Treaty of Versailles; and *The Big Money* (1936), which races headlong through the boom of the '20s to the bust of the '30s. Dos Passos reinforces the histories of his fictional characters with a sense of real history conveyed by the interpolated devices of "newsreels," artfully selected montages of actual newspaper headlines and popular songs of the day. He also interpolates biographies of such representative members of the establishment as the automobile maker Henry Ford, the inventor Thomas Edison, President Woodrow Wilson, and the financier J.P. Morgan. He further presents members of that "other nation" such as the Socialist Eugene V. Debs, the economist Thorstein Veblen, the labour organizer Joe Hill, and the Unknown Soldier of World War I. Yet another dimension is provided by his "camera-eye" technique: brief, poetic, personal reminiscences.

U.S.A. was followed by a less ambitious trilogy, *District of Columbia* (*Adventures of a Young Man*, 1939; *Number One*, 1943; *The Grand Design*, 1949), which chronicles Dos Passos' further disillusion with the labour movement, radical politics, and New Deal liberalism. The decline of his creative energy and the increasing political conservatism evident in these works became even more pronounced in subsequent works. At his death at 74, his books scarcely received critical attention.

MAO DUN

(b. July 4, 1896, Tongxiang, Zhejiang province, China—d. March 27, 1981, Beijing)

Forced to interrupt his schooling in 1916 because he ran out of money, Shen Yanbing (originally Shen Dehong), who would write under the pen name Mao Dun, became a proofreader at the Commercial Press in Shanghai, the most important publishing house of the time, and he was soon promoted to editor and translator. In 1920 he and several other young Chinese writers took over editorial control of the 11-year-old journal *Xiaoshuo yuebao* ("Short-Story Monthly"). With the support of older writers such as Zhou Zuoren, Shen and his colleagues established the Literary Research Association in the same year. Shen edited *Xiaoshuo yuebao* until 1923 and revamped it into the most important journal of "new literature" at that time.

In 1926 Shen, being one of the first members of the Chinese Communist Party (CCP), joined the Northern Expedition in Guangzhou as secretary to the propaganda department of the Kuomintang Central Executive Committee. When the Kuomintang (Nationalist Party) broke with the CCP in 1927, Shen, pleading illness, fled the confusion to Lushan, where he determined to distance himself from politics.

During the next year Shen composed three novelettes, later published as a trilogy under the title *Shi* (1930; "Eclipse"), using the pen name Mao Dun (Mao Tun), the Chinese term for "contradiction." The work, dealing with a youth's involvement in the Northern Expedition, was praised for its brilliant psychological realism. In 1930 he helped found the League of Left-Wing Writers. In the 1930s and '40s Mao Dun published six novels, including *Ziye* (1933; *Midnight*), which is commonly considered his representative work, and 16 collections of short stories and prose.

After the establishment of the communist government in 1949, Mao Dun became the first minister of culture, and, though he was active on several literary and cultural committees, he stopped writing fiction. He was dismissed from his government post in 1964 and made no public appearances during the late 1960s and early 1970s. He was elected chairman of the Chinese Writers' Association in 1978.

F. Scott Fitzgerald posing on a pier with wife, Zelda, and daughter, Frances Scott. Hulton Archive/Getty Images

F. Scott Fitzgerald

(b. September 24, 1896, St. Paul, Minnesota, U.S.—d. December 21, 1940, Hollywood, California)

A merican short-story writer and novelist Francis Scott Key Fitzgerald was famous for his depictions of the Jazz Age (the 1920s), his most brilliant novel being *The Great Gatsby* (1925). His private life, with his wife, Zelda, in both America and France, became almost as celebrated as his novels.

Fitzgerald was the only son of an unsuccessful, aristocratic father and an energetic, provincial mother. Half the time he thought of himself as the heir of his father's tradition, which included the author of "The Star-Spangled Banner," Francis Scott Key, after whom he was named, and half the time as "straight 1850 potato-famine Irish." As a result he had typically ambivalent American feelings about American life, which seemed to him at once vulgar and dazzlingly promising.

Fitzgerald also had an intensely romantic imagination, what he once called "a heightened sensitivity to the promises of life," and he charged into experience determined to realize those promises. At both St. Paul Academy (1908–10) and Newman School (1911–13) he tried too hard and made himself unpopular, but at Princeton he came close to realizing his dream of a brilliant success. He became a prominent figure in the literary life of the university and made lifelong friendships with Edmund Wilson and John Peale Bishop. He became a leading figure in the socially important Triangle Club, a dramatic society, and was elected to one of the leading clubs of the university. He fell in love with Ginevra King, one of the beauties of her generation, but he later lost her and flunked out of Princeton.

Fitzgerald returned to Princeton the next fall, but he had now lost all the positions he coveted, and in November 1917 he left to join the army. In July 1918, while he was stationed near Montgomery, Alabama, he met Zelda Sayre, the daughter of an Alabama Supreme Court judge. They fell deeply in love, and, as soon as he could, Fitzgerald headed for New York determined to achieve instant success and to marry Zelda. What he achieved was an advertising job at $90 a month. Zelda broke their engagement, and, thereafter an epic drunk, Fitzgerald retired to St. Paul to rewrite for the second time a novel he had begun at Princeton. In the spring of 1920 it was published, he married Zelda, and

> *riding in a taxi one afternoon between very tall buildings under a mauve and rosy sky; I began to bawl because I had everything I wanted and knew I would never be so happy again.*

Immature though it seems today, *This Side of Paradise* in 1920 was a revelation of the new morality of the young; it made Fitzgerald famous. This fame opened to him magazines of literary prestige, such as *Scribner's*, and high-paying popular ones, such as *The Saturday Evening Post*. This sudden prosperity made it possible for him and Zelda to play the roles they were so beautifully equipped for, and Ring Lardner called them the prince and princess of their generation. Though they loved these roles, they were frightened by them, too, as the ending of Fitzgerald's second novel, *The Beautiful and Damned* (1922), shows. *The Beautiful and Damned* describes a handsome young man and his beautiful wife, who gradually degenerate into a shopworn middle age while they wait for the young man to inherit a large fortune. Ironically, they finally get it, when there is nothing of them left worth preserving.

To escape the life that they feared might bring them to this end, the Fitzgeralds (together with their daughter, Frances, called "Scottie," born in 1921) moved in 1924 to the Riviera, where they found themselves a part of a group of American expatriates whose style was largely set by Gerald and Sara Murphy; Fitzgerald described this society in his last completed novel, *Tender Is the Night*, and modeled its hero on Gerald Murphy. Shortly after their arrival in France, Fitzgerald completed his most brilliant novel, *The Great Gatsby* (1925). All of his divided nature is in this novel, the naive Midwesterner afire with the possibilities of the "American Dream" in its hero, Jay Gatsby, and the compassionate Princeton gentleman in its narrator, Nick Carraway. *The Great Gatsby* is the most profoundly American novel of its time; at its conclusion, Fitzgerald connects Gatsby's dream, his "Platonic conception of himself," with the dream of the discoverers of America. Some of Fitzgerald's finest short stories appeared in *All the Sad Young Men* (1926), particularly "The Rich Boy" and "Absolution," but it was not until eight years later that another novel appeared.

The next decade of the Fitzgeralds' lives was disorderly and unhappy. Fitzgerald began to drink too much, and Zelda suddenly, ominously, began to practice ballet dancing night and day. In 1930 she had a mental breakdown and in 1932 another, from which she never fully recovered. Through the 1930s they fought to save their life together, and, when the battle was lost, Fitzgerald said, "I left my capacity for hoping on the little roads that led to Zelda's sanitarium." He did not finish his next novel, *Tender Is the Night*, until 1934. It is the story of a psychiatrist who marries one of his patients, who, as she slowly recovers, exhausts his vitality until he is, in Fitzgerald's words, *un homme épuisé* ("a man used up"). Though technically faulty and commercially unsuccessful, this is Fitzgerald's most moving book.

With its failure and his despair over Zelda, Fitzgerald was close to becoming an incurable alcoholic. By 1937, however, he had come back far enough to become a scriptwriter in Hollywood, and there he met and fell in love with Sheilah Graham, a famous Hollywood gossip columnist. For the rest of his life—except for occasional drunken spells when he became bitter and violent—Fitzgerald lived quietly with her. (Occasionally he went east to visit Zelda or his daughter Scottie, who entered Vassar College in 1938.) In October 1939 he began a novel about Hollywood, *The Last Tycoon*. The career of its hero, Monroe Stahr, is based on that of the producer Irving Thalberg. This is Fitzgerald's final attempt to create his dream of the promises of American life and of the kind of man who could realize them. In the intensity with which it is imagined and in the brilliance of its expression, it is the equal of anything Fitzgerald ever wrote, and it is typical of his luck that he died of a heart attack with his novel only half-finished. He was 44 years old.

THORNTON WILDER

(b. April 17, 1897, Madison, Wisconsin, U.S.—d. December 7, 1975, Hamden, Connecticut)

After graduating from Yale University in 1920, Thornton Niven Wilder studied archaeology in Rome. From 1930 to 1937 he taught dramatic literature and the classics at the University of Chicago.

His first novel, *The Cabala* (1926), set in 20th-century Rome, is essentially a fantasy about the death of the pagan gods. His most popular novel, *The Bridge of San Luis Rey* (1927; Pulitzer Prize), which was adapted for film and television, examines the lives of five people who died in the collapse of a bridge in 18th-century Peru. *The Woman of Andros* (1930) is an interpretation of Terence's *Andria*. Accused of being a "Greek" rather than an American writer, Wilder in *Heaven's My Destination* (1934) wrote about a quixotically good hero in a contemporary setting. His later novels are *The Ides of March* (1948), *The Eighth Day* (1967), and *Theophilus North* (1973).

Wilder's innovative plays engage the audience in make-believe by having the actors address the spectators directly and by discarding props and scenery. The Stage Manager in *Our Town* (1938) talks to the audience, as do the characters in the farcical *The Matchmaker* (1954). Wilder won a Pulitzer Prize for *Our Town*, becoming the only person to receive the award in both the fiction and drama categories. *The Matchmaker* was made into a film in 1958 and adapted in 1964 into the immensely successful musical *Hello, Dolly!*, which was also made into a film.

Wilder's other plays include *The Skin of Our Teeth* (1942; Pulitzer Prize), which employs deliberate anachronisms and the use of the same characters in various geological and historical periods to show that human experience is much the same whatever the time or place. Posthumous publications include *The Journals of Thornton Wilder, 1939–1961*, edited by Donald Gallup, and Wilder's correspondence with Gertrude Stein, *The Letters of Gertrude Stein and Thornton Wilder* (1996), edited by Edward Burns and Ulla E. Dydo.

WILLIAM FAULKNER

(b. September 25, 1897, New Albany, Mississippi, U.S.—d. July 6, 1962, Byhalia, Mississippi)

A s the eldest of the four sons of Murry Cuthbert and Maud Butler Falkner, William Cuthbert Faulkner (as he later spelled his name) was well aware of his family background and especially of his great-grandfather, Colonel William Clark Falkner, a colourful if violent figure who fought gallantly during the Civil War, built a local railway, and published a popular romantic novel called *The White Rose of Memphis*.

Youth and Early Writings

Born in New Albany, Mississippi, Faulkner soon moved with his parents to nearby Ripley and then to the town of Oxford, the seat of Lafayette county, where his father later became business manager of the University of Mississippi. In Oxford he experienced the characteristic open-air upbringing of a Southern white youth of middle-class parents: he had a pony to ride and was introduced to guns and hunting. A reluctant student, he left high school without graduating but devoted himself to "undirected reading," first in isolation and later under the guidance of Phil Stone, a family friend who combined study and practice of the law with lively literary interests and was a constant source of current books and magazines.

In July 1918, impelled by dreams of martial glory and by despair at a broken love affair, Faulkner joined the British Royal Air Force (RAF) as a cadet pilot under training in Canada, although the November 1918 armistice intervened before he could finish ground school, let alone fly or reach Europe. After returning home, he enrolled for a few university courses, published poems and drawings in campus newspapers, and acted out a self-dramatizing role as a poet who had seen wartime service. After working in a New York bookstore for three months in the fall of 1921, he returned to Oxford and ran the university post office there with notorious laxness until forced to resign. In 1924 Phil Stone's financial assistance enabled him to publish *The Marble Faun*, a pastoral verse-sequence in rhymed octosyllabic couplets.

His first novel, *Soldiers' Pay* (1926), given a Southern though not a Mississippian setting, was an impressive achievement, stylistically ambitious and strongly evocative of the sense of alienation experienced by soldiers returning from World War I to a civilian world of which they seemed no longer a part. A second novel, *Mosquitoes* (1927), launched a satirical attack on the New Orleans literary scene, including identifiable individuals, and can perhaps best be read as a declaration of artistic independence. Back in Oxford—with occasional visits to Pascagoula on the Gulf Coast—Faulkner again worked at a series of temporary jobs but was chiefly concerned with proving himself as a professional writer. None of his short stories was accepted, however, and he was especially shaken by his difficulty in finding a publisher for *Flags in the Dust* (published posthumously, 1973), a long, leisurely novel, drawing extensively on local observation and his own family history, that he had confidently counted upon to establish his reputation and career. When the novel eventually did appear, severely truncated, as *Sartoris* in 1929, it created in print for the first time that densely imagined world of Jefferson and Yoknapatawpha County—based partly on Ripley but chiefly on Oxford and Lafayette county and characterized by frequent recurrences of the same characters, places, and themes—which

Faulkner was to use as the setting for so many subsequent novels and stories.

The Major Novels

Faulkner had meanwhile "written [his] guts" into the more technically sophisticated *The Sound and the Fury*, believing that he was fated to remain permanently unpublished and need therefore make no concessions to the cautious commercialism of the literary marketplace. The novel did find a publisher, despite the difficulties it posed for its readers, and from the moment of its appearance in October 1929 Faulkner drove confidently forward as a writer. Crucial to his extraordinary early productivity was the decision to shun the talk, infighting, and publicity of literary centres and live instead in what was then the small-town remoteness of Oxford, where he was already at home and could devote himself, in near isolation, to actual writing. In 1929 he married Estelle Oldham—whose previous marriage, now terminated, had helped drive him into the RAF in 1918. One year later he bought Rowan Oak, a handsome but run-down pre-Civil War house on the outskirts of Oxford, restoration work on the house becoming, along with hunting, an important diversion in the years ahead. A daughter, Jill, was born to the couple in 1933, and although their marriage was otherwise troubled, Faulkner remained working at home throughout the 1930s and '40s, except when financial need forced him to accept the Hollywood screenwriting assignments he deplored but very competently fulfilled.

Oxford provided Faulkner with intimate access to a deeply conservative rural world, conscious of its past and remote from the urban-industrial mainstream, in terms of which he could work out the moral as well as narrative patterns of his work. His fictional methods, however, were the reverse of conservative. He knew the work not only of Honoré de Balzac, Gustave Flaubert, Charles Dickens, and Herman Melville but also of Joseph Conrad, James Joyce, Sherwood Anderson, and other recent figures on both sides of the Atlantic, and in *The Sound and the Fury* (1929), his first major novel, he combined a Yoknapatawpha setting with radical technical experimentation. In successive "stream-of-consciousness" monologues the three brothers of Candace (Caddy) Compson—Benjy the idiot, Quentin the disturbed Harvard undergraduate, and Jason the embittered local businessman—expose their differing obsessions with their sister and their loveless relationships with their parents. A fourth section, narrated as if authorially, provides new perspectives on some of the central characters, including Dilsey, the Compsons' black servant, and moves toward a powerful yet essentially unresolved conclusion. Faulkner's next novel, the brilliant tragicomedy called *As I Lay Dying* (1930), is centred upon the conflicts within the "poor white" Bundren family as it makes its slow and difficult way to Jefferson to bury its matriarch's malodorously decaying corpse. Entirely narrated by the various Bundrens and people encountered on their journey, it is the most systematically multi-voiced of Faulkner's novels and marks the culmination of his early post-Joycean experimentalism.

Although the psychological intensity and technical innovation of these two novels were scarcely calculated to ensure a large contemporary readership, Faulkner's name was beginning to be known in the early 1930s, and he was able to place short stories even in such popular—and well-paying—magazines as *Collier's* and *Saturday Evening Post*. Greater, if more equivocal, prominence came with the financially successful publication of *Sanctuary*, a novel about the brutal rape of a Southern college student and its generally violent, sometimes comic, consequences. A serious work, despite Faulkner's unfortunate declaration that it was written merely to make money, *Sanctuary* was actually completed prior to *As I Lay Dying* and published, in February 1931, only after Faulkner had gone to the trouble and expense of restructuring and partly rewriting it—though without moderating the violence—at proof stage. Despite the demands of film work and short stories (of which a first collection appeared in 1931 and a second in 1934), and even the preparation of a volume of poems (published in 1933 as *A Green Bough*), Faulkner produced in 1932 another long and powerful novel. Complexly structured and involving several major characters, *Light in August* revolves primarily upon the contrasted careers of Lena Grove, a pregnant young countrywoman serenely in pursuit of her biological destiny, and Joe Christmas, a dark-complexioned orphan uncertain as to his racial origins, whose life becomes a desperate and often violent search for a sense of personal identity, a secure location on one side or the other of the tragic dividing line of colour.

Made temporarily affluent by *Sanctuary* and Hollywood, Faulkner took up flying in the early 1930s, bought a Waco cabin aircraft, and flew it in February 1934 to the dedication of Shushan Airport in New Orleans, gathering there much of the material for *Pylon*, the novel about racing and barnstorming pilots that he published in 1935. Having given the Waco to his youngest brother, Dean, and encouraged him to become a professional pilot, Faulkner was both grief- and guilt-stricken when Dean crashed and died in the plane later in 1935; when Dean's daughter was born in 1936 Faulkner took responsibility for her education. The experience perhaps contributed to the emotional intensity of the novel on which he was then working. In *Absalom, Absalom!* (1936) Thomas Sutpen arrives in Jefferson from "nowhere," ruthlessly carves a large plantation out of the Mississippi wilderness, fights valiantly in the Civil War in defense of his adopted society, but is ultimately destroyed by his inhumanity toward those whom he has used and cast aside in the obsessive pursuit of his grandiose dynastic "design." By refusing to acknowledge his first, partly black, son, Charles Bon, Sutpen also loses his second son, Henry, who goes into hiding after killing Bon (whom he loves) in the name of their sister's honour. Because this profoundly Southern story is constructed—speculatively, conflictingly, and inconclusively—by a series of narrators with sharply divergent self-interested perspectives, *Absalom, Absalom!* is often seen, in its infinite open-endedness, as Faulkner's supreme Modernist fiction, focused above all on the processes of its own telling.

Later Life and Works

The novel *The Wild Palms* (1939) was again technically adventurous, with two distinct yet thematically counterpointed narratives alternating, chapter by chapter, throughout. But Faulkner was beginning to return to the Yoknapatawpha County material he had first imagined in the 1920s and subsequently exploited in short-story form. *The Unvanquished* (1938) was relatively conventional, but *The Hamlet* (1940), the first volume of the long-uncompleted "Snopes" trilogy, emerged as a work of extraordinary stylistic richness. Its episodic structure is underpinned by recurrent thematic patterns and by the wryly humorous presence of V.K. Ratliff—an itinerant sewing-machine agent—and his unavailing opposition to the increasing power and prosperity of the supremely manipulative Flem Snopes and his numerous "poor white" relatives. In 1942 appeared *Go Down, Moses*, yet another major work, in which an intense exploration of the linked themes of racial, sexual, and environmental exploitation is conducted largely in terms of the complex interactions between the "white" and "black" branches of the plantation-owning McCaslin family, especially as represented by Isaac McCaslin on the one hand and Lucas Beauchamp on the other.

For various reasons—the constraints on wartime publishing, financial pressures to take on more scriptwriting, difficulties with the work later published as *A Fable*—Faulkner did not produce another novel until *Intruder in the Dust* (1948), in which Lucas Beauchamp, reappearing from *Go Down, Moses*, is proved innocent of murder, and thus saved from lynching, only by the persistent efforts of a young white boy. Racial issues were again confronted, but in the somewhat ambiguous terms that were to mark Faulkner's later public statements on race: while deeply sympathetic to the oppression suffered by blacks in the Southern states, he nevertheless felt that such wrongs should be righted by the South itself, free of Northern intervention.

Faulkner's American reputation—which had always lagged well behind his reputation in Europe—was boosted by *The Portable Faulkner* (1946), an anthology skillfully edited by Malcolm Cowley in accordance with the arresting if questionable thesis that Faulkner was deliberately constructing a historically based "legend" of the South. Faulkner's *Collected Stories* (1950), impressive in both quantity and quality, was also well received, and later in 1950 the award of the Nobel Prize for Literature catapulted the author instantly to the peak of world fame and enabled him to affirm, in a famous acceptance speech, his belief in the survival of the human race, even in an atomic age, and in the importance of the artist to that survival.

The Nobel Prize had a major impact on Faulkner's private life. Confident now of his reputation and future sales, he became less consistently "driven" as a writer than

in earlier years and allowed himself more personal freedom, drinking heavily at times and indulging in a number
of extramarital affairs—his opportunities in these directions being considerably enhanced by a final screenwriting
assignment in Egypt in 1954 and several overseas trips
(most notably to Japan in 1955) undertaken on behalf of
the U.S. State Department. He took his "ambassadorial"
duties seriously, speaking frequently in public and to
interviewers, and also became politically active at home,
taking positions on major racial issues in the vain hope
of finding middle ground between entrenched Southern
conservatives and interventionist Northern liberals. Local
Oxford opinion proving hostile to such views, Faulkner
in 1957 and 1958 readily accepted semester-long appoint-
ments as writer-in-residence at the University of Virginia
in Charlottesville. Attracted to the town by the presence
of his daughter and her children as well as by its opportunities for horse-riding and fox-hunting, Faulkner bought
a house there in 1959, though continuing to spend time at
Rowan Oak.

The quality of Faulkner's writing is often said to have
declined in the wake of the Nobel Prize. But the central
sections of *Requiem for a Nun* (1951) are challengingly set
out in dramatic form, and *A Fable* (1954), a long, densely
written, and complexly structured novel about World
War I, demands attention as the work in which Faulkner
made by far his greatest investment of time, effort,
and authorial commitment. In *The Town* (1957) and *The
Mansion* (1959) Faulkner not only brought the "Snopes"
trilogy to its conclusion, carrying his Yoknapatawpha
narrative to beyond the end of World War II, but subtly
varied the management of narrative point of view. Finally,
in June 1962 Faulkner published yet another distinctive
novel, the genial, nostalgic comedy of male matura-
tion he called *The Reivers* and appropriately subtitled "A

Reminiscence." A month later he was dead, of a heart attack, at age 64.

Assessment

By the time of his death Faulkner had clearly emerged not just as the major American novelist of his generation but as one of the greatest writers of the 20th century, unmatched for his extraordinary structural and stylistic resourcefulness, for the range and depth of his characterization and social notation, and for his persistence and success in exploring fundamental human issues in intensely localized terms. Some critics, early and late, have found his work extravagantly rhetorical and unduly violent, and there have been strong objections, especially late in the 20th century, to the perceived insensitivity of his portrayals of women and black Americans. His reputation, grounded in the sheer scale and scope of his achievement, seems nonetheless secure, and he remains a profoundly influential presence for novelists writing in the United States, South America, and, indeed, throughout the world.

BERTOLT BRECHT

(b. February 10, 1898, Augsburg, Germany—d. August 14, 1956, East Berlin, East Germany)

Until 1924 Eugen Berthold Friedrich Brecht lived in Bavaria, where he was born, studied medicine (Munich, 1917–21), and served in an army hospital (1918). From this period date his first play, *Baal* (produced 1923); his first success, *Trommeln in der Nacht* (Kleist Preis, 1922; *Drums in the Night*); the poems and songs collected as *Die*

Hauspostille (1927; *A Manual of Piety*), his first professional production (*Edward II*, 1924); and his admiration for Frank Wedekind, Arthur Rimbaud, François Villon, and Rudyard Kipling.

During this period he also developed a violently anti-bourgeois attitude that reflected his generation's deep disappointment in the civilization that had come crashing down at the end of World War I. In Berlin (1924–33) he worked briefly for the directors Max Reinhardt and Erwin Piscator, but mainly dealt with his own group of associates. With the composer Kurt Weill he wrote the satirical, successful ballad opera *Die Dreigroschenoper* (1928; *The Threepenny Opera*) and the opera *Aufstieg und Fall der Stadt Mahagonny* (1930; *Rise and Fall of the City of Mahagonny*). He also wrote what he called "*Lehr-stücke*" ("exemplary plays")—badly didactic works for performance outside the orthodox theatre—to music by Weill, Paul Hindemith, and Hanns Eisler. In these years he developed his theory of "epic theatre" and an austere form of irregular verse. He also became a Marxist.

In 1933 he went into exile—in Scandinavia (1933–41), mainly in Denmark, and then in the United States (1941–47), where he did some film work in Hollywood. In Germany his books were burned and his citizenship was withdrawn. He was cut off from the German theatre; but between 1937 and 1941 he wrote most of his great plays, his major theoretical essays and dialogues, and many of the poems collected as *Svendborger Gedichte* (1939). The plays of these years include *Mutter Courage und ihre Kinder* (1941; *Mother Courage and Her Children*), a chronicle play of the Thirty Years' War; *Leben des Galilei* (1943; *The Life of Galileo*); *Der gute Mensch von Sezuan* (1943; *The Good Woman of Setzuan*), a parable play set in prewar China; *Der Aufhaltsame Aufstieg des Arturo Ui* (1957; *The Resistible Rise of Arturo Ui*), a parable play of Hitler's rise to power set in prewar Chicago; *Herr Puntila und sein Knecht Matti* (1948; *Herr Puntila and His Man Matti*), a Volksstück (popular play) about a Finnish farmer who oscillates between churlish sobriety and drunken good humour; and *The Caucasian Chalk Circle* (first produced in English, 1948; *Der kaukasische Kreidekreis*, 1949), the story of a struggle for possession of a child between its highborn mother, who deserts it, and the servant girl who looks after it.

Brecht left the United States in 1947 after having had to give evidence before the House Un-American Activities Committee. He spent a year in Zürich, working mainly on *Antigone-Modell 1948* (adapted from Hölderlin's translation of Sophocles; produced 1948) and on his most important theoretical work, the *Kleines Organon für das Theater* (1949; "A Little Organum for the Theatre"). The essence of his theory of drama, as revealed in this work, is the idea that a truly Marxist drama must avoid the Aristotelian premise that the audience should be made to believe that what they are witnessing is happening here and now. For he saw that if the audience really felt that the emotions of heroes of the past—Oedipus, or Lear, or Hamlet—could equally have been their own reactions, then the Marxist idea that human nature is not constant but a result of changing historical conditions would automatically be invalidated. Brecht therefore argued that the theatre should not seek to make its audience believe in the presence of the characters on the stage—should not make it identify with them, but should rather follow the method of the epic poet's art, which is to make the audience realize that what it sees on the stage is merely an account of past events that it should watch with critical detachment. Hence, the "epic" (narrative, nondramatic) theatre is based on detachment, on the *Verfremdungseffekt* (alienation effect), achieved through a number of devices that remind the spectator that he is being presented with a demonstration of human behaviour in scientific spirit rather than with an illusion of reality, in short, that the theatre is only a theatre and not the world itself.

In 1949 Brecht went to Berlin to help stage *Mutter Courage und ihre Kinder* (with his wife, Helene Weigel, in the title part) at Reinhardt's old Deutsches Theater in the Soviet sector. This led to formation of the Brechts' own company, the Berliner Ensemble, and to permanent return to Berlin. Henceforward the Ensemble and the staging of his own plays had first claim on Brecht's time. Often suspect in eastern Europe because of his unorthodox aesthetic theories and denigrated or boycotted in the West for his Communist opinions, he yet had a great triumph at the Paris Théâtre des Nations in 1955, and in the same year in Moscow he received a Stalin Peace Prize. He died of a heart attack in East Berlin the following year.

Brecht was, first, a superior poet, with a command of many styles and moods. As a playwright he was an intensive worker, a restless piecer-together of ideas not always his own (*The Threepenny Opera* is based on John Gay's *Beggar's Opera*, and *Edward II* on Marlowe), a sardonic humorist, and a man of rare musical and visual awareness; but he was often bad at creating living characters or at giving his plays tension and shape. As a producer he liked lightness, clarity, and firmly knotted narrative sequence; a perfectionist, he forced the German theatre, against its nature, to underplay. As a theoretician he made principles out of his preferences—and even out of his faults.

Federico García Lorca

(b. June 5, 1898, Fuente Vaqueros, Granada province, Spain—d. August 18 or 19, 1936, between Víznar and Alfacar, Granada province)

The Spanish poet and playwright Federico García Lorca, in a career that spanned just 19 years, resurrected and revitalized the most basic strains of Spanish poetry and theatre. He is known primarily for his Andalusian works, including the poetry collections *Romancero gitano* (1928; *Gypsy Ballads*) and *Llanto por Ignacio Sánchez Mejías* (1935; "Lament for Ignacio Sánchez Mejías," Eng. trans. *Lament for a Bullfighter*), and the tragedies *Bodas de sangre* (1933; *Blood Wedding*), *Yerma* (1934; Eng. trans. *Yerma*), and *La casa de Bernarda Alba* (1936; *The House of Bernarda Alba*).

Early Years

The eldest of four children born to a wealthy landowner and his schoolteacher wife, Lorca grew up in rural Andalusia, surrounded by images and social conditions that influenced his work lifelong. At age 10 he moved with his family to Granada, where he attended a private, secular institute in addition to a Catholic public school. Lorca enrolled in the University of Granada but was a hapless student best known for his extraordinary talents as a pianist. He took nine years to complete a bachelor's degree. Despite plans to become a musician and composer, he turned to writing in his late teens. His first experiments in prose, poetry, and drama reveal an intense spiritual and sexual malaise along with an adolescent devotion to such authors as Shakespeare, Goethe, the Spanish poet Antonio Machado, and the Nicaraguan poet Rubén Darío, father of Hispanic Modernismo, a late and decadent flowering of Romanticism.

In 1919 Lorca moved to the Residencia de Estudiantes in Madrid, a prestigious and socially progressive men's residence hall. It remained his home in the Spanish capital for the next decade. His fellow residents included the filmmaker Luis Buñuel and the artist Salvador Dalí, who later became a close companion. In Madrid, Lorca also befriended the renowned older poet Juan Ramón Jiménez and a circle of poets his own age, among them Rafael Alberti, Jorge Guillén, and Pedro Salinas.

Early Poetry and Plays

A consummate stylist, Lorca sought throughout his career to juxtapose and meld genres. His poems, plays, and prose often evoke other, chiefly popular, forms of music, art, and literature. His first book, *Impresiones y paisajes* (1918; *Impressions and Landscapes*), a prose work in the *modernista* tradition, chronicled Lorca's sentimental response to a series of journeys through Spain as a university student. *Libro de poemas* ("Book of Poems"), an uneven collection of predominantly *modernista* poems culled from his juvenilia, followed in 1921. Both efforts disappointed Lorca and reinforced his inherent resistance to publication, a fact that led to frequent delays in the publication and production of his work. Lorca preferred to perform his poems and plays, and his histrionic recitations drew innumerable admirers.

The Spanish stage director Gregorio Martínez Sierra premiered Lorca's first full-length play, *El maleficio de la mariposa* (*The Butterfly's Evil Spell* in *Five Plays: Comedies and Tragi-Comedies*, 1970), a symbolist work about a love-sick cockroach, in Madrid in 1920. Critics and audiences ridiculed the drama, and it closed after four performances. Lorca's next full-length play, the historical verse drama *Mariana Pineda* (written 1923; Eng. trans. *Mariana Pineda*), opened in 1927 in a production with sets by Dalí and received mixed notices.

In the early 1920s, Lorca began experimenting with short, elliptical verse forms inspired by Spanish folk song, Japanese haiku, and contemporary avant-garde poetics. He wrote a prodigious series of brief poems arranged in thematic "suites," later collected and published in 1983 under the title *Suites*. (Virtually all of Lorca's poetry—that contained in the volume under discussion and in the other Spanish volumes mentioned in this biography—has been translated in *Collected Poems*, 1991). In 1922 Lorca collaborated with the eminent Andalusian composer Manuel de Falla on a festival of *cante jondo* ("deep song") in Granada. The endeavour heightened Lorca's interest in popular Andalusian song, and in a blaze of inspiration he wrote a series of poems based on songs of the Andalusian Gypsies (Roma). Even more compressed than *Suites, Poema del cante jondo* (written 1921–25, published 1931; *Poem of the Deep Song*), offers a radical synthesis of the traditional and the avant-garde. The series signaled Lorca's emergence as a mature poet. His collaboration with Falla further prompted Lorca to investigate the Spanish puppet theatre tradition, and in 1923 he wrote *Los títeres de Cachiporra* ("The Billy-Club Puppets"), the first of several versions of a puppet play inspired by the classic Andalusian Grand Guignol.

From 1925 to 1928, Lorca was passionately involved with Salvador Dalí. The intensity of their relationship led Lorca to acknowledge, if not entirely

Federico García Lorca (left) *sitting at a restaurant with his close companion, Spanish Surrealist artist Salvador Dalí. Lorca's experiments with Surrealism can be attributed to Dalí's influence.* Apic/Hulton Archive/Getty Images

accept, his own homosexuality. At Dalí's urging, the poet began to experiment more boldly with avant-garde currents in the art world, notably Surrealism, although he refused to align himself with any movement. In poems such as "Oda a Salvador Dalí" (1925–26; "Ode to Salvador Dalí"), *Canciones* (written 1924, published 1926; *Songs*), and a series of abstruse prose poems, Lorca sought to create a more objective poetry, devoid of private sentiment and the "planes of reality." He joined his contemporaries in exalting Don Luis de Góngora, a 16th-century Spanish poet known for his dispassionate, densely metaphorical verse. Lorca and his fellow poets commemorated the tricentennial of Góngora's death in 1927 and became known thereafter as the "Generation of 1927." Lorca also sought to articulate in public lectures his own evolving aesthetic.

Meanwhile, Lorca continued to mine the popular Spanish tradition in his plays *La zapatera prodigiosa* (written 1924, premiered 1930; *The Shoemaker's Prodigious Wife*), a classic farce, and *El amor de don Perlimplín con Belisa en su jardín* (written 1925, premiered 1933; *The Love of Don Perlimplín with Belisa in Their Garden* in *Five Plays: Comedies and Tragi-Comedies*, 1970), a "grotesque tragedy" partially drawn from an 18th-century Spanish comic strip. Both plays reveal themes common to Lorca's work: the capriciousness of time, the destructive powers of love and death, the phantoms of identity, art, childhood, and sex.

In 1928, with Dalí's encouragement, Lorca publicly exhibited his drawings. A gifted draughtsman blessed with a startling visual imagination, Lorca produced hundreds of sketches in his lifetime.

Romancero Gitano

The publication in 1928 of *Romancero gitano* (written 1921–27; *Gypsy Ballads*), a poetry sequence inspired by the traditional Spanish *romance*, or ballad, catapulted Lorca into the national spotlight. A lyrical evocation of the sensual world of the Andalusian Gypsy, the collection enthralled Spanish readers, many of whom mistook Lorca for a Gypsy. The book's first edition sold out within a year. Throughout the work's 18 ballads, Lorca combines lyrical and narrative modes in fresh ways to form what he described as a tragic "poem of Andalusia." Formally, the poems embrace the conventions of medieval Spanish balladry: a nonstanzaic construction, *in medias res* openings, and abrupt endings. But in their wit, objectivity, and metaphorical novelty, they are brazenly contemporary. One of the collection's most famous poems, "Ballad of the Spanish Civil Guard," reads, in part:

Los caballos negros son.	*Black are the horses,*
Las herraduras son negras.	*the horseshoes are black.*
Sobre las capas relucen	*Glistening on their capes*
manchas de tinta y de cera.	*are stains of ink and of wax.*
Tienen, por eso no lloran,	*Their skulls—and this is why*
de plomo las calaveras.	*they do not cry—are cast in lead.*
Con el alma de charol	*They ride the roads*
vienen por la carretera.	*with souls of patent leather.*

("Ballad of the Spanish Civil Guard," excerpt. Reprinted by permission of Farrar, Straus and Giroux, LLC, from *Collected Poems* by Federico García Lorca. Translated by Will Kirkland. Translation copyright © 1991 by Will Kirkland. Introduction and notes copyright © 1991 by Christopher Maurer. Spanish texts copyright © 1991 by Herederos de Federico García Lorca.)

Lorca's sudden fame destroyed his privacy. This, coupled with the demise of his friendship with Dalí, the collapse of another love affair, and a profound spiritual crisis, plunged Lorca into severe depression. He sought both release and newfound inspiration by visiting New York and Cuba in 1929–30.

Later Poetry and Plays

Lorca's stay in the United States and Cuba yielded *Poeta en Nueva York* (published 1940; *Poet in New York*), a series of poems whose dense, at times hallucinatory images, free-verse lines, and thematic preoccupation with urban decay and social injustice mark an audacious departure from Lorca's previous work. The collection is redolent of Charles Baudelaire, Edgar Allan Poe, T.S. Eliot, and Stephen Crane and pays homage to Walt Whitman:

...hermosura viril	*...virile beauty,*
que en montes de carbón,	*who among mountains of coal,*
anuncios y ferrocarriles,	*billboards, and railroads,*
soñabas ser un río y dormir	*dreamed of becoming a river*
como un río	*and sleeping like a river*
con aquel camarada que pon-	*with that comrade who*
dría en tu pecho	*would place in your breast*
un pequeño dolor de ignorante	*the small ache of an ignorant*
leopardo.	*leopard.*

In Cuba, Lorca wrote *El público* ("The Audience"), a complex, multifaceted play, expressionist in technique, that brashly explores the nature of homosexual passion. Lorca deemed the work, which remained unproduced until 1978, "a poem to be hissed." On his return to Spain, he completed a second play aimed at rupturing the bounds of conventional dramaturgy, *Así que pasen cinco años* (1931; *Once Five Years Pass*), and he assumed the directorship of a traveling student theatre group, La Barraca (the name of makeshift wooden stalls housing puppet shows and popular fairs in Spain), sponsored by the country's progressive new Republican government.

With the 1933 premiere of his first Andalusian tragedy, *Blood Wedding*, an expressionist work that recalls ancient Greek, Renaissance, and Baroque sources, Lorca achieved his first major theatrical success and helped inaugurate the most brilliant era of Spanish theatre since the Golden Age. In 1933–34 he went to Buenos Aires, Argentina, to oversee several productions of his plays and to give a lecture series. While there he befriended the Chilean poet Pablo Neruda, with whom he collaborated on a tribute to Rubén Darío. Despite his new focus on theatre, Lorca continued to write poetry. With others in the Generation of 1927, he embraced a "rehumanization" of poetry, as opposed to the "dehumanization" José Ortega y Gasset had described in his 1925 essay "The Dehumanization of Art." Eloquent evidence of Lorca's return to the personal are *Divan del Tamarit* (written 1931–1934, published 1940; "The Divan at Tamarit"), a set of love poems inspired by Arabic verse forms; *Seis poemas galegos* (written 1932–1934, published 1935; "Six Galician Poems"); and *Sonetos del amor oscuro* (written 1935, published 1984; "Sonnets of Dark Love"), an 11-sonnet sequence recalling a failed love affair. The three collections underscore Lorca's abiding insistence on the interdependence of love and death:

No hay nadie que, al dar un beso,
no sienta la sonrisa de la gente sin rostro,
ni hay nadie que, al tocar un recién nacido,
olvide las inmóviles calaveras de caballo. .

There is no one who can kiss without feeling the smile of those without faces;
there is no one who can touch an infant and forget the immobile skulls of horses.

In 1934 Lorca responded to the goring and death of a bullfighter friend with the majestic *Lament for a Bullfighter*, a work famous for its incantatory opening refrain, "A las cinco de la tarde" ("At five in the afternoon"). The four-part poem, his longest, confirms Lorca as the greatest of Spain's elegiac poets.

A las cinco de la tarde.
Eran las cinco en punto de la tarde.
Un niño trajo la blanca sábana a las cinco de la tarde.
Una espuerta de cal ya prevenidaa las cinco de la tarde.
Lo demás era muerte y sólo muerte a las cinco de la tarde.

At five in the afternoon.
It was exactly five in the afternoon.
A boy brought the white sheet at five in the afternoon.
A frail of lime ready preserved at five in the afternoon.
The rest was death, and death alone at five in the afternoon.

During the last two years of his life, Lorca premiered *Yerma* (1934), the second of his Andalusian tragedies, and completed a first draft of *The House of Bernarda Alba*, his third tragedy. Childhood events and personalities inform both *Bernarda Alba* and *Doña Rosita la soltera* (written 1934, premiered 1935; *Doña Rosita the Spinster*), the most Chekhovian of Lorca's plays, as well as *Doña Rosita*'s intended sequel, the unfinished *Los sueños de mi prima Aurelia* (1936; "The Dreams of My Cousin Aurelia"). In 1935 Lorca undertook his most overtly political play, *El sueño de la vida* ("The Dream of Life"), a technically innovative work based on recent events in Spain.

Lorca was at work on *Aurelia* and *Bernarda Alba* in the summer of 1936 when the Spanish Civil War broke out. On August 16, he was arrested in Granada by Nationalist forces, who abhorred his homosexuality and his liberal views, and imprisoned without a trial. On the night of August 18 or 19 (the precise date has never been verified), he was driven to a remote hillside outside town and shot. In 1986 the Spanish government marked the 50th anniversary of Lorca's death by erecting a monument on the site of his murder. The gesture bears witness to Lorca's stature as the most important Spanish poet and playwright of the 20th century, a man whose work continues to influence writers and artists throughout the world and to speak to readers everywhere of all that is most central to the human condition.

VLADIMIR NABOKOV

(b. April 22, 1899, St. Petersburg, Russia—d. July 2, 1977, Montreux, Switzerland)

Vladimir Vladimirovich Nabokov was born into an old aristocratic family. His father, V.D. Nabokov, was a leader of the pre-Revolutionary liberal Constitutional Democratic Party (Kadets) in Russia and was the author of numerous books and articles on criminal law and politics, among them *The Provisional Government* (1922), which was one of the primary sources on the downfall of the Aleksandr Kerensky regime. In 1922, after the family had settled in Berlin, the elder Nabokov was assassinated by a reactionary rightist while shielding another man at a public meeting; and although his novelist son disclaimed any influence of this event upon his art, the theme of assassination by mistake has figured prominently in Nabokov's novels. Nabokov's enormous affection for his father and for the milieu in which he was raised is evident in his autobiography *Speak, Memory* (revised version, 1967).

Nabokov published two collections of verse, *Poems* (1916) and *Two Paths* (1918), before leaving Russia in 1919. He and his family made their way to England, and he attended Trinity College, Cambridge, on a scholarship provided for the sons of prominent Russians in exile. While at Cambridge he first studied zoology but soon switched to French and Russian literature; he graduated with first-class honours in 1922 and subsequently wrote that his almost effortless attainment of this degree was "one of the very few 'utilitarian' sins on my conscience." While still in England he continued to write poetry, mainly in Russian but also in English, and two collections of his Russian poetry, *The Cluster* and *The Empyrean Path*, appeared in 1923. In Nabokov's mature opinion, these poems were "polished and sterile."

Between 1922 and 1940 Nabokov lived in Germany and France, and, while continuing to write poetry, he experimented with drama and even collaborated on several unproduced motion-picture scenarios. By 1925 he settled upon prose as his main genre. His first short story had already been published in Berlin in 1924. His first novel, *Mashenka* (*Mary*), appeared in 1926; it was avowedly autobiographical and contains descriptions of the young Nabokov's first serious romance as well as of the Nabokov family estate, both of which are also described in *Speak, Memory*. Nabokov did not again draw so heavily upon his personal experience as he had in *Mashenka* until his episodic novel about an émigré professor of entomology in the United States, *Pnin* (1957), which is to some extent based on his experiences while teaching (1948–58) Russian and European literature at Cornell University, Ithaca, New York.

His second novel, *King, Queen, Knave*, which appeared in 1928, marked his turn to a highly stylized form that characterized his art thereafter. His chess novel, *The Defense*, followed two years later and won him recognition as the best of the younger Russian émigré writers. In the next five years he produced four novels and a novella. Of these, *Despair* and *Invitation to a Beheading* were his first works of importance and foreshadowed his later fame.

During his years of European emigration, Nabokov lived in a state of happy and continual semipenury. All of his Russian novels were published in very small editions in Berlin and Paris. His first two novels had German translations, and the money he obtained for them he used for butterfly-hunting expeditions (he eventually published 18 scientific papers on entomology). But until his best-seller *Lolita*, no book he wrote in Russian or English produced more than a few hundred dollars. During the period in which he wrote his first eight novels, he made his living in Berlin and later in Paris by giving lessons in tennis, Russian, and English and from occasional walk-on parts in films (now forgotten). His wife, the former Véra Evseyevna Slonim, whom he married in 1925, worked as a translator. From the time of the loss of his home in Russia, Nabokov's only attachment was to what he termed the "unreal estate" of memory and art. He never purchased a house, preferring instead to live in houses rented from other professors on sabbatical leave. Even after great wealth came to him with the success of *Lolita* and the subsequent interest in his previous work, Nabokov and his family (he and his wife had one son, Dmitri) chose to live (from 1959) in genteelly shabby quarters in a Swiss hotel.

The subject matter of Nabokov's novels is principally the problem of art itself presented in various figurative disguises. Thus, *The Defense* seemingly is about chess, *Despair* about murder, and *Invitation to a Beheading* a political story, but all three works make statements about art that are central to understanding the book as a whole. The same may be said of his plays, *Sobytiye* ("The Event"), published in 1938, and *The Waltz Invention*. The problem of art again appears in Nabokov's best novel in Russian, *The Gift*, the story of a young artist's development in the spectral world of post-World War I Berlin. This novel, with its reliance on literary parody, was a turning point: serious use of parody thereafter became a key device in Nabokov's art. His first novels in English, *The Real Life of Sebastian Knight* (1941) and *Bend Sinister* (1947), do not rank with his best Russian work. *Pale Fire* (1962), however, a novel consisting of a long poem and a commentary on it by a mad literary pedant, extends and completes Nabokov's mastery of unorthodox structure, first shown in *The Gift* and present also in *Solus Rex*, a Russian novel that began to appear serially in 1940 but was never completed. *Lolita* (1955), with its antihero, Humbert Humbert, who is possessed by an overpowering desire for very young girls, is yet another of Nabokov's subtle allegories: love examined in the light of its seeming opposite, lechery. *Ada* (1969), Nabokov's 17th and longest novel, is a parody of the family chronicle form. All of his earlier themes come into play in the novel, and, because the work is a medley of Russian, French, and English, it is his most difficult work. (He also wrote a number of short stories and novellas, mostly written in Russian and translated into English.)

Nabokov's major critical works are an irreverent book about Nikolay Gogol (1944) and a monumental four-volume translation of, and commentary on, Pushkin's *Eugene*

Onegin (1964). What he called the "present, final version" of the autobiographical *Speak, Memory*, concerning his European years, was published in 1967, after which he began work on a sequel, *Speak On, Memory*, concerning the American years.

As Nabokov's reputation grew in the 1930s so did the ferocity of the attacks made upon him. His idiosyncratic, somewhat aloof style and unusual novelistic concerns were interpreted as snobbery by his detractors—although his best Russian critic, Vladislav Khodasevich, insisted that Nabokov's aristocratic view was appropriate to his subject matters: problems of art masked by allegory.

Nabokov's reputation varies greatly from country to country. Until 1986 he was not published in the Soviet Union, not only because he was a "White Russian émigré" (he became a U.S. citizen in 1945) but also because he practiced "literary snobbism." Critics of strong social convictions in the West also generally hold him in low esteem. But within the intellectual émigré community in Paris and Berlin between 1919 and 1939, V. Sirin (the literary pseudonym used by Nabokov in those years) was credited with being "on a level with the most significant artists in contemporary European literature and occupying a place held by no one else in Russian literature." His reputation after 1940, when he changed from Russian to English after emigrating to the United States, mounted steadily until the 1970s, when he was acclaimed by a leading literary critic as "king over that battered mass society called contemporary fiction."

When Nabokov died in 1977, he left behind a stack of index cards filled with the text of what was to become his final novel, *The Original of Laura*. On his deathbed, he instructed his wife, Véra, to burn the unfinished work. She instead placed it in a Swiss bank vault, where it remained the object of much speculation for three decades. With

Véra's death in 1991, responsibility for the final work fell to the Nabokovs' son, Dmitri. In 2008 he announced his decision to allow its publication. *The Original of Laura*, which the younger Nabokov referred to as "the most concentrated distillation" of his father's creativity, was released in 2009. Though it proved to be in a highly incomplete state, the text was nevertheless marked by Nabokov's celebrated facility with allusion and wordplay. The story revolves around an obese intellectual, Philip, and his young, wild wife, Flora, who is the seeming subject of a scandalous novel written by one of her former lovers. The work also offers a view of Nabokov's final writings on the theme of mortality, as Philip courts his own end via an act of "auto-dissolution," a kind of willed erasure.

ELIZABETH BOWEN

(b. June 7, 1899, Dublin, Ireland—d. February 22, 1973, London, England)

The British novelist and short-story writer Elizabeth Dorothea Cole Bowen employed a finely wrought prose style in fictions frequently detailing uneasy and unfulfilling relationships among members of the upper-middle class. *The Death of the Heart* (1938), the title of one of her most highly praised novels, might have served for most of them.

Bowen was born of the Anglo-Irish gentry and spent her early childhood in Dublin, as related in her autobiographical fragment *Seven Winters* (1942), and at the family house she later inherited at Kildorrery, County Cork. The history of the house is recounted in *Bowen's Court* (1942), and it is the scene of her novel *The Last September* (1929), which takes place during the troubles that preceded Irish independence. When she was 7, her father suffered a mental illness, and she departed for England with her mother, who died when Elizabeth was 12. An only child, she lived with relatives on the Kentish coast.

With a little money that enabled her to live independently in London and to winter in Italy, Bowen began writing short stories at 20. Her first collection, *Encounters*, appeared in 1923. It was followed in 1927 by *The Hotel*, which contains a typical Bowen heroine—a girl attempting to cope with a life for which she is unprepared. *The Last September* (1929) is an autumnal picture of the Anglo-Irish gentry. *The House in Paris* (1935), another of Bowen's highly praised novels, is a story of love and betrayal told partly through the eyes of two children.

During World War II, Bowen worked for the Ministry of Information in London and served as an air raid warden. Her novel set in wartime London, *The Heat of the Day* (1949), is among her most significant works. The war also forms the basis for one of her collections of short stories, *The Demon Lover* (1945; U.S. title, *Ivy Gripped the Steps*). Her essays appear in *Collected Impressions* (1950) and *Afterthought* (1962). Bowen's last book, *Pictures and Conversations* (1975), is an introspective, partly autobiographical collection of essays and articles. *Love's Civil War: Elizabeth Bowen and Charles Ritchie: Letters and Diaries 1941–1973* (edited by Victoria Glendinning), a record of Bowen's lengthy affair with a Canadian diplomat, was published in 2009. The work, which features her letters and his diaries, provides insight into Bowen's sometimes tumultuous personal life.

KAWABATA YASUNARI

(b. June 11, 1899, Ōsaka, Japan—d. April 16, 1972, Zushi)

The sense of loneliness and preoccupation with death that permeates much of Kawabata Yasunari's mature writing possibly derives from the loneliness of his childhood (he was orphaned early and lost all near relatives while still in his youth). He graduated from Tokyo Imperial University in 1924 and made his entrance into the literary world with the semiautobiographical *Izu no odoriko* (1926; *The Izu Dancer*). It appeared in the journal *Bungei jidai* ("The Artistic Age"), which he founded with the writer Yokomitsu Riichi; this journal became the organ of the Neosensualist group with which Kawabata was early associated.

This school is said to have derived much of its aesthetic from European literary currents such as Dadaism and Expressionism. Their influence on Kawabata's novels may be seen in the abrupt transitions between separate brief, lyrical episodes; in imagery that is frequently startling in its mixture of incongruous impressions; and in his juxtaposition of the beautiful and the ugly. These same qualities, however, are present in Japanese prose of the 17th century and in the *renga* (linked verse) of the 15th century. It is to the latter that Kawabata's fiction seemed to draw nearer in later years.

There is a seeming formlessness about much of Kawabata's writing that is reminiscent of the fluid composition of *renga*. His best-known novel, *Yukiguni* (1948; *Snow Country*), the story of a forlorn country geisha, was begun in 1935. After several different endings were discarded, it was completed 12 years later, although the final version did not appear until 1948. *Sembazuru* (*Thousand Cranes*), a series of episodes centred on the tea ceremony, was begun in 1949 and never completed. These and *Yama no oto* (1949–54; *The Sound of the Mountain*) are considered to be his best novels. The later book focuses on the comfort an old man who cannot chide his own children gets from his daughter-in-law.

When in 1968 Kawabata accepted the Nobel Prize, he said that in his work he tried to beautify death and to seek harmony among man, nature, and emptiness. He committed suicide after the death of his friend Mishima Yukio.

E.B. WHITE

(b. July 11, 1899, Mount Vernon, New York, U.S.—d. October 1, 1985, North Brooklin, Maine)

Elwyn Brooks White graduated from Cornell University, Ithaca, New York, in 1921 and was a reporter and freelance writer before joining *The New Yorker* magazine as a writer and contributing editor in 1927. He married Katherine Sergeant Angell, *The New Yorker*'s first fiction editor, in 1929, and he remained with the weekly magazine for the rest of his career. White collaborated with James Thurber on *Is Sex Necessary?* (1929), a spoof of the then-current sex manuals. He also contributed a monthly column to *Harper's* (1938–43) magazine.

In 1941 White edited with his wife *A Subtreasury of American*

Charlotte's Web *by E.B. White, illustrated by Garth Williams.* PRNewsFoto/Nick Movies and Paramount Pictures/AP Images

Humor. His three books for children—*Stuart Little* (1945), *Charlotte's Web* (1952), and *The Trumpet of the Swan* (1970)—are considered classics. In 1959 he revised and published a book by the late William Strunk, Jr., *The Elements of Style*, which became a standard style manual for writing in English. Among White's other works is *Points of My Compass* (1962). *Letters of E.B. White*, edited by D.L. Guth, appeared in 1976, his collected essays in 1977, and *Poems and Sketches of E.B. White* in 1981. He was awarded a Pulitzer Prize special citation in 1978.

HART CRANE

(b. July 21, 1899, Garrettsville, Ohio, U.S.—d. April 27, 1932, at sea, Caribbean Sea)

American poet Harold Hart Crane celebrated the richness of life—including the life of the industrial age—in lyrics of visionary intensity. His most noted work, *The Bridge* (1930), was an attempt to create an epic myth of the American experience. As a coherent epic it has been deemed a failure, but many of its individual lyrics are judged to be among the best American poems of the 20th century.

Crane grew up in Cleveland, where his boyhood was disturbed by his parents' unhappy marriage, which culminated in divorce when he was 17. Emotionally ill at ease and self-destructive for the rest of his life, he was given to homosexual affairs and alcoholic bouts. He worked in a variety of jobs in New York City and Cleveland and, as his poetry began to be published in little magazines, eventually settled in New York in 1923. The clamourous vitality of urban life impressed him, and he attempted to deal with it in his poetry by insinuating into contemporary things a sense of continuity with an epic past.

His first published book was *White Buildings* (1926). It contains his long poem "For the Marriage of Faustus and Helen," which he wrote as an answer to what he considered to be the cultural pessimism of *The Waste Land,* by T.S. Eliot.

With financial assistance from his father and from the philanthropist Otto H. Kahn, Crane completed *The Bridge*. Inspired in part by the Brooklyn Bridge and standing for the creative power of man uniting the present and the past, the poem has 15 parts and is unified by a structure modeled after that of the symphony.

Crane was granted a Guggenheim Fellowship and went to Mexico City, where he planned to write another verse epic with a Mexican theme. The tensions of his life had become increasingly disturbing, however, and he did not write it, though he did write a good poem, "The Broken Tower" (1932), during his Mexican stay. On his way back to the United States he jumped from the ship into the Caribbean and was drowned.

His *Collected Poems* appeared in 1933 but was superseded in 1966 by *The Complete Poems and Selected Letters and Prose,* which incorporated some of his previously uncollected writings.

ERNEST HEMINGWAY

(b. July 21, 1899, Cicero [now in Oak Park], Illinois, U.S.—d. July 2, 1961, Ketchum, Idaho)

The first son of Clarence Edmonds Hemingway, a doctor, and Grace Hall Hemingway, Ernest Miller Hemingway was born in a suburb of Chicago. He was educated in the public schools and began to write in high school, where he was active and outstanding, but the parts of his boyhood that mattered most were summers spent with his family on Walloon Lake in upper Michigan.

Early Career

On graduation from high school in 1917, impatient for a less-sheltered environment, he did not enter college but went to Kansas City, where he was employed as a reporter for the *Star*. He was repeatedly rejected for military service because of a defective eye, but he managed to enter World War I as an ambulance driver for the American Red Cross. On July 8, 1918, not yet 19 years old, he was injured on the Austro-Italian front at Fossalta di Piave. Decorated for heroism and hospitalized in Milan, he fell in love with a Red Cross nurse, Agnes von Kurowsky, who declined to marry him. These were experiences he was never to forget.

After recuperating at home, Hemingway renewed his efforts at writing, for a while worked at odd jobs in

Chicago, and sailed for France as a foreign correspondent for the *Toronto Star*. Advised and encouraged by other American writers in Paris—F. Scott Fitzgerald, Gertrude Stein, Ezra Pound—he began to see his nonjournalistic work appear in print there, and in 1925 his first important book, a collection of stories called *In Our Time*, was published in New York City; it was originally released in Paris in 1924.

Ernest Hemingway's 1923 passport photo. **Ernest Hemingway Photograph Collection/John F. Kennedy Presidential Library**

In 1926 he published *The Sun Also Rises*, a novel with which he scored his first solid success. A pessimistic but sparkling book, it deals with a group of aimless expatriates in France and Spain—members of the postwar Lost Generation, a phrase that Hemingway scorned while making it famous. This work also introduced him to the limelight, which he both craved and resented for the rest of his life. Hemingway's *The Torrents of Spring*, a parody of the American writer Sherwood Anderson's book *Dark Laughter*, also appeared in 1926.

Paris

The writing of books occupied Hemingway for most of the postwar years. He remained based in Paris, but he traveled widely for the skiing, bullfighting, fishing, and hunting that by then had become part of his life and formed the background for much of his writing. His position as a master of short fiction had been advanced by *Men Without Women* in 1927 and thoroughly established with the stories in *Winner Take Nothing* in 1933. Among his finest stories are *The Killers, The Short Happy Life of Francis Macomber,* and *The Snows of Kilimanjaro.*

At least in the public view, however, the novel *A Farewell to Arms* (1929) overshadowed such works. Reaching back to his experience as a young soldier in Italy, Hemingway developed a grim but lyrical novel of great power, fusing love story with war story. While serving with the Italian ambulance service during World War I, the American lieutenant Frederic Henry falls in love with the English nurse Catherine Barkley, who tends him during his recuperation after being wounded. She becomes pregnant by him, but he must return to his post. Henry deserts during the Italians' disastrous retreat after the Battle of Caporetto, and the reunited couple flee Italy by crossing the border into Switzerland. There, however, Catherine and her baby die during childbirth, and Henry is left desolate at the loss of the great love of his life.

Spain

Hemingway's love of Spain and his passion for bullfighting resulted in *Death in the Afternoon* (1932), a learned study of a spectacle he saw more as tragic ceremony than as sport. Similarly, a safari he took in 1933–34 in the big-game region of Tanganyika resulted in *The Green Hills of Africa* (1935), an account of big-game hunting. Mostly for the fishing, he purchased a house in Key West, Florida, and bought his own fishing boat. A minor novel of 1937 called *To Have and Have Not* is about a Caribbean desperado and is set against a background of lower-class violence and upper-class decadence in Key West during the Great Depression.

By now Spain was in the midst of civil war. Still deeply attached to that country, Hemingway made four trips there, once more a correspondent. He raised money for the Republicans in their struggle against the Nationalists under General Francisco Franco, and he wrote a play called *The Fifth Column* (1938), which is set in besieged Madrid. As in many of his books, the protagonist of the play is based on the author. Following his last visit to the Spanish war, he purchased Finca Vigía ("Lookout Farm"), an unpretentious estate outside Havana, Cuba, and went to cover another war—the Japanese invasion of China.

The harvest of Hemingway's considerable experience of Spain in war and peace was the novel *For Whom the Bell Tolls* (1940), a substantial and impressive work that some critics consider his finest novel, in preference to *A Farewell to Arms*. It was also the most successful of all his books as measured in sales. Set during the Spanish Civil War, it tells of Robert Jordan, an American volunteer who is sent to join a guerrilla band behind the Nationalist lines in the Guadarrama Mountains. Most of the novel concerns Jordan's relations with the varied personalities of the band, including the girl Maria, with whom he falls in love. Through dialogue, flashbacks, and stories, Hemingway offers telling and vivid profiles of the Spanish character and unsparingly depicts the cruelty and inhumanity stirred up by the civil war. Jordan's mission is to blow up a strategic bridge near Segovia in order to aid a coming Republican attack, which he realizes is doomed to fail. In an atmosphere of impending disaster, he blows up the bridge but is wounded and makes his retreating comrades leave him behind, where he prepares a last-minute resistance to his Nationalist pursuers.

All of his life Hemingway was fascinated by war—in *A Farewell to Arms* he focused on its pointlessness, in *For Whom the Bell Tolls* on the comradeship it creates—and, as World War II progressed, he made his way to

London as a journalist. He flew several missions with the Royal Air Force and crossed the English Channel with American troops on D-Day (June 6, 1944). Attaching himself to the 22nd Regiment of the 4th Infantry Division, he saw a good deal of action in Normandy and in the Battle of the Bulge. He also participated in the

Ernest Hemingway with dead water buffalo, on safari in Kenya, 1953. Ernest Hemingway Photograph Collection/John F. Kennedy Presidential Library

liberation of Paris, and, although ostensibly a journalist, he impressed professional soldiers not only as a man of courage in battle but also as a real expert in military matters, guerrilla activities, and intelligence collection.

Cuba

Following the war in Europe, Hemingway returned to his home in Cuba and began to work seriously again. He also traveled widely, and, on a trip to Africa, he was injured in a plane crash. Soon after (in 1953), he received the Pulitzer Prize in fiction for *The Old Man and the Sea* (1952), a short heroic novel about an old Cuban fisherman who, after an extended struggle, hooks and boats a giant marlin only to have it eaten by voracious sharks during the long voyage home. This book, which played a role in gaining for Hemingway the Nobel Prize for Literature in 1954, was as enthusiastically praised as his previous novel, *Across the River and into the Trees* (1950), the story of a professional army officer who dies while on leave in Venice, had been damned.

By 1960 Fidel Castro's revolution had driven Hemingway from Cuba. He settled in Ketchum, Idaho, and tried to lead his life and do his work as before. For a while he succeeded, but, anxiety-ridden and depressed, he was twice hospitalized at the Mayo Clinic in Rochester, Minn., where he received electroshock treatments. Two days after his return to the house in Ketchum, he took his life with a shotgun. Hemingway had married four times and fathered three sons.

Hemingway left behind a substantial amount of manuscript, some of which has been published. *A Moveable Feast*, an entertaining memoir of his years in Paris (1921–26) before he was famous, was issued in 1964. *Islands in the Stream*, three closely related novellas growing directly out of his peacetime memories of the Caribbean island of Bimini, of Havana during World War II, and of searching for U-boats off Cuba, appeared in 1970.

Assessment

Hemingway's characters plainly embody his own values and view of life. The main characters of *The Sun Also Rises*, *A Farewell to Arms*, and *For Whom the Bell Tolls* are young men whose strength and self-confidence nevertheless coexist with a sensitivity that leaves them deeply scarred by their wartime experiences. War was for Hemingway a potent symbol of the world, which he viewed as complex, filled with moral ambiguities, and offering almost unavoidable pain, hurt, and destruction. To survive in such a world, and perhaps emerge victorious, one must conduct oneself with honour, courage, endurance, and dignity, a set of principles known as "the Hemingway code." To behave well in the lonely, losing battle with life is to show "grace under pressure" and constitutes in itself a kind of victory, a theme clearly established in *The Old Man and the Sea*.

Hemingway's prose style was probably the most widely imitated of any in the 20th century. He wished to strip his own use of language of inessentials, ridding it of all traces of verbosity, embellishment, and sentimentality. In striving to be as objective and honest as possible, Hemingway hit upon the device of describing a series of actions by using short, simple sentences from which all comment or emotional rhetoric has been eliminated. These sentences are composed largely of nouns and verbs, have few adjectives and adverbs, and rely on repetition and rhythm for much of their effect. The resulting terse, concentrated prose is concrete and unemotional yet is often resonant and capable of conveying great irony through understatement. Hemingway's use of dialogue was similarly fresh, simple, and natural-sounding. The influence of this style was felt worldwide wherever novels were written, particularly from the 1930s through the '50s.

A consummately contradictory man, Hemingway achieved a fame surpassed by few, if any, American authors of the 20th century. The virile nature of his writing, which attempted to re-create the exact physical sensations he experienced in wartime, big-game hunting, and bull-fighting, in fact masked an aesthetic sensibility of great delicacy. He was a celebrity long before he reached middle age, but his popularity continues to be validated by serious critical opinion.

*J*ORGE *L*UIS *B*ORGES

(b. August 24, 1899, Buenos Aires, Argentina—d. June 14, 1986, Geneva, Switzerland)

Borges was reared in the then-shabby Palermo district of Buenos Aires, the setting of some of his works. His family, which had been notable in Argentine history, included British ancestry, and he learned English before Spanish. The first books that he read—from the library of his father, a man of wide-ranging intellect who taught at an English school—included *The Adventures of Huckleberry Finn*, the novels of H.G. Wells, *The Thousand and One Nights*, and *Don Quixote*, all in English. Under the constant stimulus and example of his father, the young Borges from his earliest years recognized that he was destined for a literary career.

The Writing Life

In 1914, on the eve of World War I, Borges was taken by his family to Geneva, where he learned French and German and received a B.A. from the Collège de Genève. Leaving there in 1919, the family spent a year on Majorca and a year in mainland Spain, where Borges joined the young writers of the Ultraist movement, a group that rebelled against what it considered the decadence of the established writers of the Generation of 1898.

Returning to Buenos Aires in 1921, Borges rediscovered his native city and began to sing of its beauty in poems that imaginatively reconstructed its past and present. His first published book was a volume of poems, *Fervor de Buenos Aires, poemas* (1923; "Fervour of Buenos Aires, Poems"). He is also credited with establishing the Ultraist movement in South America, though he later repudiated it. This period of his career, which included the authorship of several volumes of essays and poems and the founding of three literary journals, ended with a biography, *Evaristo Carriego* (1930).

During his next phase, Borges gradually overcame his shyness in creating pure fiction. At first he preferred to retell the lives of more or less infamous men, as in the sketches of his *Historia universal de la infamia* (1935; *A Universal History of Infamy*). To earn his living, he took a major post in 1938 at a Buenos Aires library named for one of his ancestors. He remained there for nine unhappy years.

In 1938, the year his father died, Borges suffered a severe head wound and subsequent blood poisoning, which left him near death, bereft of speech, and fearing for his sanity. This experience appears to have freed in him the deepest forces of creation. In the next eight years he produced his best fantastic stories, those later collected in *Ficciones* ("Fictions") and the volume of English translations titled *The Aleph and Other Stories, 1933–69*. During this time, he and another writer, Adolfo Bioy Casares, jointly wrote detective stories under the pseudonym H. Bustos Domecq (combining ancestral names of the two writers' families), which were published in 1942 as *Seis problemas para Don Isidro Parodi* (*Six Problems for Don Isidro Parodi*). The works of this period revealed for the first time Borges's entire dreamworld, an ironical or paradoxical version of the real one, with its own language and systems of symbols.

When the dictatorship of Juan Perón came to power in 1946, Borges was dismissed from his library position for having expressed support of the Allies in World War II. With the help of friends, he earned his way by lecturing, editing, and writing. A 1952 collection of essays, *Otras inquisiciones* (*1937–1952*) (*Other Inquisitions, 1937–1952*), revealed him at his analytic best. When Perón was deposed in 1955, Borges became director of the national library, an honorific position, and also professor of English and American literature at the University of Buenos Aires. By this time, Borges suffered from total blindness, a hereditary affliction that had also attacked his father and had progressively diminished his own eyesight from the 1920s onward. It had forced him to abandon the writing of long texts and to begin dictating to his mother or to secretaries or friends.

The works that date from this late period, such as *El hacedor* (1960; "The Doer," Eng. trans. *Dreamtigers*) and *El libro de los seres imaginarios* (1967; *The Book of Imaginary Beings*), almost erase the distinctions between the genres of prose and poetry. His later collections of stories include *El informe de Brodie* (1970; *Dr. Brodie's Report*), which deals with revenge, murder, and horror, and *El libro de arena* (1975; *The Book of Sand*), both of which are allegories combining the simplicity of a folk storyteller with the complex vision of a man who has explored the labyrinths of his own being to its core.

Assessment

After 1961, when he and Samuel Beckett shared the Formentor Prize, an international award given for unpublished manuscripts, Borges's tales and poems were increasingly acclaimed as classics of 20th-century world literature. Prior to that time, Borges was little known, even in his native Buenos Aires, except to other writers, many of whom regarded him merely as a craftsman of ingenious techniques and tricks. By the time of his death, the nightmare world of his "fictions" had come to be compared to the world of Franz Kafka and to be praised for concentrating common language into its most enduring form. Through his work, Latin American literature emerged from the academic realm into the realm of generally educated readers.

NATHALIE SARRAUTE

(b. July 18, 1900, Ivanova, Russia—d. October 19, 1999, Paris, France)

The French novelist and essayist Nathalie Sarraute, born Nathalie Ilyanova Tcherniak, was one of the earliest practitioners and a leading theorist of the *nouveau roman*, the French post-World War II "new novel," or "antinovel," a phrase applied by Jean-Paul Sartre to Sarraute's *Portrait d'un inconnu* (1947; *Portrait of a Man Unknown*). She was one of the most widely translated and discussed of the *nouveau roman* school. Her works reject the "admirable implements" forged by past realistic novelists such as Honoré de Balzac, particularly the use of biographical description to create full-bodied characters.

Sarraute was two years old when her parents were divorced, and her mother took her to Geneva and then to Paris. Except for brief visits to Russia and an extended stay in St. Petersburg (1908–10), she lived in Paris thereafter, and French was her first language. She attended the University of Oxford (1921) and graduated with a *licence* from the University of Paris, Sorbonne (1925). She was a member of the French bar, 1926–41, until she became a full-time writer.

Sarraute challenged the mystique of the traditional novel in her theoretical essay *L'Ère du soupçon* (1956; *The Age of Suspicion*) and experimented with technique in *Tropismes* (1939 and 1957; *Tropisms*), her first collection of sketches. In this work she introduced the notion of "tropisms," a term borrowed from botany and meaning elemental impulses alternately attracted and repelled by each other. Sarraute described these impulses as imperceptible motions at the origin of our attitudes and actions, and forming the substrata of such feelings as envy, love, hate, or hope. Within this aggregate of minute stirrings, Sarraute portrays a tyrannical father pushing his aging daughter into marriage (*Portrait d'un inconnu*), an elderly lady enamoured of furniture (*Le Planétarium,* 1959; *The Planetarium*), and a literary coterie reacting to a newly published novel (*Les Fruits d'or,* 1963; *The Golden Fruits*). Later works include *Elle est là* (1978; "She Is There"), *L'Usage de la parole* (1980; "The Usage of Speech"), and an autobiography, *Enfance* (1983; *Childhood*).

THOMAS WOLFE

(b. October 3, 1900, Asheville, North Carolina, U.S.—
d. September 15, 1938, Baltimore, Maryland)

Thomas Clayton Wolfe's father, William Oliver Wolfe, the model for Oliver Gant of his novels, was a stonecutter, while his mother, Julia Elizabeth Westall Wolfe, the Eliza of the early novels, owned a successful boardinghouse in Asheville, North Carolina, where Wolfe grew up. He was educated privately and in 1916 entered the University of North Carolina, where he wrote and acted in several one-act plays. In 1920 he enrolled in George Pierce Baker's 47 Workshop at Harvard University, intending to become a playwright. Several of his plays were produced at Harvard, including *Welcome to Our City* (1923), in which the town of Altamont (Asheville) first appeared.

In 1923 Wolfe left Harvard for New York City, where he resided for the rest of his life. Still intending to be a playwright, he taught at Washington Square College of New York University. In 1926, while abroad, he began work on what eventually became *Look Homeward, Angel*, in which he recounted the growth of an autobiographical protagonist, Eugene Gant, in the mountain town of Altamont. The book was a success, though its publication caused a great furor in Asheville.

During the late 1920s Wolfe entered into a relationship with the theatrical designer Aline Bernstein, who appeared as Esther Jack in his last two novels and who wrote of their friendship in the novel *The Journey Down* (1938). After the publication of *Look Homeward, Angel*, Wolfe quit teaching to write full-time. His second novel,

Of Time and the River (1935), takes up the story of Eugene Gant from his leaving home to attend Harvard until his meeting with Esther Jack. Wolfe's memoir of his life in the 1930s, *The Story of a Novel* (1936), describes his close working relationship with the editor Maxwell Perkins, who helped him reduce the enormous manuscripts of his first two works down to manageable novelistic proportions.

Wolfe did not publish another novel during his lifetime, though at his death he left a prodigious quantity of manuscript, from which the editor Edward Aswell extracted two more novels, *The Web and the Rock* (1939) and *You Can't Go Home Again* (1940). These books depict the struggles of a young writer to become established in New York City and his first experiences with literary fame. A collection of Wolfe's shorter pieces and chapters of an uncompleted novel, *The Hills Beyond* (1941), and his *Letters to His Mother* (1943) were also published, as well as his *Selected Letters* (1956).

Wolfe was gifted with the faculty of almost total recall, and his fiction is characterized by an intense consciousness of scene and place, together with what is often an extraordinary lyric power. In *Look Homeward, Angel* and *Of Time and the River*, Wolfe was able to imbue his life story and the figures of his parents with a lofty romantic quality that has epic and mythopoeic overtones. Powerful emotional evocation and literal reporting are combined in his fiction, and he often alternates between dramatically effective episodes of recollection and highly charged passages of rhetoric. Though *The Web and the Rock* and *You Can't Go Home Again* contain episodes of great vividness, they are too often uncontrolled in their form and fail to sustain the epic tone of *Look Homeward, Angel*, which has become an American classic.

Langston Hughes posing in front of his home in Harlem. Hughes was a significant voice during the Harlem Renaissance, one of the most important cultural movements in African American history. Robert W. Kelley/Time & Life Pictures/Getty Images

*L*ANGSTON *H*UGHES

(b. February 1, 1902, Joplin, Missouri, U.S.—d. May 22, 1967, New
York, New York)

The black poet and writer James Mercer Langston
Hughes became, through numerous translations, one
of the foremost interpreters to the world of the black experience in the United States. Hughes's parents separated
soon after his birth, and young Hughes was raised by his
mother and grandmother. After his grandmother's death,
he and his mother moved to half a dozen cities before
reaching Cleveland, where they settled. His poem *The
Negro Speaks of Rivers,* written the summer after his graduation from high school in Cleveland, was published in *The
Crisis* (1921) and brought him considerable attention.

After attending Columbia University (1921–22), he
explored Harlem, forming a permanent attachment to
what he called the "great dark city." He also worked as a
steward on a freighter bound for Africa. Back from sea-
faring and sojourning in Europe, he won an *Opportunity*
magazine poetry prize in 1925. He received the Witter
Bynner Undergraduate Poetry Award in 1926.

While working as a busboy in a hotel in Washington,
D.C., Hughes put three of his own poems beside the plate
of Vachel Lindsay in the dining room. The next day, newspapers around the country reported that Lindsay had
discovered an African American busboy poet. A scholarship to Lincoln University in Pennsylvania followed, and
before Hughes received his degree in 1929, his first two
books had been published.

The Weary Blues (1926) was warmly received. *Fine Clothes
to the Jew* (1927) was criticized harshly for its title and for
its frankness, but Hughes himself felt it represented a

step forward. A few months after graduation *Not Without Laughter* (1930), his first prose work, had a cordial reception. In the '30s his poetry became preoccupied with political militancy; he traveled widely in the Soviet Union, Haiti, and Japan and served as a newspaper correspondent (1937) in the Spanish Civil War. He published a collection of short stories, *The Ways of White Folks* (1934), and *The Big Sea* (1940), his autobiography up to age 28.

Hughes wrote *A Pictorial History of the Negro in America* (1956), and the anthologies *The Poetry of the Negro* (1949) and *The Book of Negro Folklore* (1958; with Arna Bontemps). He also wrote numerous works for the stage, including the lyrics for *Street Scene*, an opera with music by Kurt Weill. A posthumous book of poems, *The Panther and the Lash* (1967), reflected the black anger and militancy of the 1960s. Hughes translated the poetry of Federico García Lorca and Gabriela Mistral. He was also widely known for his comic character Jesse B. Semple, familiarly called Simple, who appeared in Hughes's columns in the *Chicago Defender* and the *New York Post* and later in book form and on the stage. *The Collected Poems of Langston Hughes*, ed. by Arnold Rampersad and David Roessel, appeared in 1994.

JOHN STEINBECK

(b. February 27, 1902, Salinas, California, U.S.—d. December 20, 1968, New York, New York)

John Ernst Steinbeck attended Stanford University, Stanford, California, intermittently between 1920 and 1926 but did not take a degree. Before his books attained success, he spent considerable time supporting himself as a manual labourer while writing, and his experiences lent

Actors Henry Fonda (centre), *John Carradine* (right), *and John Qualen in a scene from a screen adaptation of John Steinbeck's novel,* The Grapes of Wrath. Henry Guttmann/Moviepix/Getty Images

authenticity to his depictions of the lives of the workers in his stories. He spent much of his life in Monterey county, California, which later was the setting of some of his fiction.

Steinbeck's first novel, *Cup of Gold* (1929), was followed by *The Pastures of Heaven* (1932) and *To a God Unknown* (1933), none of which were successful. He first achieved popularity with *Tortilla Flat* (1935), an affectionately told story of Mexican Americans. The mood of gentle humour turned to one of unrelenting grimness in his next novel, *In Dubious Battle* (1936), a classic account of a strike by agricultural labourers and a pair of Marxist labour organizers who engineer it. The novella *Of Mice and Men* (1937), which also appeared in play and film versions, is a tragic story about the strange, complex bond between two migrant labourers. *The Grapes of Wrath* (1939) summed up the bitterness of the Great Depression decade and aroused widespread sympathy for the plight of migratory farmworkers. The book won a Pulitzer Prize and a National Book Award and was made into a notable film in 1940. The novel is about the migration of a dispossessed family from the Oklahoma Dust Bowl to California and describes their subsequent exploitation by a ruthless system of agricultural economics.

After the best-selling success of *The Grapes of Wrath*, Steinbeck went to Mexico to collect marine life with the freelance biologist Edward F. Ricketts, and the two men collaborated in writing *Sea of Cortez* (1941), a study of the fauna of the Gulf of California. During World War II Steinbeck wrote some effective pieces of government propaganda, among them *The Moon Is Down* (1942), a novel of Norwegians under the Nazis, and he also served as a war correspondent. His immediate postwar work—*Cannery Row* (1945), *The Pearl* (1947), and *The Wayward Bus* (1947)— contained the familiar elements of his social criticism but were more relaxed in approach and sentimental in tone.

Steinbeck's later writings—which include *Travels with Charley: In Search of America* (1962), about Steinbeck's experiences as he drove across the United States—were interspersed with three conscientious attempts to reassert his stature as a major novelist: *Burning Bright* (1950), *East of Eden* (1952), and *The Winter of Our Discontent* (1961). In critical opinion, none equaled his earlier achievement. *East of Eden*, an ambitious epic about the moral relations between a California farmer and his two sons, was made into a film in 1955. Steinbeck himself wrote the scripts for the film versions of his stories *The Pearl* (1948) and *The Red Pony* (1949). Outstanding among the scripts he wrote directly for motion pictures were *Forgotten Village* (1941) and *Viva Zapata!* (1952).

Steinbeck's reputation rests mostly on the naturalistic novels with proletarian themes that he wrote in the 1930s. It is in these works that his building of rich symbolic structures and his attempts at conveying mythopoeic and archetypal qualities in his characters are most effective. Steinbeck received the Nobel Prize for Literature for 1962.

OGDEN NASH

(b. August 19, 1902, Rye, New York, U.S.—d. May 19, 1971, Baltimore, Maryland)

After a year at Harvard University (1920–21), Frederic Ogden Nash held a variety of jobs—advertising, teaching, editing, bond selling—before the success of his poetry enabled him to work full-time at it. He sold his first verse (1930) to *The New Yorker,* on whose editorial staff he was employed for a time. With the publication of his first collection, *Hard Lines* (1931), he began a 40-year career during which he produced 20 volumes of verse with such titles as *The Bad Parents' Garden of Verse* (1936), *I'm a Stranger Here Myself* (1938), and *Everyone but Thee and Me* (1962). Making his home in Baltimore, he also did considerable lecturing on tours throughout the United States. He wrote the lyrics for the musicals *One Touch of Venus* (1943) and *Two's Company* (1952), as well as several children's books.

His rhymes are jarringly off or disconcertingly exact, and his ragged stanzas vary from lines of one word to lines that meander the length of a paragraph, often interrupted by inapposite digressions. He said he learned his prosody from the unintentional blunders of the notoriously slipshod poet Julia A. Moore, the "Sweet Singer of Michigan," who was also parodied by Mark Twain in *Huckleberry Finn*.

CARLOS DRUMMOND DE ANDRADE

(b. October 31, 1902, Itabira, Brazil—d. August 17, 1987, Rio de Janeiro)

The poet, journalist, author of *crônicas* (a short fiction–essay genre widely cultivated in Brazil), and literary critic Carlos Drummond de Andrade is considered one of the most accomplished poets of modern Brazil and a major influence on mid-20th-century Brazilian poetry. His experiments with poetic form (including laying the foundation of what later developed into concrete poetry) and his often ironic treatment of realistic themes reflect his concern with the plight of modern man, especially Brazilian urban man, in his struggle for freedom and dignity.

After receiving his degree in pharmacy (1925), Andrade turned to poetry and joined the new group of Brazilian Modernists who were introducing colloquial language and unconventional syntax in their free-verse forms. He helped to found the literary magazine *A revista* ("Review") in 1925. The first of his numerous collections of poetry, *Alguma poesia* (1930; "Some Poetry"), demonstrates both his affinity with the Modernist movement and his own strong poetic personality.

Andrade voiced the frustrations of rural immigrants to anonymous and crushing urban centres and of bored middle-class city residents trapped in meaningless routines.

His *crônicas* reveal a special concern for children and the urban poor.

At the time of his retirement from a career of government service, in 1962, Andrade was director of the historical section of the National Historical and Artistic Heritage Service of Brazil. He was the author of approximately 15 volumes of poetry and a half dozen collections of *crônicas*. His best-known single poem is perhaps "José" (published in 1942 in *Poesias*), which depicts the boredom of an urban apartment dweller.

SHEN CONGWEN

(b. December 28, 1902, Fenghuang, Hunan province, China—d. May 10, 1988, Beijing)

Shen Congwen (Shen Ts'ung-wen), born Shen Yuehuan, was a member of the Miao ethnic minority. At age 16 he joined a regiment in Yuanling, where he spent the next few years adding to his scanty education and observing the border fighting and the lives of the local Miao people. These early experiences later became the subject matter of many of his successful stories. Shen arrived in Beijing in 1923, and, while there, he began attending classes at Peking University and writing intensely. He also became closely associated with the writer Ding Ling and her leftist companion Hu Yepin. The threesome moved to Shanghai in 1928 to begin a publishing venture, but both the venture and the friendship ultimately failed, and Shen began a teaching career. He continued to write fiction prolifically until 1949, producing a tremendous number of short stories, essays, and novellas of varying quality.

Shen was greatly influenced by the works of Western authors that he had read in translation; the influence was apparent in his loose, vernacular style. His techniques, however, were derived from both classical Chinese literature and Miao oral traditions. In stories such as "Xiaoxiao" (written 1929, revised and published 1935; filmed as *Xiangnu Xiaoxiao* in 1986), Shen examines rural values and practicality. Of Shen's longer works of fiction, *Biancheng* (1934; *The Border Town*; filmed 1984) is generally considered his best; in it he combines his doubts about modern civilization with an idealized view of the beauty of rural life. Collections of his stories published in English include *The Chinese Earth* (1947; reprinted 1982), *Recollections of West Hunan* (1992), and *Imperfect Paradise* (1995).

During the Sino-Japanese War (1937–45), Shen, out of economic necessity, taught Chinese literature at a number of universities. After the communists triumphed in 1949, the basically apolitical writer came under attack and suffered a breakdown from the pressure of "thought reform"; from that point on he produced no fiction. He managed a recovery by 1955 and was placed on the staff of the Palace Museum in Beijing, about which he wrote a work of nonfiction in 1957. He also became an authority on ancient Chinese costume. In the 1980s there was a revival of interest in his work. He is commonly considered the greatest lyric novelist in modern China.

GEORGE ORWELL

(b. 1903, Motihari, Bengal, India—d. January 21, 1950, London)

Born Eric Arthur Blair, Orwell never entirely abandoned his original name, but his first book (*Down and*

Out in Paris and London) appeared as the work of George Orwell (the surname he derived from the beautiful River Orwell in East Anglia). In time his nom de plume became so closely attached to him that few people but relatives knew his real name was Blair. The change in name corresponded to a profound shift in Orwell's life-style, in which he changed from a pillar of the British imperial establishment into a literary and political rebel.

He was born in Bengal, into the class of sahibs. His father was a minor British official in the Indian civil service; his mother, of French extraction, was the daughter of an unsuccessful teak merchant in Burma. Their attitudes were those of the "landless gentry," as Orwell later called lower-middle-class people whose pretensions to social status had little relation to their income. Orwell was thus brought up in an atmosphere of impoverished snobbery. After returning with his parents to England, he was sent in 1911 to a preparatory boarding school on the Sussex coast, where he was distinguished among the other boys by his poverty and his intellectual brilliance. He grew up a morose, withdrawn, eccentric boy, and he was later to tell of the miseries of those years in his posthumously published autobiographical essay, *Such, Such Were the Joys* (1953).

Orwell won scholarships to two of England's leading schools, Winchester and Eton, and chose the latter. He stayed from 1917 to 1921. Aldous Huxley was one of his masters, and it was at Eton that he published his first writing in college periodicals. Instead of accepting a scholarship to a university, Orwell decided to follow family tradition and, in 1922, went to Burma as assistant district superintendent in the Indian Imperial Police. He served in a number of country stations and at first appeared to be a model imperial servant. Yet from boyhood he had wanted to become a writer, and when he realized how much against their will the Burmese were ruled by the British, he felt increasingly ashamed of his role as a colonial police officer. Later he was to recount his experiences and his reactions to imperial rule in his novel *Burmese Days* and in two brilliant autobiographical sketches, "Shooting an Elephant" and "A Hanging," classics of expository prose.

In 1927 Orwell, on leave to England, decided not to return to Burma, and on January 1, 1928, he took the decisive step of resigning from the imperial police. Already in the autumn of 1927 he had started on a course of action that was to shape his character as a writer. Having felt guilty that the barriers of race and caste had prevented his mingling with the Burmese, he thought he could expiate some of his guilt by immersing himself in the life of the poor and outcast people of Europe. Donning ragged clothes, he went into the East End of London to live in cheap lodging houses among labourers and beggars; he spent a period in the slums of Paris and worked as a dishwasher in French hotels and restaurants; he tramped the roads of England with professional vagrants and joined the people of the London slums in their annual exodus to work in the Kentish hopfields.

These experiences gave Orwell the material for *Down and Out in Paris and London* (1933), in which actual incidents are rearranged into something like fiction. The book's publication in 1933 earned him some initial literary recognition. Orwell's first novel, *Burmese Days* (1934), established the pattern of his subsequent fiction in its portrayal of a sensitive, conscientious, and emotionally isolated individual who is at odds with an oppressive or dishonest social environment. The main character of *Burmese Days* is a minor administrator who seeks to escape from the dreary and narrow-minded chauvinism of his fellow British colonialists in Burma. His sympathies for the Burmese, however, end in an unforeseen personal tragedy. The protagonist of Orwell's next novel, *A Clergyman's Daughter* (1935), is an unhappy spinster who achieves a brief and accidental liberation in her experiences among some agricultural labourers. *Keep the Aspidistra Flying* (1936) is about a literarily inclined book-seller's assistant who despises the empty commercialism and materialism of middle-class life but who in the end is reconciled to bourgeois prosperity by his forced marriage to the girl he loves.

Orwell's revulsion against imperialism led not only to his personal rejection of the bourgeois life-style but to a political reorientation as well. Immediately after returning from Burma he called himself an anarchist and continued to do so for several years; during the 1930s, how-ever, he began to consider himself a socialist, though he was too libertarian in his thinking ever to take the further step—so common in the period—of declaring himself a communist.

Orwell's first socialist book was an original and unorthodox political treatise entitled *The Road to Wigan Pier* (1937). It begins by describing his experiences when he went to live among the destitute and unemployed min-ers of northern England, sharing and observing their lives; it ends in a series of sharp criticisms of existing socialist movements. It combines mordant reporting with a tone of generous anger that was to characterize Orwell's subse-quent writing.

By the time *The Road to Wigan Pier* was in print, Orwell was in Spain; he went to report on the Civil War there and stayed to join the Republican militia, serving on the Aragon and Teruel fronts and rising to the rank of second lieutenant. He was seriously wounded at Teruel, damage to his throat permanently affecting his voice and endow-ing his speech with a strange, compelling quietness. Later, in May 1937, after having fought in Barcelona against communists who were trying to suppress their political opponents, he was forced to flee Spain in fear of his life. The experience left him with a lifelong dread of communism, first expressed in the vivid account of his Spanish experiences, *Homage to Catalonia* (1938), which many consider one of his best books.

Returning to England, Orwell showed a paradoxically conservative strain in writing *Coming Up for Air* (1939), in which he uses the nostalgic recollections of a middle-aged man to examine the decency of a past England and express his fears about a future threatened by war and fascism. When war did come, Orwell was rejected for military service, and instead he headed the Indian service of the British Broadcasting Corporation (BBC). He left the BBC in 1943 and became literary editor of the *Tribune*, a left-wing socialist paper associated with the British Labour leader Aneurin Bevan. At this period Orwell was a prolific journalist, writing many newspaper articles and reviews, together with serious criticism, like his classic essays on Charles Dickens and on boys' weeklies and a number of books about England (notably *The Lion and the Unicorn*, 1941) that combined patriotic sentiment with the advocacy of a libertarian, decentralist socialism very much unlike that practiced by the British Labour Party.

In 1944 Orwell finished *Animal Farm,* a political fable based on the story of the Russian Revolution and its betrayal by Joseph Stalin. In this book a group of barnyard animals overthrow and chase off their exploitative human masters and set up an egalitarian society of their own. Eventually the animals' intelligent and power-loving leaders, the pigs, subvert the revolution and form a dictatorship whose bondage is even more oppressive and heartless than that of their former human masters. ("All animals are equal, but some animals are more equal than others.") At first Orwell had difficulty finding a publisher for this small masterpiece, but when it appeared in 1945 *Animal Farm* made him famous and, for the first time, prosperous.

Animal Farm was one of Orwell's finest works, full of wit and fantasy and admirably written. It has, however, been overshadowed by his last book, *Nineteen Eighty-four* (1949), a novel he wrote as a warning after years of brooding on the twin menaces of Nazism and Stalinism. The novel is set in an imaginary future in which the world is dominated by three perpetually warring totalitarian police states. The book's hero, the Englishman Winston Smith, is a minor party functionary in one of these states. His longing for truth and decency leads him to secretly rebel against the government, which perpetuates its rule by systematically distorting the truth and continuously rewriting history to suit its own purposes. Smith has a love affair with a like-minded woman, but then they are both arrested by the Thought Police. The ensuing imprisonment, torture, and reeducation of Smith are intended not merely to break him physically or make him submit but to root out his independent mental existence and his spiritual dignity until he can love only the figure he previously most hated: the apparent leader of the party, Big Brother. Smith's surrender to the monstrous brainwashing techniques of his jailers is tragic enough, but the novel gains much of its power from the comprehensive rigour with which it extends the premises of totalitarianism to their logical end: the love of power and domination over others has acquired its perfected expression in the perpetual surveillance and omnipresent dishonesty of an unassailable and irresistible police state under whose rule every human virtue is slowly being suborned and extinguished. Orwell's warning of the potential dangers of totalitarianism made a deep impression on his contemporaries and upon subsequent readers, and the book's title and many of its coined words and phrases ("Big Brother is watching you," "newspeak," "doublethink") became bywords for modern political abuses.

Orwell wrote the last pages of *Nineteen Eighty-four* in a remote house on the Hebridean island of Jura, which he had bought from the proceeds of *Animal Farm*. He worked between bouts of hospitalization for tuberculosis, of which he died in a London hospital in January 1950.

GEORGES SIMENON

(b. February 13, 1903, Liège, Belgium—d. September 4, 1989, Lausanne, Switzerland)

Belgian-French novelist Georges-Joseph-Christian Simenon was perhaps the most widely published author of the 20th century. He began working on a local newspaper at age 16, and at 19 he went to Paris determined to be a successful writer. Typing some 80 pages each day, he wrote, between 1923 and 1933, more than 200 books of pulp fiction under 16 different pseudonyms, the sales of which soon made him a millionaire. The first novel to appear under his own name was *Pietr-le-Letton* (1929; *The Strange Case of Peter the Lett*), in which he introduced the imperturbable, pipe-smoking Parisian police inspector Jules Maigret to fiction. Simenon went on to write 83 more detective novels featuring Inspector Maigret, as well as 136 psychological novels. His total literary output consisted of about 425 books that were translated into some 50 languages and sold more than 600 million copies worldwide. Many of his works were the basis of feature films or made-for-television movies. In addition to novels, he wrote three autobiographical works—*Pedigrée* (1948),

Quand j'étais vieux (1970; *When I Was Old*), and *Mémoires intimes* (1981; *Intimate Memoirs*), the last after the suicide of his only daughter—and a critically well-received trilogy of novellas about Africa, selections of which were published in English as *African Trio* (1979).

Despite these other works, Simenon remains inextricably linked with Inspector Maigret, who is one of the best-known characters in detective fiction. Unlike those fictional detectives who rely on their immense deductive powers or on police procedure, Maigret solves murders using mainly his psychological intuition and a patiently sought, compassionate understanding of the perpetrator's motives and emotional composition. Simenon's central theme is the essential humanity of even the isolated, abnormal individual and the sorrow at the root of the human condition. Employing a style of rigorous simplicity, he evokes a prevailing atmosphere of neurotic tensions with sharp economy.

Simenon, who traveled to more than 30 countries, lived in the United States for more than a decade, starting in 1945. He later lived in France and Switzerland. At the age of 70 he stopped writing novels, though he continued to write nonfiction.

SADEQ HEDAYAT

(b. February 17, 1903, Tehrān, Iran—d. April 4, 1951, Paris, France)

The Iranian author Sadeq Hedayat (Sadiq Hidayat, or Ṣādeq-e Hedāyat) is responsible for having introduced Modernist techniques into Persian fiction. He is considered one of the greatest Iranian writers of the 20th century. Born into a prominent aristocratic family,

Hedayat was educated first in Tehrān and then studied dentistry and engineering in France and Belgium. After coming into contact with the leading intellectual figures of Europe, Hedayat abandoned his studies for literature.

He was intensely drawn to the works of Edgar Allan Poe, Guy de Maupassant, Rainer Maria Rilke, Franz Kafka, Anton Chekhov, and Fyodor Dostoyevsky. Hedayat translated into Persian many of Kafka's works, including *In the Penal Colony*, for which he wrote a revealing introduction called "Payām-e Kafka" ("Kafka's Message"). He returned to Iran in 1930 after four years and published his first book of short stories, *Zendeh be gūr* (1930; "Buried Alive"), and the first of three plays, *Parvīn dokhtar-e Sāsān* ("Parvin, Daughter of Sasan"). These he followed with the prose works *Sāyeh-ye Moghol* (1931; "Mongol Shadow") and *Sē qaṭreh-khūn* (1932; "Three Drops of Blood").

Hedayat was the central figure in Tehrān intellectual circles and belonged to the antimonarchical, anti-Islamic literary group known as the Four (which also included Buzurg 'Alavī). He began to develop a strong interest in Iranian folklore and published *Osāneh* (1931), a collection of popular songs, and *Nīrangestān* (1932). In these, Hedayat greatly enriched Persian prose and influenced younger writers through his use of folk expressions. He also wrote a number of critical articles and translated the works of leading European authors, Chekhov and Jean-Paul Sartre among them. He began to study history, beginning with the Sāsānian period (224–651) and the Pahlavi, or Middle Persian, language, and he used this study in later fiction. In 1936–37 he went to Bombay (now Mumbai) to live in the Parsi Zoroastrian community there, in order to further his knowledge of the ancient Iranian religion.

One of Hedayat's most famous novels, *Būf-e Kūr* (1937; *The Blind Owl*), is profoundly pessimistic and Kafkaesque. A deeply melancholy man, he lived with a vision of the absurdity of human existence and his inability to effect a change for the good in Iran. He withdrew from his friends and began to seek escape from his sense of futility in drugs and alcohol. In 1951, overwhelmed by despair, he left Tehrān and went to Paris, where he took his own life.

Among Hedayat's books published in English are *Haji Agha: Portrait of an Iranian Confidence Man* (1979), *Sadeq Hedayat: An Anthology* (1979; short stories), and *The Myth of Creation* (1998; drama).

Anaïs Nin

(b. February 21, 1903, Neuilly, France — d. January 14, 1977, Los Angeles, California, U.S.)

Brought to New York City by her mother in 1914, Anaïs Nin was educated there but later returned to Europe and studied psychoanalysis with Otto Rank. She launched her literary career with the publication of *D.H. Lawrence: An Unprofessional Study* (1932). The book led to a lifelong friendship with the American author Henry Miller.

At the beginning of World War II Nin returned to New York City. There she continued — at her own expense — to print and publish her novels and short stories, and, although no critical acclaim was forthcoming, her works were admired by many leading literary figures of the time. Not until 1966, with the appearance of the first of eight volumes of her diaries, did she win recognition as a writer of significance. The success of the diary provoked interest in her earlier work *Cities of the Interior* (1959), a five-volume roman-fleuve, or continuous novel, which consists of *Ladders to Fire* (1946), *Children of the Albatross* (1947), *The*

Four-Chambered Heart (1950), *A Spy in the House of Love* (1954), and *Solar Barque* (1958).

Nin's literary contribution was a subject of controversy in her lifetime and remained so after her death. Many critics admired her unique expression of femininity, her lyrical style, and her psychological insight. Some dismissed her concern with her own fulfillment as self-indulgent and narcissistic. Opinion was further divided by the posthumous *Delta of Venus: Erotica* (1977) and later collections of previously unpublished erotic stories written on commission during the financially lean years of the early 1940s. Her other works of fiction include a collection of short stories, *Under a Glass Bell* (1944); the novels *House of Incest* (1936), *Seduction of the Minotaur* (1961), and *Collages* (1964); and three novelettes collected in *Winter of Artifice* (1939).

MARGUERITE YOURCENAR

(b. June 8, 1903, Brussels, Belgium—d. December 17, 1987, Northeast Harbor, Mount Desert Island, Maine, U.S.)

Marguerite de Crayencour was educated at home in French Flanders and spent much of her early life traveling with her father. She began writing as a teenager and continued to do so after her father's death left her independently wealthy. She led a nomadic life until the outbreak of World War II, at which time she settled permanently in the United States. She became a naturalized U.S. citizen in 1947. The name "Yourcenar," which she used as her nom de plume, is an imperfect anagram of her original name, "Crayencour."

Yourcenar's literary works are notable for their rigorously classical style, their erudition, and their psychological subtlety. In her most important books she re-creates past eras and personages, meditating thereby on human destiny, morality, and power. Her masterpiece is *Mémoires d'Hadrien* (1951; *Memoirs of Hadrian*), a historical novel constituting the fictionalized memoirs of that 2nd-century Roman emperor. Another historical novel is *L'Oeuvre au noir* (1968; *The Abyss*), an imaginary biography of a 16th-century alchemist and scholar. Among Yourcenar's other works are the short stories collected in *Nouvelles orientales* (1938; *Oriental Tales*), the prose poem *Feux* (1936; *Fires*), and the short novel *Le Coup de grâce* (1939; Eng. trans. *Coup de Grâce*). Her works were translated by the American Grace Frick, Yourcenar's secretary and life companion. Yourcenar wrote numerous essays and also translated African American spirituals and various English and American novels into French.

Membership in the Académie Française (incorporated 1635)—an exclusive literary institution with a membership limited to 40—requires French citizenship. Yourcenar had become a U.S. citizen, however, so the president of France granted her a special dual U.S.–French citizenship in 1979. In 1980 she became the first woman to be elected to the Académie.

EVELYN WAUGH

(b. October 28, 1903, London, England—d. April 10, 1966, Combe Florey, near Taunton, Somerset)

Evelyn Arthur St. John Waugh was educated at Lancing College, Sussex, and at Hertford College, Oxford. After short periods as an art student and schoolmaster, he devoted himself to solitary observant travel and to the writing of novels, soon earning a wide reputation for sardonic wit and technical brilliance. During World War II he served in the Royal Marines and the Royal Horse Guards; in 1944 he joined the British military mission to the Yugoslav Partisans. After the war he led a retired life in the west of England.

Waugh's novels, although their material is nearly always derived from firsthand experience, are unusually highly wrought and precisely written. Those written before 1939 may be described as satirical. The most noteworthy are *Decline and Fall* (1928), *Vile Bodies* (1930), *Black Mischief* (1932), *A Handful of Dust* (1934), and *Scoop* (1938). A later work in that vein is *The Loved One* (1948), a satire on the morticians' industry in California.

During the war Waugh's writing took a more serious and ambitious turn. In *Brideshead Revisited* (1945) he studied the workings of providence and the recovery of faith among the members of a Roman Catholic landed family. (Waugh was received into the Roman Catholic Church in 1930.) *Helena*, published in 1950, is a novel about the mother of Constantine the Great, in which Waugh re-created one moment in Christian history to assert a particular theological point. In a trilogy—*Men at Arms* (1952), *Officers and Gentlemen* (1955), and *Unconditional Surrender* (1961)— he analyzed the character of World War II, in particular its relationship with the eternal struggle between good and evil and the temporal struggle between civilization and barbarism.

Waugh also wrote travel books; lives of Dante Gabriel Rossetti (1928), Edmund Campion (1935), and Ronald Knox (1959); and the first part of an autobiography, *A Little Learning* (1964). *The Diaries of Evelyn Waugh*, edited by Michael Davie and first published in 1976, was reissued in 1995. A selection of Waugh's letters, edited by Mark Amory, was published in 1980.

THEODOR SEUSS GEISEL

(b. March 2, 1904, Springfield, Massachusetts, U.S.—d. September 24, 1991, La Jolla, California)

After undergraduate work at Dartmouth College, Hanover, New Hampshire, and postgraduate work at Lincoln College, Oxford, and at the Sorbonne, Theodor Seuss Geisel began working for *Life*, *Vanity Fair*, and other publications as an illustrator and humorist. After service in the army during World War II, Geisel went into advertising for a time, was made an editorial cartoonist for *PM* newspaper in New York City, and eventually in 1958 founded Beginner Books, Inc., which in 1960 became a division of Random House.

Geisel's books, most published under the pen name Dr. Seuss, were valued not only for their unique brand of humour but also for their contribution to the education of children. The books coined new nonsense words and animal characters that went far beyond the traditional primers. They include *And to Think That I Saw It on Mulberry Street* (1937), *Horton Hatches the Egg* (1940), *How the Grinch Stole Christmas* (1957), *The Cat in the Hat* (1957), *Green Eggs and Ham* (1960), and *The Lorax* (1971).

During World War II, Geisel made short films for the military effort, and, with his wife Helen Palmer Geisel, he wrote the Academy Award-winning documentary feature *Design for Death* (1947). His animated cartoon *Gerald McBoing-Boing* (1951) also won an Academy Award. He designed and produced animated cartoons for television, many of them based on his books, and in the 21st century several of his books were adapted as feature films. From 1948 until his death, Geisel lived in La Jolla, California, where he annually conducted a children's workshop at the La Jolla Museum of Art.

PABLO NERUDA

(b. July 12, 1904, Parral, Chile—d. September 23, 1973, Santiago)

Pablo Neruda, born Neftalí Ricardo Reyes Basoalto, was the son of José del Carmen Reyes, a railway worker, and Rosa Basoalto. His mother died within a month of Neruda's birth, and two years later the family moved to Temuco, a small town farther south in Chile, where his father remarried. Neruda was a precocious boy who began to write poetry at age 10. His father tried to discourage him from writing and never cared for his poems, which was probably why the young poet began to publish under the pseudonym Pablo Neruda, which he was legally to adopt in 1946. He entered the Temuco Boys' School in 1910 and finished his secondary schooling there in 1920. Tall, shy, and lonely, Neruda read voraciously and was encouraged by the principal of the Temuco Girls' School, Gabriela Mistral, a gifted poet who would, like her student, later become a Nobel laureate.

Early Publications

Neruda first published his poems in the local newspapers and later in magazines published in the Chilean capital, Santiago. In 1921 he moved to Santiago to continue his studies and become a French teacher. There he experienced loneliness and hunger and took up a bohemian lifestyle. His first book of poems, *Crepusculario*, was published in 1923. The poems, subtle and elegant, were in the

Pablo Neruda. Keystone/Hulton Archive/Getty Images

tradition of Symbolist poetry, or rather its Hispanic version, Modernismo.

His second book, *Veinte poemas de amor y una canción desesperada* (1924; *Twenty Love Poems and a Song of Despair*), was inspired by an unhappy love affair. It became an instant success and is still one of Neruda's most popular books. The verse in *Twenty Love Poems* is vigorous, poignant, and direct, yet subtle and very original in its imagery and metaphors. The poems express young, passionate, unhappy love perhaps better than any book of poetry in the long Romantic tradition.

The Experimental Poet as Diplomat

At age 20, with two books published, Neruda had already become one of the best-known Chilean poets. He abandoned his French studies and began to devote himself entirely to poetry. Three more books appeared in quick succession: *Tentativa del hombre infinito* (1926; "Attempt of the Infinite Man"); *Anillos* (1926; "Rings"), in collaboration with Tomás Lago; and *El hondero entusiasta* (1933; "The Enthusiastic Slingshooter"). Yet his poetry was not a steady source of income, so he translated hastily from several languages and published magazine and newspaper articles. Neruda's future looked uncertain without a steady job, so he managed to get himself appointed honorary consul to Rangoon in Burma (now Yangôn, Myanmar). For the next five years he represented his country in Asia. He continued to live in abject poverty, however, since as honorary consul he received no salary, and he was tormented by loneliness.

From Rangoon Neruda moved to Colombo in Ceylon (now Sri Lanka). He increasingly came to identify with the South Asian masses, who were heirs to ancient cultures but were downtrodden by poverty, colonial rule, and political oppression. It was during these years in Asia that he wrote *Residencia en la tierra, 1925–1931* (1933; *Residence on Earth*). In this book Neruda moves beyond the lucid, conventional lyricism of *Twenty Love Poems*, abandoning normal syntax, rhyme, and stanzaic organization to create a highly personalized poetic technique. His personal and collective anguish gives rise to nightmarish visions of disintegration, chaos, decay, and death that he recorded in a cryptic, difficult style inspired by Surrealism. These puzzling and mysterious poems both attract and repel the reader with the powerful and awe-inspiring vision they present of a modern descent into hell.

In 1930 Neruda was named consul in Batavia (modern Jakarta), which was then the capital of the Dutch East Indies (now Indonesia). There he fell in love with a Dutch woman, Maria Antonieta Hagenaar, and married her. In 1932 Neruda returned to Chile, but he still could not earn a living from his poetry. In 1933 he was appointed Chilean consul in Buenos Aires, Argentina. There he met the Spanish poet Federico García Lorca, who at that time was traveling in Argentina and who was to become a close friend and an enthusiastic defender of Neruda's poetry.

Communism and Poetry

In 1934 Neruda took up an appointment as consul in Barcelona, Spain, and soon he was transferred to the consulate in Madrid. His success there was instantaneous after García Lorca introduced him. Neruda's new friends, especially Rafael Alberti and Miguel Hernández, were involved in radical politics and the Communist Party. Neruda shared their political beliefs and moved ever closer to communism. In the meantime, his marriage was foundering. He and his wife separated in 1936, and Neruda met a young Argentine woman, Delia del Carril, who would be his second wife until their divorce in the early 1950s.

A second, enlarged edition of the *Residencia* poems entitled *Residencia en la tierra, 1925–35* was published in two volumes in 1935. In this edition, Neruda begins to move away from the highly personal, often hermetic poetry of the first *Residencia* volume, adopting a more extroverted outlook and a clearer, more accessible style in order to better communicate his new social concerns to the reader. This line of poetic development was interrupted suddenly by the outbreak of the Spanish Civil War in 1936, however. While García Lorca was executed by the Nationalists and Alberti and Hernández fought at the front, Neruda traveled in and out of Spain to gather money and mobilize support for the Republicans. He wrote *España en el corazón* (1937; *Spain in My Heart*) to express his feelings of solidarity with them. The book was printed by Republican troops working with improvised presses near the front lines.

In 1937 Neruda returned to Chile and entered his country's political life, giving lectures and poetry readings while also defending Republican Spain and Chile's new centre-left government. In 1939 he was appointed special consul in Paris, where he supervised the migration to Chile of many defeated Spanish Republicans who had escaped to France. In 1940 he took up a post as Chile's consul general in Mexico. He also began work on a long poem, *Canto general* (1950; "General Song," Eng. trans. *Canto general*), resonant with historical and epic overtones, that would become one of his key works. In 1943, during a trip to Peru, Neruda climbed to the ancient Inca city of Machu Picchu. The strong emotions aroused by the sight of this spectacular ruin inspired one of his finest poems, *Alturas de Macchu Picchu* (1943; *Heights of Macchu Picchu*). This powerful celebration of pre-Columbian civilization would become the centrepiece of *Canto general*.

In the meantime, Neruda suffered a stunning reversal in his native country. He had returned to Chile in 1943, was elected a senator in 1945, and also joined the Communist Party. He campaigned for the leftist candidate Gabriel González Videla in the elections of 1946, only to see President Videla turn to the right two years later. Feeling betrayed, Neruda published an open letter critical of Videla; as a consequence, he was expelled from the Senate and went into hiding to avoid arrest. In February 1948 he left Chile, crossing the Andes Mountains on horseback by night with the manuscript of *Canto general* in his saddlebag.

In exile Neruda visited the Soviet Union, Poland, Hungary, and Mexico. In Mexico he again met Matilde Urrutia, a Chilean woman whom he had first encountered in 1946. Their marriage would last until the end of his life, and she would inspire some of the most passionate Spanish love poems of the 20th century. The third volume of Neruda's *Residencia* cycle, *Tercera residencia, 1935–45* (1947; "Third Residence"), completed his rejection of egocentric angst and his open espousal of left-wing ideological concerns. His communist political beliefs receive their culminating expression in *Canto general*. This epic poem celebrates Latin America—its flora, its fauna, and its history, particularly the wars of liberation from Spanish rule and the continuing struggle of its peoples to obtain freedom and social justice. It also, however, celebrates Joseph Stalin, the bloody Soviet dictator in power at the time.

Later Years

In 1952 the political situation in Chile once again became favourable, and Neruda was able to return home. By that time his works had been translated into many languages. Rich and famous, he built a house on Isla Negra, facing the Pacific Ocean, and also maintained houses in Santiago and Valparaíso. While traveling in Europe, Cuba, and China, Neruda embarked upon a period of incessant writing and feverish creation. One of his major works, *Odas elementales* (*Elemental Odes*), was published in 1954. Its verse was written in a new poetic style—simple, direct, precise, and humorous—and it contained descriptions of everyday objects, situations, and beings (e.g., "Ode to the Onion" and "Ode to the Cat"). Many of the poems in *Odas elementales* have been widely anthologized. Neruda's poetic output during these years was stimulated by his international fame and personal happiness; 20 books of his appeared between 1958 and his death in 1973, and 8 more were published posthumously. In his memoirs, *Confieso que he vivido* (1974; *Memoirs*), Neruda summed up his life through reminiscences, comments, and anecdotes.

In 1969 Neruda campaigned for the leftist candidate Salvador Allende, who appointed him ambassador to France after being elected president of Chile. While already ill with cancer in France, Neruda in 1971 learned that he had been awarded the Nobel Prize for Literature. After traveling to Stockholm to receive his prize, he returned to Chile bedridden and terminally ill and survived by only a few days his friend Allende, who died in a right-wing military coup.

Assessment

Neruda's body of poetry is so rich and varied that it defies classification or easy summary. It developed along four main directions, however. His love poetry, such as the youthful *Twenty Love Poems* and the mature *Los versos del Capitán* (1952; *The Captain's Verses*), is tender, melancholy, sensuous, and passionate. In "material" poetry, such as *Residencia en la tierra*, loneliness and depression immerse the author in a subterranean world of dark, demonic forces. His epic poetry is best represented by *Canto general*, which is a Whitmanesque attempt at reinterpreting the past and present of Latin America and the struggle of its oppressed and downtrodden masses toward freedom. And finally there is Neruda's poetry of common, everyday objects, animals, and plants, as in *Odas elementales*.

These four trends correspond to four aspects of Neruda's personality: his passionate love life; the nightmares and depression he experienced while serving as a consul in Asia; his commitment to a political cause; and his ever-present attention to details of daily life, his love of things made or grown by human hands. Neruda was one of the most original and prolific poets to write in Spanish in the 20th century, but despite the variety of his output as a whole, each of his books has unity of style and purpose.

Neruda's work is collected in *Obras completas* (1973; 4th ed. expanded, 3 vol.). Most of his work is available in various English translations. Four essential works are *Twenty Love Poems and a Song of Despair*, trans. by W.S. Merwin (1969, reissued 1993); *Residence on Earth, and Other Poems*, trans. by Angel Flores (1946, reprinted 1976); *Canto general*, trans. by Jack Schmitt (1991); and *Elementary Odes of Pablo Neruda*, trans. by Carlos Lozano (1961).

ISAAC BASHEVIS SINGER

(b. July 14?, 1904, Radzymin, Poland, Russian Empire—d. July 24, 1991, Surfside, Florida, U.S.)

The birth date for Isaac Bashevis Singer (Yiddish: Yitskhok Bashevis Zinger) is uncertain and has been variously reported as July 14, November 21, and October 26. He came from a family of Hasidic rabbis on his father's side and a long line of Mitnagdic rabbis on his mother's side. He received a traditional Jewish education at the Warsaw Rabbinical Seminary. His older brother was the novelist I.J. Singer and his sister the writer Esther Kreytman (Kreitman). Like his brother, Singer preferred being a writer to being a rabbi. In 1925 he made his debut with the Yiddish-language story "Af der elter" ("In Old Age"), which he published in the Warsaw *Literarishe bleter* under a pseudonym. His first novel, *Der Sotn in Goray* (*Satan in Goray*), was published in installments in Poland shortly before he immigrated to the United States in 1935.

Settling in New York City, as his brother had done a year earlier, Singer worked for the Yiddish newspaper *Forverts* (*Jewish Daily Forward*), and as a journalist he signed his articles with the pseudonym Varshavski or D. Segal. He also translated many books into Yiddish from Hebrew, Polish, and, particularly, German, among them works by Thomas Mann and Erich Maria Remarque. In 1943 he became a U.S. citizen.

Although Singer's works became most widely known in their English versions, he continued to write almost exclusively in Yiddish, personally supervising the translations. The relationship between his works in these two languages is complex: some of his novels and short stories were published in Yiddish in the *Forverts*, for which he wrote until his death, and then appeared in book form only in English translation. Several, however, later also appeared in book form in the original Yiddish after the success of the English translation. Among his most important novels are *The Family Moskat* (1950; *Di familye Mushkat*, 1950), *The Magician of Lublin* (1960; *Der kuntsnmakher fun Lublin*, 1971), and *The Slave* (1962; *Der knekht*, 1967). *The Manor* (1967) and *The Estate* (1969) are based on *Der hoyf*, serialized in the *Forverts* in 1953–55. *Enemies: A Love Story* (1972; film 1989) was translated from *Sonim: di geshikhte fun a libe*, serialized in the *Forverts* in 1966. *Shosha*, derived from autobiographical material Singer published in the *Forverts* in the mid-1970s, appeared in English in 1978. *Der bal-tshuve* (1974) was published first in book form in Yiddish; it was later translated into English as *The Penitent* (1983). *Shadows on the Hudson*, translated into English and published posthumously in 1998, is a novel on a grand scale about Jewish refugees in New York in the late 1940s. The book had been serialized in the *Forverts* in the 1950s.

Singer's popular collections of short stories in English translation include *Gimpel the Fool, and Other Stories* (1957; *Gimpl tam, un andere dertseylungen*, 1963), *The Spinoza of Market Street* (1961), *Short Friday* (1964), *The Seance* (1968), *A Crown of Feathers* (1973; National Book Award), *Old Love* (1979), and *The Image, and Other Stories* (1985).

Singer evokes in his writings the vanished world of Polish Jewry as it existed before the Holocaust. His most ambitious novels—*The Family Moskat* and the continuous narrative spun out in *The Manor* and *The Estate*—have large casts of characters and extend over several generations. These books chronicle the changes in, and eventual breakup of, large Jewish families during the late 19th and early 20th centuries as their members are differently affected by the secularism and assimilationist opportunities of the modern era. Singer's shorter novels examine characters variously tempted by evil, such as the brilliant circus magician of *The Magician of Lublin*, the 17th-century Jewish villagers crazed by messianism in *Satan in Goray*, and the enslaved Jewish scholar in *The Slave*. His short stories are saturated with Jewish folklore, legends, and mysticism and display his incisive understanding of the weaknesses inherent in human nature. His works are remarkable for their rich blending of irony, wit, and wisdom, flavoured distinctively with the occult and the grotesque.

Schlemiel Went to Warsaw, and Other Stories (1968) is one of his best-known books for children. In 1966 he published *In My Father's Court*, based on the Yiddish *Mayn tatns besdn shtub* (1956), an autobiographical account of his childhood in Warsaw. This work received special praise from the Swedish Academy when Singer was awarded the Nobel Prize. *More Stories from My Father's Court*, published posthumously in 2000, includes childhood stories Singer had first published in the *Forverts* in the 1950s. His memoir *Love and Exile* appeared in 1984.

Several films have been adapted from Singer's works, including *The Magician of Lublin* (1979), based on his novel of the same name, and *Yentl* (1983), based on his story "Yentl" in *Mayses fun hintern oyvn* (1971; "Stories from Behind the Stove").

CHRISTOPHER ISHERWOOD

(b. August 26, 1904, High Lane, Cheshire, England—d. January 4, 1986, Santa Monica, California, U.S.)

Anglo-American novelist and playwright Christopher William Bradshaw-Isherwood is best known for his novels about Berlin in the early 1930s. After working as a secretary and a private tutor, Isherwood gained a measure of coterie recognition with his first two novels, *All the Conspirators* (1928) and *The Memorial* (1932). During the 1930s he collaborated with his friend the poet W.H. Auden on three verse dramas, including *The Ascent of F6* (1936). But it had been in 1929 that he found the theme that was to make him widely known. Between 1929 and 1933 he lived in Berlin, gaining an outsider's view of the simultaneous decay of the Weimar Republic and the rise of Nazism. His novels *Mr. Norris Changes Trains* (1935; *The Last of Mr. Norris*) and *Goodbye to Berlin* (1939), which were later published together as *The Berlin Stories*, established his reputation as an important writer and inspired the play *I Am a Camera* (1951; film 1955) and the musical *Cabaret* (1966; film 1972). These books are detached but humorous studies of dubious characters leading seedy expatriate lives in the German capital. In 1938 Isherwood published *Lions and Shadows*, an amusing and sensitive account of his early life and friendships while a student at the University of Cambridge.

The coming of World War II saw not merely a change of outlook in Isherwood's writing but also a permanent change of domicile. He immigrated to the United States in 1939 and settled in southern California, where he taught and wrote for Hollywood films. He was naturalized in 1946. It was also in 1939 that Isherwood turned to pacifism and the self-abnegation of Indian Vedanta, becoming a follower of Swami Prabhavananda. In the following decades, Isherwood produced several works on Vedanta and translations with Prabhavananda, including one of the *Bhagavadgita*.

Isherwood's postwar novels continued to demonstrate his personal style of fictional autobiography. *A Single Man* (1964; filmed 2009), a brief but highly regarded novel, presents a single day in the life of a lonely middle-aged homosexual. His avowedly autobiographical works include a self-revealing memoir of his parents, *Kathleen and Frank* (1971); a retrospective biography of himself in the 1930s, *Christopher and His Kind* (1977); and a study of his relationship with Prabhavananda and Vedanta, *My Guru and His Disciple* (1980). *Diaries: Volume One: 1939–1960* (1996) and *The Sixties: Diaries: 1960–1969* (2010) were published posthumously.

GRAHAM GREENE

(b. October 2, 1904, Berkhamsted, Hertfordshire, England—d. April
3, 1991, Vevey, Switzerland)

Henry Graham Greene's father was the headmaster
of Berkhamsted School, which Greene attended
for some years. After running away from school, he
was sent to London to a psychoanalyst in whose house
he lived while under treatment. He studied at Balliol
College, Oxford, and in 1926 he converted to Roman
Catholicism, partly through the influence of Vivien
Dayrell-Browning, whom he married in 1927. He moved
to London and worked for *The Times* as a copy editor
from 1926 to 1930. His first published work was a book of
verse, *Babbling April* (1925), and upon the modest success
of his first novel, *The Man Within* (1929; adapted as the
film *The Smugglers*, 1947), he quit *The Times* and worked
as a film critic and literary editor for *The Spectator* until
1940. He then traveled widely for much of the next three
decades as a freelance journalist, searching out locations
for his novels in the process.

Greene's first three novels are held to be of small
account. He began to come into his own with a thriller,
Stamboul Train (1932; also published as *Orient Express*),
which plays off various characters against each other as
they ride a train from the English Channel to Istanbul.
This was the first of a string of novels that he termed
"entertainments," works similar to thrillers in their spare,
tough language and their suspenseful, swiftly moving
plots, but possessing greater moral complexity and depth.
Stamboul Train was also the first of Greene's many novels to
be filmed (1934). It was followed by three more entertainments that were equally popular with the reading public:

A Gun for Sale (1936; also published as *This Gun for Hire*; films 1942 and, as *Short Cut to Hell*, 1957), *The Confidential Agent* (1939; film 1945), and *The Ministry of Fear* (1943; adapted as the film *Ministry of Fear*, 1945). A fifth entertainment, *The Third Man*, which was published in novel form in 1949, was originally a screenplay for a classic film directed by Carol Reed.

One of Greene's finest novels, *Brighton Rock* (1938; films 1947 and 2010), shares some elements with his entertainments—the protagonist is a hunted criminal roaming the underworld of an English sea resort—but explores the contrasting moral attitudes of its main characters with a new degree of intensity and emotional involvement. In this book, Greene contrasts a cheerful and warm-hearted humanist he obviously dislikes with a corrupt and violent teenage criminal whose tragic situation is intensified by a Roman Catholic upbringing. Greene's finest novel, *The Power and the Glory* (1940; also published as *The Labyrinthine Ways*; adapted as the film *The Fugitive*, 1947), has a more directly Catholic theme: the desperate wanderings of a priest who is hunted down in rural Mexico at a time when the church is outlawed there. The weak and alcoholic priest tries to fulfill his priestly duties despite the constant threat of death at the hands of a revolutionary government.

Greene worked for the Foreign Office during World War II and was stationed for a while at Freetown, Sierra Leone, the scene of another of his best-known novels, *The Heart of the Matter* (1948; film 1953). This book traces the decline of a kindhearted British colonial officer whose pity for his wife and mistress eventually leads him to commit suicide. *The End of the Affair* (1951; films 1955 and 1999) is narrated by an agnostic in love with a woman who forsakes him because of a religious conviction that brings her near to sainthood.

Greene's next four novels were each set in a different Third World nation on the brink of political upheaval. The protagonist of *A Burnt-Out Case* (1961) is a Roman Catholic architect tired of adulation who meets a tragic end in the Belgian Congo shortly before that colony reaches independence. *The Quiet American* (1956; films 1958 and 2002) chronicles the doings of a well-intentioned American government agent in Vietnam in the midst of the anti-French uprising there in the early 1950s. *Our Man in Havana* (1958; film 1959) is set in Cuba just before the communist revolution there, while *The Comedians* (1966; film 1967) is set in Haiti during the rule of François Duvalier. Greene's last four novels, *The Honorary Consul* (1973; adapted as the film *Beyond the Limit*, 1983), *The Human Factor* (1978; film 1979), *Monsignor Quixote* (1982), and *The Tenth Man* (1985), represent a decline from the level of his best fiction.

The world Greene's characters inhabit is a fallen one, and the tone of his works emphasizes the presence of evil as a palpable force. His novels display a consistent preoccupation with sin and moral failure acted out in seedy locales characterized by danger, violence, and physical decay. Greene's chief concern is the moral and spiritual struggles within individuals, but the larger political and social settings of his novels give such conflicts an enhanced resonance. His early novels depict a shabby Depression-stricken Europe sliding toward fascism and war, while many of his subsequent novels are set in remote locales undergoing wars, revolutions, or other political upheavals.

Despite the downbeat tone of much of his subject matter, Greene was in fact one of the most widely read British novelists of the 20th century. His books' unusual popularity is due partly to his production of thrillers featuring crime and intrigue but more importantly to his superb gifts as a storyteller, especially his masterful selection of detail and his use of realistic dialogue in a fast-paced narrative.

Throughout his career, Greene was fascinated by film, and he often emulated cinematic techniques in his writing. No other British writer of this period was as aware as Greene of the power and influence of cinema.

Greene published several collections of short stories, among them *Nineteen Stories* (1947; revised as *Twenty-one Stories*, 1954). Among his plays are *The Living Room* (performed 1952) and *The Potting Shed* (1957). His *Collected Essays* appeared in 1969. *A Sort of Life* (1971) is a memoir to 1931, to which *Ways of Escape* (1980) is a sequel. A collection of his film criticism is available in *Mornings in the Dark: The Graham Greene Film Reader* (1993). In 2007 a selection of his letters was published as *Graham Greene: A Life in Letters*. The unfinished manuscript *The Empty Chair*, a murder mystery that Greene began writing in 1926, was discovered in 2008; serialization of it began the following year.

DING LING

(b. October 12, 1904, Anfu [now Linli], Hunan province, China—d. March 4, 1986, Beijing)

Jiang Wei, who would become the popular writer Ding Ling (Ting Ling), was brought up in a school founded by her mother after her father's death in 1911. She was deeply affected by her mother's independence and anti-traditionalist views. At the beginning of 1922, Jiang Wei left Hunan for Shanghai, Nanjing, and Beijing, more to observe the intellectual life there than to study. During that period she developed an interest in anarchism. After a stint at Shanghai University, she went to Beijing, where in 1925 she met and fell in love with the leftist would-be poet Hu Yepin. With him she moved to the Western Hills outside Beijing.

Influenced by contemporary Chinese literary works and foreign literary masterpieces such as Gustave Flaubert's *Madame Bovary* and other European novels, Ding Ling began writing partly autobiographical short stories in which she developed a new kind of Chinese heroine—daring, independent, and passionate, yet perplexed and emotionally unfulfilled in her search for the meaning of life. Her chronicles of the aspirations and disappointments of modern Chinese women were an immediate success, but, because Hu Yepin was making little progress in his literary career, the couple moved to Shanghai in 1928 to start a literary magazine as a vehicle to publish his work. The venture failed, and Hu Yepin turned his attention to politics, joining the League of Left-Wing Writers. Ding Ling, however, devoted herself to writing, and by 1930 she had completed three collections of short stories and a novelette. Later that year she gave birth to a son and joined the League of Left-Wing Writers. Hu Yepin joined the Chinese Communist Party and became even more involved in politics. He was arrested by Nationalist authorities and executed in 1931. During those years Ding Ling's work shifted to reflect the lives of workers, peasants, and revolutionaries, in which sentimentalism was replaced by revolutionary passion. She held a leading position in the League of Left-Wing Writers after she joined the Communist Party in 1932.

Ding Ling's conversion to Marxism channeled her writing into a new and initially fruitful direction. Her proletarian-oriented *Shui* (1931; "Flood") was acclaimed as a model of Socialist Realism in China. She was abducted by agents of the Nationalist Party in 1933 and imprisoned until 1936, when, disguised as a soldier, she escaped and joined the communists at Yan'an. There she became friendly with Communist Party leader Mao Zedong and was linked romantically with the general Peng Dehuai. She was not completely uncritical of the communist movement, expressing her dissatisfactions openly through her stories and in journal articles. For her stories "Zai yiyuan zhong" ("In the Hospital") and "Ye" ("Night") she was censured by the authorities.

Ding Ling's officially successful proletarian novel *Taiyang zhao zai Sangganhe shang* (1948; *The Sun Shines over the Sanggan River*) was the first Chinese novel to win the Soviet Union's Stalin Prize (1951). Yet despite her triumphs, she remained in political trouble for her open criticisms of the party, especially in regard to women's rights. She was officially censured and expelled from the party as a rightist in 1957 and was imprisoned for five years during the Cultural Revolution. In 1975 she was freed, and her membership in the Communist Party was restored in 1979. Her later publications include several critical essays, short stories, and longer fictional prose. Selections of her work were published in English as *Miss Sophie's Diary and Other Stories* (1985) and *I Myself Am a Woman* (1989).

ROBERT PENN WARREN

(b. April 24, 1905, Guthrie, Kentucky, U.S.—d. September 15, 1989, Stratton, Vermont)

The American novelist, poet, critic, and teacher Robert Penn Warren was best known for his treatment of moral dilemmas in a South beset by the erosion of its traditional, rural values. He became the first poet laureate of the United States in 1986.

In 1921 Warren entered Vanderbilt University, Nashville, Tenn., where he joined a group of poets who called themselves the Fugitives. Warren was among several of the Fugitives who joined with other Southerners to publish the anthology of essays *I'll Take My Stand* (1930), a plea for the agrarian way of life in the South.

After graduation from Vanderbilt in 1925, he studied at the University of California, Berkeley (M.A., 1927), and at Yale. He then went to the University of Oxford as a Rhodes scholar. From 1930 to 1950 he served on the faculty of several colleges and universities—including Vanderbilt and the University of Minnesota. With Cleanth Brooks and Charles W. Pipkin, he founded and edited *The Southern Review* (1935–42), possibly the most influential American literary magazine of the time. He taught at Yale University from 1951 to 1973. His *Understanding Poetry* (1938) and *Understanding Fiction* (1943), both written with Cleanth Brooks, were enormously influential in spreading the doctrines of the New Criticism, which insisted on the intrinsic value of a work of art and focused attention on the work alone as an independent unit of meaning. It was opposed to the critical practice of bringing historical or biographical data to bear on the interpretation of a work.

Warren's first novel, *Night Rider* (1939), is based on the tobacco war (1905–08) between the independent growers in Kentucky and the large tobacco companies. It anticipates much of his later fiction in the way it treats a historical event with tragic irony, emphasizes violence, and portrays individuals caught in moral quandaries. His best-known novel, *All the King's Men* (1946), is based on the career of the Louisiana demagogue Huey Long and tells the story of an idealistic politician whose lust for power corrupts him and those around him. This novel won the Pulitzer Prize in 1947 and, when made into a film, won the

Academy Award for best motion picture of 1949. Warren's other novels include *At Heaven's Gate* (1943); *World Enough and Time* (1950), which centres on a controversial murder trial in Kentucky in the 19th century; *Band of Angels* (1956); and *The Cave* (1959). His long narrative poem, *Brother to Dragons* (1953), dealing with the brutal murder of a slave by two nephews of Thomas Jefferson, is essentially a versified novel, and his poetry generally exhibits many of the concerns of his fiction. His other volumes of poetry include *Promises: Poems, 1954–1956; You, Emperors, and Others* (1960); *Audubon: A Vision* (1969); *Now and Then; Poems 1976–1978; Rumor Verified* (1981); *Chief Joseph* (1983); and *New and Selected Poems, 1923–1985* (1985). *The Circus in the Attic* (1948), which included "Blackberry Winter," considered by some critics to be one of Warren's supreme achievements, is a volume of short stories, and *Selected Essays* (1958) is a collection of some of his critical writings.

Besides receiving the Pulitzer Prize for fiction, Warren twice won the Pulitzer Prize for poetry (1958, 1979) and in 1986, at the time of his selection as the first poet laureate of the United States, he was the only person ever to win the prize in both categories. In his later years he tended to concentrate on his poetry.

JEAN-PAUL SARTRE

(b. June 21, 1905, Paris, France—d. April 15, 1980, Paris)

The French novelist, playwright, and existentialist philosopher Jean-Paul Sartre wrote in a variety of genres and produced a number of philosophical works. This biography will focus on his novels and plays.

Early Life and Writings

Sartre lost his father at an early age and grew up in the home of his maternal grandfather, Carl Schweitzer, uncle of the medical missionary Albert Schweitzer and himself professor of German at the Sorbonne. The boy, who wandered in the Luxembourg Gardens of Paris in search of playmates, was small in stature and cross-eyed. His brilliant autobiography, *Les Mots* (1963; *Words*), narrates the adventures of the mother and child in the park as they went from group to group—in the vain hope of being accepted—then finally retreated to the sixth floor of their apartment "on the heights where (the) dreams dwell." "The words" saved the child, and his interminable pages of writing were the escape from a world that had rejected him but that he would proceed to rebuild in his own fancy.

Sartre went to the Lycée Henri IV in Paris and, later on, after the remarriage of his mother, to the lycée in La Rochelle. From there he went to the prestigious École Normale Supérieure, from which he was graduated in 1929. Sartre resisted what he called "bourgeois marriage," but while still a student he formed with Simone de Beauvoir a union that remained a settled partnership in life. Simone de Beauvoir's memoirs, *Mémoires d'une jeune fille rangée* (1958; *Memoirs of a Dutiful Daughter*) and *La Force de l'âge* (1960; *The Prime of Life*), provide an intimate account of Sartre's life from student years until his middle 50s. From 1931 until 1945 Sartre taught in the lycées of Le Havre, Laon, and, finally, Paris. Twice this career was interrupted, once by a year of study in Berlin and the second time when Sartre was drafted in 1939 to serve in World War II. He was made prisoner in 1940 and released a year later.

During his years of teaching in Le Havre, Sartre published *La Nausée* (1938; *Nausea*), his first claim to fame. This novel, written in the form of a diary, narrates the feeling of revulsion that a certain Roquentin undergoes when confronted with the world of matter—not merely the world of other people but the very awareness of his own body. According to some critics, *La Nausée* must be viewed as a pathological case, a form of neurotic escape. Most probably it must be appreciated also as a most original, fiercely individualistic, antisocial piece of work, containing in its pages many of the philosophical themes that Sartre later developed.

Post-World War II Work

Having written his defense of individual freedom and human dignity, Sartre turned his attention to the concept of social responsibility. Freedom itself, which at times in his previous writings appeared to be a gratuitous activity that needed no particular aim or purpose to be of value, became a tool for human struggle in his brochure *L'Existentialisme est un humanisme* (1946; *Existentialism and Humanism*). Freedom now implied social responsibility. In his novels and plays Sartre began to bring his ethical message to the world at large. He started a four-volume novel in 1945 under the title *Les Chemins de la liberté,* of which three were eventually written: *L'Âge de raison* (1945; *The Age of Reason*), *Le Sursis* (1945; *The Reprieve*), and *La Mort dans l'âme* (1949; *Iron in the Soul,* or *Troubled Sleep*). After the publication of the third volume, Sartre changed his mind concerning the usefulness of the novel as a medium of communication and turned back to plays.

What a writer must attempt, said Sartre, is to show man as he is. Nowhere is man more man than when he is in action, and this is exactly what drama portrays. He had already written in this medium during the war, and now one play followed another: *Les Mouches* (produced 1943; *The Flies*), *Huis-clos* (produced 1944, published 1945; *In Camera*, or *No Exit*), *Les Mains sales* (1948; *Crime passionel*, 1949; U.S. title, *Dirty Hands*; acting version, *Red Gloves*), *Le Diable et le bon dieu* (1951; *Lucifer and the Lord*), *Nekrassov* (1955), and *Les Séquestrés d'Altona* (1959; *Loser Wins*, or *The Condemned of Altona*). All the plays, in their emphasis upon raw human hostility, seem to be predominantly pessimistic; yet, according to Sartre's own confession, their content does not exclude the possibility of a morality of salvation. Other publications of the same period include a book, *Baudelaire* (1947), a vaguely ethical study on the French writer and poet Jean Genet titled *Saint Genet, comédien et martyr* (1952; *Saint Genet, Actor and Martyr*), and innumerable articles that were published in *Les Temps Modernes,* the monthly review that Sartre and Simone de Beauvoir founded and edited. These articles were later collected in several volumes under the title *Situations*.

Political Activities

After World War II, Sartre took an active interest in French political movements, and his leanings to the left became more pronounced. He became an outspoken admirer of the Soviet Union, although he did not become a member of the Communist Party. In 1954 he visited the Soviet Union, Scandinavia, Africa, the United States, and Cuba. Upon the entry of Soviet tanks into Budapest in 1956, however, Sartre's hopes for communism were sadly crushed. He wrote in *Les Temps Modernes* a long article, "Le Fantôme de Staline," that condemned both the Soviet intervention and the submission of the French Communist Party to the dictates of Moscow.

Over the years this critical attitude opened the way to a form of "Sartrian Socialism" that would find its expression in a new major work, *Critique de la raison dialectique* (1960; Eng. trans., of the introduction only, under the title *The Problem of Method*; U.S. title, *Search for a Method*). Though it is somewhat marred by poor construction, the *Critique* is in fact an impressive and beautiful book. A projected second volume was abandoned. Instead, Sartre prepared for publication *Les Mots*, for which he was awarded the 1964 Nobel Prize for Literature, an offer that he refused.

Last Years

From 1960 until 1971 most of Sartre's attention went into the writing of a four-volume study called *Flaubert.* Two volumes with a total of some 2,130 pages appeared in the spring of 1971. This huge enterprise aimed at presenting the reader with a "total biography" of Gustave Flaubert, the famous French novelist, through the use of a double tool: on the one hand, Karl Marx's concept of history and class and, on the other, Sigmund Freud's illuminations of the dark recesses of the human soul through explorations into his childhood and family relations. At this point he began to operate under the motto that "commitment is an act, not a word," and he often went into the streets to participate in rioting, in the sale of left-wing literature, and in other activities that in his opinion were the way to promote "the revolution." Paradoxically enough, this same radical Socialist published in 1972 the third volume of the work on Flaubert, *L'Idiot de la famille,* another book of such density that only the bourgeois intellectual can read it. It was to be his last. When he died in 1980, his funeral was attended by some 25,000 people.

Samuel Beckett, 1965. © Gisèle Freund

$\mathcal{S}$AMUEL $\mathcal{B}$ECKETT

(b. April 13?, 1906, Foxrock, County Dublin, Ireland—
d. December 22, 1989, Paris, France)

S amuel Barclay Beckett was born in a suburb of Dublin. Like his fellow Irish writers George Bernard Shaw, Oscar Wilde, and William Butler Yeats, he came from a Protestant, Anglo-Irish background. At age 14 he went to the Portora Royal School, in what became Northern Ireland, a school that catered to the Anglo-Irish middle classes.

From 1923 to 1927, he studied Romance languages at Trinity College, Dublin, where he received his bachelor's degree. After a brief spell of teaching in Belfast, he became a reader in English at the École Normale Supérieure in Paris in 1928. There he met the self-exiled Irish writer James Joyce, the author of the controversial and seminally modern novel *Ulysses*, and joined his circle. Contrary to often-repeated reports, however, he never served as Joyce's secretary. He returned to Ireland in 1930 to take up a post as lecturer in French at Trinity College, but after only four terms he resigned, in December 1931, and embarked upon a period of restless travel in London, France, Germany, and Italy. In 1937 Beckett decided to settle in Paris. (This period of Beckett's life is vividly depicted in letters he wrote between 1929 and 1940, a wide-ranging selection of which were first published in 2009.)

As a citizen of a country that was neutral in World War II, he was able to remain there even after the occupation of Paris by the Germans, but he joined an underground resistance group in 1941. When, in 1942, he received news that members of his group had been arrested by the Gestapo, he immediately went into hiding and eventually moved to the unoccupied zone of France. Until the liberation of the country, he supported himself as an agricultural labourer.

In 1945 he returned to Ireland but volunteered for the Irish Red Cross and went back to France as an interpreter in a military hospital in Saint-Lô, Normandy. In the winter of 1945, he finally returned to Paris and was awarded the Croix de Guerre for his resistance work.

Production of the Major Works

There followed a period of intense creativity, the most concentratedly fruitful period of Beckett's life. His relatively few prewar publications included two essays on Joyce and the French novelist Marcel Proust. The volume *More Pricks Than Kicks* (1934) contained 10 stories describing episodes in the life of a Dublin intellectual, Belacqua Shuah, and the novel *Murphy* (1938) concerns an Irishman in London who escapes from a girl he is about to marry to a life of contemplation as a male nurse in a mental institution. His two slim volumes of poetry were *Whoroscope* (1930), a poem on the French philosopher René Descartes, and the collection *Echo's Bones* (1935). A number of short stories and poems were scattered in various periodicals. He wrote the novel *Dream of Fair to Middling Women* in the mid-1930s, but it remained incomplete and was not published until 1992.

During his years in hiding in unoccupied France, Beckett also completed another novel, *Watt*, which was not published until 1953. After his return to Paris, between 1946 and 1949, Beckett produced a number of stories, the major prose narratives *Molloy* (1951), *Malone meurt* (1951; *Malone Dies*), and *L'Innommable* (1953; *The Unnamable*), and two plays, the unpublished three-act *Eleutheria* and *En attendant Godot* (1952; *Waiting for Godot*).

It was not until 1951, however, that these works saw the light of day. After many refusals, Suzanne Deschevaux-Dumesnil (later Mme Beckett), Beckett's lifelong companion, finally succeeded in finding a publisher for *Molloy*. When this book not only proved a modest commercial success but also was received with enthusiasm by the French critics, the same publisher brought out the two other novels and *Waiting for Godot*. It was with the amazing success of *Waiting for Godot* at the small Théâtre de Babylone in Paris, in January 1953, that Beckett's rise to world fame began. Beckett continued writing, but more slowly than in the immediate postwar years. Plays for the stage and radio and a number of prose works occupied much of his attention. (This period of Beckett's life is treated in a second volume of letters, published in 2011, covering the years 1941–56.)

Beckett continued to live in Paris, but most of his writing was done in a small house secluded in the Marne valley, a short drive from Paris. His total dedication to his art extended to his complete avoidance of all personal publicity, of appearances on radio or television, and of all journalistic interviews. When, in 1969, he received the Nobel Prize for Literature, he accepted the award but declined the trip to Stockholm to avoid the public speech at the ceremonies.

Continuity of his Philosophical Explorations

Beckett's writing reveals his own immense learning. It is full of subtle allusions to a multitude of literary sources as well as to a number of philosophical and theological writers. The dominating influences on Beckett's thought were undoubtedly the Italian poet Dante, the French philosopher René Descartes, the 17th-century Dutch philosopher

Arnold Geulincx—a pupil of Descartes who dealt with the question of how the physical and the spiritual sides of man interact—and, finally, his fellow Irishman and revered friend, James Joyce. But it is by no means essential for the understanding of Beckett's work that one be aware of all the literary, philosophical, and theological allusions.

The widespread idea, fostered by the popular press, that Beckett's work is concerned primarily with the sordid side of human existence, with tramps and with cripples who inhabit trash cans, is a fundamental misconception. He dealt with human beings in such extreme situations not because he was interested in the sordid and diseased aspects of life but because he concentrated on the essential aspects of human experience. The subject matter of so much of the world's literature—the social relations between individuals, their manners and possessions, their struggles for rank and position, or the conquest of sexual objects—appeared to Beckett as mere external trappings of existence, the accidental and superficial aspects that mask the basic problems and the basic anguish of the human condition. The basic questions for Beckett seemed to be these: How can we come to terms with the fact that, without ever having asked for it, we have been thrown into the world, into being? And who are we; what is the true nature of our self? What does a human being mean when he says "I"?

What appears to the superficial view as a concentration on the sordid thus emerges as an attempt to grapple with the most essential aspects of the human condition. The two heroes of *Waiting for Godot*, for instance, are frequently referred to by critics as tramps, yet they were never described as such by Beckett. They are merely two human beings in the most basic human situation of being in the world and not knowing what they are there for. Since man is a rational being and cannot imagine that his being thrown into any situation should or could be entirely pointless, the two vaguely assume that their presence in the world, represented by an empty stage with a solitary tree, must be due to the fact that they are waiting for someone. But they have no positive evidence that this person, whom they call Godot, ever made such an appointment—or, indeed, that he actually exists. Their patient and passive waiting is contrasted by Beckett with the mindless and equally purposeless journeyings that fill the existence of a second pair of characters. In most dramatic literature the characters pursue well-defined objectives, seeking power, wealth, marriage with a desirable partner, or something of the sort. Yet, once they have attained these objectives, are they or the audience any nearer answering the basic questions that Beckett poses? Does the hero, having won his lady, really live with her happily ever after? That is apparently why Beckett chose to discard what he regarded as the inessential questions and began where other writing left off.

This stripping of reality to its bones is the reason that Beckett's development as a writer was toward an ever greater concentration, sparseness, and brevity. Most of Beckett's plays take place in a highly abstract unreal world. *Fin de partie* (one-act, 1957; *Endgame*) describes the dissolution of the relation between a master, Hamm, and his servant, Clov. They inhabit a circular structure with two high windows—perhaps the image of the inside of a human skull. The action might be seen as a symbol of the dissolution of a human personality in the hour of death, the breaking of the bond between the spiritual and the physical sides of man. In *Krapp's Last Tape* (one-act, first performed 1958), an old man listens to the confessions he recorded in earlier and happier years. This becomes an image of the mystery of the self, for to the old Krapp the voice of the younger Krapp is that of a total stranger.

In what sense, then, can the two Krapps be regarded as the same human being? In *Happy Days* (1961), a woman, literally sinking continually deeper into the ground, nonetheless continues to prattle about the trivialities of life. In other words, perhaps, as one gets nearer and nearer death, one still pretends that life will go on normally forever.

In his trilogy of narrative prose works—they are not, strictly speaking, novels as usually understood—*Molloy*, *Malone Dies*, and *The Unnamable*, as well as in the collection *Stories and Texts for Nothing* (1967), Beckett raised the problem of the identity of the human self from, as it were, the inside. This basic problem, simply stated, is that when I say "I am writing," I am talking about myself, one part of me describing what another part of me is doing. I am both the observer and the object I observe. Which of the two is the real "I"? In his prose narratives, Beckett tried to pursue this elusive essence of the self, which, to him, manifested itself as a constant stream of thought and of observations about the self. One's entire existence, one's consciousness of oneself as being in the world, can be seen as a stream of thought. *Cogito ergo sum* is the starting point of Beckett's favourite philosopher, Descartes: "I think; therefore, I am." To catch the essence of being, therefore, Beckett tried to capture the essence of the stream of consciousness that is one's being. And what he found was a constantly receding chorus of observers, or storytellers, who, immediately on being observed, became, in turn, objects of observation by a new observer. Molloy and Moran, for example, the pursued and the pursuer in the first part of the trilogy, are just such a pair of observer and observed. Malone, in the second part, spends his time while dying in making up stories about people who clearly are aspects of himself. The third part reaches down to bedrock. The voice is that of someone who is unnamable, and it is not clear whether it is a voice that comes from beyond the grave or from a limbo before birth. As we cannot conceive of our consciousness not being there—"*I* cannot be conscious that *I* have ceased to exist"—therefore consciousness is at either side open-ended to infinity. This is the subject also of the play *Play* (first performed 1963), which shows the dying moments of consciousness of three characters, who have been linked in a trivial amorous triangle in life, lingering on into eternity.

The Humour and Mastery

In spite of Beckett's courageous tackling of the ultimate mystery and despair of human existence, he was essentially a comic writer. In a French farce, laughter will arise from seeing the frantic and usually unsuccessful pursuit of trivial sexual gratifications. In Beckett's work, as well, a recognition of the triviality and ultimate pointlessness of most human strivings, by freeing the viewer from his concern with senseless and futile objectives, should also have a liberating effect. The laughter will arise from a view of pompous and self-important preoccupation with illusory ambitions and futile desires. Far from being gloomy and depressing, the ultimate effect of seeing or reading Beckett is one of cathartic release, an objective as old as theatre itself.

Technically, Beckett was a master craftsman, and his sense of form is impeccable. *Molloy* and *Waiting for Godot*, for example, are constructed symmetrically, in two parts that are mirror images of one another. In his work for the mass media, Beckett also showed himself able to grasp intuitively and brilliantly the essential character of their techniques. His radio plays, such as *All That Fall* (1957), are models in the combined use of sound, music, and speech. The short television play *Eh Joe!* (1967) exploits the television camera's ability to move in on a face and the particular character of small-screen drama. Finally, his film script *Film* (1967) creates an unforgettable sequence of images of the observed self trying to escape the eye of its own observer.

Beckett's later works tended toward extreme concentration and brevity. *Come and Go* (1967), a playlet, or "dramaticule," as he called it, contains only 121 words that are spoken by the three characters. The prose fragment "Lessness" consists of but 60 sentences, each of which occurs twice. His series *Acts Without Words* are exactly what the title denotes, and one of his last plays, *Rockaby*, lasts for 15 minutes. Such brevity is merely an expression of Beckett's determination to pare his writing to essentials, to waste no words on trivia.

W.H. Auden

(b. February 21, 1907, York, Yorkshire, England—d. September 29, 1973, Vienna, Austria)

In 1908 Wystan Hugh Auden's family moved to Birmingham, where his father became medical officer and professor in the university. Since his father was a distinguished physician of broad scientific interests and his mother had been a nurse, the atmosphere of the home was more scientific than literary. It was also devoutly Anglo-Catholic, and Auden's first religious memories were of "exciting magical rites." The family name, spelled Audun, appears in the Icelandic sagas, and Auden inherited from his father a fascination with Iceland.

Education and Early Career

His education followed the standard pattern for children of the middle and upper classes. At 8 he was sent away to St. Edmund's preparatory school, in Surrey, and at 13 to a public (private) school, Gresham's, at Holt, in Norfolk. Auden intended to be a mining engineer and was interested primarily in science; he specialized in biology. By 1922 he had discovered his vocation as a poet, and two years later his first poem was published in *Public School Verse*. In 1925 he entered the University of Oxford (Christ Church), where he established a formidable reputation as poet and sage, having a strong influence on such other literary intellectuals as C. Day Lewis (named poet laureate in 1968), Louis MacNeice, and Stephen Spender, who printed by hand the first collection of Auden's poems in 1928. Though their names were often linked with his as poets of the so-called Auden generation, the notion of an "Auden Group" dedicated to revolutionary politics was largely a journalistic invention.

Upon graduating from Oxford in 1928, Auden, offered a year abroad by his parents, chose Berlin rather than the Paris by which the previous literary generation had been fascinated. He fell in love with the German language and was influenced by its poetry, cabaret songs, and plays, especially those by Bertolt Brecht. He returned to become a schoolmaster in Scotland and England for the next five years.

In his *Collected Shorter Poems* Auden divides his career into four periods. The first extends from 1927, when he was still an undergraduate, through *The Orators* of 1932. The "charade" *Paid on Both Sides*, which along with *Poems* established Auden's reputation in 1930, best reveals the imperfectly fused but fascinating amalgam of material from the Icelandic sagas, Old English poetry, public-school stories, Karl Marx, Sigmund Freud and other psychologists, and schoolboy humour that enters into all these works. The poems are uneven and often obscure, pulled in contrary directions by the subjective impulse to fantasy, the mythic and unconscious, and the objective impulse to a diagnosis of the ills of society and the psychological and moral defects of the individuals who constitute it. Though the social and political implications of the poetry attracted most attention, the psychological aspect is primary. The notion of poetry as a kind of therapy, performing a function somehow analogous to the psychoanalytical, remains fundamental in Auden.

The second period, 1933–38, is that in which Auden was the hero of the left. Continuing the analysis of the evils of capitalist society, he also warned of the rise of totalitarianism. In *On This Island* (1937; in Britain, *Look, Stranger!*, 1936) his verse became more open in texture and accessible to a larger public. For the Group Theatre, a society that put on experimental and noncommercial plays in London, he wrote first *The Dance of Death* (a musical propaganda play) and then three plays in collaboration with Christopher Isherwood, Auden's friend since preparatory school: *The Dog Beneath the Skin* (1935), *The Ascent of F6* (1936), and *On the Frontier* (1938). Auden also wrote commentaries for documentary films, including a classic of that genre, *Night Mail* (1936); numerous essays and book reviews; and reportage, most notably on a trip to Iceland with MacNeice, described in *Letters from Iceland* (1937), and a trip to China with Isherwood that was the basis of *Journey to a War* (1939). Auden visited Spain briefly in 1937, his poem *Spain* (1937) being the only immediate result; but the visit, according to his later recollections, marked the beginning both of his disillusion with the left and of his return to Christianity. In 1936 he married Erika Mann, the daughter of the German novelist Thomas Mann, in order to provide her with a British passport. When he and Isherwood went to China, they crossed the United States both ways, and on the return journey they both decided to settle there. In January 1939, both did so.

American Citizenship and Later Years

In the third period, 1939–46, Auden became an American citizen and underwent decisive changes in his religious and intellectual perspective. *Another Time* (1940) contains some of his best songs and topical verse, and *The Double Man* (containing "New Year Letter," which provided the title of the British edition; 1941) embodies his position on the verge of commitment to Christianity. The beliefs and attitudes that are basic to all of Auden's work after 1940 are defined in three long poems: religious in the Christmas oratorio *For the Time Being* (1944); aesthetic in the same volume's *Sea and the Mirror* (a quasi-dramatic "commentary" on William Shakespeare's *The Tempest*); and social-psychological in *The Age of Anxiety* (1947), the "baroque eclogue" that won Auden the Pulitzer Prize in 1948. Auden wrote no long poems after that.

The fourth period began in 1948, when Auden established the pattern of leaving New York City each year to spend the months from April to October in Europe. From 1948 to 1957 his summer residence was the Italian island of Ischia; in the latter year he bought a farmhouse in Kirchstetten, Austria, where he then spent his summers. In *The Shield of Achilles* (1955), *Homage to Clio* (1960), *About the House* (1965), and *City Without Walls* (1969) are sequences of poems arranged according to an external pattern (canonical hours, types of landscape, rooms of a house). With Chester Kallman, an American poet and close friend who lived with him for more than 20 years, he rehabilitated the art of the opera libretto. Their best-known collaborations are *The Rake's Progress* (1951), for Igor Stravinsky; *Elegy for Young Lovers* (1961) and *The Bassarids* (1966), for Hans Werner Henze; and *Love's Labour's Lost* for Nicolas Nabokov. They also edited *An Elizabethan Song Book* (1956). In 1962 Auden published a volume of criticism, *The Dyer's Hand*, and in 1970 a commonplace book, *A Certain World*. He spent much time on editing and translating, notably *The Collected Poems of St. John Perse* (1972). In 1972 Auden transferred his winter residence from New York City to Oxford, where he was an honorary fellow at Christ Church College. Of the numerous honours conferred on Auden in this last period, the Bollingen Prize (1953), the National Book Award (1956), and the professorship of poetry at Oxford (1956–61) may be mentioned.

Assessment

In the early 1930s W.H. Auden was acclaimed prematurely by some as the foremost poet then writing in English, on the disputable ground that his poetry was more relevant to contemporary social and political realities than that of T.S. Eliot and William Butler Yeats, who previously had shared the summit. By the time of Eliot's death in 1965, however, a convincing case could be made for the assertion that Auden was indeed Eliot's successor, as Eliot had inherited sole claim to supremacy when Yeats died in 1939.

Auden was, as a poet, far more copious and varied than Eliot and far more uneven. He tried to interpret the times, to diagnose the ills of society and deal with intellectual and moral problems of public concern. But the need to express the inner world of fantasy and dream was equally apparent, and, hence, the poetry is sometimes bewildering. If the poems, taken individually, are often obscure—especially the earlier ones—they create, when taken together, a meaningful poetic cosmos with symbolic landscapes and mythical characters and situations. In his later years Auden ordered the world of his poetry and made it easier of access; he collected his poems, revised them, and presented them chronologically in two volumes: *Collected Shorter Poems 1927–57* (1967) and *Collected Longer Poems* (1969).

℞ICHARD ℘RIGHT

(b. September 4, 1908, near Natchez, Mississippi, U.S.—d. November 28, 1960, Paris, France)

Richard Wright's grandparents had been slaves. His father left home when he was five, and the boy, who grew up in poverty, was often shifted from one relative to another. He worked at a number of jobs before joining the northward migration, first to Memphis, Tennessee, and then to Chicago. There, after working in unskilled jobs, he got an opportunity to write through the Federal Writers' Project. In 1932 he became a member of the Communist Party, and in 1937 he went to New York City, where he became Harlem editor of the Communist *Daily Worker*.

He first came to the general public's attention with a volume of novellas, *Uncle Tom's Children* (1938), based on the question: How may a black man live in a country that denies his humanity? In each story but one the hero's quest ends in death.

Wright's fictional scene shifted to Chicago in *Native Son*. Its protagonist, a poor black youth named Bigger Thomas, accidentally kills a white girl, and in the course of his ensuing flight his hitherto meaningless awareness of antagonism from a white world becomes intelligible.

Richard Wright. Hulton Archive/Getty Images

The book was a best-seller and was staged successfully as a play on Broadway (1941) by Orson Welles. Wright himself played Bigger Thomas in a motion-picture version made in Argentina in 1951.

In 1944 he left the Communist Party because of political and personal differences. Wright's autobiography, *Black Boy*, is a moving account of his childhood and young manhood in the South. The book chronicles the extreme poverty of his childhood, his experience of white prejudice and violence against blacks, and his growing awareness of his interest in literature.

After World War II, Wright settled in Paris as a permanent expatriate. *The Outsider* (1953), acclaimed as the first American existential novel, warned that the black man had awakened in a disintegrating society not ready to include him. Three later novels were not well-received. Among his polemical writings of that period was *White Man, Listen!* (1957), which was originally a series of lectures given in Europe. *Eight Men*, a collection of short stories, appeared in 1961.

The autobiographical *American Hunger*, which narrates Wright's experiences after moving to the North, was published posthumously in 1977. Some of the more candid passages dealing with race, sex, and politics in Wright's books had been cut or omitted before their original publication, but unexpurgated versions of *Native Son*, *Black Boy*, and his other works were published in 1991. A novella, *Rite of Passage* (1994), and an unfinished crime novel, *A Father's Law* (2008), were also published posthumously.

NELSON ALGREN

(b. March 28, 1909, Detroit, Michigan, U.S.—d. May 9, 1981, Sag Harbor, New York)

The son of a machinist, Nelson Algren grew up in Chicago, where his parents moved when he was three years old. He worked his way through the University of Illinois, graduating in journalism in the depth of the Great Depression. Sometime after graduating, he adopted a simplified spelling of the original name, Ahlgren, of his Swedish grandfather, who had converted to Judaism and taken the name Abraham. He went on the road as a door-to-door salesman and migratory worker in the South and Southwest, then returned to Chicago, where he was employed briefly by a WPA (Works Progress Administration) writers' project and a venereal-disease control unit of the Board of Health. In this period, too, he edited with the proletarian novelist Jack Conroy the *New Anvil*, a magazine dedicated to the publication of experimental and leftist writing.

Algren's first novel, *Somebody in Boots* (1935), relates the driftings during the Depression of a young poor-white Texan who ends up among the down-and-outs of Chicago. *Never Come Morning* (1942) tells of a Polish petty criminal who dreams of escaping from his squalid Northwest Side Chicago environment by becoming a prizefighter. Before the appearance of Algren's next book—the short-story collection *The Neon Wilderness* (1947), which contains some of his best writing—he served as a U.S. Army medical corpsman during World War II.

In 1947 Algren met the French writer and feminist Simone de Beauvoir. The two began a transatlantic relationship that lasted 17 years. De Beauvoir dedicated her novel *Les Mandarins* (1954; *The Mandarins*) to him, limning him in the character Lewis Brogan.

Algren's first popular success was *The Man with the Golden Arm* (1949; filmed 1956), which won the first National Book Award for fiction. Its hero is Frankie Machine, whose golden arm as a poker dealer is threatened by shakiness connected with his drug addiction. In *A Walk on the Wild Side* (1956; filmed 1962) Algren returned to the 1930s in a picaresque novel of New Orleans bohemian life. After 1959 he abandoned the writing of novels (though he continued to publish short stories) and considered himself a journalist. His last novel, *The Devil's Stocking*, which he completed in 1979, was rejected by many publishers but was published posthumously in 1983.

Algren's nonfiction includes the prose poem *Chicago, City on the Make* (1951) and sketches collected as *Who Lost an American?* (1963) and *Notes from a Sea Diary: Hemingway All the Way* (1965). Algren was elected to the American Academy and Institute of Arts and Letters three months before he died.

His novels depicting the lives of the poor are lifted from routine naturalism by his vision of their pride, humour, and unquenchable yearnings. He also catches with poetic skill the mood of the city's underside: its juke-box pounding, stench, and neon glare.

$\mathcal{E}UDORA$ $\mathcal{W}ELTY$

(b. April 13, 1909, Jackson, Mississippi, U.S. — d. July 23, 2001, Jackson)

American short-story writer and novelist Eudora Welty focused with great precision on the regional manners of people inhabiting a small Mississippi town that resembles her own birthplace and the Delta country. She attended Mississippi State College for Women before transferring to the University of Wisconsin, from which she graduated in 1929. During the Great Depression she was a photographer on the Works Progress Administration's

Guide to Mississippi, and photography remained a life-long interest. *Photographs* (1989) is a collection of many of the photographs she took for the WPA. She also worked as a writer for a radio station and newspaper in her native Jackson, Mississippi, before her fiction won popular and critical acclaim.

Welty's first short story was published in 1936, and thereafter her work began to appear regularly, first in little magazines such as the *Southern Review* and later in major periodicals such as *The Atlantic Monthly* and *The New Yorker*. Her readership grew steadily after the publication of *A Curtain of Green* (1941; enlarged 1979), a volume of short stories that contains two of her most anthologized stories—"The Petrified Man" and "Why I Live at the P.O." In 1942 her short novel *The Robber Bridegroom* was issued, and in 1946 her first full-length novel, *Delta Wedding*. Her later novels include *The Ponder Heart* (1954), *Losing Battles* (1970), and *The Optimist's Daughter* (1972), which won a Pulitzer Prize. *The Wide Net and Other Stories* (1943), *The Golden Apples* (1949), and *The Bride of Innisfallen and Other Stories* (1955) are collections of short stories, and *The Eye of the Story* (1978) is a volume of essays. *The Collected Stories of Eudora Welty* was published in 1980.

Welty's main subject is the intricacies of human relationships, particularly as revealed through her characters' interactions in intimate social encounters. Among her themes are the subjectivity and ambiguity of people's perception of character and the presence of virtue hidden beneath an obscuring surface of convention, insensitivity, and social prejudice. Welty's outlook is hopeful, and love is viewed as a redeeming presence in the midst of isolation and indifference. Her works combine humour and psychological acuity with a sharp ear for regional speech patterns.

One Writer's Beginnings, an autobiographical work, was published in 1984. Originating in a series of three lectures she gave at Harvard, it beautifully evoked what Welty styled her "sheltered life" in Jackson and how her early fiction grew out of it.

EUGÈNE IONESCO

(b. November 26, 1909, Slatina, Romania—d. March 28, 1994, Paris, France)

Romanian-born French dramatist Eugène Ionesco (born Eugen Ionescu) was taken to France as an infant but returned to Romania in 1925. After obtaining a degree in French at the University of Bucharest, he worked for a doctorate in Paris (1939), where, after 1945, he made his home. While working as a proofreader, he determined to learn English; the formal, stilted commonplaces of his textbook inspired the masterly catalog of senseless platitudes that constitutes his one-act "antiplay" *La Cantatrice chauve* (1949; *The Bald Soprano*). In its most famous scene, two strangers—who are exchanging banalities about how the weather is faring, where they live, and how many children they have—stumble upon the astonishing discovery that they are indeed man and wife; it is a brilliant example of Ionesco's recurrent themes of self-estrangement and the difficulty of communication. The play inspired a revolution in dramatic techniques and helped inaugurate the Theatre of the Absurd.

In rapid succession Ionesco wrote a number of plays, all developing the "antilogical" ideas of *The Bald Soprano*. These included brief and violently irrational sketches and also a series of more elaborate one-act plays in which many of his later themes—especially the fear and horror of death—begin to make their appearance. Among these, *La Leçon* (1951; *The Lesson*), *Les Chaises* (1952; *The Chairs*), and *Le Nouveau Locataire* (1955; *The New Tenant*) are notable successes. In *The Lesson*, a timid professor uses the meaning he assigns to words to establish tyrannical dominance over an eager female pupil. In *The Chairs*, an elderly couple await the arrival of an audience to hear the old man's last message to posterity, but only empty chairs accumulate on stage. Feeling confident that his message will be conveyed by an orator he has hired, the old man and his wife commit a double suicide. The orator turns out to be afflicted with aphasia, however, and can speak only gibberish.

In contrast to these shorter works, it was only with difficulty that Ionesco mastered the techniques of the full-length play: *Amédée* (1954), *Tueur sans gages* (1959; *The Killer*), and *Le Rhinocéros* (1959; *Rhinoceros*) lack the dramatic unity that he finally achieved with *Le Roi se meurt* (1962; *Exit the King*). This success was followed by *Le Piéton de l'air* (1963; *A Stroll in the Air*). With *La Soif et la faim* (1966; *Thirst and Hunger*) he returned to a more fragmented type of construction. In the next decade he wrote *Jeux de massacre* (1970; *Killing Game*); *Macbett* (1972), a retelling of Shakespeare's *Macbeth*; and *Ce formidable bordel* (1973; *A Hell of a Mess*). *Rhinoceros*, a play about totalitarianism, remains Ionesco's most popular work.

Ionesco's achievement lies in having popularized a wide variety of nonrepresentational and surrealistic techniques and in having made them acceptable to audiences conditioned to a naturalistic convention in the theatre. His tragicomic farces dramatize the absurdity of bourgeois life, the meaninglessness of social conventions, and the futile and mechanical nature of modern civilization. His plays build on bizarrely illogical or fantastic situations using such devices as the humorous multiplication of objects on stage until they overwhelm the actors. The clichés and tedious maxims of polite conversation surface in improbable or inappropriate contexts to expose the deadening futility of most human communication.

Ai Qing

(b. March 27, 1910, Jinhua, Zhejiang province, China—d. May 5, 1996, Beijing)

The son of a well-to-do landowner, Jiang Haicheng— who would become known as Ai Qing (Ai Ch'ing)—was encouraged to learn Western languages. He studied painting in Paris from 1928 to 1932, and he developed an appreciation for Western literature. Imprisoned for his radical political activities, he began to write poetry under his pen name. His first collection of verse, *Dayanhe* (1936), reflects his concern for the common people of China; the title poem recalls the foster nurse (called Dayanhe in the poem) who reared him. He went to Yan'an in 1941 and eventually accepted the literary teachings of the Chinese Communist Party leader Mao Zedong. Ai Qing published a number of additional volumes in the 1940s, such as *Kuangye* (1940; "Wildness"), *Xiang taiyang* (1940; "Toward the Sun"), and *Beifang* (1942; "North"). An advocate of free expression and the role of the writer as social critic, Ai Qing used simple language and a free style in creating his socially oriented poems.

After 1949 Ai Qing served on various cultural committees, but in 1957 he was officially censured as a rightist for criticizing the communist regime. He remained silent for 21 years and was interned in labour camps in Heilongjiang and Xinjiang. He began writing again in 1978, publishing books such as *Guilai de ge* (1980; "Song of Returning"). *Selected Poems of Ai Qing* was published in 1982, and his entire oeuvre was published as *Ai Qing quanji* ("The Complete Works of Ai Qing") in 1991. His son Ai Weiwei (b. 1957) is a noted artist and also an activist.

CHAIM GRADE

(b. April 5, 1910, Vilna, Russian Empire [now Vilnius, Lithuania]—d. June 26, 1982, New York, New York, U.S.)

Yiddish poet, short-story writer, and novelist Chaim Grade was one of the last surviving secularized Yiddish writers to have been educated in a European yeshiva (rabbinical seminary). His fiction reflects an intimate knowledge of the complexities and breadth of that vanished culture and tradition.

Grade traced his descent from one of Napoleon's officers, who was wounded during the Napoleonic wars and cared for by a Jewish family in Vilna; he later married into the family and converted to Judaism. Grade's father, a strong-willed rabbi and Zionist, died when Grade was a boy and his mother, a poor street vendor, struggled to raise money for a traditional Jewish education for her son. Grade studied at several yeshivas and was part of the pietistic movement known as Musar. At age 22, however, he gave up his religious studies to become a writer. A leading member of Yung Vilne ("Young Vilna"), a group of avant-garde Yiddish writers and artists, Grade began publishing poems in Yiddish periodicals. His first published book was the poetry collection *Yo* (1936; "Yes"): it includes poems of spiritual struggle and the destruction of Jewish life and conveys Grade's premonition of the Holocaust, a concern that informed much of his work from this period. Many of his poems were later recited by Jews in the Vilna ghetto and in Auschwitz. After the German invasion in 1941, he escaped to Russia but returned to Vilna after the war and discovered that his wife and mother had been killed and that the culture in which he had been nurtured had been destroyed. Grade then moved to Paris, where he wrote searing poetry about the Holocaust. In 1948 he went to New York City with his second wife.

Most of Grade's subsequent works deal with issues related to the culture and tradition of his Jewish faith. *Mayn krig mit Hersh Rasseyner* (1950; *My Fight with Hersh Rasseyner*) is a "philosophical dialogue" between a secular Jew deeply troubled by the Holocaust and a devout friend from Poland. Grade's novel *Di agune* (1961; *The Agunah*) concerns an Orthodox woman whose husband is missing in action in wartime and who, according to Orthodox Jewish law, is forbidden to remarry, lest she enter into an adulterous union. In the ambitious two-volume *Tsemakh Atlas* (1967–68; *The Yeshiva*), Grade reveals Jewish life under the Torah and what some critics saw as his revelation of the Pauline spirit of Judaism. Among his other notable works of fiction are a novella, *Der brunem* in *Der Shulhoyf* (1967; Eng. trans. *The Well*), and many short stories and poems. Grade's memoir, *Der mame's Shabosim* (1955; *My Mother's Sabbath Days*), provides a rare portrait of prewar Vilna, as well as a description of refugee life in the Soviet Union and Grade's return to Vilna after the war.

JEAN ANOUILH

(b. June 23, 1910, Bordeaux, France—d. October 3, 1987, Lausanne, Switzerland)

Jean Anouilh was a playwright who became one of the strongest personalities of the French theatre and achieved an international reputation. His plays are intensely personal messages; often they express his love of the theatre as well as his grudges against actors, wives, mistresses, critics, academicians, bureaucrats, and others. Anouilh's characteristic techniques include the play within the play, flashbacks and flash forwards, and the exchange of roles.

The Anouilh family moved to Paris when Jean-Marie-Lucien-Pierre was a teenager, and it was there that he studied law and worked briefly in advertising. At age 18, however, he saw Jean Giraudoux's drama *Siegfried*, in which he discovered a theatrical and poetic language that determined his career. He worked briefly as the secretary to the great actor-director Louis Jouvet.

L'Hermine (performed 1932; *The Ermine*) was Anouilh's first play to be produced, and success came in 1937 with *Le Voyageur sans bagage* (*Traveller Without Luggage*), which was soon followed by *La Sauvage* (1938).

Anouilh rejected both naturalism and realism in favour of what has been called "theatricalism," the return of poetry and imagination to the stage. Technically he showed a great versatility, from the stylized use of Greek myth, to the rewriting of history, to the *comédie-ballet*, to the modern comedy of character. Anouilh developed his own view of life highlighting the contradictions within human reality, for example, or the ambiguous relationships between good and evil. He called two major collections of his plays *Pièces roses* ("Rose-coloured Plays") and *Pièces noires* ("Black Plays"), in which similar subjects are treated more or less lightly. His dramatic vision of the world poses the question of how far the individual must compromise with truth to obtain happiness. His plays show men or women facing the loss of the privileged world of childhood. Some of his characters accept the inevitable; some, such as the light-headed creatures of *Le Bal des voleurs* (1938; *Thieves' Carnival*), live lies; and others, such as *Antigone* (1944), reject any tampering with ideals.

With *L'Invitation au château* (1947; *Ring Around the Moon*), the mood of Anouilh's plays became more sombre. His aging couples seem to perform a dance of death in *La Valse des toréadors* (1952; *The Waltz of the Toreadors*). *L'Alouette* (1953; *The Lark*) is the spiritual adventure of Joan of Arc, who, like Antigone and Thérèse Tarde (*La Sauvage*), is another of Anouilh's rebels who rejects the world, its order, and its trite happiness. In another historical play, *Becket ou l'honneur de Dieu* (1959; *Becket, or, The Honour of God*), friendship is crushed between spiritual integrity and political power.

In the 1960s Anouilh's plays were considered by many to be dated compared with those of the Absurdist dramatists Eugène Ionesco or Samuel Beckett, but in the following decade other new plays appeared to confirm his place as a master entertainer, including *Cher Antoine; ou, l'amour raté* (1969; *Dear Antoine; or, The Love That Failed*), *Le Directeur de l'opéra* (1972), *Le Scénario* (1976), *Vive Henry IV* (1977), and *La Culotte* (1978; "The Trousers").

JEAN GENET

(b. December 19, 1910, Paris, France — d. April 15, 1986, Paris)

Jean Genet was a French criminal and social outcast turned writer who, as a novelist, transformed erotic and often obscene subject matter into a poetic vision of the universe and, as a dramatist, became a leading figure in the avant-garde theatre, especially the Theatre of the Absurd.

Genet, an illegitimate child abandoned by his mother, Gabrielle Genet, was raised by a family of peasants. Caught stealing at the age of 10, he spent part of his adolescence at a notorious reform school, Mettray, where he experienced much that was later described in the novel *Miracle de la rose* (1945–46; *Miracle of the Rose*). His autobiographical *Journal du voleur* (1949; *The Thief's Journal*) gives a complete and uninhibited account of his life as a tramp, pickpocket, and male prostitute in Barcelona, Antwerp, and various other cities (*c.* 1930–39). It also reveals him as an aesthete, an existentialist, and a pioneer of the Absurd.

He began to write in 1942 while imprisoned for theft at Fresnes and produced an outstanding novel, *Notre-Dame des Fleurs* (1943; *Our Lady of the Flowers*), vividly portraying the prewar Montmartre underworld of thugs, pimps, and perverts. His talent was brought to the attention of Jean Cocteau and later Jean-Paul Sartre and Simone de Beauvoir. Because Genet in 1948 was convicted of theft for the 10th time and would have faced automatic life imprisonment if convicted again, a delegation of well-known writers appealed on his behalf to the president of the French republic, and he was "pardoned in advance."

After writing two other novels, *Pompes funèbres* (1947; *Funeral Rites*) and *Querelle de Brest* (1947; *Querelle of Brest*, film 1982), Genet began to experiment with drama. His early attempts, by their compact, neoclassical, one-act structure, reveal the strong influence of Sartre. *Haute Surveillance* (1949; *Deathwatch*) continues his prison-world themes. *Les Bonnes* (1947; *The Maids*), however, begins to explore the complex problems of identity that were soon to preoccupy other avant-garde dramatists such as Samuel Beckett and Eugène Ionesco. With this play Genet was established as an outstanding figure in the Theatre of the Absurd.

His subsequent plays, *Le Balcon* (1956; *The Balcony*), *Les Nègres* (1958; *The Blacks*), and *Les Paravents* (1961;

The Screens), are large-scale, stylized dramas in the Expressionist manner, designed to shock and implicate an audience by revealing its hypocrisy and complicity. This "Theatre of Hatred" attempts to wrest the maximum dramatic power from a social or political situation without necessarily endorsing the political platitudes of either the right or the left.

Genet, a rebel and an anarchist of the most extreme sort, rejected almost all forms of social discipline or political commitment. The violent and often degraded eroticism of his experience led him to a concept of mystic humiliation.

ELIZABETH BISHOP

(b. February 8, 1911, Worcester, Massachusetts, U.S.—d. October 6, 1979, Boston, Massachusetts)

E lizabeth Bishop was reared by her maternal grandparents in Nova Scotia and by an aunt in Boston. After graduating from Vassar College in 1934, she traveled abroad often, living for a time in Key West, Florida (1938–42), and Mexico (1943). She was consultant in poetry at the Library of Congress (now poet laureate consultant in poetry) from 1949 to 1950. During most of the 1950s and '60s she lived with Lota de Macedo Soares in Petrópolis, Brazil, near Rio de Janeiro, later dividing the year between Petrópolis and San Francisco. Her first book of poems, *North & South* (1946), captures the divided nature of Bishop's allegiances: born in New England and reared there and in Nova Scotia, she eventually migrated to hotter regions. This book was reprinted in 1955, with additions, as *North & South: A Cold Spring*, and it won a Pulitzer Prize.

Much of Bishop's later work also addresses the frigid-tropical dichotomy of a New England conscience in a tropical sphere. *Questions of Travel* (1965) and *Geography III* (1976) offer spare, powerful meditations on the need for self-exploration, on the value of art (especially poetry) in human life, and on human responsibility in a chaotic world. The latter collection includes some of Bishop's best-known poems, among them "In the Waiting Room," "Crusoe in England," and the exquisite villanelle "One Art." A collection entitled *The Complete Poems* was published in 1969.

Bishop taught writing at Harvard University from 1970 to 1977, and she was elected to the American Academy of Arts and Letters in 1976. Her posthumously published poetry collections include *The Complete Poems, 1927–1979* (1983) and *Edgar Allen Poe & the Juke-Box* (2006), the latter of which contains previously unpublished material. *The Collected Prose*, a volume of fiction and nonfiction, appeared in 1984. A selection of her letters was published under the title *One Art* in 1994. *Elizabeth Bishop: Poems, Prose, and Letters* (2008) is a comprehensive collection of her published and unpublished work.

Bishop also wrote a travel book, *Brazil* (1962), and translated from the Portuguese Alice Brant's Brazilian classic, *The Diary of Helena Morley* (1957). She edited and translated *An Anthology of Twentieth-Century Brazilian Poetry* (1972). Bishop also was an artist, and *Exchanging Hats* (1996) is a collection of more than 50 of her paintings.

TENNESSEE WILLIAMS

(b. March 26, 1911, Columbus, Mississippi, U.S. — d. February 25, 1983, New York City)

Tennessee Williams. Bill Pierce/Time & Life Pictures/Getty Images

Thomas Lanier Williams became interested in playwriting while at the University of Missouri (Columbia) and Washington University (St. Louis) and worked at it even during the Depression while employed in a St. Louis shoe factory. Little theatre groups produced some of his work, encouraging him to study dramatic writing at the University of Iowa, where he earned a B.A. in 1938.

His first recognition came when *American Blues* (1939), a group of one-act plays, won a Group Theatre award. Williams, however, continued to work at jobs ranging from theatre usher to Hollywood scriptwriter until success came with *The Glass Menagerie* (1944). In it, Williams portrayed a declassed Southern family living in a tenement. The play is about the failure of a domineering mother,

Amanda, living upon her delusions of a romantic past, and her cynical son, Tom, to secure a suitor for Tom's crippled and painfully shy sister, Laura, who lives in a fantasy world with a collection of glass animals.

Williams's next major play, *A Streetcar Named Desire* (1947), won a Pulitzer Prize. It is a study of the mental and moral ruin of Blanche Du Bois, another former Southern belle, whose genteel pretensions are no match for the harsh realities symbolized by her brutish brother-in-law, Stanley Kowalski.

In 1953, *Camino Real*, a complex work set in a mythical, microcosmic town whose inhabitants include Lord Byron and Don Quixote, was a commercial failure, but his *Cat on a Hot Tin Roof* (1955), which exposes the emotional lies governing relationships in the family of a wealthy Southern planter, was awarded a Pulitzer Prize and was successfully filmed, as was *The Night of the Iguana* (1961), the story of a defrocked minister turned sleazy tour guide, who finds God in a cheap Mexican hotel. *Suddenly Last Summer* (1958) deals with lobotomy, pederasty, and cannibalism, and in *Sweet Bird of Youth* (1959), the gigolo hero is castrated for having infected a Southern politician's daughter with venereal disease.

Williams was in ill health frequently during the 1960s, compounded by years of addiction to sleeping pills and liquor, problems that he struggled to overcome after a severe mental and physical breakdown in 1969. His later plays were unsuccessful, closing soon to poor reviews. They include *Vieux Carré* (1977), about down-and-outs in New Orleans; *A Lovely Sunday for Crève Coeur* (1978–79), about a fading belle in St. Louis during the Great Depression; and *Clothes for a Summer Hotel* (1980), centring on Zelda Fitzgerald, wife of novelist F. Scott Fitzgerald, and on the people they knew.

Williams also wrote two novels, *The Roman Spring of Mrs. Stone* (1950) and *Moise and the World of Reason* (1975), essays, poetry, film scripts, short stories, and an autobiography, *Memoirs* (1975). His works won four Drama Critics' awards and were widely translated and performed around the world.

CZESŁAW MIŁOSZ

(b. June 30, 1911, Šateiniai, Lithuania, Russian Empire [now in Lithuania]—d. August 14, 2004, Kraków, Poland)

The son of a civil engineer, Czesław Miłosz completed his university studies in Wilno (now Vilnius, Lithuania), which belonged to Poland between the two world wars. His first book of verse, *Poemat o czasie zastygłym* (1933; "Poem of Frozen Time"), expressed catastrophic fears of an impending war and worldwide disaster. During the Nazi occupation he moved to Warsaw, where he was active in the resistance and edited *Pieśń niepodległa* (1942; "Independent Song: Polish Wartime Poetry"), a clandestine anthology of well-known contemporary poems.

Miłosz's collection *Ocalenie* (1945; "Rescue") contained his prewar poems and those written during the occupation. In the same year, he joined the Polish diplomatic service and was sent, after briefly working during 1946 in the Polish embassy in New York City, to Washington, D.C., as cultural attaché, and then to Paris, as first secretary for cultural affairs in Paris. There he asked for political asylum in 1951. Nine years later he immigrated to the United States, where he joined the faculty of the University of

California at Berkeley. Miłosz became a naturalized citizen of the United States in 1970.

There are several volumes of English translations of Miłosz's poetry, including *The Collected Poems 1931–1987* (1988) and *Provinces* (1991). His prose works include his autobiography, *Rodzinna Europa* (1959; *Native Realm*), *Prywatne obowiązki* (1972; "Private Obligations"), the novel *Dolina Issy* (1955; *The Issa Valley*), and *The History of Polish Literature* (1969).

Though Miłosz was primarily a poet, his best-known work became his collection of essays *Zniewolony umysł* (1953; *The Captive Mind*), which condemned the accommodation of many Polish intellectuals to communism. This theme is also present in his novel *Zdobycie władzy* (1955; *The Seizure of Power*). His poetic works are noted for their classical style and their preoccupation with philosophical and political issues. An important example is *Traktat poetycki* (1957; *Treatise on Poetry*), which combines a defense of poetry with a history of Poland from 1918 to the 1950s. The critic Helen Vendler wrote that this long poem seemed to her "the most comprehensive and moving poem" of the latter half of the 20th century.

NAGUIB MAHFOUZ

(b. December 11, 1911, Cairo, Egypt—d. August 30, 2006, Cairo)

Naguib Mahfouz was the son of a civil servant and grew up in Cairo's Al-Jamāliyyah district. He attended Fu'ād I University (now Cairo University), where in 1934 he received a degree in philosophy. He worked in the Egyptian civil service in a variety of positions from 1934 until his retirement in 1971.

Mahfouz's earliest published works were short stories. His early novels, such as *Rādūbīs* (1943; "Radobis"), were set in ancient Egypt, but he had turned to describing modern Egyptian society by the time he began his major work, *Al-Thulāthiyyah* (1956–57), known as *The Cairo Trilogy*. Its three novels—*Bayn al-qaṣrayn* (1956; *Palace Walk*), *Qaṣr al-shawq* (1957; *Palace of Desire*), and *Al-Sukkariyyah* (1957; *Sugar Street*)—depict the lives of three generations of different families in Cairo from World War I until after the 1952 military coup that overthrew King Farouk. The trilogy provides a penetrating overview of 20th-century Egyptian thought, attitudes, and social change.

In subsequent works Mahfouz offered critical views of the old Egyptian monarchy, British colonialism, and contemporary Egypt. Several of his more notable novels deal with social issues involving women and political prisoners. His novel *Awlād ḥāratinā* (1959; *Children of the Alley*) was banned in Egypt for a time because of its controversial treatment of religion and its use of characters based on Muhammad, Moses, and other figures. Islamic militants, partly because of their outrage over the work, later called for his death, and in 1994 Mahfouz was stabbed in the neck.

Mahfouz's other novels include *Al-Liṣṣ wa-al-kilāb* (1961; *The Thief and the Dogs*), *Al-Shaḥḥādh* (1965; *The Beggar*), and *Mīrāmār* (1967; *Miramar*), all of which consider Egyptian society under Gamal Abdel Nasser's regime; *Afrāḥ al-qubba* (1981; *Wedding Song*), set among several characters associated with a Cairo theatre company; and the structurally experimental *Ḥadīth al-ṣabāḥ wa-al-masā'* (1987; *Morning and Evening Talk*), which strings together in alphabetical order dozens of character sketches. Together, his novels, which were among the first to gain widespread acceptance in the Arabic-speaking world, brought the genre to maturity within Arabic literature. In 1988 he became the first Arabic writer to be awarded the Nobel Prize for Literature.

Mahfouz's achievements as a short-story writer are demonstrated in such collections as *Dunyā Allāh* (1963; *God's World*). *The Time and the Place, and Other Stories* (1991) and *The Seventh Heaven* (2005) are collections of his stories in English translation. Mahfouz wrote more than 45 novels and short-story collections, as well as some 30 screenplays and several plays. *Aṣdāʾ al-sīrah al-dhātiyyah* (1996; *Echoes of an Autobiography*) is a collection of parables and his sayings. In 1996 the Naguib Mahfouz Medal for Literature was established to honour Arabic writers.

JOHN CHEEVER

(b. May 27, 1912, Quincy, Massachusetts, U.S.—d. June 18, 1982, Ossining, New York)

American short-story writer and novelist John Cheever described, often through fantasy and ironic comedy, the life, manners, and morals of middle-class, suburban America. He has been called "the Chekhov of the suburbs" for his ability to capture the drama and sadness of the lives of his characters by revealing the undercurrents of apparently insignificant events. Known as a moralist, he judged his characters from the standpoint of traditional morality.

Cheever himself was born into a middle-class family, his father being employed in the shoe business then booming in New England. With the eventual failure of the shoe industry and the difficulties of his parents' marriage, he had an unhappy adolescence. His expulsion at age 17 from the Thayer Academy in Massachusetts provided the theme for his first published story, which appeared in *The*

New Republic in 1930. During the Great Depression he lived in New York City's Greenwich Village. Cheever married in 1941 and had three children. In 1942 he enlisted in the army to train as an infantryman, but the army soon reassigned him to the Signal Corps as a scriptwriter for training films. After the war Cheever and his wife moved from New York City to the suburbs, whose culture and mores are often examined in his subsequent fiction.

Cheever's name was closely associated with *The New Yorker*, a periodical that published many of his stories, but his works also appeared in *The New Republic*, *Collier's*, *Story*, and *The Atlantic*. A master of the short story, Cheever worked from "the interrupted event," which he considered the prime source of short stories. He was famous for his clear and elegant prose and his careful fashioning of incidents and anecdotes. He is perhaps best-known for the two stories "The Enormous Radio" (1947) and "The Swimmer" (1964; filmed 1968). In the former story a young couple discovers that their new radio receives the conversations of other people in their apartment building but that this fascinating look into other people's problems does not solve their own. In "The Swimmer" a suburban man decides to swim his way home in the backyard pools of his neighbours and finds on the way that he is a lost soul in several senses. Cheever's first collection of short stories, *The Way Some People Live* (1943), was followed by many others, including *The Enormous Radio and Other Stories* (1953) and *The Brigadier and the Golf Widow* (1964). *The Stories of John Cheever* (1978) won the Pulitzer Prize for fiction.

Cheever's ability in his short stories to focus on the episodic caused him difficulty in constructing extended narratives in his novels. Nonetheless, his first novel, *The Wapshot Chronicle* (1957)—a satire on, among other subjects, the misuses of wealth and psychology—earned him the National Book Award. Its sequel, *The Wapshot Scandal*

(1964), was less successful. *Falconer* (1977) is the dark tale of a drug-addicted college professor who is imprisoned for murdering his brother. *Oh What a Paradise It Seems* (1982) is an elegiac story about a New Englander's efforts to preserve the quality of his life and that of a mill town's pond. *The Letters of John Cheever*, edited by his son Benjamin Cheever, was published in 1988, and in 1991 *The Journals of John Cheever* appeared. The latter is deeply revealing of both the man and the writer.

PATRICK WHITE

(b. May 28, 1912, London, England — d. September 30, 1990, Sydney, New South Wales, Australia)

Australian novelist and playwright Patrick Victor Martindale White was born in London while his parents were there on a visit, and he returned to England (after 12 years in Australia) for schooling. He then worked for a time at his father's sheep ranch in Australia before returning to study modern languages at King's College, Cambridge. By the time he served in the Royal Air Force during World War II, he had already published some early work, traveled extensively, and been involved with the theatre. After 1945 he returned to Australia, but he also lived intermittently in England and in the United States.

White's first novel, *Happy Valley* (1939), was set in New South Wales and showed the influence of D.H. Lawrence and Thomas Hardy. The material of White's later novels is distinctly Australian, but his treatment of it has a largeness of vision not limited to any one country or period. White saw Australia as a country in a highly volatile process of growth and self-definition, and his novels explore the possibilities of savagery to be found within such a context. His conception of Australia reflected in *The Tree of Man* (1955), *Voss* (1957), *Riders in the Chariot* (1961), *The Solid Mandala* (1966), and *The Twyborn Affair* (1979) is the product of an individual, critical, poetic imagination. His style is dense with myth, symbol, and allegory. His deepest concern is for man's sense of isolation and his search for meaning. In 1973 he won the Nobel Prize for Literature.

White wrote plays, including *The Season at Sarsaparilla* (produced 1962; published in *Four Plays*, 1965), *Night on Bald Mountain* (produced 1964), and *Signal Driver* (1982); short stories; the autobiographical *Flaws in the Glass* (1981); a screenplay; and a book of poems.

JORGE AMADO

(b. August 10, 1912, Ferradas, near Ilhéus, Brazil—d. August 6, 2001, Salvador)

Jorge Amado grew up on a cacao plantation, Auricídia, and was educated at the Jesuit college in Salvador and studied law at Federal University in Rio de Janeiro. He published his first novel at age 19. Three of his early works deal with the cacao plantations, emphasizing the exploitation and the misery of the migrant blacks, mulattoes, and poor whites who harvest the crop and generally expressing communist solutions to social problems. The best of these works, *Terras do sem fim* (1942; *The Violent Land*), about the struggle of rival planters, has the primitive grandeur of a folk saga.

Amado became a journalist in 1930, and his literary career paralleled a career in radical politics that won him election to the Constituent Assembly as a federal deputy representing the Communist Party of Brazil in 1946. He was imprisoned as early as 1935 and periodically exiled for his leftist activities, and many of his books were banned in Brazil and Portugal. He continued to produce novels with facility, most of them picaresque, ribald, unforgettable tales of Bahian city life, especially that of the racially conglomerate lower classes. *Gabriela, cravo e canela* (1958; *Gabriela, Clove and Cinnamon*) and *Dona Flor e seus dois maridos* (1966; *Dona Flor and Her Two Husbands*; film, 1978) both preserve Amado's political attitude in their satire. His later works include *Tenda dos milagres* (1969; *Tent of Miracles*), *Tiêta do agreste* (1977; *Tieta, the Goat Girl*), *Tocaia grande* (1984; *Show Down*), and *O sumiço da santa* (1993; *The War of the Saints*). Amado published his memoirs, *Navegaçãu de cabotagem* ("Coastal Navigation"), in 1992.

ALBERT CAMUS

(b. November 7, 1913, Mondovi, Algeria—d. January 4, 1960, near Sens, France)

Less than a year after Albert Camus was born, his father, an impoverished worker, was killed in World War I during the First Battle of the Marne. His mother, of Spanish descent, did housework to support her family. Camus and his elder brother Lucien moved with their mother to a working-class district of Algiers, where all three lived, together with the maternal grandmother and a paralyzed uncle, in a two-room apartment. Camus's first published collection of essays, *L'Envers et l'endroit* (1937; "The Wrong Side and the Right Side"), describes the physical setting of these early years and includes portraits of his mother, grandmother, and uncle. A second collection of essays, *Noces* (1938; "Nuptials"), contains intensely lyrical meditations on the Algerian countryside and presents natural beauty as a form of wealth that even the very poor can enjoy. Both collections contrast the fragile mortality of human beings with the enduring nature of the physical world.

Early Years

In 1918 Camus entered primary school and was fortunate enough to be taught by an outstanding teacher, Louis Germain, who helped him to win a scholarship to the Algiers *lycée* (high school) in 1923. (It was typical of Camus's sense of loyalty that 34 years later his speech accepting the Nobel Prize for Literature was dedicated to Germain.) A period of intellectual awakening followed, accompanied by great enthusiasm for sport, especially football (soccer), swimming, and boxing. In 1930, however, the first of several severe attacks of tuberculosis put an end to his sporting career and interrupted his studies. Camus had to leave the unhealthy apartment that had been his home for 15 years, and, after a short period spent with an uncle, Camus decided to live on his own, supporting himself by a variety of jobs

Albert Camus. **Michael Ochs Archives/Moviepix/Getty Images**

while registered as a philosophy student at the University of Algiers.

At the university, Camus was particularly influenced by one of his teachers, Jean Grenier, who helped him to develop his literary and philosophical ideas and shared his enthusiasm for football. He obtained a *diplôme d'études supérieures* in 1936 for a thesis on the relationship between Greek and Christian thought in the philosophical writings of Plotinus and St. Augustine. His candidature for the *agrégation* (a qualification that would have enabled him to take up a university career) was cut short by another attack of tuberculosis. To regain his health he went to a resort in the French Alps—his first visit to Europe—and eventually returned to Algiers via Florence, Pisa, and Genoa.

Camus's Literary Career

Throughout the 1930s, Camus broadened his interests. He read the French classics as well as the writers of the day—among them André Gide, Henry de Montherlant, André Malraux—and was a prominent figure among the young left-wing intellectuals of Algiers. For a short period in 1934–35 he was also a member of the Algerian Communist Party. In addition, he wrote, produced, adapted, and acted for the Théâtre du Travail (Workers' Theatre, later named the Théâtre de l'Équipe), which aimed to bring outstanding plays to working-class audiences. He maintained a deep love of the theatre until his death. Ironically, his plays are the least-admired part of his literary output, although *Le Malentendu* (*Cross Purpose*) and *Caligula,* first produced in 1944 and 1945, respectively, remain landmarks in the Theatre of the Absurd.

In the two years before the outbreak of World War II, Camus served his apprenticeship as a journalist with

Alger-Républicain in many capacities, including those of leader- (editorial-) writer, subeditor, political reporter, and book reviewer.

He enjoyed the most influence as a journalist during the final years of the occupation of France and the immediate post-Liberation period. As editor of the Parisian daily *Combat*, the successor of a Resistance newssheet run largely by Camus, he held an independent left-wing position based on the ideals of justice and truth and the belief that all political action must have a solid moral basis. Later, the old-style expediency of both Left and Right brought increasing disillusion, and in 1947 he severed his connection with *Combat*.

By now Camus had become a leading literary figure. *L'Étranger* (U.S. title, *The Stranger*; British title, *The Outsider*), a brilliant first novel begun before the war and published in 1942, is a study of 20th-century alienation with a portrait of an "outsider" condemned to death less for shooting an Arab than for the fact that he never says more than he genuinely feels and refuses to conform to society's demands. The same year saw the publication of an influential philosophical essay, *Le Mythe de Sisyphe* (*The Myth of Sisyphus*), in which Camus, with considerable sympathy, analyzed contemporary nihilism and a sense of the "absurd." He was already seeking a way of overcoming nihilism, and his second novel, *La Peste* (1947; *The Plague*), is a symbolical account of the fight against an epidemic in Oran by characters whose importance lies less in the (doubtful) success with which they oppose the epidemic than in their determined assertion of human dignity and fraternity. Camus had now moved from his first main concept of the absurd to his other major idea of moral and metaphysical "rebellion." He contrasted this latter ideal with politico-historical revolution in a second long essay,

L'Homme révolté (1951; *The Rebel*), which provoked bitter antagonism among Marxist critics and such near-Marxist theoreticians as Jean-Paul Sartre. His other major literary works are the technically brilliant novel *La Chute* (1956) and a collection of short stories, *L'Exil et le royaume* (1957; *Exile and the Kingdom*).

In 1957, at age 44, Camus received the Nobel Prize for Literature. With characteristic modesty he declared that had he been a member of the awarding committee his vote would certainly have gone to André Malraux. Less than three years later he was killed in an automobile accident.

Assessment

As novelist and playwright, moralist and political theorist, Albert Camus after World War II became the spokesman of his own generation and the mentor of the next, not only in France but also in Europe and eventually the world. His writings, which addressed themselves mainly to human isolation in an alien universe, the estrangement of the individual from himself, the problem of evil, and the pressing finality of death, accurately reflected the alienation and disillusionment of the postwar intellectual. He is remembered, with Sartre, as a leading practitioner of the existential novel.

GLOSSARY

Acmeist Member of a small group of early-20th-century Russian poets reacting against the vagueness and affectations of Symbolism.

alexandrine A line of verse of 12 syllables consisting regularly of 6 iambs with a caesura after the third iamb.

asperity Harshness.

belle époque A period of high artistic or cultural development that took place in France toward the end of the 19th century.

bildungsroman A novel about the moral and psychological growth of the main character.

calligramme A design in which the letters of a word (as a name) are rearranged so as to form a decorative pattern or figure.

demimonde A class of women on the fringes of respectable society supported by wealthy lovers.

Expressionism Literary style that arose as a reaction against materialism, complacent bourgeois prosperity, rapid mechanization and urbanization, and the domination of the family within in pre-World War I European society.

facile Easily accomplished or attained.

gunrunning Trafficking in contraband arms and ammunition.

hagiographic Of, relating to, or being an idealizing or idolizing biography.

histrionic Deliberately affected; theatrical.

Imagist Any of a group of American and English poets who wrote succinct verse of dry clarity and hard outline in which an exact visual image made a total poetic statement.

inapposite Not apt or pertinent.

in medias res In or into the middle of a narrative or plot.

jingoistic Characterized by extreme chauvinism or nationalism marked especially by a belligerent foreign policy.

juvenilia Compositions produced in the artist's or author's youth.

laconic Using or involving the use of a minimum of words.

libretto The text of a work (as an opera) for the musical theatre.

martinet A strict disciplinarian.

Modernism In the arts and literature, a radical break with the past and the concurrent search for new forms of expression.

Modernismo Late 19th- and early 20th-century Spanish-language literary movement that emerged in the late 1880s. The poets of the Modernismo movement used free verse and sensuous imagery to express their own highly individual spiritual values.

mordant Biting and caustic in thought, manner, or style.

mythopoeic Of or relating to a creating of myth.

nihilism Any of various philosophical positions that deny that there are objective foundations for human value systems.

Noh Classic Japanese dance-drama having a heroic theme, a chorus, and highly stylized action, costuming, and scenery.

nouveau roman Avant-garde novel of the mid-20th century that marked a radical departure from the conventions of the traditional novel in that it ignores such elements as plot, dialogue, linear narrative, and human interest.

objective correlative Something (as a situation or chain of events) that symbolizes or objectifies a particular emotion and that may be used in creative writing to evoke a desired emotional response in the reader.

paean A work that praises or honours its subject.

panegyric A eulogistic oration or writing.

polemicist One trained in art or practice of disputation or controversy.

prosody A particular system, theory, or style of versification, or the systematic study of metrical structure.

quatrain A unit or group of four lines of verse.

realism In the arts and literature, the accurate, detailed, unembellished depiction of nature or of contemporary life.

recondite Difficult or impossible for one of ordinary understanding or knowledge to comprehend.

roman-fleuve Series of novels, with each book complete in itself, that deals with one central character, an era of national life, or successive generations of a family.

Romanticism Literary, artistic, and philosophical movement that began in Europe in the 18th century and lasted roughly until the mid-19th century. Romanticism emphasized the individual, the subjective, the irrational, the imaginative, the personal, the spontaneous, the emotional, the visionary, and the transcendental.

sahib A European official or settler in a largely non-European population.

sinecured Of or pertaining to an office or position that requires little or no work and that usually provides an income.

Socialist Realism Officially sanctioned theory and method of artistic and literary composition in the Soviet Union from 1932 to the mid-1980s that purported to serve as an objective mirror of life. Instead

of critiquing society, however, it took as its primary
theme the struggle to build socialism and a class-
less society and called for the didactic use of art to
develop social consciousness.

Symbolism A loosely organized literary and artistic
movement that originated with a group of French
poets in the late 19th century, spread to painting
and the theatre, and influenced the European and
American literatures of the 20th century to varying
degrees. Symbolists sought to express individual emotional experience through the subtle and suggestive
use of highly symbolized language.

tropism Response or orientation of an organism to a
stimulus that acts with greater intensity from one
direction than another.

Ultraist Of or relating to the movement in Spanish and
Spanish American poetry after World War I, characterized by a tendency to use free verse, complicated
metrical innovations, and daring imagery and symbolism instead of traditional form and content.

villanelle A chiefly French verse form running on two
rhymes and consisting typically of five tercets (three-
line verses) and a quatrain in which the first and third
lines of the opening tercet recur alternately at the end
of the other tercets and together as the last two lines
of the quatrain.

BIBLIOGRAPHY

Noteworthy studies of some of the early modern authors covered in this volume include G.K. Chesterton, *George Bernard Shaw* (1909, reprinted 2010); Michael Holroyd, *Bernard Shaw*, 4 vol. (1988–92), also available as *Bernard Shaw: The One-Volume Definitive Edition* (1997); John G. Peters, *The Cambridge Introduction to Joseph Conrad* (2006); Zdzisław Najder, *Joseph Conrad: A Life*, 2nd extensively rev. English-language ed. (2007); Simon Karlinsky (ed.), *Anton Chekhov's Life and Thought: Selected Letters and Commentaries* (1973, reprinted 1997); Donald Rayfield, *Anton Chekhov: A Life* (1997); R.F. Foster, *W.B. Yeats: A Life*, 2 vol. (1997–2003); Charles Carrington, *Rudyard Kipling: His Life and Work*, rev. ed. (1978); Norman MacKenzie and Jeanne MacKenzie, *The Life of H.G. Wells*, rev. ed. (1987); Henri Troyat, *Gorky* (1989); Alan Sheridan, *André Gide: A Life in the Present* (1999); Edmund White, *Marcel Proust: A Life* (2009); Jean-Yves Tadié, *Marcel Proust* (2000; originally published in French, 1996); Jerome Loving, *The Last Titan: A Life of Theodore Dreiser* (2005); Lawrance Thompson, *Robert Frost*, 3 vol., vol. 3 coauthored with R.H. Winnick (1966–76); Jay Parini, *Robert Frost: A Life* (1999); Hermann Kurzke, *Thomas Mann: Life as a Work of Art* (2002; originally published in German); Ritchie Robertson (ed.), *The Cambridge Companion to Thomas Mann* (2002); Ralph Freedman, *Life of a Poet: Rainer Maria Rilke* (1996); David E. Pollard, *The True Story of Lu Xun* (2002); Hermione Lee, *Virginia Woolf* (1996); Panthea Reid, *Art and Affection: A Life of Virginia Woolf* (1996); Richard Ellmann, *James Joyce*, new and rev. ed. (1982); Edna O'Brien, *James Joyce* (1999, reprinted as *James Joyce: A Life*, 2011); Nicholas

Murray, *Kafka* (2004); John Worthen, *D.H. Lawrence, the Early Years, 1885–1912* (1991); Mark Kinkead-Weekes, *D.H. Lawrence, Triumph to Exile, 1912–1922* (1996); David Ellis, *D.H. Lawrence, Dying Game, 1922–1930* (1997); Ira Bruce Nadel, *Ezra Pound: A Literary Life* (2004); Anthony David Moody, *Ezra Pound: Poet: A Portrait of the Man and His Work, 1, The Young Genius, 1885–1920* (2007), the first volume of a projected monumental study; Arthur Gelb and Barbara Gelb, *O'Neill*, enlarged ed. (1973, reissued 1987); Arthur Gelb and Barbara Gelb, *O'Neill: Life with Monte Cristo* (2000); Stephen A. Black, *Eugene O'Neill: Beyond Mourning and Tragedy* (1999); Joseph Blotner, *Faulkner: A Biography*, rev. and shortened ed. (1984, reissued 2005); Maria M. Delgado, *Federico García Lorca* (2008); Leslie Stainton, *Lorca: A Dream of Life* (1998); Carlos Baker, *Ernest Hemingway: A Life Story* (1969, reissued 1988); James R. Mellow, *Hemingway: A Life Without Consequences* (1992); James Woodall, *Borges: A Life* (1996, also published as *The Man in the Mirror of the Book: A Life of Jorge Luis Borges*); Edwin Williamson, *Borges: A Life* (2004); Volodia Teitelboim, *Neruda: An Intimate Biography* (1991; originally published in Spanish, 1984); Adam Feinstein, *Pablo Neruda: A Passion for Life* (2004); Kenneth Thompson and Margaret Thompson, *Sartre: Life and Works* (1984); Ronald Hayman, *Sartre* (1987, reissued 1992); Annie Cohen-Solal, *Sartre: A Life* (1987, originally published in French); Anthony Cronin, *Samuel Beckett* (1996); Lois Gordon, *The World of Samuel Beckett, 1906–1946* (1996); James Knowlson, *Damned to Fame* (1996); Charles Osborne, *W.H. Auden: The Life of a Poet* (1979, reprinted 1995); Humphrey Carpenter, *W.H. Auden: A Biography* (1981, reissued 2010); Morvan Lebesque, *Portrait of Camus: An Illustrated Biography* (1971; originally published in French, 1963); Herbert R. Lottman, *Albert Camus* (1979, reissued 1997); Patrick McCarthy, *Camus* (1982); and Olivier Todd, *Albert Camus* (1997), an abridged and edited translation of the original French (1996).

INDEX